Shared Traditions

 Southern History and Folk Culture

Charles Joyner

University of Illinois Press

Urbana and Chicago

© 1999 by the Board of Trustees of the University of Illinois
Manufactured in the United States of America
1   2   3   4   5   C   P   5   4   3   2

∞ This book is printed on acid-free paper.

Library of Congress Cataloging-in-Publication Data
Joyner, Charles W.
Shared traditions : Southern history and folk culture /
Charles Joyner.
p.   cm.
Includes bibliographical references (p.   ) and index.
ISBN 0-252-01521-5 (acid-free paper)
ISBN 0-252-06772-X (pbk. : acid-free paper)
1. Southern States—Social life and customs. 2. Folklore—
Southern States. 3. Folklore and history—Southern States.
4. Plantation life—Southern States—History. I. Title.
F209.J69   1999
975—ddc21   98-40082
CIP

Shared Traditions

To Hannah and Wesley

Contents

Acknowledgments

The essays in this book all reflect an interest in the relationship between history and culture, and particularly between southern history and folk culture, that has occupied most of my academic life.

Much of the education that set me on this path—what I consider my *real* education—came about during the course of two continuing seminars. The first was informal, held with my apartment mates, fellow graduate students, and lifelong friends Dan T. Carter, John B. Edmunds Jr., M. Hayes Mizell, and Selden K. Smith, at 1015 Henderson Street, Columbia, South Carolina, from 1960 to 1963. The camaraderie, intellectual curiosity, social commitment, ambition, self-doubt, and mutual support that we shared there is beyond my ability to convey in words. I shall always cherish the experience. The second seminar was only nominally more formal. It was the teaching team for "The American Experience," the senior-year installment of the interdisciplinary general education program at St. Andrews Presbyterian College. The team included Carl D. Bennett from the English department; Harry L. Harvin Jr. from history; and (at various times) George Fouke and John Hill from politics; Leslie Bullock, Douglas Hix, and the late Spencer Ludlow from philosophy and religion; and occasional others. Being part of that team was for me something of a postdoctoral residency in other disciplines. We began as specialists contributing from our individual training to a *multi*disciplinary teaching and learning experience. But we did not end with that approach. I believe it was the anthropologist Ralph Linton who first said that *inter*disciplinary approaches work best when the disciplines involved are all in one head. As we taught not only our students but also one another, we found that the approaches and viewpoints of other disciplines had become intrinsic to our own approaches and viewpoints.

The opportunity to be a part of the Southern Intellectual History Circle, the Australian and New Zealand American Studies Association, and the European Southern Studies Forum has enhanced the influence of those formative seminars in Columbia and at St. Andrews on my thinking. While the three groups are quite different from one another in most ways, they have welcomed me (in their unique styles) with a rare combination of supportive encouragement and penetrating interdisciplinary criticism. I know of nobody else who has enjoyed the hospitality of all three groups, and I feel particularly privileged to have had the opportunity.

Perhaps one should not attempt to straddle the humanities and the social sciences unless one has very long legs. But I must gratefully acknowledge financial support during the course of these investigations from both the National Endowment for the Humanities and the Social Science Research Council, as well as the South Carolina Humanities Council.

I am grateful to Coastal Carolina University for the warm and supportive environment it has provided and for the friendship and intellectual companionship of my colleagues and students. I wish to thank especially Ronald R. Ingle, president; John Idoux, provost; John B. Durrell, dean of humanities and the fine arts; Roy Talbert, chair of the department of history; the Coastal Education Foundation; and the Horry County Higher Education Commission for their support and encouragement. I have been privileged at Coastal Carolina to occupy the Franklin A. and Viola B. Burroughs Chair in Southern History and Culture, established by the late Henry Burroughs in memory of his parents. It has provided not only time for research and writing but also travel support and funds for research.

My research trips have taken me to numerous libraries, including the South Caroliniana Library at the University of South Carolina; the Southern Historical Collection and the Southern Folklife Collection in the Wilson Library at the University of North Carolina, Chapel Hill; the South Carolina Historical Society in Charleston; the Manuscripts Division of the Perkins Library at Duke; the Widener, Baker, and Houghton Libraries at Harvard; the Archive of Folk Culture at the Library of Congress in Washington; the Newberry Library in Chicago; the William Ransom Hogan Jazz Archive at Tulane; the University of California Library at Berkeley; the University of Pennsylvania Library; the John Davis Williams Library at the University of Mississippi; the Gorgas Library at the University of Alabama; the William A. Kimbel Library at Coastal Carolina; and the private library of the late Kenneth S. Goldstein.

It is not only the size of its collections but also the skill of its staff that enhances the value of any research library. I am grateful to the splendid staffs of all the above institutions, but I wish to express special thanks to Allen Stokes and Thomas L. Johnson at the South Caroliniana Library, David Moltke-Hansen at the Southern Historical Collection, Michael Taft at the Southern Folklife Collection, Joseph C. Hickerson at the Archive of Folk Culture, and Peggy Bates at the William A. Kimbel Library.

Three visiting professorships—at the University of California, Berkeley, in 1986; at the University of Mississippi in 1987; and at the University of Sydney, Australia, in 1993—and an associateship at the W. E. B. Du Bois Center for Afro-American Research at Harvard University in 1989–90 gave me time for writing and enabled me to share ideas with scholars who had similar interests but varying perspectives. I am particularly grateful to Leon F. Litwack and Lawrence W. Levine for the opportunity to be a part of the history department at Berkeley, to William R. Ferris, Charles Reagan Wilson, and Robert Haws for inviting me to be a Ford Foundation Professor of Southern Studies at Ole Miss, to Shane White and Graham White for arranging for me to teach in the remarkable history department at Sydney, and to the late Nathan Huggins for the invitation to be an associate of the Du Bois Center.

It is an impossible task to thank everyone who has contributed to what has gone into this book. I must acknowledge at the outset the influence and encouragement of J. Morgan Kousser, who (in a review of one of my earlier efforts) foresaw the possibility of my writing this book even before I did. The many historians, folklorists, and anthropologists whose works I have plundered are acknowledged in the notes. In the paragraphs that follow I wish to express my thanks to those who along the way have contributed specifically to this book.

I have shamelessly exploited a number of friends and fellow scholars by foisting one or another of these essays upon them for their advice and counsel. I am deeply indebted to C. Vann Woodward, Bertram Wyatt-Brown, and Roger D. Abrahams for reading the entire manuscript and offering astute suggestions that have made this a better book. I am grateful to historians Peter Bastian, James L. Baumgarner, Orville Vernon Burton, Edward D. C. Campbell Jr., Dan T. Carter, Avery O. Craven, Warren Ellem, Drew Gilpin Faust, Paul Finkelman, Roy E. Finkenbine, David

Hackett Fischer, Walter J. Fraser Jr., William W. Freehling, David Gold-field, Rhys Isaac, Hannah Joyner, William McFeely, George E. Martin, David Moltke-Hansen, Winfred B. Moore Jr., Michael O'Brien, Ted Own-by, Kym S. Rice, John Salmond, Melvin I. Urofsky, Deborah Gray White, Graham White, Shane White, Stephen J. Whitfield, Bernard Wax, and Charles Reagan Wilson; folklorists Barbara Allen, Hermann Bausinger, Dan Ben-Amos, Rolf Bredknecht, Jan Harold Brunvand, Guy and Candie Carawan, Camilla Collins, Linda Degh, Alan Dundes, William R. Ferris, Alan Jabbour, Jay Mechling, Venetia Newall, Maja Povrzanovic, Dunja Rihtman-Augustin, Klaus Roth, J. Barre Toelken, John Michael Vlach, and Charles G. Zug III; American Studies scholars Richard H. King and Helen Taylor; journalist Jack Bass; and historical archaeologists Jerome Handler and Teresa Singleton. For any errors of fact or judgment that have survived their scrutiny (and the careful editorial process at the University of Illinois Press) I alone am responsible.

Richard Wentworth, director of the University of Illinois Press, is one of the giants of academic publishing. My debt to him, in this and in other endeavors, is more than a brief acknowledgment can convey. His encouragement over more than two decades and his perceptive readings have been much appreciated. Also at Illinois, I want to acknowledge the literary sensibility Carol Bolton Betts has brought to the task of transforming my manuscript into a book. Possessed of not only a keen eye but also an acute ear for the nuances of language, she has helped me to avoid all sorts of repetitions, opaque passages, and other infelicities.

These essays were written over several years. Some of them were published in journals not regularly perused by historians, some in journals not readily available in the United States. Some are published here for the first time. All except "'Guilty of Holiest Crime'" have been revised, most of them substantially, in an effort to unify the book.

An earlier version of "'Let Us Break Bread Together': Cultural Interaction in the Old South" was published as "'A Single Southern Culture': Cultural Interaction in the Old South," in *Black and White: Cultural Interaction in the Antebellum South*, edited by Ted Ownby (Jackson: University Press of Mississippi, 1993), 3–22. "'In His Hands': The World of the Plantation Slaves" appeared, in a slightly different form, in *Before Freedom Came: African-American Life and Labor in the Antebellum South*, edited by Edward D. C. Campbell Jr. and Kym S. Rice, published for the Museum of the Confederacy by the University Press of Virginia (Charlottesville,

1991), 51–99. "'Guilty of Holiest Crime': The Passion of John Brown" was published in *His Soul Goes Marching On: New Views of the John Brown Raid*, edited by Paul Finkelman (Charlottesville: University Press of Virginia, 1995), 296–334. A preliminary version of "The South as a Folk Culture: David Potter and the Southern Enigma" was published in *The Southern Enigma: Essays on Race, Class, and Folk Culture*, edited by Walter J. Fraser Jr. and Winfred B. Moore Jr. (Westport, Conn.: Greenwood Press, 1983), 157–67. An earlier and shorter account of "The Sounds of Southern Culture: Blues, Country, Jazz, and Rock" was published as "African and European Roots of Southern Culture: The 'Central Theme' Revisited," in *Dixie Debates: Perspectives on Southern Cultures*, edited by Richard H. King and Helen Taylor (London: Pluto Press, 1996), 12–30. A shorter version of "Sea Island Legacy: Folk Tradition and the Civil Rights Movement" was published as the foreword to *Ain't You Got a Right to the Tree of Life: The People of Johns Island, South Carolina—Their Faces, Their Words, and Their Songs*, edited by Guy and Candie Carawan, revised and expanded edition (Athens: University of Georgia Press, 1989), vii–x. An earlier rendering of "Folklore and Social Transformation" was published as "Prica o dvije discipline: folkloristika i historija," in *Folklor i povijesni proces*, edited by Dunja Rihtman-Augustin and Maja Povrzanovic (Zagreb: Zavodza istrazivanje folklora, 1989), 9–22. "Endangered Traditions: Resort Development and Cultural Conservation on the Sea Islands" was published, in slightly different form, as the foreword to Patricia Jones-Jackson, *When Roots Die: Endangered Traditions in the Sea Islands* (Athens: University of Georgia Press), ix–xviii.

My family has shared the making of this book from the beginning, accompanying me on field trips and visits to the archives. My wife, Jeannie, has read and commented on various drafts of the various essays, always questioning, always seasoning her candid and rigorous criticism with encouragement. As our daughter, Hannah, and our son, Wesley, grew up, they too have had various of these essays thrust upon them. Hannah has become a historian herself, teaching at Gallaudet University and writing her own book. Wesley is a budding anthropologist with special interests in folk music and ethnomusicology. They, too, have learned to season their criticism with encouragement (and their encouragement with "suggestions"). My debt to Jeannie is certainly no less now than it was when I dedicated *Down by the Riverside* to her. But the fact that I am dedicating this book to Hannah and Wesley is a token both of my pride in them and my gratitude to them for all the ways in which they have enriched my life.

Shared Traditions

Introduction

Let me tell you a story. A middle-aged woman and a young boy sat together in a swing on the lawn of Hibben House, on the shores of Charleston Harbor in Mt. Pleasant. It was 1944, and she was tutoring him in the Presbyterian Shorter Catechism. The youngster learned his catechism; but the woman taught him much more, inflaming his youthful imagination with the local history of Mt. Pleasant and Christ Church Parish, especially of the Gullah-speaking slaves who had labored on the rice plantations along the Cooper River. She told him of the beautiful hand-coiled rice "fanner baskets" they made there, like the ones their ancestors had made in Africa. She taught him that if he wished to understand the South Carolina lowcountry, the small place that constituted her native soil, he must first learn a great deal about three continents—North America, Europe, and Africa. The woman was Petrona Royall McIver. I was the young boy. I have since come to refer to what I learned from "Miss Petey" as "asking large questions in small places." The phrase is mine, but the concept was hers.

One of the largest questions has been whether there is a distinctive southern culture, and the answers proffered by our predecessors—whether they posed the question in terms of central theme, collective character, or general outlook—might well serve as a warning to any present-day scholar contemplating a similar undertaking. "The possibilities for embarrassment," as C. Vann Woodward has noted, "are obviously numerous."[1]

The most conspicuous efforts have traditionally sought to find southern identity in the social and political behavior of the region's dominant white males. The Georgia-born historian Ulrich B. Phillips, for instance, found what he considered an entirely adequate key to southern culture in the racial attitudes and policies of white southerners. The determination to maintain white supremacy, he declared in a 1928 essay, is "the cardinal test of a Southerner and the central theme of Southern history."[2] A variation of this analysis is the familiar claim of politicians, journalists, and a few scholars that the South is "quintessentially conservative." According to the historian Eugene D. Genovese, the southern tradition—the *only* southern tradition—is conservatism; and such conservatives as the Nashville Agrarians and their latter-day disciples Richard Weaver and M. E. Bradford "have had every right to speak simply of *the* Southern tradition." Genovese makes much of their "special kind of conservatism" that made incarnate in southern history nothing less than the "essentials" of "Western Christian civilization." Genovese parts company with Phillips in disavowing what he calls the "legacy of racism" that has often animated southern conservatism. But he too proposes an interpretation of the whole region generalizing from the attitudes of a group of white southern men.[3]

Other and more plausible explanations have been nominated to account for southern distinctiveness. The distinguished historians C. Vann Woodward and David Potter advance interpretations emerging not merely from a small group of atypical white men but from the common experience of all southerners, black and white, men and women, past and present. Woodward, in his seminal essay "The Irony of Southern History," finds the South's defining characteristics rooted in its historical experience.[4] No longer can any interpretation of the South be taken seriously without the historical dimension. Still, the region's history can be only partly understood in isolation from the culture within which it was experienced. Potter, in his own notable essay "The Enigma of the South," bases the South's claims to a distinctive tradition in what he calls "the culture of the folk," a culture that has managed to endure all the homogenizing effects of commercial popular culture.[5]

While neither Woodward nor Potter explores the mutual implications of their explanations, the relation of history to folk culture would seem to be an essential starting point for any effort to understand the South. The region's historical experience has endowed the men and women of the South with a rich folk culture, a culture not confined to elite whites but shared by all southerners, a culture that finds its unity in the region's racial, class, and ethnic diversity.

I have spent much of my career attempting to build upon the wisdom of Woodward and Potter in an effort to understand the interplay of history and folk culture in the South. I have found in folk culture insights into

the history of men and women previously ignored by mainstream historical scholarship; and I have found in history insights into the folk culture
created by those men and women. The history of the South is first and
foremost the history of the folk, who were not just the central characters
in the drama but constituted the very essence of society itself. As the sociologist Howard Odum noted, "because they are so elementally powerful and necessary, and because they are not understood by most and are
forgotten by many, it is of the utmost importance to re-examine and re-
capture the meaning and role of the folk in both the understanding and
directing of society."[6]

When I was a graduate student in history my involvement in the civil
rights movement brought me into direct contact with the overwhelming
power of traditional African-American preaching styles in mass meetings.
Time and again I felt the heart-stirring inspiration of the magnificent old
black spirituals with their exciting new "freedom" lyrics. I became convinced that to understand history, at least to understand the kind of history I wanted to write about, I would have to understand folk culture. Soon
I was recording white tradition-bearers as well, in the form of banjo pickers, ballad singers, storytellers, and dulcimer makers in the Appalachians
and the Ozarks. By the early 1970s I was taking my portable tape recorder to England, Scotland, Northern Ireland, and Newfoundland as well.
Although I had already completed a doctorate in history at the University of South Carolina, I came to realize that I would have to undertake further graduate study in order to draw upon the insights of anthropology
and folklife studies if I were to understand the history of the folk. Since
earning a Ph.D. in folklore and folklife at the University of Pennsylvania
I have been profoundly influenced in my approach to the study of folk
culture by contemporary developments in the fields of folklore, linguistics, and anthropology, as well as history.

What is this folk culture, and why should we regard it as important? Folk
culture may be regarded as what human beings remember not because it
is reinforced by the church, the state, the school, or the press, but simply
because it is unforgettable. Our popular culture, while widely known in
the short run, is essentially disposable. A popular song rarely lasts more
than six weeks on the charts. After that it is a moldie oldie. Popular culture is created for the moment, folk culture—like great art—for the ages.
But unlike the creations of a self-conscious artist, unlike those of, say, a

William Faulkner or a Eudora Welty, whose works embody their individual visions and values, folk culture embodies in its traditional chain of transmission the visions and values of the folk themselves.

It would be difficult to overemphasize the importance of *tradition* in folk culture. Imagine that you make up a story, or a song—both the words and the music—but nobody knows it is your story or your song. It is presumed to belong to everyone. Anyone who wishes can change it in any way, for any reason. If people cannot understand part of it, find some part of it offensive, think they can improve on some part, or simply forget a part, they are free to change your song to their heart's content for the next decade, the next generation, the next century. It is unlikely that all of your story or song will survive that process of weeding out everything unintelligible, inartistic, offensive, or simply forgettable. But what does survive will be what you have in common with everyone who became a link in the chain of tradition. Some of the folktales and folksongs still alive in southern tradition are centuries old. What remains, after forgetting everything that is not truly memorable, is something primal, something very close to the basic poetic impulse of the human species. People neither remember nor forget without reason.

Because the elements of folk culture are often uncomplicated, folk cultures often appear simple to outside observers. But the elements are so intricately woven into a complex fabric that the totality is highly complicated in ways not always comprehended even by those who have inherited the tradition.[7] The old songs and the old tales, the old prayers and the old personal expressiveness are more than just quaint cultural artifacts. They provide the present generation with a sense of continuity with generations gone before, a precious lifeline to courageous ancestors, a source of strength that still enables us to cope with the hail and upheaval of life.

In the pages that follow I have certainly not attempted to meet the need for a full-scale history of the southern folk. Southern folk culture reflects what Howard Odum once called the "variegated fabric" of southern folk society, with a small plantation aristocracy, middle-class business people and yeoman farmers, free persons of color, and black slaves. In the South, beginning in the seventeenth century, Europeans of various ethnic backgrounds converged with Africans of various ethnic backgrounds and with Native Americans of various ethnic backgrounds. The folk traditions of all southerners, natives and newcomers alike, stimulated and modified one another. It is obviously impossible to cover the whole vast field in a single volume.[8]

Readers will doubtless note that in the sections devoted to the Old South the great majority of white southerners receive less attention than do slaves and slaveholders (especially in considering the cultural influence of the former on the latter). It is true that most southerners, the very bedrock of southern society, comprised a large group variously called "plain folk," "poor whites," "common whites," "crackers," and other derogatory names. Few southerners could live the life of a privileged planter.[9] Scholars have found it difficult even to *define* this majority, much less to delineate its culture. David Potter's lament that scholars are "far from agreeing about so basic a question as the nature of ante-bellum society" is as true today as when he voiced it in 1967.[10]

In their pathbreaking work in the 1940s, Frank L. Owsley and his students at Vanderbilt University identified this white majority as prosperous, fairly well educated, middle-class landowners who took pride in being called *plain folk* and in the solid virtues that the term meant to them. The Owsley group argued that the Old South was both a political and an economic democracy, and that the plain folk had plausible prospects of upward mobility. In this interpretation landless families were becoming landowners, and nonslaveholders were becoming masters. They supported the plantation system because it served their ends.[11]

Some owned a few slaves (and often worked beside them in the fields); most did not. To Owsley and his followers, *a few* slaves meant as many as ten. If yeomen are defined a priori as affluent slaveowners, the conclusion that they were prosperous supporters of slavery is hardly surprising. More recently Steven Hahn and Lacy Ford have limited their yeomen to five slaves or fewer, while Stephanie McCurry *broadened* her definition to include farmers who owned as much as 150 acres of cultivated land and possessed as many as nine slaves.[12] But none of the modern scholars define yeoman slaveholding as generously as did Daniel R. Hundley in 1860. "As a general rule," he noted "they own no slaves; and even in case they do, the wealthiest of them rarely possess more than ten to fifteen."[13]

According to the Owsley group, the yeomen identified with the spirit and manners of the gentry. "They were not class-conscious in the Marxian sense, for with rare exceptions they did not regard the planters and men of wealth as their oppressors," Owsley wrote. "On the contrary, they admired them as a rule and looked with approval on their success; and they assumed, on the basis of much tangible evidence, that the door of economic opportunity swung open easily to the thrust of their own ambitions."[14] But other writings, from Roger Shugg's pioneering 1939 analy-

sis to modern studies, have challenged the yeoman-democracy thesis and
suggested that yeomen and planters were locked in vigorous class conflict.[15] Eugene D. Genovese's "hegemonic" interpretation portrays the
yeomen as being utterly dominated by the slaveholders: "The hegemony
of the slaveholders, presupposing the social and economic preponderance
of the great slave plantations, determined the character of the South."
Nonetheless the plain folk supported the planters, against their class interest, for a variety of noneconomic reasons. Genovese explains that the
Gramscian concept of hegemony implies not only "class antagonisms,"
but also "the ability of a particular class to contain those antagonisms on
a terrain in which its legitimacy is not dangerously questioned."[16]

In a bold and controversial ethnocultural interpretation, the historians
Grady McWhiney and Forrest McDonald highlight the long-neglected
Celtic influence on southern culture. They contend that the plain folk were
not class conscious but led precisely the kind of life they wished, just as
their Celtic forebears had done. "A list of southern traits most observed
by contemporaries," McWhiney avers, "reads like an inventory of traditional Scottish, Irish, and Welsh cultural characteristics." Gracious manners, reckless drinking, and impetuous propensity to violence were legendary. "Courteous, modest, and even deferential," the white majority
could be "deadly if provoked." This "cracker culture," as McWhiney dubs
it, contrasted sharply with the English-derived culture of the North.[17]
David Hackett Fischer, in an equally controversial study of the transplant-
ing of British regional folk culture to American regions, emphasizes the
influence of folkways from the English-Scottish border to the southern
backcountry.[18]

It is easier to call for fresh studies of the plain folk than to undertake
one. We know considerably more about the cultural artifacts this white
majority has preserved than we do about the cultural meaning of those
artifacts to their makers and users.[19] There are no bodies of evidence for
the non-elite white majority analogous to the Federal Writers Project interviews with former slaves or even to the abolitionist-sponsored autobiographies of the self-emancipated. Evidence of their views and values
are easier to find in the twentieth century than in the nineteenth. Nonetheless, in the book as a whole I have attempted to draw upon the whole
range of the southern population.

The volume opens with "Southern Folk Culture: Unity in Diversity," an
exposition of the significance of folk culture and a survey of its major

forms in the South. That is followed by two sections designed to illustrate the importance of folk culture to the study of history, treating folk culture historically as it has taken various forms over time, dropping back into early America for origins and causes, and leaping forward into the present for a glance at achievements and consequences. Interspersed between the two is a section examining three scholars (two historians and one folklorist) who have been concerned in one way or another with southern culture and tradition. A fourth section argues the importance of the historical dimension to the study of folk culture, and the final section meditates on the future of endangered southern folk traditions.

Part 1, "The Old South," opens with "'Let Us Break Bread Together,'" an examination of cultural interaction emphasizing the diversity of antebellum southern culture. "'In His Hands'" is a historical ethnography of the world of the plantation slaves, an effort to reveal the vitality of the emergent African-American folk culture without blinking the ugliness and horror of slavery. "History as Ritual" is more analytical, appraising how rituals were used on the slave plantations by both masters and slaves. The slaveholders employed rites of power to try to bolster their authority and legitimacy, while the slaves used rites of resistance to foster community solidarity and undermine emotional dependence upon slaveholders. "'Guilty of Holiest Crime'" is less historical ethnography than ethnographic history, using Victor Turner's anthropological theory of "social drama" to explore an unresolved historical problem—the cultural causes and consequences of John Brown's uncharacteristically Christlike demeanor on the gallows.

Following is a section of "Three Historiographical Forays," commentaries on scholars who have written on southern culture. "The South as a Folk Culture" closely examines the thesis of David Potter's 1961 essay "The Enigma of the South" and attempts to appraise its insights and its implications. "The Bold Fischer Man" considers David Hackett Fischer's massive study of the British sources of American folk culture and its implications for the South. And "The Narrowing Gyre" uses Henry Glassie's monumental meditation on Irish folklife as the basis for a comparative approach to southern folk culture.

The New South is treated in part 3. It opens with "A Community of Memory," which surveys the Jews of Georgetown—a folk group defined by ethnicity—from 1761 to 1904 and assesses their complex blend of cultural assimilation and cultural preservation. "The Sounds of Southern Culture" examines both the pivotal role black and white southern musicians have played in the creation of the blues, country music, jazz, and rock

and also the ways those musical forms have become metaphors for southern culture. "Sweet Music" reveals how southern cultures become symbolically embodied in particular objects and practices, often ones that are
more important in their message than in their actual origins and usage.
"Sea Island Legacy" appraises the important role played by folk tradition
in the civil rights movement.

Most of this book elaborates the significance of folk culture to the understanding of history. But the penultimate section highlights the importance of history to the understanding of folk culture. "Alice of the Hermitage" reveals that history—in the sense both of the history of the legend
itself and of the historical context of the legend—is crucial to the modern redefinition of the genre. "A Model for the Analysis of Folklore Performance in Historical Context" points out the continuing usefulness of
history to the modern rhetorical theories of folkloristic analysis. "Folklore and Social Transformation" explores the interactions of historians
and folklorists in the last half of the twentieth century.

The final essay, "Endangered Traditions," studies the impact of large-
scale resort development on the folk culture of the Sea Islands and muses
on the future of folk culture, finding at least tentative optimism in the fact
that, while folk culture may be endangered, it is not fragile.

Embedded in the very idea of *folklore*—a neologism of nineteenth-century thinkers seeking to grasp the dynamics of their century's disorienting
social changes and trying to fashion some kind of order out of its apparent chaos—was a romantic conviction that traditional folk culture was
rapidly being swept away. While the folk were forging new patterns of
culture in response to new forces, folklorists foresaw, with a minimum of
doubt, the impending demise of folk culture. Thus the origins of folklore
as a scholarly pursuit are inseparable from both a profound historical
consciousness—an acute awareness of the potential of political and economic forces to transform society and culture—and a naive romantic
nostalgia for the "last leaves" of folklore.

I would not deny that my own research interests have been motivated
by both impulses. My career has been shaped by a deep and longstanding
commitment to folklore as a means of recalling to memory the forgotten
men and women of history, a commitment dating back to 1957 when I began to use folksongs as clues to the mentality of early twentieth-century
Rocky Mountain miners in their radical response to the industrial system's

social effects. My more recent investigations in the folk culture of Appalachian whites and Gullah blacks have undoubtedly been inspired by an apprehension that a precious and hard-earned heritage is endangered by rapid resort development in the mountains and on the coast.

Unquestionably the southern Appalachians and the Sea Islands are areas of endangered traditions as well as endangered natural resources. But it would be premature to publish an obituary yet. The belief that this or that folk culture is dying out would appear to be a folkloristic perennial, pronounced by each successive generation of folklorists. Traditions always appear to be endangered at any given time, but seen from the perspective of history (that is, in the future's rear-view mirror) it is apparent that they are also forever transforming themselves in the face of social change.

Whatever else might be said about relationships between history and folk culture, they can hardly be said to be trivial. On the contrary, I believe those relationships are far deeper than we have yet comprehended. There is an old folk proverb: "You can't tell the depth of a well by the length of the pumphandle." Like the shadows cast on the walls of Plato's cave, folk expressions are tangible and visible manifestations of intangible and invisible realities, of hidden and unseen motivations, motivations that folklorists and historians ignore at some peril to their understanding.

What is most striking about the transformations that have taken place in the South is that southern folk culture has become something more than merely a repository of the dead or dying artifacts of European or African folk culture. It is the dynamic product of rich and complex interactions by the descendants of Europeans and Africans with one another and with Native Americans. Because of those interactions every southerner, regardless of race, shares both African and European traditions. Out of the cultural triangle of Europe, Africa, and the American South has emerged a profound and creative exchange that has given the region a distinctive folk culture of great strength and of great beauty, a folk culture that unites all the South's people, perhaps in deeper ways than we even yet understand.

1

Southern Folk Culture

Unity in Diversity

In William Faulkner's *Absalom, Absalom!* the culture-haunted southerner Quentin Compson sits in his Harvard dormitory room with his Canadian roommate, Shreve McCannon, attempting to deconstruct a group of oral narratives he had heard from various people in Yoknapatawpha County, his Mississippi home. Quentin believes that these narratives hold the key to understanding the South's tragic history. To Shreve, the objective but obtuse outsider, the South is simply an exotic place: "The South. The South. Jesus. No wonder you folks all outlive yourselves by years and years and years." But Quentin, the quintessential insider, is obsessed by the burden of southern history, a burden he finds all too personal. Neither can really understand the South without the other.

"I do wish you could see Mississippi," wrote the great southern writer Eudora Welty to a friend in New York, because she was certain the friend would like what she called "the folk quality to the little adventures and stories and the directness and simplicity, really the dignity in the way they find and hold their beliefs, and the feeling of the legendary . . . that you get when you see some of the ruins and haunted houses." She strongly associated what she called "the folk quality" with place. "One place comprehended," she writes in her famous essay *Place in Fiction*, "can make us understand other places better." A sense of place is the necessary compass that people carry within themselves, a compass that enables them to find the universal in the particular. "Sense of place gives equilibrium," she notes. "It is by knowing where you stand that you grow able to judge where you are."

Southern folklife involves everything southerners do, think, hope, and fear in our short existence on this planet. It has been a means of preserving the memorable experiences of southerners. It has been a means of protesting—humorously, bitterly, or militantly—the hard life imposed by nature, or society, or by the inhumanity of some men toward other men; a means of commenting on manners and morals, on the trivial and the transcendental in gropings of southern men and women for a life of meaning and dignity. Not only folktales and folksongs, but folk speech, proverbs, legends, fiddle tunes, square dances, and material folk culture—foodways, folk arts, and vernacular architecture—have served a variety of purposes in the South. They admonish, they lull to sleep, they call to battle, they ring with joy for the lover, sorrow for the loser, hope for the prisoner, threat for the jailer. Folklore tells of childbirth, childhood, wedlock, work, fun, murder, love (all kinds—shared, rejected, or betrayed), courting, complaint, celebration, melancholy, and joy. Southern folklife is rooted in the real hungers, the real needs, and the real struggles of southern men and women.

Folklife is a broader concept than *folklore.* The pioneer American folklife scholar Don Yoder describes folklife as an "exciting totality of the verbal, spiritual, and material aspects of a culture." During the first half of the twentieth century, while many American folklorists were preoccupied with lore (the texts of oral tradition), European folklife scholars were more interested in the folk themselves, embracing in their work the customs and material culture of the folk as well as their oral traditions. According to Yoder, "not only does the researcher study the verbal arts of folksong, folktale, riddle, etc.—which the folklorist has long ago made his province—but also agriculture and agrarian history, settlement patterns, dialectology or folk speech, folk architecture, folk cookery, folk costume, the folk year, arts and crafts." The term folklife denotes "the total range of folk-cultural phenomena."

Attempts to define the South have proved even more difficult than attempts to define folk society, folk culture, and folklife. Perhaps a minimum definition would include the states of the former Confederacy, although there might be disputes over whether *all* of Texas is southern. Other definitions add Kentucky, Maryland, Missouri, Oklahoma, and/or West Virginia. A few add Delaware. At least one scholar speaks of a "Southern diaspora" that includes not only Harlem, Watts, and southside Chicago, but Bakersfield, California, and Flint, Michigan, as well. Wherever its borders are drawn, the South displays enormous diversity within them. From the

Sea Islands to the Appalachians, from the Black Belt to the Ozarks, from the bayous of Louisiana to the Rio Grande valley, the South is diverse.

The student of southern folklife cannot limit study to only one group of southerners. The folk culture of the South is not merely the legacy brought by European settlers but is the result of the rich and complex interaction of three major cultural groups—white, red, and black. The origins of southern folklife are found in the story of a small minority of English men and women interacting with a large majority not only of Germans, French, Jews, Highland Scots, Scotch-Irish, Spanish, and Swiss, but also of Catawbas, Cherokees, Choctaws, Creeks, Lumbees, Seminoles, and Tuscaroras, as well as Ashantis, Fantes, Fulas, Ibos, Mandingos, and Yorubas, and more recently of Cubans, East Indians, West Indians, Greeks, Irish, Italians, Lebanese, Vietnamese, and many others. And yet, as W. J. Cash notes, "if it can be said there are many Souths, the fact remains that there is also one South." One who would understand southern folklife must examine the complex ways that its strands have been interwoven over the past three centuries, exemplifying the ways that the lives of diverse groups of southerners have been intertwined. For the rich patterns of southern folklife were woven by black, red, and white southerners.

It is through language that people not only communicate with and entertain one another but link themselves into a community, give shape to a common culture, and pass that culture on to their posterity. At its simplest, folk speech is defined (rather vaguely) as traditional deviations from standard speech. If we define "standard speech" in the South as the language taught in the schools (rather than the language actually spoken by southerners) we shall have to conclude that "folk speech" is a very broad category, including variations in grammar, pronunciation, and vocabulary.

Any discussion of southern folk speech should also include such paralinguistic phenomena as the Rebel Yell; distinctive southern patterns in naming people and places; colorful expressions used as stylistic enhancers in front-porch conversation or storytelling (such as *liked to* for *almost* or *lickety-split* for *in a hurry*); and the sometimes bombastic conglomerations of incomprehensible phraseology that constitute traditional southern political and pulpit oratory. Folk speech is not confined to the rural South. Southerners in the region's cities retain in their speech much of the old regional distinctiveness, but they have also developed new regional characteristics.

The South may be the nation's most distinctive speech region, but there is little uniformity among its speakers. In fact southern speech is more diverse than that of any other region of the nation. Neither the stereotypical southern "drawl" nor even the widespread second-person plural pronoun y'all, perhaps the region's most famous example of folk speech, is ubiquitous. However, although southern speech varies with race, class, and ethnicity, most southerners acquire more than one variety and command the ability to shift styles quickly and naturally. Southern speech also varies with locality, the best-known varieties being those of the Appalachians, the Ozarks, the Virginia tidewater, the South Carolina lowcountry, the Outer Banks of North Carolina, the Florida keys, and New Orleans. But many southerners are able to discern linguistic differences in localities as close as nine miles apart. (A doctoral dissertation has explored linguistic differences among various neighborhoods in Charleston, South Carolina).

While there are few southerners who speak no English, many southerners speak a language other than English as their primary or secondary tongue. Acadian, or Cajun, is a variety of French widespread in southwestern Louisiana, where Francophone refugees from Nova Scotia created a unique culture. Spanish is also common in the South—one variety spoken by Mexican-Americans, known as *Tejanos*, in Texas; another by Central and South Americans in Dallas and Houston; and yet another by Cubans in south Florida. Rather different varieties of German survive among a declining number of speakers within the Austin–Houston–San Antonio triangle of Texas and among Mennonites in western Virginia. All these varieties of French, Spanish, and German have been influenced by the southern speech with which they interact. Many of the Native American languages have become extinct, but Chickasaw, Creek, and Shawnee are spoken in Oklahoma; Choctaw in Oklahoma, Mississippi, and Louisiana; Cherokee in Oklahoma and North Carolina; and Seminole in Oklahoma and Florida.

Linguists call the process by which two or more languages converge to form a new native tongue "creolization" and the product of that process a creole language. Two creole languages developed in the South. In the new physical and social environment of the South the various languages of enslaved Africans were often mutually unintelligible. Out of the convergence of their various African languages and the language of their masters, slaves in the lowcountry of South Carolina and Georgia developed a common creole language called Gullah. Gullah and English had a reciprocal influence upon one another. While Gullah retained thousands of African words, most of the active vocabulary was English. But the grammar—the basic structure that governs how speakers put elements of vocabulary together to generate meaning—embodied constructions most widely shared among a variety of African languages. Similarly, in early Louisiana the dominant language was French. There, out of the convergence of French with their various native languages, enslaved Africans created a creole language and a creolized culture. As in Carolina and Georgia, the new language combined grammatical elements from native African languages with a mostly French vocabulary. And, in Louisiana as in the Carolina and Georgia, the creole culture of black southerners proved to be influential upon white southerners.

Other forms of linguistic folklore include such genres as proverbs, legends, and folktales. Proverbs have served several generations of southerners as guides to appropriate behavior and as informal channels of education. They are still in widespread use today. Though relatively simple in form, proverbs are perhaps the most complex of all folklore genres in their extreme sensitivity to context. The meaning and distinctiveness of the southern proverb lies neither in its form or content, but in the context of its use. And those contexts range as widely and deeply as southern life itself. Embodying the emphasis of the folk on generalized wisdom, proverbs serve southerners as metaphors of collective experience. The proverb repertoire seems to serve some southerners as a set of universal laws against which individual experience may be measured. With their characteristic use of metaphor and their perceptions of similarity and difference, southern proverbs remain close to both poetry and philosophy.

The South has proved to be fertile ground for legends, especially legends of haunted places and revenants, some coming back to complete some unfinished task, others to warn the living of impending disasters. Wherever Spanish moss waves low from the live-oak trees, ghostly legends can be found in profusion. The region also abounds in legends of mysterious lights; of ghostly hitch-hikers; of hags, haunts, and plat-eyes; of historical figures; of local eccentrics; and of natural disasters or narrow escapes.

Generations of southerners have delighted in folktales of the audacious animal trickster Buh Rabbit. Slave storytellers originally blended ancestral African elements with elements of the American historical experience to spin tales of Buh Rabbit's struggle for mastery with his more powerful but less intelligent adversary Buh Bear and in tales of the no-less-audacious slave trickster and his struggle for mastery with his more powerful but less intelligent adversary Ole Massa. Trickster tales taught slave children many valuable lessons. One was that the powerless must learn the ways of the powerful in order to survive. Another was that one must learn how to sidestep a trick as well as how to perpetrate one. These stories, portraying the weak defeating the strong by using their wits, promoted the idea of freedom even within the confines of slavery. Young slaves could identify with Buh Rabbit, the trickster, while Buh Bear, the fool, seemed a great deal like "Ole Massa," the man who claimed to own them. Young slaves learned that ethics appropriate in some situations might not be useful in others. The obligations of friendship were expected within the slave community; but, when dealing with the master, one had much to gain and little to lose by adopting the ethics of the trickster. The slave trickster was called John, John Henry, John the Conqueror, or High John among English-speaking narrators. Not only do Buh Rabbit and John tales continue to live in southern tradition, but such modern black tricksters as Stagolee, Shine, and the Signifyin' Monkey are the stars of long epic poems called toasts.

Other southern folktales are inherited from the European *märchen* tradition, but southern narrators often developed distinctive versions. For instance, Europe's famous "Cinderella" story has been collected in a variety of forms in southern tradition. The traditional North Carolina mountain folktale entitled "Mutsmag" is found in many European collections under the title given it by the Brothers Grimm—"Hansel and Gretel." Yet another story, known throughout Europe as "Beauty and the Beast," still lives in Arkansas, North Carolina, and Virginia, as well as in a fascinating Kentucky version entitled "The Girl Who Married the Flop-Eared Hound Dog." Distinctive southern versions of "The Taming of the Shrew" have also been collected in Virginia, Kentucky, Arkansas, and Texas.

The form now known as the tall tale was used by Native Americans from what is now South Carolina to regale Spanish audiences as early as the 1520s. Tall tales were being told throughout the backwoods South by the nineteenth century, especially in Georgia, Alabama, and Mississippi— the Old Southwest. There is also an Appalachian cycle of tall tales known as "Jack Tales," in which the clever farm boy Jack topples giants and outwits the Devil. Tall tales were often told in liars' contests in which frontier narrators topped one another in spinning yarns about "The Split Dog," "The Snakebit Hoehandle," mythical beasts, crops that grew overnight, and impossible weather. Many of these tall tales are known to posterity by having been published as a new kind of fiction known as "Southwest humor." Humorous folk narratives have also enabled black and white southerners to comment on such matters as rural-urban conflicts and racial tensions. And behind the mask of laughter, a popular cycle of preacher stories cautions southern folk against clerical hypocrisy and the fallibility of fundamentalist religion.

Folktales of European origin have been collected from black southerners, tales of African origin have been collected from white southerners, and both African and European tales have been collected among the Natchez, the Creeks, and the Seminole. Old World tales apparently entered Native American tradition through both Europeans and Africans.

Southern folk customs and rituals are associated with seasonal cycles and with the special events of such rites of passage as childbirth, marriage, and death. Rituals such as "sitting up," a southern version of the wake honoring the dead, and the "shivaree," honoring the newly married couple, seem to be declining in the region. But southern traditions of folk medicine remain strong, functioning mainly as an adjunct rather than as an alternative to formal health care. Southern folk medicine embodies a cultural system centering around a broad spectrum of vernacular healers from midwives and herbalists to conjurers, root doctors, and faith healers. Southern women often play crucial roles as healers who reassure their patients by embodying traditional concepts of health and illness even as they modernize traditional healing practices with elements of scientific medicine. They are aided in their ministrations by various substances such as herbs, roots, and over-the-counter drugs that are considered to help achieve or restore health. Many folk medical practices (and the belief systems they represent) flourish even in the cities.

Material culture was another notable example of culture change in the South. Black southerners imposed an African sensibility upon new materials in a new environment to create new material objects and a new material culture, while white southerners imposed a European sensibility upon new materials in a new environment to create new material objects and a new material culture.

The importance of food to southerners is perhaps best revealed in two proverbs: "a full belly makes strong arms an' a willin' heart," but "hunger tame wild beast." Blacks and whites alike ate the fruits, vegetables, grains, and meats grown in the southern environment. Some southern cuisine consisted of foodstuffs imported from Europe; other foods—such as okra, yams, and rice—were African. Maize, or corn, was adopted from Native

Americans. But to those shared material ingredients black cooks applied
African methods of cooking and spicing, remembered recipes, and ancestral taste preferences. In other words, the "vocabulary" of slave foodways
was *encountered;* the "grammar" (the appropriate ways to put those ingredients together to generate meaning) was *remembered.* The combination
created a distinctive southern cuisine, originated and perfected by black
cooks in white kitchens as well as in their own homes.

Corn, for instance, became central not only to southern cuisine but to
southern cultural identity. It could be eaten on the cob, off the cob, and
in scores of varieties of corn bread, such as hoe cake, johnny cake, spoon
bread, hush puppies, and corn dodgers. And the leftovers could feed the
livestock. But corn's importance was not confined merely to foodways.
Southerners could stuff a mattress with the shucks; braid a collar for the
mule or a mat for the floor; or make a doll for the kids. Or they could mix
corn squeezings with some pure branch water, run it through some copper tubing, and find solace for long winter evenings and perhaps a little
extra cash. By the spoonful or by the glass, corn became a symbol of southern identity (and a staple of southern humor).

Folk arts in the South are rooted not in the individual values of the artist
but in the traditional values of the folk group, the community and the
family. While folk arts are often called primitive or naive by outsiders, they
proclaim the values of a past that is deemed worthy of preservation. When
southern folk artists fashion patchwork quilts or braided rugs, sweetgrass
baskets or split-oak chairs, bottle trees or tractor-tire planters, reed flutes
or cornshuck dolls, designed for beauty and made with skill, they proclaim
by their creations that life can be enriched by one's own efforts. They
proclaim by their creations that the people from whom they learned their
craft (almost always older members of the community) were artists worthy of imitation. They proclaim by their creations that *re*-creation is pref-
erable to new creation, that tradition deserves to survive.

Southern women have produced distinctive and distinguished folk arts,
especially in textiles, quilts, and such needlework as needlepoint, petit-
point, crewelwork, drawnwork, and cross-stitch. Quilts are perhaps the
most colorful of the southern folk arts. Getting together at night, after the
day's other work, women have created warm and beautiful patchwork
quilts, not only to keep their families warm but also to create something
beautiful for the home. Quilters create a design from numerous bits and
pieces (or patches) of cloth. Many of the works of white quilters display

continuities with a rich legacy of European textile art in which the repeated motif is the basic cultural and design unit. Although black quilters learned many techniques from European quilting traditions, many of the quilts of black southerners display continuities with a rich legacy of African textile art in which improvisation, asymmetry, bright colors, strips, and large designs are basic design principles.

Basketmaking comprises three major traditions in the South—black, white, and red—each using somewhat different materials and designs. The famous Gullah baskets of coastal South Carolina are coiled from sweetgrass sewn with palmetto fronds, while Mississippi Choctaw baskets are plaited from cane, and Appalachian baskets are woven from straight-grained hardwoods such as white oak and hickory. Gullah basketmakers have long been admired for the beauty and quality of their baskets, but less attention has been paid to the region's Native American or Anglo-American basketmakers. Anglo-American basketmaking seems to vary little from Virginia to Texas, but Native American basketmaking differs radically from the Atlantic states to Oklahoma.

Black southern blacksmiths have not only shod horses but have also made the beautiful wrought-iron gates so prized in South Carolina and Louisiana. Charleston's Philip Simmons, carrying on a family tradition stretching back eight generations, has become one of the South's most honored folk artists. Other southern folk artists have specialized in creating such musical instruments as fiddles, banjos, and guitars. Among the prominent makers of musical instruments, especially of the distinctive Appalachian dulcimer, are Leonard Glenn, Edsel Martin, and Edd Presnell of North Carolina, Homer Ledford of Kentucky, and Lynn McSpadden of Arkansas.

Pottery has been produced in the South since earliest times. In York County, South Carolina, Catawba Indian pottery exemplifies a fascinating blend of cultural conservatism and cultural innovation. Catawba potters continue to produce pottery in a traditional hand-built and pit-fired manner little changed from the precontact era, but Catawba designs are often strikingly innovative, influenced by increased recognition and growing sales among white collectors. On the slave plantations talented black potters incorporated elements of both African and Native American pottery traditions to make a low-fired unglazed earthenware known as Colono Ware. But the dominant southern pottery tradition has been stoneware, often produced by the same families for generations. Stoneware in the Upper South was glazed by throwing salt in the kiln at the height of firing to form a transparent glass coating over the clay. Salt-glazing was imported from Europe, but alkaline-glazing was created in the South by the potters of Edgefield District, South Carolina. Edgefield potters used slaked wood ashes or lime to help melt the clay and sand and produce green to brown hues with a characteristic runny finish. Alkaline-glazed stoneware has remained distinctive to the South but unknown in the North. The North Carolina pottery tradition included lead-glazed earthenware as well as both salt-glazed and alkaline-glazed stoneware. The most prominent early North Carolina potters were the Moravians, but stoneware production eventually centered in the Seagrove area of the eastern piedmont where some two hundred potters have turned and burned their wares. Although salt glazes prevail among Seagrove potters, alkaline glazes have become the distinctive hallmark of southern pottery from the Carolinas to Texas. The Meaders family of North Georgia, carrying on a multigeneration tradition of alkaline-glazed pottery, created grotesque "face jugs" that have become popular with collectors, filmmakers, folklife scholars, and other potters. Among the region's most celebrated potters have been Georgia's Lanier Meaders, North Carolina's Ben Owen, and the early nineteenth-century Edgefield slave known only as Dave. Their artistic works have been displayed in folk art collections throughout the country.

Talented southern builders, both black and white, fashioned a stunning variety of folk house types, including the log cabin, the I house, the T house, the saddlebag, the dogtrot, and the shotgun. The saddlebag house is one room deep, with a rectangular shape featuring a central chimney and two front doors. The I house is a structure two rooms wide, one room deep, and two rooms tall. The ubiquitous T house, combining vernacular and formal traditions with popular building fashions, comprises a projecting gable wing two rooms deep, straddled by a wing one room deep. Perhaps the most distinctively southern house-types are the dogtrot and the shotgun. The dogtrot is a house with an open hallway separating two rooms under a common roof. The shotgun house, characteristic of black southerners' homes, is one room wide and three rooms long, under a gable roof. It is distinctive because, alone among southern vernacular house-types, its gable end faces the street. The roots of the dogtrot are in Europe; those of the shotgun are in the Caribbean and ultimately Africa.

Southerners inherited from Europe (especially from England and Scotland) a repertory of ballads (or narrative songs) that enabled them to make artistic comments on the human condition. Among ballads surviving in

southern tradition, a common plot involves the difficulty of transcending the rigid class divisions between rich and poor through love. A classic example of this theme is "Lord Thomas," often known as "The Brown
Girl." In a typical version, collected in Murrells Inlet, South Carolina, a
poor girl (Fair Ellender) has fallen in love with a rich young man (Lord
Thomas). When he asks his parents what he should do, his mother urges
him to marry someone of his own station:

> The Brown Girl she has house and land
> Fair Ellender she has none
> I would advise you as a good mother
> To bring the Brown Girl home

Having agreed to marry the Brown Girl, Lord Thomas rides to Fair Ellender's door to invite her in person to his wedding. When she arrives at the
wedding, dressed in scarlet red, Lord Thomas introduces her to his new
bride:

> This is my bride, Lord Thomas said
> This bride belongs to me
> I love the end of your little finger
> Better than her whole body

In a fit of jealous rage, the bride then draws her "little pen knife" and
pierces Fair Ellender's heart. The rich young husband is shocked and
heartbroken:

> He took the Brown Girl by the hand
> And led her through the hall
> He pulled off his sword and cut her head off
> and kicked it against the wall

> Go dig my grave Lord Thomas said
> Dig it both wide and deep
> Bury Fair Ellender in my arms
> And the Brown Girl at my feet

In other ballads it is a poor boy who falls in love with a rich girl, but pa-
rental interference brings equally tragic results. "The Drowsy Sleeper" has
been collected in Virginia, West Virginia, Kentucky, North and South
Carolina, Georgia, Florida, Mississippi, Arkansas, and Missouri. The poor
boy asks the rich girl to marry him. Despite her love for him, she rejects

him, because her parents are violently opposed to the match. By her father's side, she tells him, is a golden dagger to kill the one that she loves
best. In most versions the two lovers commit suicide.

Three types of ballads have been collected in the South. Most prized
by ballad scholars have been the traditional ballads of England and Scotland, often called "Child ballads" after the ballad scholar Francis James
Child, who published a canon under the title *The English and Scottish Popular Ballads*. These include such widely collected ballads as "Lord Thomas" (Child 73) and "Barbara Allen" (Child 84). A second ballad type consists of more recent British broadside ballads, such as "The Butcher Boy"
or "The Drowsy Sleeper." They are often more sensational in plot and less
poetic in language. A third ballad type consists of ballads British in style
and form but American in origin, including ballads on subjects of local and
regional interest, often featuring scandals and tragedies, such as "Naomi
Wise" or "The Titanic." Although the ballad was a European song form,
ballads have been collected from black southerners as well as white, and
some of the best known of the American ballads, such as "John Henry,"
"Delia," and "Frankie and Johnny," were created by black southerners.

The grand and stately spirituals were southern creations, bringing together the structure and rhythm of African music with the melodic and
textual elements of British song. Seemingly concerned with a better life
after death in a literal heaven, the troubles of this world left behind, the
spirituals expressed both a reaffirmation of human dignity and a ringing
condemnation of the wicked ways of the world, offering the slaves both
escape from reality and meaning for life as they struggled for spiritual
survival on the slave plantations.

White spirituals arose in the nineteenth century in the wake of the
religious revivals of the Second Great Awakening. Such white spirituals
as "Wondrous Love" were harmonized and compiled into shape-note
songbooks, such as *The Southern Harmony* and *The Sacred Harp*. Shape
notes, in the form of circles, diamonds, rectangles, and triangles, provided a simple system of reading music, and song leaders "lined out" each
line of the song before the group sang it. *The Southern Harmony* went out
of print in the 1840s, but *The Sacred Harp* is still in active use today in
northern Alabama, northern Mississippi, and southern Tennessee. In
many ways black and white spirituals have paralleled each other, with
many exchanges of melody, rhythm, and lyric. Despite the reciprocity,
each tradition retained distinctive characteristics. In particular, the slave
spirituals were distinguished by an explicit sorrow over the actual woes

of the world, an indignation against oppression, and a resonating cry for freedom that had little counterpart in the white spirituals. By the dawn of the twentieth century, the parallel black and white traditions developed faster-paced "gospel" styles that became popular among southern audiences, often featuring such black or white family groups as the Chosen Sisters or the Blackwood Brothers.

The spirituals reflect the religious life of black southerners, but few of their secular songs were meant for the ears of the Lord, much less those of Ole Massa. Out of the field hollers of the Old South developed the most important black music of the New South—the blues, first recorded on "race records" in the 1920s, featuring such acoustic "country blues" artists as Mississippi's Charley Patton and Robert Johnson and Texas's Blind Lemon Jefferson. In the blues, stark, full, human passions expressed a fundamental and universal emotion of the human heart, a kind of disillusionment without defeat that might be called existential. In Memphis and, following the Great Migration, in southside Chicago, southern artists such as Muddy Waters and B.B. King developed "urban blues" on electric instruments.

Across the South, most white southerners grew up with the songs of black southerners falling upon their ears. Despite themselves, most southern whites understood that the songs of black southerners somehow captured the essence of the southern irony, of the southern tragedy, and of the southern hope. Despite themselves, they were profoundly influenced by the songs of their black neighbors. These cultural seeds would sprout exciting new hybrids in the American South. Cultural traditions mixed in new and exciting ways, providing clues to the expansion of southern cultural boundaries. In the convergence of various African cultures and European cultures in the American South, white southerners had their old cultures Africanized by their black neighbors and black southerners had their old cultures Europeanized by their white neighbors.

The interaction of musical traditions gave rise to new genres of music, serving as the catalyst for ragtime, black brass band music, and ultimately jazz on one hand, and for southern mountain hoedowns, hillbilly, and eventually country music on the other. Over the decades the verse forms of ballads and folksongs evolved into country music, first recorded on "hillbilly" records in the 1920s by such southern musicians as Mississippi's Jimmie Rodgers and Virginia's Carter Family. White singers from the Deep South such as Jimmie Rodgers and later Hank Williams were heavily influenced by the blues because they grew up among black southerners and were influenced by their music. Bluegrass music is a post-1945 development in acoustic stringband music that adapts the archaic fiddle tunes and vocal styles of traditional British folk music to supercharged rhythms and complex, blues-influenced picking on mandolin and banjo. Bill Monroe was the central figure in the emergence of bluegrass music; and his band, the Blue Grass Boys, served as a training ground for such future stars of bluegrass as Lester Flatt and Earl Scruggs, Mac Wiseman, Don Reno, and Sonny Osborne.

The rich diversity of southern ethnicity is reflected in the Cajun music of southwest Louisiana, combining elements of African, British, Spanish, and French traditions; the zydeco music of Louisiana's black Creoles, blending elements of Cajun music with heavy doses of the blues and complex Caribbean rhythms; and the *norteno conjunto* music of the Texas *barrios*, intermingling elements of Mexican and German music. Cajun performers such as Dennis McGee and Nathan Abshire, zydeco performers such as Amadie Ardoin and Clifton Chenier, and *conjunto* performers such as Santiago Jimenez and Narciso Martinez pioneered these ethnic musical forms. More recently the Cajun fiddler Michael Doucet and his group Beausoleil, the zydeco accordionist Queen Ida, and the *conjunto* accordionist Flaco Jimenez have brought renewed popularity to the music.

Beginning in the 1930s such southern folksingers as Kentucky's Aunt Molly Jackson, Oklahoma's Woody Guthrie, and Louisiana's Huddie Ledbetter, better known as "Leadbelly," used southern folk music to attract support for labor unions, civil rights, and social change in the region. In the 1960s Bernice Johnson Reagon, of Albany, Georgia, and the Freedom Singers of the Student Nonviolent Coordinating Committee continued that tradition, attracting both moral and financial support for the civil rights movement.

§

Out of the convergence of African and European traditions, so different yet so alike, emerged a new southern folk culture, a folk culture with both an African and a European heritage yet as different from either as water is from hydrogen and oxygen. I believe that the sharing of cultural traditions in the South is more responsible than any other single factor for the extraordinary richness of southern culture. The new synthesis has been a dynamic, evolving tradition, deeply affected by the ideals, frustrations, anxieties, and hopes of all the southern people by whom it was created.

Central to the richness of southern folk culture has been racial integration, but it was not obvious for a long time. One reason was that earlier folklorists, conceptualizing their task as the preservation of "cultural survivals," sought the "purest" survivals of European and African traditions. Thus ballad collectors went to the Appalachians or the Ozarks, and spiritual collectors went to the Sea Islands or the Black Belt. Other southerners, black or white, were free to sing without fear of being interrupted by strangers with notebooks or microphones. Another reason it was not obvious was that the white elite—the so-called "leaders" of the white South—spent a great deal of time, money, and energy in an effort to create and maintain a racially segregated society. But, like Huck and Jim on their raft, black and white folk southerners recognized that they were in the same boat. They continued to swap recipes and cultural styles, songs and stories, accents and attitudes. Folk culture simply refused to abide by any color line, however rigidly it may have been drawn.

Unlike other purported explanations of southern identity, folklife rests upon the shared cultural past of all southerners, rather than upon that of white southerners alone. "The black Southerner and the white Southerner are locked to the land and to history," the novelist Maya Angelou says, "a painful history of guilt and cruelty and ignorance. It clings to us like the moss on the trees." Jack Burden, the aptly named protagonist of Robert Penn Warren's *All the King's Men*, tells "how if you could not accept the past and its burden there was no future, for without one there cannot be the other, and how if you could accept the past you might hope for the future, for only out of the past can you make the future." The history of the South's racially mixed folk culture offers southerners a different perspective from which they might, if they will, understand and accept their past. The American South was multicultural from its very beginnings. "Our cultural patterns are an amalgam of black and white. Our destinies are tied together," declared Martin Luther King Jr. "Somewhere along the way the two must join together, black and white together, we shall overcome, and I still believe it." From that vantage point, the great tradition of southern folklife has a special contribution to make to the region's future.

PART ONE

The Old South

2

"Let Us Break Bread Together"
Cultural Interaction in the Old South

Some years ago, I was speaking on the subject of southern music to a large, racially mixed, adult audience at one of the community colleges in North Carolina. I told them I wanted to begin by playing taped selections of two southern musicians. I told them the two shared a great deal. Each came from a rural Mississippi background. Each sang about everyday southern life. One was white and one was black. One went into country music and one went into jazz. I did not identify the musicians. After I played the songs I asked the audience to discuss what they had heard. The audience spoke of the racial characteristics of the music. It was immediately evident from the comments that they thought the country musician was white and the jazz musician was black. After I had identified the musicians as Charlie Pride and Mose Allison, I explained to a more receptive audience than usual that musical styles are cultural rather than genetic, and that each of the musicians was playing in a racially mixed musical tradition.

Most Americans know about Mississippi and the blues, one of America's greatest cultural achievements. They know about B.B. King, and Muddy Waters, and James "Son" Thomas. Many know about John Lee Hooker, Howlin' Wolf, Mississippi John Hurt, and Fred McDowell. Some even know about Tommy Johnson, Robert Johnson, and Charley Patton (although some don't know Diddley). Most Americans also know that Mississippi plays a central role in country music and country comedy. They know about Conway Twitty, and Tammy Wynette, and Jerry Clower. And many Americans know about Mississippi and jazz. At least they know about Lester Young. These artists became stars performing in the style more or less expected of them by most Americans.

But Mississippians know, better than other Americans, that not everyone sounds like they are expected to sound. They know that the leading
contralto of the Metropolitan Opera, before her retirement, was a black
woman from Laurel, Mississippi—Leontyne Price. They know, better than
other Americans, that one of the leading stars of country music is a black
man from Sledge, Mississippi—Charley Pride. They know, better than
other Americans, that one of America's leading jazz pianists, famed for
his funky chords and blues-drenched vocals, is a white man from Tippo,
Mississippi—Mose Allison. They know, better than other Americans, that
one of America's leading blues singers, Johnny Winter, is a white Mississippian. Many of them know that a native of Woodville, Mississippi,
William Grant Still, was the first black conductor to conduct a major symphony orchestra, the first black composer to have a symphony performed
by a major symphony orchestra, and the first black conductor to conduct
a major symphony orchestra in the South. They know that cultural styles
have always refused to observe any color line.

And they know something about musical integration, too. They know
that in the 1920s Jimmie Rodgers, a white Mississippian, fused the twelve-
bar country blues of his black neighbors with the "Swiss yodels" of white
vaudeville music, to become the first great star of country music. And they
know that in the 1950s another white Mississippian, Elvis Presley, combined the urban blues of black southerners, the country music of white
southerners, and the gospel music of both into a new synthesis, which was
soon labeled rock 'n' roll.[1]

That the folk culture of white southerners has its roots in European—
mainly British—sources has been so commonly assumed that its demonstration hardly seemed necessary. That the folk culture of white southerners also has roots in African sources has seemed so patently absurd that
few scholars have bothered to explore the question. Recent scholarship
has challenged the orthodoxy on white southern culture in two ways. One
has been an emphasis on *Celtic* rather than *English* sources of southern
culture, the other an emphasis on specific regional British roots for specific
regional American cultures, North and South.

Grady McWhiney, in his *Cracker Culture*, contends that "a list of southern traits most observed by contemporaries reads like an inventory of
traditional Scottish, Irish, and Welsh cultural characteristics." McWhiney's "list of Southern traits" constitutes a daunting catalog of negative
stereotypes. Southerners were, he writes, lazy, idle, and illiterate folk who
loafed except when forced to work; they ate, drank, smoked, chewed,

gambled, and fought to excess, but were highly musical and fond of dancing. Were McWhiney not of southern birth, rearing, and residence, and did his surname not begin with a Celtic *Mac*, surely someone would complain that the South in general and Celts in particular had been victimized by vile Yankee slander. Many slaveholders in the Old South ascribed the same cultural traits to black southerners, citing them as sufficient evidence of African genetic inferiority to justify slavery. An alternative hypothesis might be that all these traits the masters complained about were in fact characteristics learned by the slaves from Celtic whites.[2]

In *Albion's Seed,* it is David Hackett Fischer's bold thesis that the major dialects of American speech, the major regional patterns of American life, the continuing conflicts between customary ways of thinking about order, power, and freedom, and the complex dynamics of American politics, all derive principally from four British regional folkways brought to America between 1629 and 1775. Folk from each of these British regions spoke distinctive dialects of English, had distinctive folkways by which they conducted their everyday lives, and had distinctive customs and conceptions of order, power, and freedom. The culture of Virginia, for instance, derives specifically from Royalists and indentured servants from the south and west of England, Fischer notes, who brought their folkways with them. Similarly, the culture of the southern backcountry derives from settlers from the borderlands of north Britain and Ireland.[3]

Not only have the African sources of the white southern folk culture long gone unacknowledged, the African sources of *black* southern folk culture were denied by all but a few until the 1970s. In fact, the question of the nature and origin of the folk culture of black southerners has remained one of the most controversial topics in the controversial literature of southern history and culture.

One school of thought, identified with the black sociologist E. Franklin Frazier, emphasizes the influence of European culture upon enslaved Africans. No major contemporary scholar embraces this school in an overall sense, although some researchers do emphasize white influence in specific fields, such as language or religion. According to John Boles, for instance, religion was the principal channel through which European culture reached the slaves. John Blassingame seems to share Boles's view insofar as it applies to slave religion. "The church," he notes in the second edition of his *The Slave Community,* "was the single most important institution for the 'Americanization' of the bondsman." It should be emphasized that both Boles and Blassingame acknowledge African and European cultural interaction. Neither argues exclusively British or European sources in the formation of slave culture. But they are imprecise on either the proportions or the process of cultural interaction in the Old South.[4]

An opposite school of thought, emphasizing the "Africanity" of slave culture, derives from the work of the white anthropologist Melville J. Herskovits. A leading contemporary spokesman for this school, Sterling Stuckey, argues in his *Slave Culture* that the distinctive attributes of African-American Christianity were outward and visible manifestations of inward and invisible African cognitive orientations. Most important, according to Stuckey, "by operating under cover of Christianity, vital aspects of Africanity, which were considered eccentric in movement, sound, or symbolism, could more easily be practiced openly." Stuckey writes from an Afrocentric critical perspective, using African rather than European ideals as a standpoint from which to understand the culture of the African diaspora. "Christianity," as he sees it, was "shot through with African values." What Blassingame describes as "the 'Americanization' of the bondsman" Stuckey calls the "Africanization of Christianity."[5]

Before celebrating the insights or lamenting the myopia of either of these schools of thought, I would like to review the scholarly traditions behind them. As Ralph Ellison says, "If you would tell me who I am, at least take the trouble to discover what I have been."[6] In the first half of the twentieth century, the leading university historian of slavery was Yale's Georgia-born scholar Ulrich Bonnell Phillips. His *American Negro Slavery*, published in 1918, remained the standard work on the subject until the 1950s. Although Phillips was ambivalent regarding the influence of Africa on African Americans, his view of Africa was terribly negative. "No people is without its philosophy and religion," he admitted, but "of all regions of extensive habitation equatorial Africa is the worst." As for the Africans, "the climate in fact not only discourages but prohibits mental effort of severe or sustained character, and the negroes have submitted to that prohibition as to many others, through countless generations, with excellent grace." Such African continuities as he acknowledged, he deplored. Slavery he regarded as a school—mostly successful—for civilizing savages.[7]

According to what has been called the catastrophist school of American sociological thought, African Americans, alone among all the peoples that made up the United States, had lost their entire native culture. Following the position enunciated in 1919 by the University of Chicago sociologist Robert E. Park, the catastrophists regarded black folkways as an

imperfect accommodation to an American culture derived from Europe.[8]
E. Franklin Frazier was the foremost figure of the catastrophist school.
"Probably never before in history," Frazier wrote, "has a people been so
completely stripped of its social heritage as the Negroes who were brought
to America." The positive result of losing their African heritage, however, was that they had "gradually taken over the more sophisticated American culture."[9] The classic sociological studies of the South Carolina Sea
Islands in the 1930s followed the catastrophist interpretation of Park and
Frazier. In his *Folk Culture on St. Helena Island*, Guy B. Johnson traced the
genealogy of African-American speech, songs, and folk beliefs mainly to
white sources. Other studies in the St. Helena project by Guion Griffis
Johnson and T. J. Woofter Jr. were in the same tradition.[10]

For the most part folklorists of the period tended to publish large collections of lore without drawing many conclusions about the folk. For
example, the white folklorist Elsie Clews Parsons collected African-American folklore in the Sea Islands off South Carolina and in the Caribbean.
She refrained from inferences, but her careful annotations showed the
similarity of her material to folklore collected in Africa. On the other
hand, Newbell Niles Puckett, another white folklorist, said in his *Folk
Beliefs of the Southern Negro*, that while most whites believed African-American "superstitions" to be relics of African heathenism "in four cases out
of five it is a European dogma." The black folklorist Zora Neale Hurston
suggested in her *Mules and Men* that there was a more complex relationship between African and European elements underlying African-American folklore, but she was somewhat vague about their proportions.[11]
Hurston, in a letter to her anthropological mentor Franz Boas, pointed out
with feigned naivete how easily Western religion might be interpreted in
the same "primitive" terms that Western scholars apply to African religions. "Is it safe for me to say that baptism is an extension of water worship as a part of pantheism," she asked, "just as the sacrament is an extension of cannibalism?" "Isn[']t the use of candles in the Catholic chu[r]ch
a relic of fire worship? Are not all the uses of fire upon the altars the same
thing? Is not the [C]hristian ritual rather one of attenuated nature-wor-
ship, in the fire, water, and blood? Might not the frequently mentioned fire
of the Holy Ghost not [*sic*] be an unconscious fire worship. May it not be a
deification of fire?"[12] Both Parsons and Hurston were trained anthropologists who had studied with Boas at Columbia University. Boas, in a pro-
lific series of books, articles, and platform addresses, inaugurated what
would ultimately become a massive campaign for the recognition that cul-

ture is not racial—that is to say, biological—but social. Eager to combat
the evolutionary tradition in anthropology that considered blacks to be
at an earlier, less advanced level of civilization than whites, Boas denied
any enduring influence of African culture.[13]

The year 1944 saw the publication of Gunnar Myrdal's *An American
Dilemma*, an erudite and influential exploration of the tensions inherent
in America's attempt to encompass both racial prejudice and democratic
ideals of equality at the same time. Myrdal's social analysis was trenchant,
but his understanding of black culture simply reiterated the catastrophist position. "American Negro culture," the Swedish scholar insisted, "is
not something independent of general American culture. It is a distorted
development, or a pathological condition, of the general American culture."[14] Even as late as 1963, the catastrophist interpretation continued to
dominate American social science. In that year Nathan Glazer and Daniel
Patrick Moynihan echoed Park and Frazier in their *Beyond the Melting Pot*:
"The Negro," they wrote, "is only an American and nothing else. He has
no culture and values to guard and protect."[15]

But in the 1930s one anthropologist was beginning to ask if scholars
might not, upon close examination of African-American culture, find
"some subtle elements left of what was ancestrally possessed." Himself a
student of Boas, Melville J. Herskovits had early in his career scorned the
idea that there were even lingering traces of Africa among African Americans and had doubted that there was any separate African-American culture. As he began to conduct comparative research in New World African-American cultures, however, Herskovits began to question his earlier
position.[16]

In 1941, following several years of fieldwork in the Caribbean, in Bra-
zil, and in West Africa, Herskovits published his most significant work,
The Myth of the Negro Past. In it he proposed a general theory of culture
change that posited the persistence of African "survivals" in African-
American culture, survivals such as the Savannah Unit of the Federal
Writers Project had already demonstrated the previous year in *Drums and
Shadows: Survival Studies among the Georgia Coastal Negroes*. But *Drums and
Shadows* met with indifference, while *The Myth of the Negro Past* was im-
mediately controversial. Nearly all American intellectuals, black and
white, denounced the Herskovits thesis as misguided and exaggerated.
Racial equalitarians such as E. Franklin Frazier and Guy B. Johnson were
concerned that segregationists might use Herskovits's arguments to build
a case that African-Americans were unassimilable. Herskovits, a longtime

foe of white supremacy, was no supporter of segregation (even though much of his *Myth of the Negro Past* was built upon the scholarship of Ulrich B. Phillips, whom he quoted approvingly a dozen times). But few Americans other than ardent white supremacists were prepared to accept his thesis of African survivals in the New World.[17]

Given the ideologies of our own time it is not easy to understand the widespread aversion to Africa among those most strongly committed to racial equality. Why were most black intellectuals reluctant to acknowledge their African heritage? The answer lies in their understanding of the place Africa held in white racism. Behind white racism was the image of Africa as "the dark continent," a land of backwardness and savagery. Those who held black people in bondage and claimed to own them justified their claims by defining African Americans as inherently different—and inherently inferior. Behind white racism was the widespread conviction that blacks, once freed from the restraints so beneficently bestowed by slavery, were in imminent danger of reverting to the savage state presumed natural to their African origins. It is now easy enough to see that a more constructive response to white racism would have been to promote a better understanding of Africa. But in the first half of the twentieth century, for African Americans to acknowledge a continuing African heritage was tantamount to acknowledging that they had a very tenuous hold on "civilization." Like present-day liberals, they found it easier simply to run from the label and its pejorative identification.[18]

There is merit in each of the scholarly traditions under consideration, but each has serious shortcomings as a perspective from which to understand the nature of southern culture. To underestimate the Africanity of African-American culture is to rob the slaves of their heritage. But to overestimate the Africanity of that culture is to deny the slaves their creativity. Africans were creative in Africa; they did not cease to be creative when they became involuntary settlers in America. African-American Christianity, for example, was neither a continuation of African religion disguised as Christianity nor a dark version of the Christianity preached by slaveholders, but a complex amalgam drawing upon many traditions, African and European.

What may be considered a third school of thought is exemplified by Mechal Sobel, who contends in her *The World They Made Together* that stressing the relative autonomy of slave culture overlooks the cultural interaction of Africans and Europeans in the colonial Chesapeake. Not only was African-American culture shaped by exposure to white culture, she writes, but emergent forms of white culture were also shaped by close association with bearers of African tradition. "Blacks and whites played together as children, danced, drank, and 'slept' together as adults," she writes. "As a result a new culture emerged in the American South that was a mix of both African and English values."[19]

The convergence of African and European elements varied widely, of course, conditioned by specific environmental and demographic features. There was more than one acculturation process going on in the Old South. African and European cultures on the whole were converging and modifying each other, but an interchange between European cultures—English, Scottish, Scotch-Irish, Welsh, French, German, and Spanish, in particular—was also taking place in the Old South. And in the new physical and social environment of such places as the Carolina and Georgia lowcountry, where enslaved Africans and their descendants constituted 80 to 90 percent of the population for most of the eighteenth and nineteenth centuries, many African cultures were intersecting and altering one another. African men and women of different ethnic groups mixed in ways that did not occur in Africa. Whether Fullah or Fante, Gola or Guinea, or whatever African ethnic group, on any given morning in a lowcountry rice field, an enslaved African would meet more Africans from more ethnic groups than he or she would encounter in a lifetime in Africa. The varied African cultures were fused increasingly in combinations that did not exist in Africa. A new culture, predominantly African in origin but different from any particular African culture, began to take shape.[20]

I have tried to explain this cultural transformation with the concept of creolization. Perhaps it can best be illustrated by looking first at one element of the slaves' culture change: their acquisition of a common language. It is through language that people not only communicate with and entertain one another but link themselves into a community, give shape to a common culture, and hand down that culture to their posterity. The slaves' various African languages were often mutually unintelligible, but through creolization a common language evolved. Lowcountry slaves, for example, developed Gullah. Combining English vocabulary with African grammar, Gullah was strikingly similar to the creole languages of Jamaica and Barbados.[21]

Another product of convergence, the Acadian, or Cajun, culture centered in southwest Louisiana rests upon a foundation of western French folkways, but it also includes influences from English, Scottish, Irish, Native American, Caribbean, German, Spanish, and African folk tradition.

One of the early Cajun recordings was *Blues Nègres,* a ten-inch 78 rpm record with vocal by Cléoma Falcon and accordion and guitar accompaniment.[22]

Language was, of course, only one element of the transformation from African to African-American culture. But it provides a model for explaining other elements of culture change. What I have called the "creolization of culture" involves the unconscious "grammatical" principles of culture—the "deep structure" that generates specific cultural patterns. Such "grammatical" principles survived the middle passage and governed the selective adaptation of elements of both African and European culture in a complex amalgam. Enslaved Africans, herded together with others with whom they shared only a common condition of servitude and some degree of cultural overlap, employed their African creativity in creating a new language, a new religion, and a new culture.[23]

A striking example of cultural creolization was the mutual transformation of African religious systems and Christianity in the South. Black southerners imposed an African religious grammar on encountered Christian traditions. Christianity is a universal religion, not just a white religion. Nevertheless enslaved Africans encountered Christianity largely through their masters. At the vocabulary level—that is, in its theology—there is little difference between the religious beliefs of black and white Christians in the South. There may be a difference in emphasis. Black Christians, it is said, emphasize salvation and redemption, while white Christians emphasize sin and damnation. That may be denominationally specific. White evangelists, especially those of a Calvinist persuasion, did indeed stress sin and damnation. And the appeal of a doctrine of salvation and redemption in a heaven yet to come is readily understandable. Nonetheless, black Christians did believe in sin and damnation; and even Calvinists believed in salvation and redemption (if only for the elect). At the vocabulary level, African-American Christianity would seem to be a prime example of cultural borrowing. At the grammatical level, however—that is, at the level of how the vocabulary of Christianity was used to generate meaning, to worship God—the differences between black Christianity and white Christianity are so profound that typically each group thinks nothing very religious is going on in the worship services of the other. Black Christians tend to think white Christians go to church to hear a lecture. In that supposition they are not, of course, altogether mistaken. White Christians tend to think black Christians go to church to have a good time. The concept of "having a good time in the name of the Lord" is not normally a part of white Christianity. The slaves did not simply adopt the God and the faith of the white missionaries. In establishing a spiritual life for themselves, they reinterpreted elements of Christianity in terms of deep-rooted African cognitive (or "grammatical") orientations—mental rules governing appropriate behavior—that profoundly affected their Christianity. The result was more than a dark reflection of white religion.[24]

On the slave plantations of the Old South necessity was upon the slaves to make their own music, their own songs. They sang on the way to the fields in the morning, they sang while they plowed and hoed under the broiling sun, they came in singing from the fields. Most slaveholders liked for their slaves to sing while working, and few could prevent it in any case. After the day's work was done, slaves entertained their children with play songs and at night sang them to sleep with lullabies.[25]

On Saturday nights, from Virginia and the Carolinas through Alabama and Mississippi to Louisiana and Texas, the slaves held dances and frolics.[26] Slave religious services were especially marked by music. Whether the slaves slipped away into the woods on Sunday evenings or had general prayer meetings on Wednesday nights at slave chapels, they would often "turn de wash pot bottom upwards so de sound of our voices would go under de pot." Then they "would have a good time shouting, singing, and praying just like we pleased."[27] Deeply expressive of the life of the slaves, and at the same time deeply revealing of the Old South, the spirituals rank among the classic folk expressions. The songs offered escape from reality and meaning for life. But they also expressed something much more specific. When the slaves sang, "Go Down, Moses, way down in Egypt land, tell old Pharaoh to let my people go," the Pharaoh they envisioned often looked just like Ole Massa. The slaves knew that Moses had set his people free, but only after plagues had been visited upon the Egyptian power structure. And when they sang, "Jordan's river is chilly and wide, milk and honey on the other side" and "Jordan's river is chilly and cold, chills the body but not the soul," the Jordan they were singing of may have flowed between the banks of the Potomac or the Ohio. And what could the slaves have meant by "Steal away, steal away. . . . I ain't got long to stay here"?[28]

A shared spiritual tradition touched the lives of both blacks and whites in the antebellum South. A European traveler witnessed one example of black-white musical interaction near Charleston, South Carolina. "By degrees the people began to assemble," she wrote, "the white people on one side, the black on the other." As they sang, she assumed that "most likely the sound proceeded from the black portion of the assembly, as their number was three times that of the whites, and their voices are naturally beautiful and pure." She characterized the massed sounds as "a magnificent choir." Another observer reported on religious services in Virginia: "White people or black, and sometimes both together, would begin to sing, and being affected would begin to pray, and others would join with them, and they would continue their cries till some of them would find peace in their souls."[29]

Singlehandedly the spirituals debunk the stereotype that enslaved Africans brought no culture with them to the New World, that the slaves were cultural beggars waiting for a few crumbs of culture to be tossed to them, that the slave plantations were schools for civilizing savages. The slaves were not merely receivers of European culture, they were also donors of African culture, and they rank among the creators of southern culture.[30]

For the slaves on southern plantations, as for their African ancestors, the funeral was life's true climax. At once a religious ritual, a major social event, and a community pageant, the slave funeral drew upon cherished African tradition. A northern teacher in Louisiana wrote in her diary, "This evening a negro . . . died suddenly—about 9 ocl'k. . . . Heard a sound of distant music. It was a lament for the dead. . . . The negroes assemble and spend a great part of the night praying and singing." A Georgia slave recalled, "The mourners beat the drum while on the way to the cemetery; after arriving they marched around the grave in a ring and beat the drum and shouted." A slave funeral in Virginia was witnessed by Frederick Law Olmsted in 1853. "An old negro," he wrote, "raised a hymn, which soon became a confused chant—the leader singing a few words alone, and the company then either repeating them after him or making a response to them."[31]

As they cleared the fields, planted and harvested the crops, and built the plantations and cities of the South, black southerners sang. Whether alone in field hollers or together in choruses of cotton pickers, timing the swing of their singing to the rhythmic motions of their labor, black southerners sang. Singing seemed to make the work go easier. Singing seemed to ease the aches of backs and the aches of hearts.[32]

The long-range impact of cultural interaction in the Old South was profound. Minstrel songs, composed by whites in imitation of slave melodies, were more influential than was once suspected. Minstrel songs filtered back from professional entertainers to both white and black folk musicians across the South, stimulating new fusions, such as jazz and country music.[33]

Ernest Roubleau, a light-skinned black banjo and guitar player from New Orleans, toured and recorded with a racially mixed hillbilly band in the 1930s. Operating out of Johnson City, Tennessee, in the Smoky Mountains, the band had four musicians—two white and two black. The quartet played square dances around the Tennessee–North Carolina border area.[34]

When Steve Brown was interviewed by Richard Allen for the Jazz Archive at Tulane, Allen asked him, "Were the Dorseys in here anywhere?" Brown, who had played in a band called "Brown's Band" or "Brown's Ragtime Band" before 1913, replied that "they, uh, no colored have never played with us." Allen rephrased his question. "No, I mean Jimmy and Tommy Dorsey." Brown answered, "Oh, you mean Dorseys!" Allen said, "Yeah." Brown replied, "I thought you said darkies." But Brown did acknowledge to Allen that he had employed a black bass player in New Orleans and that he had jammed with Louis Armstrong in Chicago.[35]

Country music has its roots in the music of the early settlers. One can find in country music echoes of the old ballad styles of singing, of bagpipes and fiddle sounds of the British Isles, minstrel show songs and sentimental songs of the nineteenth century. But another major influence on country music was the music of black southerners, especially the blues, from which this emerging popular music of white southerners borrowed both chords and color. African-American melodic, textual, and instrumental styles influenced white musicians, who enriched their music without losing their own identity. Bill C. Malone emphasizes that, despite overlapping song repertoires, "a mutually cherished hymn like 'Amazing Grace,' or a commonly performed fiddle tune like 'Old Zip Coon,' assumed radically different forms when winnowed and shaped in the styles of black and white performers."[36]

Thus the intersection of cultural styles in the Old South not only engendered an important shared heritage of repertoires and performance styles but also stimulated distinctive new forms of expression among both black and white performers. This mixing of cultural traditions—operating on so many levels and generating so many new cultural forms—is more responsible than any other factor for the extraordinary richness of southern culture.

3

"In His Hands"

The World of the Plantation Slaves

Little Jacob was a slave. At the age of eight he was assigned to help take care of his master's stable of fine horses. One day a groom began to beat him with a switch for no apparent reason. It was the first time he had been whipped by anyone except his parents. He cried out in pain, but he thought to himself that he would tell his father. Father would take care of that groom. When at last his oppressor quit beating him, Jacob ran to his father. His father, William, only told him there was nothing he could do. He told Jacob to be a good boy and go back to work. But Jacob's mother, Chloe, complained to the groom. The groom took his whip and began to flog *her*. Jacob ran back and forth between them until the groom stopped beating her and gave *him* another whipping.

Soon Jacob's whippings became daily ordeals. Eventually he told his parents he would put up with the whippings no longer. He would fight back. William forbade him, because the master would think his parents had advised him to fight. That would make life harder for the whole family. William told Jacob to keep silent and do his work as well as he could. Frustrated, Jacob complained that he did not know why he should be whipped. He had done nothing wrong. The groomsman simply whipped him because he felt like it. William replied sadly that the only thing he could do was to pray to the Lord to hasten the time when such things should all be done away.

Chloe burst into tears when she saw the wounds upon Jacob's back, but there was little she could do to comfort him. She said she would not mind it so much except that Jacob was so small. If she told the master, she believed he would forbid the groomsman to treat the child so cruelly. She had grown up with her master, she said, and he would listen to her. But William was skeptical. If the master stopped the groomsman from whipping Jacob, William said, the groomsman would only avenge himself through the overseer. The best thing for them to do would be to pray over it. The time would come when the children would be free, though their parents might not live to see it. Chloe cried out that she wished they would take her son out of this world so he would be out of pain. If he were in heaven, his parents would not have to fret so about him. William told the boy not to worry, he would be a man eventually. Jacob thought if small boys are treated so cruelly, how much worse would it be when he became a man?

Suddenly Jacob realized for the first time what slavery really meant, realized that he and the rest of his fellow slaves were doomed to arbitrary treatment through life. And there was nothing he could do about it. Not only was he unable to defend himself, his parents could not defend him either. They, too, were forced to submit to the same degradation. At bedtime the family knelt in prayer. William's prayer seemed more anguished and more genuine to Jacob that night than ever before, especially when he prayed that the Lord would hasten the time when the children would be free men and women. Jacob expected that the Lord would answer his father's prayer in two or three weeks at the latest. He could not know then that his father would die the following year, or that it would be six more years before emancipation.[1]

The story of little Jacob Stroyer contains within it most of the great themes inherent in the world of plantation slaves—coming of age in bondage, the agony of discovering one's degraded status, the drudgery of work and the arbitrariness of punishment, the consolations and limitations of religion and family, the advantages and limits of personal relations between slaves and masters. Jacob's ordeal thus simultaneously reveals the strengths and the weaknesses of the emergent folk culture created by the slave community and exposes the cruelty and inhumanity of the slave experience. It is easy to overemphasize either the achievements of the community or the constraints of the institution, and it is difficult to assess the proportions of these two great truths. The cultural achievement of the slave community was real, but the story of Jacob Stroyer is a moving reminder that it was accomplished against almost overwhelming odds.

᪣

Cotton was the dominant crop of the Old South, but some regions with the highest concentrations of slaves were not part of the Cotton Kingdom. There were tobacco plantations in the Chesapeake, rice plantations in the lowcountry of South Carolina and Georgia, and sugar plantations in Louisiana. But whether on cotton, tobacco, rice, or sugar plantations, most slaves were field workers. Slave workdays began before dawn. The slaves were summoned to the fields by the sound of a bell, horn, or conch. And at harvest time virtually all of the slaves on the plantation were pressed into field work, regardless of their usual occupations.

Cotton was a hazardous crop. Cato, a Georgia driver, wrote to his master, "The heavy rains in August & hot Sun has damaged us in the cotton much. All the unmanured ground is more or less blighted & in Spots looks like winter but the manured ground though diseased holds on well. But sometimes success could come when least expected." With a justifiable tone of pride, Cato added, "The marsh has astonished every boddy that has seen it. It is very fine cotton & especially all the oldest stocks from the first planting, we have now all the women picking cotton & from appearance will have no more time to do anything else. It is opening finely & is very white & pretty cotton. I think we will make Thirty Bales unless I am much deceived."[2]

Former slaves, interviewed by field researchers of the Federal Writers Project in the 1930s, remembered their work vividly. Ebenezer Brown, a slave on a Mississippi cotton plantation, sang, "Watch de sun, see how she run; / Niver let her ketch yo' wit yer wurk undun."[3] Slaves on cotton plantations "listed" the ground—that is, broke it up with a broad cotton-field hoe. A full hand was expected to "list" half an acre per day. "June month," the slaves agreed, "was a ha'd month." The sun was hot and the weeds grew fast in June. As the slaves moved across the cotton fields, keeping time to the rise and fall of their hoes, they sang a favorite tune:

What y'u gwine t'do fo' June month?
    Jerusalem Jerusalem.
Pull off y'u coat an' go t'work.
    Jerusalem Jerusalem.
June month's a ha'd month.
    Jerusalem Jerusalem.
Jerusalem in the mornin'.
    Jerusalem Jerusalem.

At harvest time, a full hand was expected to pick at least ninety pounds of cotton a day:

> Way down in the bottom—whah the cotton boll's a rotten
>   Won' get my hundud all day
> Way down in the bottom—whah the cotton boll's a rotten
>   Won' get my hundud all day.[4]

If the master owned a cotton gin, it was usually operated by male slaves. Packing the cotton in with their feet was hard and tiring work.

Virginia slaves had vivid memories of setting out the tobacco plants in the spring. "Dey w'uld 'ave de land all hilled up fur de plants, an' de 'bacco plants w'uld be put in a wagon an' de wagon w'uld be drawn by six oxen. De 'bacco rows w'uld be one mile long. I 'ave seen 50, 60, or 75 'ands settin' ert 'bacco plants. Dey always had one or two plants in their 'ands, so if one want good dey w'uld use de 'toter one. Aftur de 'bacco grew dey w'uld prime de le'ves off, de lower ones, le'vin de good ones on. Den dey w'uld worm 'hit e'ery day."[5]

It was very important to keep worms off the tobacco during the growing season. Young children were assigned the daily task of examining the tobacco leaves, pulling off the worms, if there were any, and killing them. Simon Stokes said that his overseer "wuz de meanes ole hound you'se eber seen, he hed hawk eyes fer seein' de worms on de terbaccer." If a slave did not get them all, he or she would "habe ter bite all de worms dat yo' miss into, or git three lashes on yo' back wid his ole lash." The overseer's lash, he recalled, "wuz powfull bad, wusser dan bittin' de worms, fer yo' could bite right smart quick, and dat wuz all dat dar wuz ter it; but dem lashes done last a pow'full long time." Simon Stokes "sho' didn't like dat job, pickin' worms off de terbaccer plants."[6]

"Guess I was a girl 'bout five or six," Nancy Williams remembered, "when I was put wid de other chillun pickin' de bugs off de terbaccy leaves. Gal named Crissy was wukin' on nex' row, an' kep' whisperin' to me to pick em all off. Didn' pay no 'tention to her, any dat fell off I jus' let lay dere." Soon her master came by, checking on the children's progress. He saw that she had been missing some of the tobacco worms. Nancy Williams would never forget what happened next: "Picked up a hand full of worms, he did, an' stuffed 'em inter my mouth; Lordy knows how many of dem shiny things I done swallered, but I sho' picked em off careful arter dat."[7]

By midsummer it was harvest time. "Got to pick dem leaves what's jus' startin' to brown," Gabe Hunt pointed out. "Pick 'em too soon dey don't cure, an' you pick 'em too late dey bitters." Matilda Perry agreed. One would "git a lashin'," she said, "effen you cut a leaf fo' its ripe." It was important to break the tobacco leaves off clean at the stem and not twist them. If they were bruised they would spoil. Hunt would never forget the tactile sensation of tobacco: "Hands git so stuck up in dat old tobaccy gum it git so yo' fingers stick together. Dat ole gum was de worse mess you ever see. Couldn't brush it off, couldn't wash it off, got to wait tell it wear off." After picking the tobacco leaves, slaves would spread them on a cart and drag it to the tobacco barn. There slave women would place the stem of each between two pieces of board and tie the ends together. "Den hand 'em all up in dat barn an' let it smoke two days an' two nights," Hunt explained. "Got to keep dat fire burnin' rain or shine, 'cause if it go out, it spile de tobaccy. Ev'ybody happy when de tobaccy curin' is done, 'cause den ole Marse gonna take it to market an' maybe bring back new clothes fo' de slaves."[8]

Rice culture was labor intensive; plantations had a larger number of slaves per unit than did cotton or sugar plantations. Work was apportioned according to the task system. Each day a certain task was allotted. When it was completed to the driver's satisfaction, the slave had the rest of the day to use for his or her own purposes. The hoe, as in Africa, was the principal all-purpose tool for preparing the soil. But plantation slaves also used gourds for sowing, sickles for harvesting, wooden flails for threshing, and mortars and pestles for pounding the rice. Much of the work was drudgery. At its best, rice culture was exacting hand labor. A visitor was appalled at the slaves' constant exposure to extremely unhealthy conditions: "The labor required for the cultivation is fit only for slaves," she wrote, "and I think the hardest work I have seen them engaged in."[9]

The annual cycle would begin in December or January. The fields had to be prepared during the winter by turning or hoeing; and trunks, canals, and ditches had to be cleaned and repaired. Planting began in mid-March and continued through April. Seed was dropped at twelve-inch intervals into shallow trenches about three inches wide. Then the floodgates—or trunk docks—were opened at the next high tide and the fields were flooded. A sequence of flooding and draining followed until harvest time.

> John say you got to reap in the harvest what you sow
> John say you got to reap in the harvest what you sow
> If you sow it in the rain, you got to reap it jus' the same
> You got to reap in the harvest what you sow.[10]

The water was drained a final time, and the slaves cut the stalks with sickles. They bound the dried stalks in sheaves about a foot thick and brought the sheaves in to the threshing ground. Threshers, armed with wooden flailing sticks, began to separate the grain from the husk.

At first nearly all plantations used the mortar and pestle to hull and polish the rice grains for market, although eventually some plantations had pounding mills. Pestles had a sharp end for bruising and removing the husks and a flat end for polishing the grain. Mortars were hollowed out of cypress or pine logs. Women or boys would hold the pestles in the middle, raising and lowering them quickly and evenly to a rhythmic chant:

> I gwine t' beat dis
> Gwine t' beat 'um so
> Gwine t' beat 'um until the hu'ks come off
> Ah hanh hanh (nasal)
> Ah hanh hanh.[11]

Harvesting, threshing, and pounding were not finished until early November. The four winter months were scarcely long enough for the amount of work that had to be accomplished before March, when the first planting was begun. Threshing, pounding, and shipping to market had to be completed. Then the stubble had to be burned, the land had to be turned, and the annual cycle began again.

On sugar plantations, planting began in January and continued through April, employing three gangs of slaves. One gang drew a stalk of cane from a stack and cut off its top. The second gang planted the stalk. The third gang used their hoes to cover the planted stalks with about three inches of dirt. Within four weeks the cane sprouted and began to grow rapidly. Until early August it required careful hoeing. In mid-September the slaves harvested and stacked the seed cane. The general harvest began in October. "Cutting cane was an employment that suited me," Solomon Northup wrote. For three years straight Northup held the lead row on a Louisiana sugar plantation, heading a gang of one hundred slaves. Wielding cane knives with very sharp fifteen-inch blades, the slaves sheared the tops from the stalks down as far as the stalks were green. It was important to keep the green part of the stalk from the ripe, for the juice of green cane would sour the molasses. Then the slaves chopped the stalks off at the root and threw them into a cart bound for the sugar house.[12]

At the sugar house the carts were unloaded by slave children, who placed the stalks on conveyor belts. The belts ran between two iron rollers that crushed the stalks. The juice fell into a conductor beneath the rollers and was channeled through five filters before being boiled in an iron pan. As the molten syrup passed over coolers with fine sieve bottoms, it crystallized. The molasses fell through the sieves into a cistern below. The remaining sugar was packed in hogsheads and shipped to market. The molasses was then refined by another process into brown sugar. In January the fields were prepared for planting another crop.[13]

But many jobs besides field work had to be done on the slave plantations of the Old South. A large corps of slave craftspersons—blacksmiths, bricklayers, cabinetmakers, carpenters, coopers, shoemakers, and spinners—was necessary for the efficient operation of the plantations. Jacob Stroyer's African-born father was a hostler. He took care of his master's many horses and mules. Jacob's mother was a field hand. But she came from a family of slave craftspersons and house servants.

The driver was a slave with authority. He had direct responsibility for the slaves' day-to-day work. The driver, more than any other person, determined the plantation's success or failure. Jacob Stroyer's Uncle Esau was a driver on his plantation. The master, according to Jacob, thought more of Uncle Esau than he did of his overseer. The driver also meted out punishments—usually whippings—for offenses against plantation rules. Jacob considered his Uncle Esau to be "more cruel than any white man master ever had on his plantation."[14]

On rainy days female slaves were sent to the "loom room," where they would spin, weave, and dye cloth. There was a heavy emphasis on durability in slave clothing. In some districts all slave clothing was made on the plantations. Each slave woman was expected to make most of her own family's clothes. But across the South there was also a great market for coarse clothing made in New England mills. One set each of winter and summer clothing was usually distributed to each slave in ceremonies arranged by the master or mistress. Large plantations with one hundred or more slaves could save money by having a cobbler who did nothing but make shoes for the slaves. The condition of the slaves' clothing on her husband's plantation shocked Fanny Kemble, an English actress married to a Georgia slaveholder, Pierce Butler. Many of the slaves went barefoot even in midwinter. Each slave was allowed annually two pairs of shoes, a certain number of yards of flannel, and a small allocation of a rough, uncomfortable cloth called "plains."[15]

The men's clothing consisted of pants, shirts, and coats. Children wore long-tailed shirts, and no undergarments. They seldom had pants until late childhood. Lou Smith remembered his Oklahoma mistress, "she said us kids didn't need to wear any clothes and one day she told us we could jest take 'em off as it cost too much to clothe us."[16] Women's clothes, however, were not entirely devoid of ornament and fashion. A Mississippi slave recalled his mother had a blue dress with pictures of gourds upon it. According to Clara Walker, her Arkansas mistress "was good to me. She gives me lots of good clothes." Nannie Bradfield, an Alabama ex-slave, recalled that "Miss give me a brown dress and hat." John Matthews remembered, "De white wimen wore hoop skirt, but I neber seed a black woman wid one. Dey jes' starched deir petticoats an' made deir dresses stand out like hoop under dem."[17] In this small way, slave women not only expressed a desire to be stylish, they also refused to accept complete defeminization.

Day-to-day, household slaves were in more frequent contact with the plantation mistress than field hands were. As a result of working in such close proximity to their mistress's house, servants experienced both some of the best and some of the worst conditions of slavery. They received greater attention from the whites due to their greater contact, but that attention was not necessarily a positive influence on their situation. It is true that slaves in the Big House had the advantage of obtaining better food, clothing, and furniture, but their working hours were irregular and they were always under the careful scrutiny of the whites. A plantation mistress discovered that one little girl, barely five years old, had been taught to knit by her mother. She at once took the child away from her mother and put her in a room in the Big House. Such actions were considered by the plantation mistresses to be extending a generous opportunity to the slave child. The fact that it simultaneously broke up a slave family was not always recognized.[18]

A few house servants seem to have identified less with the slave families in the quarters than with the master's family in the Big House. "When I was a small child and lived in the house with the white folks," said Ann May of Mississippi, "I despised for anyone to call me a 'nigger'—that would make me fighting mad. Now I don't want them to call me that yet. I am black, but I was raised with white folks and got no nigger ways."[19] A few such house servants even earned reputations among the slave community as spies for the masters. For example, a slave named Frances worked as a maid in Pharaoh Carter's plantation Big House in Mississippi by day. But by night she spied on the cabins.

Despite their different situations, black slaves and white mistresses who lived and worked together could occasionally forge bonds of genuine friendship and mutual dependency across the color bar. Sometimes slaves and mistresses worked so closely with each other that real affection developed between owner and owned. But there were also relationships of another type. Sarah Colbert remembered that her mistress "was very mean to the slaves, whipped them regularly every morning to start the day right."[20]

For slaves in such situations, everything they could learn about the plantation mistress's strengths and weaknesses gave them leverage in the close and continuing relationships of the Big House. House servants often gained their mistress's confidence by playing the part of surrogate mothers and sisters. With each of the mistress's secrets they carried, the slaves could feel a little freer. Esther Easter took revenge on a cruel mistress by revealing to her master that his wife was having an affair. "The mistress didn't know I knows her secret," she recalled many years later, "and I'm fixen to even up for some of them whippings she put off on me."[21]

Slaves were introduced to work almost as soon as they passed infancy. Much of the herding was done by children. Boys and girls would also carry water to the adults in the field, kindle fires, sweep the yard, and other minor tasks that had to be done but would have cost valuable time if a field hand had to take care of them. In their early teen years slaves were socialized into culturally defined sex roles. A few years later they joined a work gang and were initiated into what were often overwhelmingly male or female worlds.

Women often worked in female work groups—hoeing, spinning, weaving, sewing, or quilting—apart from men. In female company most of the day, they spent most of their nonworking hours sharing joys, concerns, and heartbreaks with one another as well. They learned to depend upon one another for midwifery, medical care, and child care. Elderly women in the slave community enjoyed high status as nurses, midwives, and caretakers of children. But aged slaves received less care and attention from their masters than from their friends and relatives. Some slaveholders simply freed slaves too old to work rather than assume the responsibility for their food, clothing, and housing.

Sickness often visited the slave plantations. Masters hired doctors to care for their expensive property, but the slaves placed little confidence in them. Some large plantations had infirmaries. Fanny Kemble found the infirmary at her husband's Georgia plantation "a wretched abode of wretchedness." She wrote a vivid description in her journal: "Here lay women expecting every hour the terror and agonies of childbirth, others who had just brought their doomed offspring into the world, others who were groaning under the anguish and bitter disappointment of miscarriages—here lay some burning with fever, others chilled with cold and aching with rheumatism, upon the hard cold ground, the draughts and damp of the atmosphere increasing their sufferings, and dirt, noise, stench, and every aggravation of which sickness is capable combined in their condition." Her heart went out to those whom she described as "these poor wretches [who] lay prostrate on the earth, without bedstead, bed, mattress, or pillow, with no covering but the clothes they had on and some filthy rags of blanket in which they endeavored to wrap themselves as they lay literally strewing the floor, so that there was hardly room to pass between them."[22]

Preserving the health and well being of slaves was normally considered the responsibility of the plantation mistress. She took it upon herself to prescribe medicines for the slaves' illnesses. Physicians were summoned only if her cures did not work. Alabama's Anthony Abercrombie said, "She was jes' as good to me as she could be. She useta dose me up wid castor oil, jimson root and dogwood tea when I'd be feelin' po'ly." Carrie Davis recalled her Alabama mistress's healing the wounds of slaves after beatings: "Ol' Mistus has put salve on a heap of backs so dey could git deir shirts off." It was also the mistress's responsibility to ensure that valuable slave infants were brought to term by improving their mothers' diet and reducing their work load. Some dedicated mistresses made daily rounds to the cabins of sick slaves or to the infirmaries set aside for the sick, the invalid, and the infant members of the slave community. One former slave recalled that her Alabama mistress "used to go 'roun' de quarters eve'y mornin' to see 'bout her sick niggers. She always had a little basket wid oil, and teppentine." Mary, an Alabama slave, remembered, "Once when I was awful sick, Mistis' Ma'y Jene had me brung in de Big House an put me in a room dat sot on de 'tother side of the kitchen so she could take kere of me herself."[23]

Other slaves had to make do with their own resources. According to one Mississippi slave, Smitty Hodges, "When slaves was sick, dey went to de woods and got roots an' herbs ter doctor 'em wid." Old slave women made "teas" for various ailments. Red oak bark was used to combat dysentery, and other remedies were tried to reduce menstrual problems. Herbs were also worn in pouches as a preventative. Silvia Durant, a South

Carolinian, recalled that one popular charm was a dime worn around the ankle or elsewhere to ward off sickness or worms in children. Sarah Colbert said, "Slaves went to witch doctors for remedies or charms against cruel mistress."[24]

Most slave children were delivered by slave midwives. An Arkansas midwife, Clara Walker, recalled being hired out to other plantations to deliver white as well as black babies. "When I come home I made a lot o' money for Old Miss." According to Ank Bishop, an Alabamian, "all de women on Lady Liza' place had to go to de fiel' ev'y day an' dem what had suckerlin' babies would come in 'bout nine o'clock in de mawnin' an' when de bell ring at twelve an' suckerlin' en." Hannah Jones recalled of her Missouri grandmother, "Three days after her first baby was born dey made her git up and make twelve stiff-front, tucked white shirts for her old mistress' boy who be goin' off to college and she was so sick and weak, some of the stitches was crooked. . . . Old miss ordered de overseer to take her out and beat her 'bout it."[25]

Few slaves in the antebellum South could reasonably expect to find a partner for a stable marriage on their own plantation. The possibility of finding a husband or a wife was as much affected by a plantation's structure of sex and age as by its size. The number of potential partners from which one could select a mate was very limited even on very large plantations. If a slave had extensive kinship ties, the pool of eligible mates might be even further reduced. Nevertheless, in spite of the limited choices with which they were confronted, they seem to have been able to find partners. By courting slaves who lived on other plantations they managed to increase the size of the pool to which they were exposed. While Laura Montgomery's father wooed her mother, he brought gifts to her on a nearby plantation. "Some time he would bring er bucket of 'lasses, an' some time a watermelon an' one time he brung some apples," Laura recalled.[26]

Masters were not above promoting slave marriages by buying men and women and matching up couples. "Jacob," said one Mississippi master, "I brung you a young woman, take her an' live wid her."[27] But forced unions could cause as great a strain within the slave community as forced separations. Sometimes a husband or wife had to be purchased from his or her owner in order to facilitate a marriage. Some slaves were able to purchase title to their wives or other members of their families. One master allowed the slaves on his Mississippi plantation to work a cotton patch that would yield a sixty-dollar bale for themselves. "Uncle Dollie did this for a number of years," Oliver Jones recalled, "until he had saved $500 and paid this money to Moster for a girl for his wife, Aunt Onie, and his Moster had him to build them a house out from the quarters as he set her free, but Uncle Dollie continued a slave."[28]

Slave marriages had no legal standing. Nevertheless, slaves, slaveholders, and preachers all performed rituals that signified the permanence of slave unions. "The marsters married the slaves without any papers," a North Carolina slave recalled. "All they did was to say perhaps to Jane and Frank, 'Frank, I pronounce you and Jane man and wife.' But the woman did not take the name of her husband, she kept the name of the family who owned her." Another North Carolina slave testified, "I reckon 'bout the funniest thing 'bout our plantation wuz de marryin. . . . A couple got married by sayin' dat dey wuz, but it couldn't last for longer dan five years. Dat wuz so iffen one of 'em got too weakly ter have chilluns de other one could git him another wife or husban."[29] Andrew Simms, a former Florida slave, said that on his plantation the slaves "just jumped the broomstick and goes to living with somebody else I reckon."[30] In Louisiana, as an ex-slave recalled, "De couple steps over de broom laid on de floor, dey's married den." And according to an Alabama ex-slave,

> De way dey done at weddings dem days, you picks out a girl and tells your boss. If she was from another plantation you had to git her bosses 'mission and den dey tells you to come up at night and get hitched up. They says to de girl, "You's love dis man?" Dey say to de man, "You loves dis girl?" If you say you don't know, it's all off, but if you say yes, dey brings in de broom and holds it 'bout a foot off de floor and say to you to jump over. Den he says you's married. If either of you stumps yor toe on de broom, dat mean you got trouble comin' 'tween you, so you sho' jumps high.[31]

"Jumping the broom" was nearly universal in the slave South as a wedding ritual.

Sometimes the brides were dressed in the cast-off finery of the plantation mistress. According to Matila Pugh, a former slave in Mississippi, "we wuz ma'ied [married] in de parlor, an' wo' [wore] a party dress of Miss Sara's." Katherine Eppes, an Alabamian, recalled, "Ol miss gin me my weddin' dress an' a long veil down to my foots." But not everyone was so favored. Another Alabama slave, Silvia Witherspoon, recalled, "I ma'ied dat ole nigger in a dirty work dress an' my feets was bare jus' lak dey is now."[32]

Slave marriages, based on the complementary roles played by husband and wife, were surprisingly egalitarian. Since male slaves did not control property or other culturally valued subsistence goods, slave women were more independent of husbands than were southern white women. It was not easy for slaves to preserve their marriages within the constraints of bondage, but love and affection played important roles. Whether a marriage was based on romance or on more pragmatic considerations, the family helped socialize slave children into familial roles and enabled them to create an identity beyond their condition of servitude.

The relationship between wives and husbands was ultimately superseded by that between mothers and children. Motherhood played a central role in the slave community. Slave marriages were fragile; at any time a husband or wife could be sold away. But the breakup of a slave family was experienced differently by women and men. Wives might lose husbands, but husbands typically lost both wives and children.

Child raising was largely communal due to the dictates of the master. This had led some to believe that the ties between slave children and their parents were not strong. On most plantations, mothers had to leave their children and resume work as soon as they were able. Nursing infants were commonly placed on a quilt beside the fields so that their mothers could feed them from time to time. Adelaide J. Vaughn recalled an Arkansas slave who was brought down to the auction block without knowing that her master intended to sell her. When she realized that she was going to be separated from her child, "She broke away from her mistress and said, 'I can't go off and leave my baby.' And they had to git some men and throw her down and hold her to keep her from going back to the house. They sold her away from her baby boy."[33]

Older children or women too old to work watched the youngest children, who were fed from a trough or a pot with "pot likker" along with milk. When not engaged in small labors that helped ease them into the plantation work system, slave children played various folk games in the quarters, ranging from pastimes (running, jumping, skipping, jumping poles, walking on stilts, riding stick horses) to games of skill (jump rope, ball, marbles, horseshoes). Often the master's children were playmates. Games of concealment, such as "I Spy," "Blindfold and Tag," "Peep Squirrel Peep," and "You Can't Catch Me," taught young slaves potentially useful skills. Sometimes they also made bows and arrows. According to a slave in the South Carolina upcountry, "Some games children played was hiding switches, marbles, and maybe others. Later on, some of de nigger boys started playing cards and got to gambling; some went to de woods to gamble." Charlie Barbour, a former North Carolina slave, recalled, "I 'minds me of de days when as a youngin' I played marbles an' hide an' seek. Dar wuzn't many games den, case nobody ain't had not time for 'em. De grownups had dances an' sometimes corn shuckins an' de little niggers patted dere feets at de dances an' hepter shuck de co'n."[34]

During puberty, boys and girls became more interested in the opposite sex, and parents became more apprehensive. Female slaves experienced menarche around the age of fifteen but delayed childbearing for about two years. Giving birth was a life-affirming act that bolstered the status of the slave women, but it made their workdays all the more exhausting. On the slave plantations as well as in traditional Africa, motherhood was the most important rite of passage for black women. The slaves did not condemn what the white world called "illegitimacy." It was common for a slave woman to marry the father of her first child after its birth. This pattern reflected continuity with an ancient African custom that considered marriage consummated only after a woman had demonstrated her ability to bear children.

The most dramatic threat to the well-being of the slave family was the auction block. It is clear that settlement of the old Southwest was accompanied by widespread disruption of slave families back in the East. Slaves in the Deep South, cotton lands opened up in the 1820s and 1830s, came from many different states. Parvenu cotton planters acquired their labor forces on the auction blocks of the older slave states.

Slaves were not sold only as stock for new plantations but also as gifts or part of estate settlements. The slave auction was one of the strongest forms of psychological control any slaveholder possessed. Henry Walker remembered his Arkansas mistress saying, "'If you don't be good and mind we'll send yare off and sell you wid 'em.'" That threat, he recalled, frightened him more than any beating he ever received.[35]

Some former slaves disclaimed any knowledge of families being separated. North Carolina's Jane Arrington maintained that she "never saw a grown slave whupped or in chains and I never saw a slave sold. Jackson May would not sell a slave. He didn't think it right. He kept 'em together." But not all slaves were spared the horrors of being separated from family and friends. Viney Baker vividly recalled slavery days in North Carolina: "One night I lay down on de straw mattress wid my mammy," she said, "an' de nex mo'nin I woked up an' she wuz gone. A speculator comed dar de night before an' wanted ter buy a 'oman. Dey had come an' got my mammy widout wakin' me up. I has always been glad somehow dat I wuz asleep."[36] It was not uncommon for a master to present his daughter with a slave as a wedding present. Such a gift might represent an act of kindness from father to daughter; in breaking up the slave's family it had a contrary effect. An Alabama slave contended that "Mistis never 'lowed no mistreatin' of de slaves, 'cas dey was raisin' slaves for de market, an' it wouldn't be good bizness to mistreat 'em." Shipping slaves to the market became so common in Virginia that the slaves made up a song about it—"Massa's Gwine Sell Us Tomorrow."[37]

Another major threat to the stability of the slave family was the sexual liberty taken by some white men with female slaves. If a slave family had an attractive daughter, she could be taken from her home and moved to the Big House where the "young masters could have the run of her," as a former Virginia slave described it. In his memoirs, Henry Clay Bruce, an escaped slave, wrote, "we would have been pure black, were it not that immoral white men, by force, injected their blood into our veins, to such an extent, that we now represent all colors from pure black to pure white, and almost entirely as a result of the licentiousness of white men." Another writer complained, "one of the reasons why wicked men in the South uphold slavery, is the facility which it affords for a licentious life. Negroes tell no tales in courts of law of the violation by white men of colored females." One who thus upheld slavery was South Carolina's leading man of letters, William Gilmore Simms. In his *Morals of Slavery* (1838), Simms characterized slavery as a beneficial institution because it protected the purity of white women by allowing slaveholders to vent their lust "harmlessly" upon slave women.[38]

House servants were perhaps more often at risk of sexual exploitation by their masters or his guests than were field hands. One of the Reverend Charles Colcock Jones's household slaves gave birth to a mulatto child. Jones, convinced that the father was a man who had been a visitor in his home, was outraged. He chastised the man for daring "to offer to me personally and to my family and to my neighbors so vile and so infamous an insult. You are the only man who has ever dared to debauch my family servants . . . and to defile my dwelling with your adulterous and obscene pollutions."[39]

Overseers were also known to exploit slave women sexually. On Argyle Island the twenty-four-year-old overseer was too familiar with the slaves to suit Louis Manigault, his employer. He sided with the slaves against their drivers, joined them in their prayer meetings, and fathered a mulatto son in the slave quarters. According to Fanny Kemble both the father and son who successively managed her husband's plantations sexually abused the female slaves and fathered mulatto children by them. It would be hard to find "a more cruel and unscrupulous" man, she wrote of the younger, "even among the cruel and unscrupulous class to which he belonged."[40]

Mulatto children fathered by the master were rarely acknowledged on the slave plantations. According to Mary Boykin Chesnut, mistress of Mulberry Plantation in South Carolina, a slaveholder's "wife and daughters in the might of their purity and innocence are supposed never to dream of what is plain before their eyes as the sunlight, and they play their parts of unsuspecting angels to the letter."[41] The large numbers of plantation mulattoes contributed to the hostility felt by some mistresses toward their slaves. They considered black women promiscuous and directed their anger toward the slaves instead of toward their husbands. Under the slavery system, Mary Chesnut lamented, "we live surrounded by prostitutes. . . . God forgive us, but ours is a *monstrous* system and wrong and iniquity. Perhaps the rest of the world is as bad—this *only* I see. Like the patriarchs of old our men live all in one house with their wives and their concubines, and the mulattoes one sees in every family exactly resemble the white children—every lady tells you who is the father of all the mulatto children in every body's household, but those in her own she seems to think drop from the clouds, or pretends so to think."[42] Mothers resented the young slaves who attracted their sons, and wives feared the female slaves who attracted their husbands. Such slaves threatened the position of the plantation mistress.

A few slaveholders flaunted their relations with slave women, risking condemnation by the public and by their own families. After his wife died, David Dickson of Georgia lived openly with his slave mistress and their children. Josias Grey scandalized Louisiana society when he took his mulatto children to public places. Governor Leroy Pope of Alabama consorted publicly with his mulatto mistress. The well-publicized relationship humiliated Pope's wife and set tongues wagging in his home town. She became so angry that she forced him to send the slave to another plantation. Thereupon the governor spent most of his time at the other plantation, until social pressure forced him to sell the woman.[43]

James Henry Hammond, former governor of South Carolina, was somewhat more clandestine about his relationships. Hammond took an eighteen-year-old slave to be his mistress. When her daughter reached the age of twelve, Hammond made her his mistress too. When he brought his slave mistress into the Big House, his wife moved out and refused to return until he sent the mistress away. The slave mistress moved out, and the wife returned. But soon the slave mistress returned as well.[44]

A classic example of the tensions inherent in such situations is the story told by Mary Reynolds, a former slave in Louisiana:

> Once Massa goes to Baton Rouge and brung back a yaller gal dressed in fine style. She was a seamster nigger. He builds her a house 'way from the quarters. This yaller gal breeds fast and gits a mess of white young-uns. She larnt them fine manners and combs out they hair. Oncet two of them goes down the hill to the dollhouse where the Missy's children am playing. They wants to go in the dollhouse and one of the Missy's boys say, "That's for white children." They say, "We ain't no niggers, 'cause we got the same daddy as you has, and he comes to see us near every day."

As the children quarrel, the plantation mistress hears their conversation from her bedroom window. Mary Reynolds recalled vividly what happened later that day.

> When Massa come home his wife hardly say nothin' to him, and he asks her what the matter, and she tells him, "Since you asks me, I'm studying in my mind 'bout them white young-uns of that yaller nigger wench from Baton Rouge." He say, "Now, Honey, I fotches that gal just for you, 'cause she a fine seamster." She say, "It look kind of funny they got the same kind of hair and eyes as my children, and they got a nose look like yours." He say, "Honey, you just paying 'tention to talk of little children that ain't got no mind to what they say." She say, "Over in Mississippi I got a home and plenty with my daddy and I got that in mind." Well, she didn't never leave, and Massa bought her a new span of surrey hosses. But she don't never have no more children, and she ain't so cordial with the Massa. That yaller gal has more white young-uns, but they don't never go down the hill no more."[45]

It was difficult for wives to get out of such marriages in the Old South. In North Carolina, Samuel Hansley's wife sued him for divorce because of his relationship with his slave Lucy. The Hanover County Superior Court granted the decree in 1845, but it was reversed by the North Carolina Supreme Court in 1849.

The position of a plantation mistress involved in such a triangle was a difficult one. Sometimes a master's infidelity prompted a mistress's cruel and unfair behavior toward the slaves. For example, one former slave,

Sarah Wilson, recalled, "When I was eight years old, old mistress died and grandmammy told me why old mistress picked on me so. She told me about my being half Mister Ned's blood."[46] Henry Ferry told of a childless Virginia plantation mistress whose husband had fathered a son by one of his slaves.

> Ole Marse John ain't never had no chillun by his wife. His wife was pow'ful jealous of Martha an' never let her come near de big house, but she didn't need to, 'cause marsa was always goin' down to the shacks where she lived. Marse John used to treat Martha's boy, Jim, jus' like his own son, which he was. Jim used to run all over de big house, an' Missus didn't like'it, but she didn't dare put him out. One day de Parson come to call. He knew Marse John but didn't know Missus Mamie. He come to de house an' Jim come runnin' down de stairs to meet him. He took de little boy up in his arms an' rubbed his haid, an' when Missus come, tol' her how much de boy look like his father and mother. "'Course it favor its father most," de preacher say, tryin' to be polite, "but in de eyes, de lookin' glass of de soul, I kin see dat he's his mother's boy."[47]

The mistress did not let on to the preacher that the boy was not hers, but she never again let him come in the house.

Some slave women may have given their sexual favors more or less willingly in an effort to gain favors, special treatment, or perhaps even manumission. As one woman slave recalled, "Some did it because they wanted to."[48] Solomon Northup described a vain and beautiful young slave, Maria, who told her companions in the slave pen that she was willing to be a concubine but she had no desire to be a field hand on some plantation. She had no doubt that as soon as they were put on the auction block in New Orleans, she would be immediately purchased by some wealthy and unmarried gentleman.[49]

Whether they were willing or not, slave women had little recourse. "Any man with money can buy a beautiful and virtuous girl, and force her to live with him in a criminal connection," the former slave William Craft wrote in his memoir, "and as the law says a slave shall have no higher appeal than the mere will of the master, she cannot escape unless it be by flight or death."[50] Others were forced to submit through coercion, force, and violence. In Edgefield District, South Carolina, Charlotte's lecherous master tried to force her into a sexual relationship. She resisted, but he stripped her and forced her to sit naked upon a pile of manure until she finally submitted. Later, after she had borne him a child, he passed her on to his cousin, to whom she bore another child.[51]

Slave women fought back and so did their families. Robert Elliott recalled that on the Virginia plantation where he had lived, a white man tried to molest his sister one day. When his father realized what was happening, he "jumped up and grabbed him in the chest. He pointed at the Big House and said, 'If you don't get in that house right now, I'll kill you with my bare hands.'"[52]

In this instance, the white man backed off and left the girl and her father alone. But other efforts to deter white sexual aggression were less successful. In one case a cruel master lusted after a woman in the slave quarters. Regularly he would come to her cabin, wake her family, and tell her husband to leave the house while he used the wife for his sexual gratification. One night the husband waited outside for the white man. When the master had finished with the woman and was leaving the cabin, the slave husband strangled him. For this "crime" the husband was swiftly executed.[53]

Masters were sometimes inclined to sell their mulatto children in order to protect them from the abuse of their stepmothers, half-brothers, and half-sisters. Frederick Douglass noted, "As cruel as the deed may strike anyone to be, for a man to sell his own children to human flesh-mongers, it is often the dictate of humanity for him to do so: for unless he does this, he must not only whip them himself, but must stand by and see the white son tie up his brother, of but a few shades darker complexion than himself, and ply the gory lash to his naked back."[54]

The white slaveowners' slave kin, if they were not sold, were quite often made personal slaves in the Big House. In many cases the body servants of the young people were their half-brothers or half-sisters. In rare instances such brothers and sisters developed close bonds. Ed Domino said, "my mudder 'n' my mistus claim half-sisters. My mistus wouldn' 'low nobuddy t' touch me 'r my mudder."[55]

There were also instances in which mulatto children grew up with the love and affection of the white family. Dora Franks, who had been a slave in Choctaw County, Mississippi, recalled, "My daddy was my young Marster. His name was Marster George Brewer and my mammy always told me dat I was his'n. I knew dat dere was some difference 'tween me and de rest o' chillen, 'cause dey was all coal black, and I was even lighter dan I is now. Lord, it's been to my sorrow many a time, 'cause de chillen used to chase me round and holler at me, 'Old yellow nigger.'" But she recalled her mistress with affection: "I stayed in de house most o' de time with Miss Emmaline. . . . I loved her 'cause she was so good to me." Her master and his wife had no young children left, and they loved her and treated her as a granddaughter. "She and Marse Bill had about eight chillen, but most of 'em was grown when I come along. Dey was all mighty good to me and wouldn't allow nobody to hurt me." On one occasion she asked an old slave cook for a piece of white bread like the whites ate. "She haul off and slap me down and call me all kind o' names dat I didn't know what dey meant. My nose bled and ruint de nice dress I had on. When Mistis come back Marse George was with her. She asked me what on earth happen to me and I told her. Dey call Caroline in de room and asked her if what I saw was de truth. She tell em it was, and dey sent her away. I hear tell dat dey whip her so hard dat she couldn't walk no more."[56]

Occasionally a master's slave offspring were reared as though free. James Calhart James recalled that his father gave him money and good clothes. He would buy toys and games. He was educated with his half-brothers and half-sisters, and he was allowed to attend the white church with the other children of the household. Lizzie Williams, who had been a slave near Selma, Alabama, told of a similar case: "Emily, she look like a white gal. She was treated just like she white. Her daddy was a white man. . . . But de missy she was good to her. She never stay in de quarters; she stay in de house with de white folks. But Emily had de saddest look on her yaller face 'cause de other niggers whisper about her pappy."[57]

Nevertheless, status was never secure in a slave society. In his memoirs, Levi Coffin tells of a child born to a white slaveowner and a quadroon slave. When the boy was three years old the master had family problems and sent him away from the plantation. He was given a good education and grew up as a free man, never knowing that he was a slave until his father died and his white relatives sold him to a slave dealer.[58]

Being victimized by the master's lust was only part of the sexual exploitation visited upon slave women. After legal slave importations were ended in 1807, the reproductive capacity of almost all slave women was manipulated for the slaveholders' profit. Male slavery rested on the work that men were required to perform; female slavery was based not only on their work, but also on their bearing and rearing children to replenish their masters' labor force.

As early as 1831 the Reverend Charles Colcock Jones delivered an eloquent sermon urging slaveholders to instruct their slaves in the principles of the Christian religion. Not only would religious instruction save the slaves' souls, he said, it would also create "a greater subordination" among the slaves and teach them "respect and obedience [to] all those whom God in his providence has placed in authority over them."[59] Pastor of Savannah's First Presbyterian Church, the Reverend Jones was also master of three rice plantations and more than one hundred slaves in coastal Georgia. As a pastor his concern for the salvation of his slaves' souls was genuine. But as a master he also consciously and deliberately used Christianity as an instrument of discipline and control. After all, he believed a faithful servant was more profitable than an unfaithful servant. So he tailored the Christianity he taught to his slaves to serve his desire to keep slaves reconciled to their bondage.

Some slaveholders were simply indifferent to the religious education of their slaves. At Cannon's Point Plantation on St. Simons Island, Georgia, a Swedish visitor, Fredrika Bremer, tried to teach a gathering of the slave children to recite the Lord's Prayer. "The children grinned, laughed, showed their white teeth," she said, "and evinced very plainly that none of them knew what that wonderful prayer meant nor that they had a Father in heaven."[60]

Other slaveholders actively opposed efforts to Christianize the slaves. Such slaveholders maintained that the slaves were not fully human creatures. Thus they were not capable of reasoning and learning the truths of the Christian religion. The slaveholders especially feared the intense emotionalism preferred by the slaves as the appropriate way to worship God. The whole enterprise seemed to them as pernicious as it was useless. The Reverend Jones and slaveholders of similar inclinations wanted their slaves delivered from what they considered the savage heathenism of Africa to the true light of the Christian Gospel, preferably of the Episcopal or Presbyterian variety. Ultimately those of the evangelistic persuasion were able to prove to their more doubtful brethren's satisfaction that they favored only quiet and sedate worship services.

The kind of Christianity slaveholders wanted for their slaves is revealed in the incessant references to the spiritual and physical welfare of the slaves in the Jones family correspondence. "I trust that you are holding on to your high profession of the Gospel of our Lord and Savior Jesus Christ at all times, and constantly watch and pray," he wrote to his head slave carpenter, Sandy Maybank. "You know our life and health are in His hands," Jones constantly counseled his driver Cato, "and it is a great comfort to me to have a good hope that you love Him, and do put all your trust in our Lord and Savior Jesus Christ, who is a precious Savior to us in life and in death." And he was very pleased when another driver, Andrew, sent back such replies as "it is no light thing to be a christian, for we may play with the lightning and the rattle snake, but dont trifle with Almighty God 'lest he tear you to pieces in his anger and then be never to deliver you.'"[61]

The religious indoctrination of the slaves began early on most plantations. "There was Sabbath School each Sunday afternoon, under the big live oaks," a planter's daughter recalled. "My Father would read from the Bible and we would tell simple stories to the children and many grownups, who came with them." According to the former slave Mattie Logan, "All the slaves who wanted religion was allowed to join the Methodist church, because that was the Mistress' church." An Alabama slave said, "Miss Dell was a good mistis an' she useter hab Sunday School ebber' Sund'y mornin' at de Big House an' all us li'l niggers went up dar for her to teach us 'bout de Bible an' Jesus." Hattie Clayton remembered, "Ol Mistus useter take all de littlee scamps dat was too little for church an' read de book to dem under de big oak tree in de front yahd." Another mistress "uster read de Bible to us niggers. She would talk to us 'bout de Good Book an' have prayer meetin' wid us," Emma Jones recalled. "At night some of de house niggers would gather 'roun de fire, an' mistis would read us de scriptures, an' de white chilluns get tired an' slip out de do' but us little niggers couldn't ford to do dat; us hadda stay dere whether us liked it or not."[62]

Slaveholders were quite selective in the Christianity they taught their slaves. They often attempted to use religion as a means of asserting control. In the master's church the most important thing that was preached to them "was how to serve their master and mistiss," an Arkansas slave recalled. "Dey read the Bible and told us to obey our marster," according to Hannah Crasson, a North Carolinian, "for der Bible said obey your marster."[63]

Most slaves belonged to Baptist or Methodist churches. Despite their masters' fears, the slaves' style of worship was emotional. As Lewis Jefferson explained, "Ebery time I feel de Spirit move me I jes' gib him de reigns an' I tells de wurld I is happy. I tells the whole wurld. I is gwine to Heaben when I die."[64]

Immanent in slave religion was the gaining of freedom, and not merely freedom from sin:

> O, Lord cum free dis nigger,
> O, Lord cum free dis nigger,
> O, Lord cum free dis nigger,
> For I can't wurk all de day.[65]

Slaves had prayer meetings out in the quarters, "with abundance of preaching and praying, (for they all exhorted, men as well as women)." Or they would gather secretly in wooded areas, away from the plantations and patrols. Charlie Van Dyke, a former Alabama slave, recalled that slaves often heard white preachers exhort them to be "good." He said, "church is what they called it, but all that preacher talked about was for us slaves to obey our masters and not to lie or steal. Nothing about Jesus, was ever said."[66]

In their secret prayer meetings, the slaves would pray for deliverance from bondage. "I remember one old song we used to sing when we met down in the woods back of the barn. My mother she sing an' pray to the Lord to deliver us out of slavery," recalled W. L. Bost of North Carolina.

> As I went down in the valley to pray
> Studyin' about the good old way
> Who should wear that starry crown
> Good Lord show me the way
> Oh, Mother, let's go down,
> Down in the valley to pray.[67]

Slave Christians often looked for freedom through some heavenly decree. If they put all their faith in the Lord, he would deliver them from the House of Bondage as he had delivered the Hebrew children from Egypt in the Bible. Broder Coteney, a slave preacher, likened his flock of slave Christians to a flock of sheep:

> An dem buckra dat beat dem nigger onjestly an onmusefully, jes kase de po nigger cant help e self, dems de meanest buckra ob all, an berry much like de sheep-killin dog dat cowud to take sumpn dat cant help e self. Dat berry ting dat de nigger cant fend e self an helpless, mek de gentleman buckra berry pashunt an slow to punish dem nigger. An de berry fack dat de Lawd sheep is po helpless ting, mek de Lawd pity an lub we mo, an mek we pen pun Him an cry fur Him in de time ob trouble an danejur. An dat wha de Lawd want, fur we feel we own weakness an trust in Him strenk. De mudder lub de morest de chile dats de weakest an dat need um de morest, and so wed de Sabeyur an e lettle wuns dat pend only pun Him.[68]

Nevertheless, expressing even such mild sentiments could be dangerous. Who could tell when slaves might begin to ask the Lord not merely to deliver them in the next world, but to aid their own efforts to cast off the shackles of this one? Some slaveholders, like Mississippi's Pharaoh

Carter, forbade prayer meetings entirely. A house servant named Frances betrayed such a secret prayer meeting to Carter, who had the slave worshippers savagely beaten.[69]

Music was central to slave worship services. Booker T. Washington recalled listening to the slave songs as a child during the Civil War. "Some one individual, who had already gained a reputation as a leader in singing," he noted, would lead off "in clear distinct tones," whereupon the congregation "would join in, some hundred voices strong." To young Washington, "there was something wild and weird about that music, such as will never again be heard in America." Fredrika Bremer described one such service near Columbia, South Carolina: "They sang so that it was a pleasure to hear, with all their souls and with all their bodies in unison; for their bodies wagged, their heads nodded, their feet stamped, their knees shook, their elbows and their hands beat time to the tune and the words which they sang with evident delight." After witnessing a similar service, Mary Boykin Chesnut wrote in her diary, "I would very much have liked to shout, too." A white Presbyterian minister in Virginia was moved to say that of all the sacred music he had heard, if he were asked "which of all seemed most like the praise of God," he would have to answer, "the united voices of a thousand slaves." But few whites perceived that such singing also functioned as a means of criticism and comment on the circumstances of this world and the next. Washington recalled that during the war, "most of the verses of the plantation songs had some reference to freedom. True, they had sung those same verses before, but they had been careful to explain that the 'freedom' in those songs referred to the next world, and had no connection with life in this world. Now they gradually threw off the mask, and were not afraid to let it be known that the 'freedom' in their songs meant freedom of this body in this world."[70]

Some slaveholders continued to oppose teaching slaves about Christianity, believing that it was not safe to teach any religion to the slaves. Candus Richardson said that they had no Bible on the Scott plantation, for it meant a beating or "a killing if you'd be caught with one." With or without the blessings of their "earthly masters," however, slave Christians found ways to worship. As a North Carolina slave put it, "I reckon somethin' inside jes told us about God and that there was better place hereafter. We would sneak off and have prayer meetin'."[71]

Various supernatural beliefs, stemming from both African and European folk sources, were incorporated within slave religion. There was considerable continuity with African patterns of folk belief on the slave plantations of the New World. Ghosts or haunts—the spirits of the dead—returned to trouble the living: "I know dere is ghosts cause when I was a little boy my mammy come in from de field and laid across de bed and I was sittin' in front of de fireplace and a big somethin' like a cow without no head come in de door," recalled an Alabama slave. Another time, he said, "dis spirit like an angel come to my mammy and told her to tell de white lady to read de Bible backwards three times."[72] Gabe Butler, from Mississippi, recalled that "w'en I wus a chile I wus skeered uf ha'nts. W'en ebber I went by de grave yard on de hill I cud hear dem callin' me, den I cud feel deir breath blowin' hot on me, en den I wud run en no body cud kotch me. Yes dey did git atter me. I niver seed 'em but I kno'd dey sho' is spirits. I kno' case I outrun dem."[73] Jane Smith of Spartanburg, South Carolina, recalled hearing a ghost once. The night after her master had killed himself, she heard doors being shut, windows slamming, and chairs rocking on the front porch when there was no wind. The slaves used various charms to ward off the spirits' unwelcome visits.[74]

African spirit beliefs were incorporated into slave Christianity, but voodoo (or hoodoo) continued an underground existence outside of and hostile to Christian tradition. Other slave folk beliefs included signs—if "a screech owl lit on your chimney and hollered," it signified that "somebody in dat house was goin' to die." Certain practices were designed to ward off misfortune. Burning salt could prevent the death predicted by the screech owl. A rabbit's foot could bring good luck and guard against magic. Many slaves also planted by the phases of the moon to ensure a good crop.[75]

Slaves often took their problems to plantation conjurers. The conjurers, assisted by various substances that were held to be magical, would cast spells upon enemies and protect against "ruin or cripplin' or dry up de blood." Conjurers enjoyed a considerable reputation among the slaves, who sought their aid in all sorts of matters. They would mix hair, nails, thimbles, and needles in a "conjure bag," or "have a li'l bottle and have roots and water in it and sulphur." On the Sea Islands of South Carolina conjurers were known to "put bad mouth on you." Not all slaves believed in conjure. "Dem conjure-folks can't hurt you lessen you believe in 'em," one slave contended. Another said, "Ma told us chillen voodoo was a no 'count doin' of de devil, and Christians was never to pay it no attention." But others took no chances. "I been a good Christian ever since I was baptized," an Oklahoma slave said, "but I keep a little charm here on my neck anyways."[76]

"Funeral services," the Reverend Charles Colcock Jones once observed, "are much esteemed by the Negroes," although little care was given to the deceased on some plantations.[77] One escaped slave, Henry Bibb, wrote that less care was "taken of their dead bodies than if they were dumb beasts." But more commonly residents of the slave quarters would sing and pray through the night after a death. Slave Christians would "thank God that brother Charles, or brother Ned or sister Betsy, is at last free, and gone to heaven where bondage is never known. Some who are left behind, cry and grieve that they, too, cannot die and throw off their yoke of slavery, and join the company of the brother and sister who has just gone."[78] When a slave died, the other slaves would "go to the overseer, and obtain leave to sit up all night with their dead, and sing and pray. This is a very solemn season. First, one sings and another prays, and this they continue every night until the dead body is buried."[79]

On some plantations all work was suspended until the dead were buried. Slaves from adjoining plantations would receive passes to come. On others, according to a traveler's account of a funeral in Virginia, "when a slave dies, the master gives the rest a day, of their own choosing, to celebrate the funeral. This, perhaps a month after the corpse is interred, is a jovial day with them; they sing and dance and drink the dead to his new home, which some believe to be in old Guinea." A Georgia slave recalled, "The mourners beat the drum while on the way to the cemetery; after arriving they marched around the grave in a ring and beat the drum and shouted."[80]

Fanny Kemble described in her journal a slave funeral on St. Simons Island in which she had participated during the winter of 1838.

> Yesterday evening the burial of the poor man Shadrach took place. . . . The coffin was laid on trestles in front of the cooper's cottage, and a large assemblage of the people had gathered round, many of the men carrying pine-wood torches. . . . Presently the whole congregation uplifted their voices in a hymn, the first high wailing notes of which—sung all in unison, in the midst of these unwonted surroundings—sent a thrill through all my nerves.[81]

Grave decoration followed cherished African tradition. "Negro graves were always decorated with the last article used by the departed," according to a Georgia planter's daughter, "and broken pitchers and broken bits of colored glass were considered even more appropriate than the white shells from the beach nearby. Sometimes they carved rude wooden figures like images of idols, and sometimes a patchwork quilt was laid upon the grave."[82]

Not all of the slaves in the antebellum South embraced Christianity. There was a considerable Islamic presence on the South Carolina and Georgia coasts. Moslem slaves deliberately sought Moslem marriage partners in the second generation. "On Sapelo Island near Darien," a Georgia rice planter's daughter recalled, "I used to know a family of Negroes who worshipped Mahomet. They were all tall and well-formed, with good features. They conversed with us in English, but in talking among themselves they used a foreign tongue that no one else understood. The head of the tribe was a very old man called Bi-la-li. He always wore a cap that resembled a Turkish fez. These Negroes held themselves aloof from the others as if they were conscious of their own superiority.[83]

The old man was Bilali Mohomet. Shadrach Hall, his great-grandson, remembered him as being "coal-black." A devout Moslem, he said his prayers three times a day facing Mecca while kneeling on his sheepskin prayer rug. Bilali and other Moslem slaves carefully observed Moslem fasts and feast days. Bilali Mohomet and his wife, Phoebe, prayed at sunrise, when the sun was directly overhead, and at sunset, according to Katie Brown, his great-granddaughter. Shad Hall recalled that when they prayed they bowed to the sun while kneeling on a prayer rug. They had beads on a long string. According to his descendants, Bilali would pull the beads while saying, "Belambi, Hakabara, Mahamadu." His wife would say, "Ameen, Ameen." Many former slaves on the Georgia coast remembered their ancestors praying in that fashion, When Bilali died, he was buried with his prayer rug and his Koran.[84]

The slaves' lives were controlled from dawn to dusk, but from dusk to dawn the slave community created its own social and cultural life. People got together to socialize—to converse, to sing, to dance, and to enjoy one another's company. Most plantations gave the slaves Saturday afternoons and Sundays off. The slaves would divide the time tending their gardens, patching clothes and doing other household chores, hunting, and fishing. One popular pastime was visiting other plantations, whether or not one could get a pass. Ben Horry dodged the patrols to visit his first girlfriend, Teena, on a neighboring rice plantation in the South Carolina lowcountry. If he had been caught without a pass, he would have received a severe beating. But he said she was worth the risk. An Alabama slave, Sylvester Brooks, recollected the "pattyrollers," or patrols, all too clearly, "'cause dey whip me every time dey cotches me without my pass. Dat de way dey make us stay home at night."[85]

As in peasant cultures around the world, the slaves alternated long days of toil in the cotton, tobacco, sugar, and rice fields with periods of ritual festivity. Harvest time was one such occasion. "After the cotton was picked dey would eat barbecue, and dance, and have a big time," a Georgia slave remembered. In addition, there were corn shuckings, wedding parties, and celebrations on various holidays. Midge Burnett recalled that in North Carolina, "We had square dances dat las' all night an holidays an' we had a Christmas tree an' a Easter egg hunt an' all dat, case Marse William intended ter make us a civilized bunch of blacks." In the South Carolina upcountry, slaves went to barbecues on the Fourth of July after morning chores were finished. Some Virginia slaves had a Whitsun holiday. "On dem days we would play ring plays, jump rope, and dance. Then nights we'd dance juba." Whitsun holidays appear to have been rare, but slaves typically celebrated Christmas and Easter.[86]

Christmas was the most important holiday in the annual cycle on the plantations. On many plantations, the slaves gathered early on Christmas morning at the Big House to receive greetings and small presents from the masters, extra rations of pork, beef, molasses, and tobacco. In Georgia, Christmas

> am the day for the big time. A tree am fix, and some present for everyone. The white preacher talk 'bout Christ. Us have singing and 'joyment all day. Then at night, the big fire builded, and all us sot round it. There am 'bout hundred hog bladders save from hog killing. So, on Christmas night, the children takes them and puts them on the stick. First they is all blowed full of air and tied tight and dry. Then the children holds the bladder in the fire and pretty soon, "BANG!" they goes. That am the fireworks.[87]

A Missouri slave's report seems scarcely credible: "During Christmas time and de whole month of January, it was de rulin' to give de slaves a holiday in our part of de country. A whole month to go and come as much as we pleased and go for miles as far as we wanted to, but we had better be back by de first of February."[88] Whatever the situation in Missouri, Christmas for most slaves meant two or three days of released time for celebration.

Slaves eagerly looked forward to Christmas because it meant not only days off from work but also gifts of food, candies, and alcoholic beverages from the master. On many plantations dances were held at night during the holiday season. The patrols were eased up as masters allowed greater freedom of movement than usual. The John Canoe festival (so beloved in Jamaica) was an exotic part of the Christmas celebration as far north as North Carolina. Bands of dancers, keeping time to the beat of the "gumbo box," triangles, and jawbones, begged donations from spectators. Most slave drinking was confined to such holidays and dances. Masters gave liquor rations out at Christmas, and ex-slaves told of drinking during dances. A Louisiana slave reported, "The men would save money out of the crops to buy their Christmas whiskey. It was all right for the slaves to get drunk on Christmas and New Year's Day; no one was whipped for getting drunk on those days." Frederick Douglass believed slaveholders deliberately got slaves drunk in order "to disgust their slaves with freedom, by plunging them into the lowest depths of dissipation." Such holidays, he believed, were "among the most effective means in the hands of the slaveholders in keeping down the spirit of insurrection."[89]

Corn shuckings were also festive occasions. George Woods recalled that in the South Carolina upcountry both whites and blacks gathered to shuck corn and have a good time. Once the corn was shucked, the slaves chased the master until they caught him. Then they hoisted him upon their shoulders and carried him around the house, laughing and singing all the while. Finally they took him inside the Big House, placed him in a chair, combed his hair, crossed his knees, removed his hat, and threw it in the fire. According to tradition, the master had to have a new hat for a new crop. After a day of shucking corn everyone was served a large meal, followed by a dance. Some slaves recalled the reel as the most popular dance.[90]

Singing, dancing, and making music were especially significant folk performances on the slave plantations, although some slaveholders did not approve of their slaves singing. "Dey didn't allow us to sing on our plantation," an Alabama slave recalled, "'cause if we did we just sing ourselves happy and get to shouting and dat would settle de work."[91]

Fanny Kemble found the melodies of the slaves' rowing songs on the Georgia coast "wild and striking." She believed the slaves had a natural gift of music. She was especially interested in what she considered the unusual structure of the slave songs: "The way in which the chorus strikes in with the burden, between each phrase of the melody chanted by a single voice, is very curious and effective, especially with the rhythm of the rowlocks for accompaniment."[92]

Some of the slave songs commented directly and satirically on the world of the plantation. Ebenezer Brown, who had been a slave in Mississippi, recalled the slaves singing as they worked in the cotton fields:

Howdy my brethen, Howdy's yo' do
Since I bin in de lan'
I do mi'ty well, an' I thank de Lord, too,
Since I bin in de lan'
O yes, O yes, Since I bin in de lan'
O yes, O yes, Since I bin in de lan'
I do mi'ty well, an' I thank de Lord, too,
Since I bin in de lan'.[93]

Laura Montgomery, another ex-slave from the same Mississippi county, had learned a somewhat different version.

Howdy my brethren, How d' yer do,
Since I'se bin in de lan,'
I do mighty po,' but I thank de Lord sho'
Since I'se bin in de lan.'
O, yes! O, yes! Since I'se bin in de lan'.[94]

These two versions of the same song reflect the complexities of the slaves' cultural response to slavery in the American South. One song was sung by people hard at work when out in the fields under white supervision. The other was learned by the narrator in the privacy of the slave quarters, out of white earshot, where slaves could feel freer to express their true feelings.

On Saturday nights, from Virginia and the Carolinas through Alabama and Mississippi to Louisiana and Texas, the slaves held dances and frolics. Talented slave "musicianers" played such old-time songs as "Arkansas Traveller," "Black Eyed Susie," "Jimmy Long Josey," "Soldier's Joy," and "Old Dan Tucker." According to a Mississippi slave, when the fiddler played the old reels, "you couldn't keep your foots still." A North Carolina slave exclaimed, "Oh, Lord, that fiddle could almost talk." Slave dances, like white dances of the age, centered upon fiddle music. In Mississippi dances called the "back step" and the "pigeon-wing" were popular. In coastal Georgia the slaves danced an old African dance called the "buzzard lope."[95]

Some masters had slaves dance to amuse their white guests, who were as amazed at the slaves' strange moves as at their great enthusiasm for dancing. A northern visitor condescendingly described one such musical gathering on a South Carolina rice plantation: "The little nigs, only four or five years old, would rush into the ring and shuffle away at the breakdowns till I feared their short legs would come off; while all the darkies joined in the songs, till the branches of the old pines above shook as if they too had caught the spirit of the music."[96] Slave music and dance served an important function on the plantations—temporary release from the soul-crushing burdens of bondage.

The folk speech of the slaves included a wide variety of folk linguistic phenomena, ranging from lexical, syntactical, or phonological variations from standard speech to full-blown creole languages such as Gullah. The slaves' folk expressions made colorful and explicit comments on the experience of slavery. The slaves worked "from can to can't." They had to "root like a pig or die." The master "didn't give me sweat off de black cat's eye." But slavery made the slaves tough; the "buzzards laid me and de sun hatch me." A significant element of slave folk speech had to do with onomastics, or naming patterns. Not only were Akan day names still found among slaves as late as the 1860s, but African *patterns* of naming persisted to an even greater extent. Kin-names were passed on in families, and surnames (or "titles") were in wide use within the slave community before emancipation.[97]

The African penchant for proverbial ways of speaking—that is, speaking by indirection—was reflected in slave proverbs, which served as metaphors of social experience. Some African proverbs survived almost unchanged: the Hausa "Chattering doesn't cook the rice" continued in the South Carolina lowcountry as "Promisin' talk don' cook rice." But others underwent local changes. The Bantu "Every beast roars in its own den" became the Gullah "Every frog praise its own pond [even] if it dry." Some spoke directly to the experiences of the slave plantation: "Ol' Massa take keer o' himself, but de niggah got to go ter God." Others could take on heightened meaning in the context of slavery: "Dere's a fambly coolness twixt de mule an' de singletree" could be employed as a comment on master/slave relations. "Yuh mought as well die wid de chills ez wid de feber" could be employed as a comment on the relative merits of trying to escape or remaining in bondage.[98]

Across the South, slaves narrated legends (folk narratives set in historical time that are told *as though* true) of "Ole Nat" (Nat Turner), "Moses" (Harriet Tubman), Frederick Douglass, John Brown, and Abraham Lincoln. According to one such legend, "I was looking right in Lincoln's mouth when he said, 'The colored man is turned loose without anything. I am going to give a dollar a day to every Negro born before Emancipation until his death—a pension of a dollar a day.' That's the reason they killed him."[99]

Another form of legend purported to explain how things came to be. Many such legends persisted as humorous stories (or etiological tales) even after the belief factor had eroded. Slaves in Winnsboro, South Carolina, told a story of the biblical Nicodemus the publican:

> In the days of the disciples there was a small colored man named Niggerdemos, that was a Republican and run a eating-house in Jerusalem. He done his own cooking and serving at the tables. He heard the tramp, tramp, tramp of the multitude a-coming, and he asked: "what that going on outside?" They told him the disciples done borrowed a colt and was having a parade over the city. Niggerdemos thought the good Lord would cure him of the lumbago in his back. Hearing folks a-shouting, he throwed down his dishrag, jerked off his apron, and run for to see all that was gwine on, but having short legs he couldn't see nothing. A big sycamore tree stood in the line of the parade, so Niggerdemos climbed up it, going high enough for to see all. The savior tell him: "Come down; we gwine to eat at your house Niggerdemos." Niggerdemos come down so fast, when he hear that, he scrape the bark off the tree in many places. Niggerdemos was sure cured of the lumbago, but sycamores been blistered ever since. Next time you pass a sycamore tree, look how it is blistered![100]

The folktales of the slaves included tall tales (or improvements on reality, with smart slaves smarter, bad weather worse, and big crops bigger), outrageous falsehoods narrated with a straight face in the sober tones of truth. "One day I was walking past a forty acre patch of corn," one begins, "and the corn was so high and thick, I decide to ramble through it. 'Bout halfway over, I hears a commotion. I walks on and peeps. There stands a four-ox wagon backed up to the edge of the field, and two niggers was sawing down a stalk. Finally they drag it on the wagon and drives off. I seen one of them, in a day or two, and asks 'bout it. He say: 'We shelled 356 bushels of corn from that one ear, and then we saw 800 feet of lumber from the cob.'"[101]

Trickster tales, with their theme of the struggle for mastery between the trickster (usually a small but sly, weak but wily animal such as Buh Rabbit) and his bigger and more powerful adversary, were the most popular tales on the plantations. Robert Pinckney, of Wilmington Island off the Georgia coast, told stories of the trickster defeating his rival by outwitting him. The story of the magic hoe was widespread in Africa. It was especially well known in Hausa and Ashanti folklore.

> Bruh Rabbit and Bruh Wolf wuz alluz tryin tuh git duh bes uh one anudduh. Now Bruh Wolf he own a hoe an it wuk fuh crop all by itsef. Bruh Wolf jis say, "Swish," tuh it. Den he sit down in duh fiel an duh hoe do all duh wuk.

Bruh Rabbit he wahn dat hoe. He hide behine bush an watch how duh wolf make it wuk. One day wen duh wolf way, Bruh Rabbit he steal duh hoe. He go to he own fiel an he stan duh hoe up an he say, "Swish." Duh hoe staht tuh wuk. It wuk and it wuk. Fo long duh crop is done finish. Den rabbit want hoe tuh stop, an he call out an he call out but hoe keep right on wukin. Bruh Rabbit dohn know wut wud tuh say tuh stop it. Pretty soon duh hoe cut down all Bruh Rabbit wintuh crop an still it keep on wukkin an wukkin. Bruh Rabbit wring he hans. Ebryting he hab is gone. Jis den Bruh Wolf come long an he laugh an he laugh out loud wen he see how Bruh Rabbit steal he hoe an how it done ruin all duh crop. Bruh Rabbit he keep callin out, "Swish, swish," an duh hoe go fastuhn fastuh. Wen he see Bruh Wolf, he ax um tuh make duh hoe stop. Bruh Wolf wohn say nuttn uhtall cuz he mad dat Bruh Rabbit steal he hoe. Den attuh a time he say, "Slow, boy," an duh hoe he stop wukkin. Den Bruh Wolf he pick up he hoe an carry um home.[102]

The slaves also narrated a cycle of human trickster stories featuring the slave John and his never-ending contest with the master: "One day John killed one of his master's hogs, and he catch him, and he ask him, 'What's that you got there?' John said, 'A possum.' The master said, 'Let me see.' He look and seen it was a hog. John said, 'Massa, it may be a hog now, but it was a possum a while ago when I put 'im in this sack.'"[103] In such tales as these, as in other elements of their rich folk culture, the slaves used language as symbolic action. By manipulating the words that defined their world, they verbally rearranged it and turned it symbolically upside down.

§

Folk cultural expression was also exemplified in slave foodways. At sunset in the slave quarters one could smell the aromas of cornbread, peas and rice, pork or fish cooking over wood fires.

Rations were given out on Saturdays and usually included cornmeal, lard, meat, molasses, peas, greens, and, on occasion, flour and soda. William Ballard of upcountry South Carolina recalled that "we was allowed three pounds o' meat, one quart o' molasses, grits and other things each week—plenty for us to eat." Another slave reported that "we were given plenty of milk and sometimes butter. We were permitted to have a fowlhouse for chickens, separate from the white folks."[104]

A former slave recollected that "each slave cabin had a stone fireplace in the end, and over the flames at daybreak was prepared the morning meal. That was the only meal the field negroes had to cook. All the other meals were fixed up by an old man and woman who was too old for field trucking. The peas, the beans, the turnips, the potatoes, all seasoned up with fat meats and sometimes a ham bone, was cooked in a big iron kettle and when meal time come they all gathered around the pot for a-plenty of helpings! Corn bread and buttermilk made up the rest of the meal."[105]

Fanny Kemble, told that her husband's slaves had "sufficient" food, found that it was prepared by elderly cooks in the cookhouse. For lunch, cooked and eaten during breaks from field work, they doled out grits or occasionally rice that was unfit for market. For supper, six hours later, they occasionally varied the menu with crabs, oysters, and freshwater fish, which they spooned into the slaves' small cedar vessels. The slaves mostly ate with crude wooden spoons or by using their fingers, as the children did. They had neither knives nor forks, nor tables nor chairs.[106]

For many slaves, however, their diet remained largely unsatisfactory. But slave gardens, hunting, and fishing added additional variety to the cuisine. Hunting was one way in which slaves were allowed to supplement their rations. Mississippi slave Jim Martin used to sing

> Come 'long boys an' lets go er huntin',
> Come 'long boys an' lets go er huntin',
> Come 'long boys an' lets go er huntin',
> Fur I heered de dogs bark,
> an' I know dey treed sumptin'.[107]

Most of the plantation provisions were raised by the slaves. They herded livestock, raised foodstuffs, and helped slaughter and dress meat. Much of the herding was done by children. Most slave families also cultivated gardens in their off time, raising potatoes, pumpkins, watermelons, and other fruits and vegetables. Typically each family had its own garden plot from which to supplement its weekly allocation of rations.

On some plantations slaves who ran out of food before the end of the week could get a little more. For the most part, however, if the weekly ration proved insufficient, slaves had to find other sources of nourishment. Food theft became so common on the plantations that slaves had a song about it.

> Some folks say dat a nigger wont steal
> I caught two in my corn field
> One had a bushel
> One had a peck
> An' one had rosenears [roasting ears]
> Strung 'round his neck.[108]

Biscuits were a rare delicacy for most slaves. An Alabama slave described them as the plantation mistress's Sunday treat. "Ebery Sunday mawnin'," he said, "she'd make de older slaves bring all de little niggers up to de Big House, so she could read de Bible to 'em and den she give us plenty of dem good biscuits and taters. . . . I really thought Mistus was an angel!" A Mississippi slave recalled that when he was a child and his mistress planned to punish him, she would first lure him out of hiding with a biscuit.[109]

Even rarer were alcoholic beverages, although on some plantations, slaves "always made at least one barrel of peach brandy and one of cider. That would be vinegar 'nough by spring. 'Simmon beer was good in the cold freezing weather too. We make much as we have barrels if we could get the persimmons."[110] Slaves ate the foodstuffs of the plantation environment; but slave cooks applied to them African methods of cooking and spicing, remembered recipes, ancestral tastes. They thus not only maintained cultural continuity with African foodways but also creatively adapted African traditions to the New World.[111]

Folk architecture was strikingly exemplified in the slave cabins, varying from slave quarters built of stone reported in Kentucky to "old rugged huts made out of poles" in Alabama. On one Mississippi plantation, slaves lived in large wooden houses with brick chimneys and up to six rooms. Such elaborate housing, however, was unique in that county. It marked the slaveholder's great wealth and generous paternalism. On another, "about three hundred negro families living in box-type cabins made it seem like a small town. Built in rows, the cabins were kept white-washed, neat and orderly, for the Master was strict about such things." Some slave cabins were described by ex-slaves as "good houses, weatherboarden with cypress and had brick chimneys." A Georgia slave recalled, "We lived in weatherboard houses. Our parents had corded-up beds with ropes and we chillun slept on the floor for the most part or in a hole bored in a log. Our house had one window jest big enough to stick your head out of, and one door, and this one door faced the Big House which was your master's house. This was so that you couldn't git out 'less somebody seen you."[112]

More commonly slave dwellings were built of logs. Sometimes the logs were covered with slabs. Some cabins were large. A Missouri slave reported that "de hewed log house we lived in was very big, about five or six rooms." Far more typical was the one- or two-room cabin in which as many as a dozen people might sleep on "an old pile o' rags in de corner." One former slave said he had lived in a "little one room log cabin, chinked and daubed." A Tennessee slave reported, "We lived in one-room log huts. There was a long string of them huts. We slept on the floor like hogs. Girls and boys slept together—jest everybody slept every what." A Mississippi slave reported, "we live in log huts, and when I left home grown, I left my folks living in the same log huts." But to others log cabins would have seemed a luxury. A Georgia ex-slave reported having lived in "old ragged huts made out of poles and some of the cracks chinked up with mud and moss and some of them wasn't." On some plantations, "dey wasn't fitten for nobody to live in. We just had to put up with 'em." The cracks between the logs were chinked with mud or clay, not always successfully. A Texas slave reported that "the cold winds in the winter go through the logs like the walls was somewhere else." Some cabins had plank floors, but others did not. A Georgia slave recalled, "Dey no floor in dem houses, 'cept what God put in dem." According to a Mississippi slave, "My ma never would have no board floor like de rest of 'em, on 'count she was a African." Furniture was simple and hand made. Beds were often made with a post or two and a mattress of moss or straw. A more elaborate bed had ropes plaited to form a support for a feather mattress. Other furniture consisted of simple benches and chairs. The chimneys were usually built of sticks, clay, and mud, with a coat of clay daubed over them. All too often the chimneys caught fire. "Many the time we have to get up at midnight and push the chimney away from the house to keep the house from burnin' up."[113]

Talented slave artisans created beautiful crafts. On the rice plantations of the South Carolina lowcountry, slaves made wide fanner baskets with low sloping sides after the African method of coiled basketry. In Georgia slave basketmakers made plaited baskets and mats. Throughout the South slave women made quilts—often in strip patterns—both to keep their families warm and to provide beautiful objects in their cabins. A North Carolina slave described how "the womenfolks carded and spun and wove cloth, then they dyed it and made clothes. And we knit all the stockings we wore." Slave blacksmiths not only shod horses and other livestock but also made striking wrought-iron gates and grilles. And slave craftspersons were adept at making musical instruments that were beautiful both to see and to hear. There were fiddles made from gourds, banjoes made from sheep hides, "bones" made from beef ribs, and quills made from willow stalks: "You takes de stick and pounds de bark loose and slips it off, den split de wood in one end and down one side, puts holes in de bark and put it back on de stick. De quill plays like de flute."[114]

Most slaves never had the opportunity to learn to read and write. Both law and custom in the Old South conspired to keep slaves illiterate, to prevent them from attaining positions closer to equality with their masters. "White folks didn't teach us to read or write," Lindy Patton, a former slave in Alabama, testified in the 1930s. According to Sam T. Stewart of North Carolina, his owners "never taught me to read and write, and most slaves who got any reading and writing certainly stole it. There were rules against slaves having books." Those rules were sometimes ruthlessly enforced. The former slave Elijah Green of South Carolina said, "An' do for God's sake don't let a slave be catch with pencil an' paper. That was a major crime. You might as well had kill your master or missus." Henry Brown, another Charleston ex-slave, added that for such an offense "in slavery he would be whip' 'til not a skin was lef' on his body."[115] But despite legal prohibitions against slave literacy, many masters and more mistresses taught at least some of their slaves to read and write. An ex-slave reported, with a touch of envy, that "Miss Jane Alice was very fond of little Bob and taught him to read and write." Some slaves, such as Prince, coachman on a South Carolina rice plantation, even acquired a reputation for being somewhat "bookish." And the former slave Filmore Ramsey recalled that Mary Stewart, his mistress in Mississippi, had taught him to read, write, and recite poems and speeches.[116]

The mixture of kindness and cruelty so prevalent throughout slave society is evident in slaveholders' efforts to teach slaves to read and write. According to Harriott Robinson, "Mistress Julie used to drill her chillen in spelling any words. At every word them chillen missed, she gave me a lick 'cross the head for it. Meanest woman I ever seen in my life."[117]

Some slaves learned to read and write from the white children rather than from the mistress. "When the white children studied their lessons," according to John Bectom in North Carolina, "I studied with them. When they wrote in the sand I wrote in the sand too. The white children, and not the marster or mistress, is where I got started in learnin' to read and write."[118]

Later, after emancipation, the importance of literacy would become obvious to all. Mary Vereen Magill, wife of a South Carolina rice planter with a reputation for cruelty, taught one of her slaves, young Bruce Williams, to read and write. After emancipation he became a minister, helped found Bethel A.M.E. Church in Georgetown, and served as a senator in the South Carolina legislature from 1876 to 1902. For those slaves who had been denied literacy in slavery, emancipation only set in motion an un-equal contest between former slave and former master. Ben Horry ex-pressed the dilemma very well: "You had the learning in you head! Give me that pencil to catch up dem thing. I couldn't to save my life."[119]

§

Former slaves often described those who had claimed to own them in three basic categories—"good masters," "temperamental masters," and "mean masters." A Virginia slave recalled, "Good masters had good slaves 'cause they treated 'em good, an' bad masters had lyin' thievin' slaves 'cause they made 'em that way."[120]

A "good" master tempered the physical punishments dealt out to the slaves. The Mississippi slave Gabe Butler said his master was "de best white man who ebber liv'd. He low'd no overseer to beat his darkies." According to another Mississippi slave, his master "wus a good man. He never 'lowed his slaves to be brutalized. He made them wurk, but he nev-er 'lowed the driver to strip the women folks in whip dem. En ernuther thing he never 'lowed a woman who wus breedin' to be whip'd." But, as one former North Carolina slave, Sam T. Stewart, recalled, "When a slave owner treated his slaves unusually good, some other slave owner would tell him he was raising slaves who would rise against him."[121]

The testimonies of ex-slaves characterizing the former masters as "good" while simultaneously describing brutal punishments meted out must be approached with caution. "I ain't a'complaining," Frank Adam-son recalled, choosing his words carefully. "He was a good master, best-est in de land, but he just had to have a whipping post, 'cause you'll find a whole passle of bad niggers when you gits a thousand of them in one flock." A similar variation on the "good master" theme was gingerly put forward by Victoria Adams: "De massa an' messus was good to me," she said, "but sometimes I was so bad they had to whip me. I 'members she used to whip me every time she tell me to do something and I take too long to move 'long and do it."[122]

"Temperamental" masters were "good" except when angered. As Laura Montgomery noted of her masters, "Dey was all fine folks 'ceptin old Marse Bill when he got mad he was mighty bad." "Mean" masters pun-ished often and cruelly, and they made their slaves work very hard. Victoria Perry recalled her master as cruel and frightening. When he got mad at any slave he whipped them all. And he got mad often. He tied them to a post or tree, stripped their clothes to the waist, and whipped them until he grew tired. She said she had seen her mother whipped in such a manner until she bled. Orris Harris considered his Mississippi master, Pharaoh Carter, to have been the "meanest white man dat eber lived." But the question of who was the "meanest white man" was disputed among the slaves. Sam Anderson contended that *his* master, Hillery Quinn, was "de meanest white man dat eber drew breath. He cudnt sleep if he didnt whup a nigger fore de sun went down." Another Mississippi master was said to have urged his overseer to whip slaves even harder with such statements as "dat will loosen up deir hides so dey ken wurk better."[123]

If masters and overseers were inhumane, slaves went to the plantation mistress for help, for protection, for justice. And "Ole Miss" did frequently induce masters and overseers to be more lenient with their punishments. According to Ben Horry, when slaves on his South Carolina rice plantation broke into the barn and stole rice, his mistress made the overseers give them more rice rather than punish them for trying to steal it. "Anybody steal rice and they beat them, Miss Bessie cry and say, 'Let 'em have rice! My rice—my nigger!'"[124]

But plantation mistresses were not always successful in such efforts. Fanny Kemble was particularly incensed at the driver's harsh punishments of women on her husband's plantation. In her journal, she described how on one occasion several slave women were "fastened by their wrists to a beam or a branch of a tree, their feet barely touching the ground, so as to allow them no purchase for resistance or evasion of the lash, their clothes turned over their heads, and their backs scored with a leather thong." She complained to her husband of "the brutal inhumanity of allowing a man to strip and lash a woman, the mother of ten children; to exact from her, toil, which was to maintain in luxury idle young men, the owners of the plantation." But her complaint was to no avail. Such punishments continued on the Butler plantations.[125]

One Alabama mistress was so angry about the treatment of a house servant that she rebuked her husband. "You know I don't allow you to tech my house servants," she exclaimed. "I ruther see dem marks on my own shoulders dan to see 'em on mammy's." Jane Montgomery, an Oklahoma ex-slave, recalled that her "mistress never whip us and iffen master would[,] mistress would git a gun and make him stop." Another former slave, Lindy Patton, recalled an occasion on her Alabama plantation when the master was going to whip one of the slaves. "De Misstis tol' him to leave de ole fool alone, said it warn't worth the trouble." But the mistress was not always aware of beatings that took place on the plantation. One Alabamian, Henry Cheatam, recalled, "A heap of times old Miss didn't know nothin' 'bout it, an' de slaves better not tell her, 'caze dat oberseer-er whup 'em iffen he finds out dat dey done gone an' tol.'"[126]

A "good" master might have a "mean" wife. Charles Ball, a Georgia slave, wrote that his master, "when left to pursue his own inclinations, was kind and humane in his temper, and conduct towards his people." If it had not been for his master's wife, he said "I should have had a tolerable time of my servitude with him; and should, in all probability, have been a slave in Georgia until this day." His mistress, however, "gave us a specimen of her character, on the first morning after her arrival amongst us, by beating severely, with a raw cow-hide, the black girl who nursed the infant, because the child cried, and could not be kept silent. When enraged," according to Ball, "she would find some victim to pour her fury upon, without regard to justice or mercy."[127]

The plantation mistress could be as cruel as the master. According to Sarah Wilson, who had been a slave in Oklahoma, "Old Mistress just as bad, and she took most of her wrath out hitting us children all the time." In fact in some cases it was the master who restrained his wife. Another Oklahoma slave recalled, "When Master was there he made her treat us good, but when he was gone she made our lives a misery to us." Frank Cooper testified that his back was broken when "three white women beat me because they had no butter for their biscuits and cornbread. Miss Burton used a heavy board while the missus used a whip. While I was on my knees beggin' them to quit, Miss Burton hit the small of mah back with the heavy board." According to Jacob Branch, his mistress in Texas punished another slave simply because he had never received a whipping before. "Missy think he gettin' it too good, 'cause he ain't never been whipped. She clumb over de fence and start down des row with de cowhide."[128]

But physical assaults upon male slaves by white women were infrequent. More often, cruel plantation mistresses turned their ire upon female slaves. The cruelties a mistress inflicted were often prompted by a slave's failure to perform some task to the mistress's satisfaction. For example, Ida Henry recalled that "when passing around the potatoes, Old Mistress felt one as if hit wasn't soft done. She exclaimed to de cook, 'What you bring these raw potatoes out here for?' and grab a fork and stuck it in her eye and put hit out." George G. King recalled seeing his mother abused by the mistress, "pull his mammy's clothes over her head so's the lash would reach the skin." While his mother writhed in pain, "the mistress walk away laughing."[129]

Slaves were frequently punished for circumstances beyond their control. Jacob Branch, a Texan, recalled, "My poor mama! Every washday old Missy give her a beatin'. She couldn't keep de flies from speckin' de clothes overnight." Delia Garlic remembered vividly the temper of her Arkansas mistress: "She pick up a stick of stovewood an' flails it agin' my head. I didn't know nothin' more till I come to, lyin' on de floor. I heard de Mistus say to one of de girls: 'I thought her thick skull and cap of wool could take it better than that.'" But the mistress's temper led her to more horrible punishments. "One day I was playin' wid de baby. It hurts its li'l han' an' commenced to cry, an' she whirl on me, pick up a hot iron an' run it all down my arm an' han'. It took off de flesh when she done it."[130]

The worst punishments were reserved for slaves who attempted to emancipate themselves by flight. Jack Frowers was captured during an escape attempt near Aiken, South Carolina. "Just as soon as Master Holley got me home, he set the dogs to worry and bite me, and the scars on my legs and arms are what they did with their teeth. After he got tired of that fun, he took me to a blacksmith, who put a ring around my ankle, bending the ends in when it was red hot." Even slaveholders who were otherwise considered "good" masters meted out harsh reprisals against runaways to serve as examples to the other slaves. The South Carolina rice planter Plowden C. J. Weston, for example, routinely sold recaptured runaways far away from their wives and children.[131]

§

Slaves might pretend to be satisfied with their lot around whites, but it is untrue that the slaves accepted their condition because they had no concept of freedom. As a former slave put it, "De white folks had ebery thing fine an' ebery thing dey wanted, an' cud cum an' go wid out de patroller gittin' dem, but de slaves wanted to do de same thing; dat is de reason dey all wanted to be sot free." To see the advantages whites had that they lacked was to perceive all too clearly the difference between freedom and slavery.[132]

Slaves did not always accept their situation passively. Their response took many forms. They pretended to be sick, slowed work, fought back, committed suicide or homicide, and emancipated themselves by flight. Whatever its form, slave resistance created a problem of discipline for slaveholders. Whether mild and sporadic or bold and persistent, acts of resistance threatened property or safety. Acts of resistance also had the ultimate potential to weaken or even destroy an institution that held human beings in bondage.[133]

At the center of the slave community was a communications network known as the "grapevine." The grapevine was a crucial element of slave resistance. "We used to carry news from one plantation to the other I reckon, 'cause mammy would tell about things going on some other plantation and I know she never been there," recalled Phyllis Petite, a former slave. How did slaves learn what was going on in the larger world? According to Benjamin Russell, who had been a slave in South Carolina, "many plantations were strict about this, but the greater the precaution the alerter became the slaves, the wider they opened their ears and the more eager they became for outside information. Among the sources were girls that waited on the tables, the ladies' maids, and the drivers; they would pick up everything they heard and pass it on to the other slaves." Slaves also used "field calls and other kinds of whoops and hollers, what had a meanin' to 'em."[134]

Malingering—pretending to be sick in order to get out of work—was one way that slaves engaged in day-to-day resistance to slavery. A Georgia slave reported that his father had "beat ol' marster out o' 'bout fifteen years work. When he didn't feel like workin' he would play like he wus sick an' ol' marster would git de doctor for him."[135] The slave narratives suggest that women were more likely than men to feign sickness as a form of passive resistance. But women may also have been more susceptible to genuine illness, especially disorders associated with the menstrual cycle and with childbirth.

A more subtle method of resistance was for slaves to perform assigned work poorly, sabotaging the system through intentional failure. Texas slaves even had a song for this form of slave resistance: "Fool my master seven years / Goin to fool him seven more / Hey diddle, de diddle, de diddle, de do." One slaveholder told Frederick Law Olmsted that his slaves "never do more than just enough to save themselves from being punished, and no amount of punishment prevents their working careless and indifferently. Moreover, it always seems on the plantation as if they took great pains to break all the tools and spoil all the cattle that they possibly can, even when they know they'll be directly punished for it."[136]

One of the most prominent methods by which slaves resisted was stealing. By theft a slave could simultaneously take revenge upon oppressors and supplement a family's meager food supply. Few acts of slave resistance irritated the masters more. Food was the primary object of slave theft. Children began at an early age to take food from pantries and henhouses. Sometimes older slaves punished the children for such deeds, but they rarely informed on them to the masters.

Slave thieves were not always as successful as Buh Rabbit, and the punishment was often more severe than the briar patch. A Mississippi slaveholder caught "Uncle Irwin," an elderly slave, pulling apart the boards of the plantation smoke house in an effort to get in. The master had him whipped. Later, the slaveholder noticed that his corn supply was going down faster than he had expected. He set a trap to ensnare the corn culprit and apprehended the old man again. This time the slaveholder forced him to dance as he was whipped.[137]

Literacy could be used as one form of slave resistance. Learning how to read and write was of great advantage to the slaves for sabotage and day-to-day resistance. Frederick Douglass's master forbade his wife to teach the young slave to read and write. The master said it would make him "unfit to be a slave." Douglass concluded that "the pathway from slavery to freedom" was literacy. An Alabama slave came to the same conclusion. "Ol' Miss taught de niggers how to read an' write an' some of 'em got to be too good at it, 'case dey learned how to write too many passes so's de pattyrollers wouldn't cotch 'em."[138]

Slaves moving about after dark, whether visiting wives or sweethearts on other plantations or making an escape attempt, were subject to capture and punishment by slave patrols with dogs, horses, and whips. Each of the slave states required men—whether they owned slaves or not—to serve on the patrols as a means of controlling unauthorized slave movements, especially at night. The slave community's dread of the patrols is reflected in the lines of a song sung by a Mississippi slave: "Run, nigger run, de patroller git you / Run, nigger run, it is almost day."[139] The "pattyrollers" were considered the most virulent elements of white society by the slaves.

Sometimes slaves fought back. One effective method was arson, a more obviously rebellious act than stealing. A patroller who had been engaged in harassing slaves might suddenly awake at night to find his barn aflame. Puzzled for several years at the number of structures on his plantation that mysteriously burned to the ground, Edmund Ruffin eventually came to realize that his slaves were torching the buildings as retaliation against a hated overseer. Ruffin, in fact, dismissed three overseers in succession for cruelly mistreating his slaves.[140]

Some slaves took their own lives rather than continue to submit. Adeline Marshall, a former slave, told of a Texas slave who "done hang himself to 'scape he mis'ry." But others turned violence upon their oppressors rather than upon themselves. The overseer on a Mississippi plantation attempted to beat a slave named Mose. Pulling up the stakes intended to hold him down, Mose attacked the overseer with one of the stakes before being clubbed unconscious. Mose's master, however, abandoned his effort to break the slave and auctioned him off.[141]

Women resisted as fervently as men. "Ole Miss," according to John Rudd, "had a long whip hid under her apron and began whippin' Mama across the shoulders 'thout tellin' her why. Mama wheeled around from whar she was slicin' ham and started runnin' after Old Missus Jane. Ole Missus run so fas' Mama couldn't catch up wif her so she throwed the butcher knife and struck it in the wall!" The grandmother was sold. Mary Armstrong, a former slave in Texas, recalled her master and mistress as "the meanest two white folks what ever live, cause they was always beatin' on their slaves. . . . Old Polly, she was a Polly devil if there ever was one, and she whipped my little sister what was only nine months old, and just a baby, to death. She come and took the diaper offen my little sister and whipped till the blood just ran—just 'cause she cry like all babies do, and it kilt my sister." Mary Armstrong never forgave her mistress for killing her baby sister. Eventually she had an opportunity to take revenge on her. "You see, I'se 'bout ten year old and I belongs to Miss Olivia, what was that old Polly's daughter, and one day Old Polly devil comes to where Miss Olivia lives after she marries, and tries to give me a lick out in the yard, and I picks up a rock about as big as half your fist and hits her right in the eye and busted the eyeball, and tells her that's for whippin' my baby sister to death." Seven decades after emancipation, Mary Armstrong had still not forgiven her mistress: "But that Old Polly was mean like her husband, Old Cleveland, till she die, and I hopes they is burnin' in torment now." Age did not always prevent slaves from fighting back. After her young master whipped her, an elderly Mississippi mammy took a pole from her loom and beat him "nearly to death," shouting with each stroke, "'I'm goin' to kill you. These black titties sucked you, and you come out here to beat me!'"[142]

Sometimes the slaves' revenge was even more forceful. An Alabama exslave told "about a mean man who whupped a cullid woman near 'bout to death. She got so mad at him dat she tuk his baby chile what was play-in' roun' de yard and grab him up an' th'owed it in a pot of lye dat she was usin' to wash wid. His wife come a'hollerin' an' run her arms down in de boilin' lye to git de chile out, an' she near 'bout burnt her arms off, but it didn't do no good 'case when she jerked de chile out he was daid."[143] An Oklahoma slave, unwilling to endure the indignities of slavery any long-er, suddenly turned upon his tormenters and "just killed all of 'em he could."[144]

Running away was perhaps the most important form of protest against human bondage. Those who sought permanent freedom naturally tried to get out of the South altogether. According to a former slave in South Carolina, "I 'member seein' one big black man, who tried to steal a boat from Charleston. He stole away one night from Master Mobley's place and got to Charleston, befo' he was caught with. He tell the overseer who questioned him after he was brought back: 'Sho', I try to get away from this sort of thing. I was goin' to Massachusetts, and hire out 'till I git 'nough to carry me to my home in Africa.'" To attempt self-emancipation was to undertake a perilous flight for freedom in the dead of night along danger-ous and unfamiliar paths. "Every once in a while slaves would run away to de North," recalled an Alabama slave. "Most times dey was caught an' brought back. Sometimes dey would git desp'rit an' would kill demse'ves 'fore dey woud stand to be brought back."[145]

Those who pondered escape from slavery had to consider that their chances of success were poor and the penalty for failure was dire. Most of the time a flight for freedom ended in failure. Punishment was certain. Except for slaves in border states self-emancipation seemed totally im-practical. The North and freedom were all but unattainable for the great majority of slaves. Instead of striking out in quest of freedom against all odds, many chose the less rewarding but more practical approach of steal-ing away from the plantation and hiding out in the woods for a time. An escapee from a South Carolina plantation dug a hillside cave and took up residence in the woods, slipping out at night to obtain food. When the slave catchers apprehended him five months later, he had in his posses-sion a hog, two geese, some chickens, and some dressed meat apparently stolen from a smokehouse.[146]

Simon, a slave of Virginia's Colonel Landon Carter, ran away in 1766. After a month he was spotted and shot in the leg and foot. Eleven days later he was apprehended by the foreman. The other slaves, however, tried to make it appear to Carter that Simon had come in on his own. Despite

Simon's having been shot, Carter believed his limp was faked and had him
punished for shamming. Bart, another Carter slave, returned a week later after having been "out" about four months. He had run away after having been accused of bringing in only one load of wood. He contended he
had brought in two. According to Carter, "he is the most incorrigible vil-
lain I believe alive, and has deserved hanging." Bart was tied and locked
up but escaped once again.[147]

Often slave resistance was prompted by clear personal grievances or
directed at individual offenses. Perhaps most slaves ran away for reasons
other than seeking permanent freedom. Cruelty was certainly one reason,
although slaves of kindly masters sought freedom as eagerly as those of
cruel ones. A former slave in the South Carolina upcountry reported seeing a slave turn on a cruel white overseer and beat him. "Once a nigger
whipped the overseer," William Ballard explained, "he had to run away
in the woods and live so he wouldn't get caught."[148]

But slaves did not necessarily have to be prodded by any specific punishment or incident to take flight. Sharper and Stepney, two slaves in the
Abbeville District of South Carolina, slipped away from their plantation
in 1862. Their bemused overseer informed the slaveholder that "I was
uncertain whether they had run away or were only absenting themselves
from work and particularly as they had not reason for leaving no fault
being found with them or punishment inflicted."[149]

Young Harriet Jacobs, who inherited her father's sense of self-worth and
rebellion, was determined to emancipate herself or die trying. To gain her
freedom she enacted desperate and complicated schemes with the aid of
fellow blacks who were willing to risk everything. A free black who helped
Jacobs to escape told her, "I don't forget that your father was my best friend,
and I will be a friend to his children as long as God lets me live."[150]

Slave women were less likely than men to run away, not because they
loved freedom less, but because their mobility—crucial to a successful
escape—was limited by their responsibility for the care of their children.
Fugitive slaves typically were between fifteen and thirty-five years of age.
Most slave women in this age group were either pregnant, nursing an
infant, or had a small child to care for. When slave women did resort to
flight, it was more often in response to immediate personal grievances
than to an effort to emancipate themselves. For instance, Martha Bradley, an Alabama slave, was "workin' in de field and de overseer he come
'round and say sumpin' to me he had no bizness say. I took my hoe and
knocked him plum down. I knowed I'se done sumpin bad so I run to de

bushes." Her escape was short lived, however. "Marster Lucas come and got me and started whoopin me. I say to Marster Lucas whut dat overseer sez to me and Marster Lucas didn' hit me no more."[151]

But slave women were often intimately involved in planning and aiding the escape attempts of others. Even trusted house servants were conspirators in runaway efforts. Mary, a "highly favored servant . . . in charge of the house with the keys" on a South Carolina rice plantation, helped many of her family to escape in 1864. Not only did her sons run off, but also her daughter and her daughter's family and her brother and all of his family. Ultimately her mistress became suspicious. There were, she wrote a friend, "too many instances in her family for me to suppose she is ignorant of their plans and designs."[152]

Aiding and abetting fugitive slaves could be as dangerous as an escape attempt itself. Harriet Miller's grandfather ran away from his master's Mississippi plantation to escape an overseer's brutality. He hid out nearby, and his family secretly supplied him with food and information. But the overseer came to the man's cabin and questioned his family about his whereabouts. When the man's daughter refused to answer, the overseer beat her to death.[153]

When slave catchers attempted to apprehend them, runaways rarely surrendered peacefully. Fugitives, facing severe punishment and perhaps death if returned to slavery, often elected to stand and fight. Occasionally the slaves had the better of the battle. "Lots of times when de patterollers would git after de slaves dey would have de worse fight," an Alabama slave recalled, "an' sometimes de patterollers would git killed."[154] But more often freedom seekers fell to overwhelming odds. A slave catcher in South Carolina sued for damages caused by the slave he had attempted to apprehend.

> A runaway slave named George, the property of a Gentleman of Chester District, stole two horses, broke open several houses and committed other offences in Richland District for which a warrant was issued against him but it was found impossible to arrest him. He was at length taken in Columbia on the 4 July last but broke from custody. A hue and cry was immediately raised and your petitioner joined in the pursuit and first overtook the fellone where a contest ensued between them in which the slave cut out your petitioner's eye with a razor blade—The fellone has since been tried, convicted, and executed.[155]

A slave attempting to escape from North Carolina was attacked by patrollers. "He say he tired standin' so many beatin's, he jus can't stan' no mo."

He tried to fight the patrollers. But there were too many for him, and he was killed.[156]

Some runaways formed armed maroon bands, hiding out in the woods or in the swamps and raiding storehouses for arms and food. One such group was reported in South Carolina during the Civil War.

> On [M]onday I commenced hunting down Cosawhatchie Swamp, during the afternoon the dogs struck a warm trail which we followed about one mile into the swamp through water and bog sometimes swimming and sometimes bog down when the dogs trailed a negro boy; belonging to the Est. of Harry You-mans, who has been out since August last. [T]he said boy stated that there was two others with him that day and four at the camp seven or eight miles below— all armed with guns and pistols. . . . On the 1st of Feby a gentleman from St. Luke's Parish who lives on the Swamp came to this camp and reported that the day before some runaways had broken into a house in his neighborhood and stole all the ammunition and some provisions—I believe it is a part of the same gang.[157]

The most drastic form of slave resistance was insurrection. At least six major insurrectionary plots disturbed the consciousness of the slave South before the slaves were emancipated: the Stono rebellion in South Carolina in 1739, Samba's conspiracy in Louisiana in 1763, the Gabriel Prosser uprising in Virginia in 1800, the great Louisiana slave revolt of 1811, the Denmark Vesey plot in South Carolina in 1822, and the Nat Turner insurrection in Virginia in 1831. There were also numerous smaller uprisings. Since most of them were aborted, their full dimensions remain unknown. Among them was one in French Louisiana in July 1776, the same month that the Declaration of Independence was adopted. In 1802, there was one involving sixteen slaves in Bertie County, North Carolina, and another of undetermined strength in Georgetown County, South Carolina. There was a second in Georgetown County in 1810, sufficient to cause a hasty mobilization of the militia. At least three slaves were executed for their part in a third slave uprising in Georgetown County in 1829. And there is evidence of a slave conspiracy in Adams County, Mississippi, in 1861.[158]

The most important of the rebellions was the one led by Nat Turner. According to the escaped slave Henry Clay Bruce, it caused "no little sensation amongst the slaveholders."[159] Stories of "Ole Nat" lived in oral tradition among Virginia slaves. Allen Crawford, a Virginia ex-slave, described the rebellion vividly. "It started out on a Sunday night. Fust place he got to was his mistress' house. Said God 'dained him to start the fust war with forty men. When he got to his mistress' house he commence to grab him missus baby and he took hit up, slung hit back and fo'h three times. Said hit was so hard for him to kill dis baby 'cause hit had bin so playful setting on his knee and dat chile sho did love him. So third sling he went quick 'bout hit—killing baby at dis rap." The insurrectionists then went to another house, according to Crawford, and "went through orchard, going to the house—met a school mistress—killed her."[160] Another Virginia slave remembered well the fear of the white folks. According to Fannie Berry, "I can remember my mistress, Miss Sara Ann, coming to de window an' hollering, 'De niggers is arisin', De niggers is arisin', De niggers is killin' all de white folks—killin' all de babies in de cradle!'"[161] Harriet Jacobs wrote in her memoirs, *Incidents in the Life of a Slave Girl*, that she thought it strange that the whites should be so frightened "when their slaves were so 'contented and happy'!"[162]

The following day the militia was mustered to search the quarters of all slaves and free blacks. Harriet Jacobs said the militia planted false evidence to implicate some slaves in the rebellion: "The searchers scattered powder and shot among their clothes, and then sent other parties to find them, and bring them forward as proof that they were plotting insurrection."[163] Allen Crawford recalled that "Blues and Reds—name of soldiers—met at a place called Cross Keys, right down here at Newsome's Depot. Dat's whar they had log fires made and every one dat was Nat's man was taken bodily by two men who catch you and hold yer bare feet to dis blazing fire 'til you tole all you know'd 'bout dis killing."[164] In the wake of the Turner insurrection, Henry Box Brown wrote in his memoirs, many slaves were "half-hung, as it was termed—that is, they were suspended from some tree with a rope about their necks, so adjusted as not quite to strangle them—and then they were pelted by men and boys with rotten eggs." The air was filled with shrieks and shouts. Harriet Jacobs said she "saw a mob dragging along a number of colored people, each white man, with his musket upraised, threatening instant death if they did not stop their shrieks." Jacobs could not contain her indignation. "What a spectacle was that for a civilized country!" she exclaimed. "A rabble, staggering under intoxication, assuming to be the administrators of justice!"[165]

According to Crawford, "Ole Nat was captured at Black Head Sign Post, near Cortland, Virginia—Indian town. He got away. So after a little Nat found dem on his trail so he went back near to the Travis place whar he fust started killing and he built a cave and made shoes in this cave. He came out night fur food dat slaves would give him from his own missus plantation." After about a month Nat Turner's hiding place was discovered and he was taken into custody. Turner's captors, Crawford said, "brought him to Peter Edwards's farm. 'Twas at this farm whar I was born. Grandma ran out and struck Nat in the mouth, knocking the blood out and asked him, 'Why did you take my son away?' In reply Nat said, 'Your son was as willing to go as I was.' It was my Uncle Henry dat they was talking about." Then, Crawford said, Virginia "passed a law to give the rest of the niggers a fair trial and Nat, my Uncle Henry, and others dat was caught was hanged."[166]

Nat Turner's revolt was followed by the appearance of a new and militant abolitionist newspaper, William Lloyd Garrison's *The Liberator.* Slaves took heart. White southerners concentrated their energies on trying to defend slavery against the criticism of a critical and unfriendly world. The institution that many white southerners had once considered an evil destined for eventual elimination was now praised as a positive good, the secret of the region's fancied perfection. They staked everything—their fortunes, their honor, the lives of their sons—on its defense. Unlike slaveholders anywhere else, they went to war to preserve their "Peculiar Institution."

§

When the Civil War finally broke out, most slaves had been expecting it for some time. They heard their masters boast of quick victory, and watched the women wave their men off to war. Confederate officers, as gentleman, of course required body servants. Like many other slaves, James Cornelius followed his master into war. By the 1930s he was living on a pension from the state of Mississippi. "I'se proud I'se a old sojer," he said.[167]

During the war, white plantation families keenly felt the absence or loss of family members. Sometimes they expressed their frustration by taking out their anger on their bondsmen. Harriet Robinson's mistress blamed the war on the slaves. "She say 'your master's out fighting and losing blood trying to save you from them Yankees.' Then Miss Julia would take me by my ears and butt my head against the wall." Hearing slaves mention the prospects of freedom often enraged plantation whites. When Sam McAllum's Mississippi mistress "heard de Nigger talkin' 'bout bein' free, she wore em out wid a cowhide."[168] An Alabama slave was caught praying for freedom. After a severe beating he slipped away and joined the Union Army.

The slaves watched as masters and sons returned home from the front, some in boxes, some with crutches or empty sleeves, some to die of wounds and illness. "De Massa had three boys to go to war," a Georgia slave remembered, "but dere wuzn't one to come home. All the chillun he had wuz killed. Massa, he los' all his money and de house soon begin droppin' away to nothin'. Us niggers one by one lef' de ole place and de las' time I seed de home plantation I wuz a standin' on a hill. I looked back on it for de las' time through a patch of scrub pines and it look' so lonely."[169]

The slaves learned from the whites of the advance of Union forces and felt the approach of freedom. A North Carolina slave recalled vividly the coming of the Union troops: "I remember the Yankees. I will remember seein' them til I die. I will never forgit it. I thought it was the last of me. The white folks had told me the Yankees would kill me or carry me off."[170]

But most slaves were thrilled at the coming of the Yankees, even if their owners were not. When Anna Williamson was impressed by the brass buttons on the Yankee uniforms, "my old mistress slapped me till my eye was red cause one day I says 'Ain't dem men pretty?'"[171] Midge Burnett recalled that her North Carolina master had not shared the slaves' enthusiasm about the arrival of the northerners. "Marse William ain't eber hit one of us a single lick till de day when we heard dat de Yankees wus a'comin. One big nigger jumps up an' squalls, 'Lawd bless de Yankees!' Marse yells back, 'God damn de Yankees!' an' he slaps big Mose a summerset right outen de do'." After that, "nobody else doesn't say Yankees ter de marster."[172]

When Sherman's troops marched through South Carolina and many masters fled their plantations for safer ground, slaves sang

> Master gone away
> But darkies stay at home
> The year of jubilee is come
> And freedom will begun.[173]

A Mississippi slave recalled that the Yankees "come ridin' up on fine horses. Dey was all dressed in blue coats an all had guns. I thought dey was comin' to sot us free." They had not come to free the slaves, however. They had come to commandeer food supplies and to burn cotton.[174] "De Yankees come in and dey pulled de fruit off de trees and et it," according to a Georgia slave, William Colbert. "Dey et de hams and cawn, but dey neber burned de houses. Seem to me lak dey jes' stay aroun' long enough to git plenty somp'n t'eat, kaze dey lef' in two or three days, an' we neber seed 'em since."[175] Another Mississippi slave said, "I 'member de time of de Civil Wah', an' de Yankee sojers comes marchin' to town and smashed in sto' doahs' an' windows an' all us lil' chillun' sho' did have a fine time 'cause we got pies an' candy an sech lak—much as we could eat. We wished de Yankees would come every day!"[176]

Some slaves struck out for the Union lines in pursuit of freedom. Zias, a slave on the McDowell plantation in Mississippi, took off with a pony. Zias came back in a blue uniform with the promise of forty acres and a mule. But he came back on foot. The Yankees had taken the pony.[177]

As defeated masters dragged themselves back to their plantations, the slaves could sense that the war was over. Nelson Dickerson's master called his former slaves together and announced that they were free. He offered wages if they would stay.[178] Many ex-slaves remained on the plantations when the war was over, feeling that they had no other place to go. But some slaveholders never bothered to tell their slaves they were free. Amanda Oliver recalled, "Old Mistress didn't tell us when we was free, but another white woman told my mother and I remembuh one day Old Mistress told my mother to git to that wheel and git to work, and my mother said, 'I ain't gwinter, I'm jest as free as you air.'"[179] Pharaoh Carter did not tell his slaves, but they learned from freedmen on other plantations. Carter had a slave woman arrested on trumped-up charges of having stolen a bale of cotton. Her husband came to the jail with a group of white men and freed her. Such a bold move by any black man would have been unthinkable a year earlier.[180]

Freedom did not always live up to expectations. Gabe Butler, the Mississippi slave, recalled, "Sum of de slaves sed when dey wud be sot free dey wud git forty acres uf land frum Mr. Lincoln an' sum sed dey wud git plenty uf good things to eat an' sum sed dey wudn't have to wurk any more, kaze Mr. Lincoln wud give dem everything."[181] It did not work out that way. For many former slaves life scarcely changed. Katie Darling said, "Missy whip me after the War just like she did before. She has a hundred lashes up for me now."[182] One resentful mistress rued the day that slaves had been taught religion. According to a former slave, the mistress claimed that it was the prayers of the slaves that "cause you young folks to be free today."[183] Whatever his mistress thought, he was pleased to have done what he could. However circumscribed freedom might be, however limited the opportunities available to former slaves, his children would be born free. Never again in the United States would human beings be bought and sold at auction into slavery.

4

History as Ritual

Rites of Power and Resistance on the Slave Plantation

What was the source of the power relations between masters and slaves? So much has been written on the sectional politics of the slavery question that the sheer volume of the literature tends to conceal a lack of explanation of the *internal* politics of slavery. Viewed in retrospect, how did so few masters, with limited powers of coercion, exert such compulsion over so many slaves? The question, to be sure, is not an easy one. To discuss the problem adequately would be to analyze all the social relations on the slave plantation. But it is enough to record here that the real source of the master's power rested less on his use of brute force than on his ability to get the slaves to recognize his authority. And the remarkable extent to which the master was able to do that was in large part due to his ability to exploit symbolic behavior as an instrument of power. As Orlando Patterson notes in *Slavery and Social Death*, "Herein lies the source of authority. Those who exercise power, if they are able to transform it into a 'right,' a norm, a usual part of the order of things, must first control (or at least be in a position to manipulate) appropriate symbolic instruments."[1] Such symbolic behavior was exemplified on the plantation in ceremonial, highly formalized rituals of interaction. In these rituals, ideas were acted out in actual social interaction.[2]

Granting that symbolic behavior comprised only one dimension of the complex power relations that made up the slave plantation, and conceding that the threat of violence was always present, the fundamental fact remains that one cannot hope to unravel the tangled strands of plantation power relations without taking account of rituals of interaction. Acknowledging problems of precise definition, Jack Goody points to ritual as "a category of standardized behavior (custom) in which the relationship between the means and the end is not 'intrinsic.'"[3] In the conventionalized and obligatory patterns of ritual, human beings express the most fundamental values of their communities. Any activity may be stylized into dramatic performance and thus made the focus of ritual.[4] When the experience being symbolized is a persisting one, well-defined symbolic patterns often develop.[5] With no disposition to insist that anthropological means offer any infallible path to historical ends, one might at least observe that the study of ritual would seem to be of special value in the effort to discover the internal politics of the slave plantation.

The relationship between symbolic behavior and plantation power relations can best be tested in the crucible of a particular slave community, where the unity of the society and the integration of the culture were realities, rather than the mental constructs of scholars. An examination of rituals of interaction on the rice plantations of All Saints Parish, Georgetown District, South Carolina, should reveal the ritual process and its influence on the question of power relations. The rice plantations of All Saints Parish, however, were certainly not of average size, wealth, or importance. Lying between the Waccamaw River and the Atlantic Ocean, All Saints Parish was once the site of the richest rice plantations in the South Carolina lowcountry. Here the slaves lived—and shaped the patterns of their folk culture—within a distinctive economic, ecological, and demographic environment. They lived on larger plantations than slaves elsewhere. The smallest plantation in All Saints Parish in 1860 had 90 slaves, the largest 1,121. The mean number of slaves was 292. They lived in an environment virtually devoid of free blacks and mulattoes, with a higher median age, a lower ratio of males to females, and a smaller proportion of youth and aged than was true of the South as a whole. Perhaps most important, because more Africans came to South Carolina than anywhere else on the North American mainland, and because the nine blacks to each white in All Saints Parish throughout the nineteenth century was the highest ratio of blacks to whites in South Carolina, slave culture in All Saints Parish may be regarded as a seedbed of black culture in the United States.[6]

Many of the interactions between master and slaves on the plantation, such as the weekly distribution of provisions and the semiannual distribution of clothing and blankets, were treated as paternalistic rituals. Such ritual behavior may have several meanings at once. By dramatizing a sense of mutual obligations between master and slaves, the ritual was designed to help promote a sense of community on the plantation. But beyond that, in transforming a necessary task of labor organization into a ritual of personal largesse, the All Saints rice planter simultaneously underscored his own dominant status in contrast with the slaves' position of dependence. Thus the ceremonial giving in itself served to emphasize the master's reputed benevolence and to promote the slaves' gratitude, while at the same time it was designed to enhance the master's aura of status and power.[7]

Another occasion for ritual in the interaction of slaves and master in All Saints Parish was the investiture of drivers. This is a natural process of ritual: people not only move from one status to another, but they mark such moves with appropriate rituals. Drivers were invested with their powers by the masters in public ceremonies. In some cases their authority was confirmed by the clergy. The appointment of a slave named Daniel to be driver for Benjamin Allston was confirmed by a bishop, for example. Ceremony played an important role in the confirmation of status. By seeming to place the authority of the master behind the elevation of the driver to office and status, ritual simultaneously underscored the legitimacy of the office and the accountability of its exercise. In such prescribed formal rituals, the very act of delegating authority symbolically enhanced both the dominance of the driver over other slaves and the sovereignty of the master over the driver. While such ritual sanctions did not ensure that drivers would never misuse their power, the rituals did promote an almost mystical aura of high seriousness in the delegation of command.[8]

Rituals accompanying such "life crises" as birth, marriage, and death are often called "rites of passage." The general power of such rituals as weddings and funerals is to cushion the transition from one status to another, which cannot be effected without social and individual disturbance. Slave weddings and funerals in All Saints Parish represented focused gatherings in which both master and slaves on the rice plantations were engrossed in a common flow of activity and related to one another in terms of that flow. One of the most important rituals in the life cycle was marriage. Christmas was the most popular time for slave weddings in All Saints Parish, but whether celebrated at Christmas or at some other time, the weddings of slaves were occasions of great festivity. At Hagley plantation, for instance, weddings were said to be "kept with good cheer; wedding cards were sent out to all their friends; the master gives them cake, turkeys, hams, molasses, coffee &c., and they are always allowed three days' holiday." Louisa Brown, who had been a slave at Turkey Hill plantation, recalled the wedding feasts many years later: "Hot supper, cake, wine, and

all. Kill cow, hog, chicken, and all. That time when you marry, so much to
eat." The novelist Julia Peterkin, who spent part of her early life on an All
Saints rice plantation, recalled that the white owners joined the celebrants
in wishing health and happiness to the bride and groom. Ceremonies were
performed in the yard of the Big House, and the wedding cakes were often baked in the master's kitchen. Such rituals of largesse were designed
to enhance the master's aura of status and power.[9]

Slave funerals, marked by considerable pageantry and display, were as
elaborate a part of the slave life-cycle in All Saints Parish as weddings. The
slaves emphasized the necessity of an appropriate funeral to prevent the
spirits of the dead from returning, possibly in malevolent form. This represented a direct line of continuity with West African funeral tradition.
The processions to and from the burial ground as well as the graveside
services were marked by music—mournful songs on the way to the bury-
ing ground, happier music on the return. Generally the slaves preferred
their own preachers at funerals, but the presence of white ministers and
mourners was not uncommon. Even rites of passage from this world to
the next provided opportunities for symbolic enhancement of the master's authority.[10]

As Christians, the rice planters were committed to the religious instruction of their slaves, but the religion to be taught to the slaves also called
the masters to account. That the masters were as subject as the slaves to
the requirements of Christianity created for the masters a serious problem of role boundaries on the rice plantations, because boundary transgressions gave rise to unavoidable tensions and contradictions within the
social system. While the masters employed themselves in teaching highly selected precepts of Christianity to the slaves, the slaves applied their
creolized version of Christianity to every aspect of plantation life and
made European religious forms serve African functions.[11]

The question of role boundaries was also involved in the reluctance of
the master class to permit their slaves to imbibe intoxicating liquors. The
rice planters were keenly sensitive to the potential of alcohol to disrupt
what they regarded as normal role boundaries in a slave society. Even the
slightest transgressions were enough to send forth ripples of alarm. The
disruptive potential of alcohol was memorably epitomized in the apho-
rism of Hagar Brown, an All Saints slave who later recalled, "Likker'll
make you not know you mama." While some masters may, as Frederick
Douglass suspected in Maryland, have used alcohol as a means of slave
control, most of the All Saints planters strictly limited slave imbibing to

such ritual celebrations as Christmas and weddings. Some of them forbade their overseers to allow any slave to imbibe without a physician's
orders. Not all slaves, however, confined their drinking to occasions sanctioned by the master. Define Horry, one of the slaves at Brookgreen plantation, stole rice from the fields, threshed it in the woods, and sold it for
money to buy liquor.[12]

The social relations between masters and slaves were dynamic rather
than static, and constantly shifted in equilibrium. Thus rituals of punishment on the rice plantations were as much a part of the paternalistic system as the rewards for faithful service, the Christmas largesse, or the slave
wedding feasts. The masters regarded the resort to overt use of force as a
confession of weakness rather than as evidence of strength, yet every slaveholder and every overseer had to contend with troublesome slaves at some
point. Surrounded by such difficulties and seeing that attempts to impose
discipline on sullen and rebellious bondsmen made a grim and ugly contrast to the public face of paternalism, the master—when he supervised
or administered punishments, no less than when he dispensed gifts and
favors—did so in rituals that contrasted the dependent position of the
slaves with his own status of dominance. The ritual of slave punishment
was a dramatization of fundamental status concerns. And what ritualized
punishment says of those status concerns is that they are matters of life
and death. Thus formalized public punishment—the "deep play" of ritual—dramatized in a particularly acute way the enforcement of rules of
deference and social behavior, free of etiquette, euphemism, and illusion.[13]

But symbolic behavior on the slave plantation did not merely enhance
the authority of the master; it also promoted the cohesiveness of the slave
community and served to explain, in the language of symbols, the nature
of the slavery experience. In mythic terms, such slave rituals as storytelling functioned to give symbolic form to the validating concepts and beliefs of the slave worldview. If the master was able to manipulate certain
rituals of interaction between blacks and whites to enhance his own authority, the slaves were able to manipulate rituals of interaction among
themselves in such a way as to undermine the master's authority and to
enhance their own self-image.

The slaves in any slave system, according to W. L. Westermann, had
"definite rights—not legal but actual, and sanctioned by custom," which
the slaves "both accept and insist upon." The time provided by such customs away from work was not "leisure time" in the usual sense, but part
of the moral economy of the plantation, time (as one of the masters de-

scribed it) when "the people may work for themselves." The slaves' expressive behavior within the special temporal contexts set aside as "off
time" embodied a great deal of symbolic enactment. This time, so highly
charged with symbolic behavior, provided them a means of focusing, of
remembering, and of understanding their experience.[14]

To attempt to delineate the nature of power relations on the slave plantation without taking into consideration the evidence of the slaves' folk
tales is to ignore the medium through which they spoke from their very
souls. Such questions as to what extent the slaves "accepted" the authority of the masters as legitimate will remain egregious speculation until
careful analysis is made of the storytelling engaged in by slaves when the
master was not around. Whether or not such narratives actually took place
as told (even those told as personal experiences) is less significant than
the fact that narrating such experiences had cultural meaning for the slaves
who told and for the slaves who listened. The animal and human trickster tales of All Saints slaves exemplified language used as symbolic action. By manipulating the words that defined their world the slaves could
verbally rearrange that world and could turn it symbolically inside out.[15]

Among the principal determinants of such symbolic action as storytelling were social relationships. Storytelling as ritual, storytelling as everyday symbolic enactment, provided a frame for experience. There was a
special kind of expectancy at the ritual time or place. The customary "once
upon a time" created a special mood receptive to soaring imagination.
Such frames could limit experience by shutting in desired themes and
shutting out undesired ones. Thus framed, even the least action was capable of carrying special significance. Storytelling sessions thus functioned as both inspiration and education. They were transformed from
pure rhetoric into quasireligious ritual. Verbal action evoked a behavioral response, both of which were part of a continuum of social action. The
ex-slave Sabe Rutledge, recalling his childhood on an All Saints rice plantation, said his mother and father told "all those Buh Rabbit story" to keep
him and his brothers and sisters awake as the whole family worked in their
cabin until late at night.[16]

The most obvious feature of the animal trickster tales told by the slaves
of All Saints Parish was their emphasis on small but sly creatures, weak
but wily animals who continually got the better of their larger and more
powerful adversaries through superior cunning. Despite physical puni-

ness, the tiny trickster had a personality marked by audacity, egotism, and rebellion. Through the symbolic identification of nature with society, the animal trickster tales define the trickster and his actions as both necessary and good. Such symbolic identification serves as a means of transforming the unavoidable into the desirable, and of giving a certain freedom of individual action despite group restrictions.[17]

These tales of thoroughly humanized animals, as narrated by the slaves of All Saints Parish, exemplify the process of symboling. The animals think and behave as human beings, they experience human emotions, and they live in a realistic world clearly like that of their narrators. But they also remain recognizably animals. The big animals are usually strong and powerful but not very bright: they are constantly being duped by the less powerful trickster figures. This combination of realism and fantasy made it possible for storytellers and their audiences on the rice plantations of All Saints Parish (as for their ancestors in Africa) to identify with the animal characters without the identification becoming rigid or allegorical. That the animal trickster tales provided slaves with a satirical depiction of the society in which they lived has been somewhat obscured by overemphasis on similarities between the trickster and the slave. A people's perception of their social and economic system grows out of their identification of the people with nature and their perception of nature in terms of social categories. Thus the struggle between Buh Rabbit (the slave) and Buh Bear (the master) could be perceived as founded in nature and thus inevitable.[18]

In one All Saints trickster tale Buh Rabbit is competing with Buh Wolf for the favors of a "pretty girl." Rabbit decides to demonstrate to her that Wolf is nothing more than his saddle horse: "Start to party. Budder Rabbit ax Budder Wolfe to be he riding horse. Budder Rabbit so tricky. Got near where the dancing house Budder Rabbit spur 'em. All the pretty girl is see Budder Rabbit fine riding horse. All laughed at Budder Wolfe."[19]

Here the trickster does more than simply defeat his rival. He thoroughly humiliates him, takes his woman, and reduces him to servility. This symbolic inversion of roles performs a function identical to the symbolic inversions in ritual, providing psychic relief from the emotional constraints of slavery, symbolic attacks on oppressive masters and overseers, and—most important of all—a continuing reminder that existing power relationships are not necessarily *natural* power relationships. Here one can see the important role played by such folktales in shaping the worldview of the slaves.

A notable theme of the trickster tales is the punishment of those who refuse to live up to the obligations of friendship or to come to the aid of their fellow creatures in time of need. The All Saints versions of the classic Tar Baby folktales exemplify the rhetorical device that shows things getting worse as the result of the neglect of sacred duties. The other animals seek revenge on Buh Rabbit for his not sharing water from his secret well during a drought. He tells them he gets up early in the morning to drink the dew. One night Billy Goat watches Buh Rabbit and discovers the secret well. Billy Goat hastens back to tell the other animals. They decide to teach Buh Rabbit a lesson, and set a trap—the tar baby—for him near his well.

> When Buh Rabbit comes for a drink, he says "Hey, oh deah, Putty Gal!" but the tar baby does not answer. Buh Rabbit becomes angry. "You bettah talk wid me! Oh, ef I slaps you one time wid my right han', I broke you jaw!" The tar baby does not answer and Buh Rabbit hits her. His hand sticks. "Ef I slaps you wid my lef' han' one time, I slaps you face one-sided!" The same result. "Ef I kicks you wid dis foot, I buss you belly open!" The same result again. "Oh, I wouldn' wantuh kick you wid muh lef' foot—Oh, Gal, ah ain' know whut 'e done fo you!" Both hands and feet are soon stuck. "Well, I knows one ting! Uh got uh belly! I ain' wantah butt you wid muh belly tall-tall. Uh got uh belly hyuh. I butt you wid my belly, buss you open!"

Eventually even his head and teeth are stuck to the tar baby. Then the goat and other animals come and chastise him for lying about the dew, and then release him. Buh Rabbit's selfishness is the reason *why* the other animals revenge themselves upon him, but his vanity, boastfulness, and stupidity are the keys to *how* they are able to accomplish that revenge, a valuable lesson to slaves.[20]

Unlike Buh Rabbit, the slave trickster John was neither allegorical nor remote. He expressed the values and attitudes of his fellow slaves directly. In his inevitable victories over the more powerful master (and thus over the slave system), John provided his fellow slaves with perspective by incongruity. Buh Rabbit tales might be narrated to the master's family as well as to one's fellow slaves, but John tales were for telling only within the slave community. He expressed in symbolic action their plight and their hope, and thus their very identity.[21]

To comprehend fully the significance of slave storytelling, one must look beyond the surface themes of the trickster tales. The enhancement of self-image, of identity, and the promotion of autonomy, were important functions of the trickster tales in All Saints Parish (however difficult those functions may be to examine). Like Buh Rabbit, slaves had to make do with their natural resources and learn to maneuver with what they had. The trickster tales may thus be seen as exemplifying in symbolic behavior a definition of the situation that encompassed within itself a strategy for dealing with that situation. The importance of self-reliance—as indicated in the trickster tales—was underscored in the proverb of one of the All Saints slaves, Hagar Brown, who noted, "Every tub stand on its own bottom." Survival in the slave system depended upon the slaves' ability always to remember who and where they were, and upon their ability to "put yuh bess foot fo moss" (that is, put your best foot forward) in any crisis.[22]

Thus the trickster tales served as inspiration for and justification of some forms of antisocial behavior and simultaneously served as a release valve for even more aggressive and antisocial repressed desires. In so doing they both promoted day-to-day resistance to slavery and at the same time lessened the likelihood that a large-scale slave rebellion might attempt to overthrow the whole slave system. The historian Eric Hobsbawm, in his study of "primitive rebels," noted a similar phenomenon in the peasant celebration of such bandit-heroes as Robin Hood in song and story. Not the least important part of the slaves' deft blend of accommodation and resistance, the trickster tales were in fact a crucial element in the development of an adaptive African-American culture. That culture was the most significant form of resistance against the spiritual and psychological, if not the physical, effects of slavery.[23]

The fact that the slaves developed a cohesive new culture out of their various African heritages and the necessities of the New World environment promoted a sense of group solidarity even in the face of the most dehumanizing attacks of the slave system. Conceding that slavery must be recognized as a total institution, one need not conclude that such total institutions necessarily lead to the total dehumanization of their denizens. The creolized culture created by the slaves served as a buttress to courage, confidence, and self-esteem, and as a buffer to infantilism and dependency. Not only was the masters' stereotype of the slaves as ignorant, carefree, and childlike rejected by the slaves as a self-concept, but, in being perceived by the slaves as denigration, the stereotype actually promoted their sense of solidarity. A common (although unintended) result of denigration is to promote a sense of homogeneity and cohesion even in a heterogeneous situation. Such examples of traditional expressive behavior as storytelling were among the most striking means by which the slaves proclaimed and reinforced their sense of autonomy.[24]

The range of symbolic behavior examined here suggests but one dimension of the power relations on the slave plantation. Many more questions must be posed and resolved before full understanding of the power relations of the "Peculiar Institution" can be achieved. The understanding must be complex, and some of its manifestations may sit uneasily with present-day preconceptions of varying persuasions and of varying motivations. But if a subject as inherently controversial as slavery can be explored with enough detachment and patience, scholars may find a promising approach to the problem in the analysis of symbolic behavior.

5

"Guilty of Holiest Crime"
The Passion of John Brown

> But let me not die without a huge effort,
> nor let me dishonorably die, but in the
> brave doing of some great deed let me go,
> that men yet to be may hear of what happened.
>   — Homer, *The Iliad*

> Loved I shall be with him whom I have loved,
> Guilty of holiest crime.
>   — Sophocles, *Antigone*

> Thus, in succession, flame awakening flame
> Fulfilled the order of the fiery course.
>   — Aeschylus, *Agamemnon*

It was an hour before noon that Friday morning when they took John Brown from jail. The prisoner neither protested nor acquiesced. His arms were tied down above the elbows, leaving his forearms free. At the door of the jail an open wagon awaited him. Lying on its bed was a large poplar box, within which was a black walnut coffin. Almost deliberate in his movements, without haste or fumbling, he climbed onto the wagon and sat down upon the box. The sheriff and the jailer sat down beside him, and the wagon moved off toward a field southeast of town. A column of soldiers escorted them, and two more columns of riflemen stood shoulder-to-shoulder along their route. The prisoner observed the military display without comment.[1]

It was bleak and chill that morning as the wagon made its way toward the field. At eleven o'clock it was about as warm as it was going to get. Tension hovered in the quiet, crisp December air. Even the houses appeared huddled close together, watchful and apprehensive. Brown broke the silence. "This is beautiful country," he said pleasantly to his companions on the wagon. "I never had the pleasure of seeing it before." In the distance they could see the company of troops already in possession of the field and, looming over everything, the gallows. They were almost there.[2]

"Old Brown," as he seemed to be universally known, was fifty-nine years old. He wore the same shabby black suit he had worn at Harpers Ferry and at his trial, the black contrasting vividly with his white shirt and socks and his incongruous red slippers. His frame was tall but gaunt now almost to emaciation, and his grizzled beard was shorter than he had worn it in Kansas. The deep saber cut on the back of his neck, received at Harpers Ferry forty-six days before, was now a scar. His unflinching gray eyes, described by a supporter as possessing "great mesmeric power," were serious but wore no expression of melancholy that morning. Whatever his inner feelings, he showed no fear. His demeanor was characterized by an unexpected serenity.[3]

Now they were there. A group of soldiers surrounded the wagon and the scaffold. They allowed no one to come between them and the prisoner. Pickets were posted at various points, and the crowd was held back at bayonet point. "Why are none but military allowed in the enclosure?" Brown asked in that incongruously soft, pleasant voice. "I am sorry the citizens have been kept out." But if John Brown looked around him for sympathy and support it was in vain. As his pale gray eyes wandered over the stern, haggard faces of the crowd and the soldiers, he could not help but know that his hour had come. The elaborate security precautions were not necessary. The crowd was quite orderly. They had not come to rescue John Brown; they had come to see him die. Could the tranquil figure who stood immobile before them now, gaunt and impotent, be the demon they had been conditioned to hate and fear?[4]

The earth immediately about the scaffold was bare. The prisoner turned, not hurriedly or even quickly, but just easily, and ascended the steps to the gallows. And still with no haste, but no pause either, he shook hands with Sheriff James Campbell and jailer John Avis. "Gentlemen, goodbye," he told them. His quiet voice did not falter in the least. He stood where they told him to stand and held his head to one side so the sheriff could place the noose about his neck. Then Brown turned slowly, standing erect above the held breaths, and looked down upon the crowd with an invincible fatalism. One can only imagine with what sensations the crowd gazed upon this ritual, with its studied ceremony and show of courtesy. Colonel Thomas J. Jackson was there, commanding a detachment of his cadets from the Virginia Military Institute. So was the aging fire-eater Edmund Ruffin, who had borrowed a cadet's uniform so that he could stand nearer the scaffold for a better view of the hanging. The soldiers and the crowd looked up at the prisoner standing there—frail, shabby, insignificant, yet somehow exalted, too, still wearing that expression of serenity, a martyr to the terrible simplicity of his idea, calling blood to the regeneration of human freedom. Before he left his cell that morning, Brown had written a note to his wife in his thin, cramped script, enclosed in which was a statement for public release: "I John Brown am now quite *certain* that the crimes of this guilty, *land: will* never be purged *away*, but with Blood. I had *as I now think: vainly* flattered myself that without *very much* bloodshed; it might be done."⁵

The sheriff asked the prisoner if he would like a handkerchief to drop as a signal. The prisoner replied quietly, "No, I don't care. I don't want you to keep me waiting unnecessarily." No preacher stood beneath the scaffold to pray for the convicted man's soul: Brown had declined the services of any minister who approved of, or even consented to, the enslavement of human beings. Now they put a white hood over his head. Jailer Avis asked him to step forward onto the trapdoor. "You must lead me," Brown responded dispassionately, "for I cannot see." He stood there for nearly ten minutes, erect, unflinching, unable to see the military units march and countermarch into position. Nor could he see the crowd, some standing motionless with bowed heads, others staring alternately at one another and at the distant figure upon the gallows. But Brown was not blind to the fact that his whole life up to this moment was meaningless compared to the incontestable goodness he believed he could bequeath to it now. He stood there upon the trapdoor, which was supported on the north side by hinges and on the south side by a rope.

When the troops had finally wheeled about into formation, their colonel announced to the sheriff, "All ready." The sheriff appeared not to understand the order, and the colonel had to repeat it. Then the sheriff struck the rope a sharp blow with a hatchet, springing the trap. John Brown fell through the trapdoor until his knees were even with the platform. His arms, below the elbows, flew up horizontally, with fists clinched, and gradually, with recurring spasms, fell. Then all was quiet. And in the hush that suddenly enveloped the whole somber assemblage, his body swung to and fro. The crowd stared. They would remember it, watching John Brown's body sway to and fro like that. Thomas J. Jackson, shortly to be likened to a stone wall, sent up a prayer that Brown's soul might be saved. "Awful was the thought," Jackson would write to his wife that night, "that he might in a few minutes receive the sentence, 'Depart, ye wicked, into ev-

erlasting fire.' I hope that he was prepared to die, but I am doubtful."
Brown's pulse did not stop beating for thirty-five minutes. Then they cut
him down and sent him back to his wife in the black walnut coffin.[6]

So they took him home to the hard and sterile acres of his farm at North
Elba, New York, and buried him in the shadow of a great rock, among the
rugged hills of the Adirondacks, by the quiet waters of Lake Placid. As the
frigid day passed, the abolitionist Wendell Phillips addressed the mourners at the graveside. "How our admiration, loving wonder has grown, day
by day," Phillips marveled, "as he has unfolded trait after trait of earnest,
brave, tender, Christian life!" Phillips's pious and practiced voice rang out
over the fields to the hills beyond. "We see him walking with radiant, serene face to the scaffold, and think what an iron heart, what devoted
faith!" Then the chief mourner moved beyond eulogy to apotheosis:
"Thank God for such a master. Could we have asked a nobler representative of the Christian North putting her foot on the accursed system of slavery?" His rich voice ringing, Phillips challenged those assembled, "How
can we stand here without a fresh and utter consecration?"[7]

Freed at last of time and flesh, absolved of mortality, John Brown was
a far more palpable presence in death than he had been in life. Had it not
been for the symbolic significance of his passion, John Brown might have
been little noted nor long remembered. Measured by his grandiose ambitions, his whole life was a pitiful failure. His various bankruptcies had
prompted charges of flagrant dishonesty on his part. He was accused of
stealing horses and of murdering five unarmed proslavery settlers at Pot-
tawatomie, Kansas. From 1856 on he depended for his livelihood on the
donations of sympathizers, but he proved to be an incompetent revolutionary. His raid on the federal arsenal at Harpers Ferry, quickly put down
by federal troops, was ill conceived, ill planned, and ill executed. The slave
rebellion he anticipated never took place.[8]

But John Brown's significance lies less in the inadequacies of his life than
in the manner of his death. "Let no man pray that Brown be spared," proclaimed the Reverend Henry Ward Beecher before the execution. "Let Virginia make him a martyr. Now, he has only blundered. His soul was noble; his work miserable. But a cord and a gibbet would redeem all that,"
Beecher declared, "and round up Brown's failure with a heroic success."[9]
John Brown's execution was a beginning rather than an end. When his body
was laid to molder in the grave, his soul was released into the public do-
main. Speechmakers, pamphleteers, and editorialists in the North and the
South lost no time in constructing a mythic John Brown. His historical

significance rests upon his passion, and upon the reactions of men and women on both sides of the Mason-Dixon line to what they read into it.

History and folklore converge in John Brown's passion. His wild career of violence in Kansas and at Harpers Ferry had a legendary dimension, larger than life. And his calm acceptance of death had a mythic, fatalistic quality. But how did John Brown come to his unexpected serenity on the gallows? What was the root of his commitment to the Christian ideal of martyrdom—of emphasizing the ultimate worth of his cause by consciously laying down his life for it? What accounts for the depth of the responses to his execution? These central problems demand deeper analysis than they have yet received. One promising approach to such an analysis is offered by the conceptual tools of cultural anthropology: the passion of John Brown can be analyzed as a "social drama" in much the same fashion that anthropologists have analyzed events in preliterate societies. The situational approach developed by Victor Turner to analyze disputes among central African villagers would seem particularly useful in this regard. The rhetoric and symbolic gestures of the major actors in the John Brown affair were not, in fact, unlike those of preliterate tribesmen.[10]

There is, of course, a major difference between the passion of John Brown and a relatively localized crisis in a small-scale, and possibly preliterate, society. All the tensions of an emerging capitalist nation undergoing rapid social transformation were immanent within the John Brown crisis. At the same time, the form and content of its discourse derived from major, long-standing traditions of Western thought. Such a crisis stood at the nexus of slavery and freedom in its own time but could stand as well at the nexus of structure and conjuncture, of event and process, in ours. John Brown's actions constitute a crucial dramatic link in the chain stretching from the compromises of the Constitutional Convention through the Missouri Compromise and the Compromise of 1850 to the uncompromisable secession crisis, the Civil War, and ultimately emancipation.

The concept of social drama, as elaborated by Turner, is very useful for analyzing events manifesting social conflict. Turner's four-stage model may be thought of as a drama in four acts. The first act opens with the breach of some crucial social relationship. The second act dramatizes a phase of rapidly expanding crisis, a phase that tends to polarize the social group. During the third act attempts are made to apply legal or ritual means of reconciliation. Depending on the success or failure of such efforts, the final act expresses either social reconciliation or irremediable schism. This four-act structure results not from the historical actors' instincts or improvisation but from basic models and metaphors—cultural paradigms—carried in their heads.[11] Social dramas are structured in time rather than in space, and they develop in phases. At any point in the process social relations are thus likely to be incomplete. But ideas and images, patterned by actual social events, manifest themselves as symbols somewhere between consciousness and the unconscious. Originating in human passion, these vernacular symbols then precipitate social action. In crises of cross-purposes and competing interests, they mediate between ideals and action.[12] Many opposing values clashed in the social drama of John Brown's passion: conflicts over secular and religious sources of authority, honor and conscience as ethical systems, aristocratic and bourgeois notions of liberty, and seigneurial versus market relations, as well as the more obvious slavery issue. All these conflicts, and more, were caught up in the social drama of John Brown and all these social conflicts were supported by sharply contrasting cultural paradigms.[13]

To study the structure of social drama, then, is to study the vernacular symbols people employ to achieve their goals. To understand social drama is to understand the process of communication among groups and within groups. Actions in a social drama are guided less by rules or customs than by subjective paradigms existing in the heads of the actors. Such root paradigms, moreover, affect the form and style of behavior even when the actors are not consciously aware of them. Allusive, metaphorical, and existential, root paradigms reach toward the fundamental assumptions that undergird society and are thus available to anyone who chooses to act upon them. Inherently bound up with religion, root paradigms often involve self-sacrifice as a symbol of ultimate victory. Bowed down by the painful shadow of death that nothing could make endurable, Brown knew there was no hope for him. He knew that for the rest of his days, frail and racked, he would live in the hazy presence of a purifying terror. Between his capture at Harpers Ferry and his execution at Charleston, John Brown came under the sway of such a root paradigm.[14]

The passion of John Brown not only marks his passage from the degraded status of condemned prisoner to the exalted status of martyr but also invokes elaborate ritual and serene self-sacrifice in an effort to cure slavery—the nation's leading affliction. Thus the social drama of John Brown may be seen not only as a functional equivalent to the kinds of "rites of passage" that mark changes in social status but also as equivalent to the "rituals of affliction" that are invoked to cure illness or dispel misfortune.[15]

Act 1: The Breach

The first phase of a social drama opens with the breach of some crucial relationship within the social system—a dramatic symbol of dissidence. The attack by John Brown and his men on the federal arsenal at Harpers Ferry, Virginia, constituted the "symbolic trigger of confrontation or encounter." Brown acted—or believed he was acting—on behalf of enslaved African Americans, although in fact he had little contact with African Americans. Governor Henry A. Wise of Virginia contended that Brown had broken the law of the land and thus sought to begin the drama at the redressive stage, with Virginia as judge. Brown countered that it was not so much that he had broken manmade laws but that the slave states had breached God's laws by holding human beings in bondage. For their part, slaveholders held that it was the free states that had breached the constitutional agreement not to meddle in Southern domestic institutions. At stake, however, was not whose breach of what had instigated the crisis, but who could prevail in the test of wills. Virginia sought to provoke an immediate showdown on the sectional issue while the terms of the dispute appeared to be in her favor. Both proslavery forces and antislavery forces sought to muster their resources of wealth, power, and influence. And the breach quickly became a crisis, a deepening crisis so severe that the normal means of redress would soon prove inadequate.[16]

There was a strange calm just before both slaveholders and abolitionists realized the nature and the implications of the social drama toward which they were being impelled. In South Carolina, the South's hotspur state, initial press reaction was deceptively mild. On October 20, the *Charleston Daily Courier* appeared relatively unruffled, remarking that the raid itself "only demonstrates the impregnable safety of the South, when awakened to her own defense." But Southern impregnability hardly mitigated the offense to Southern honor. "Let the law be vindicated," the *Courier* demanded, "and questions of jurisdiction and process be settled afterwards." The *Edgefield Advertiser* used more colorful rhetoric in its denunciation of the raid a few days later, labeling the affair "a harebrained demonstration by a pack of crazy fanatics and poor deluded slaves." Nevertheless, the incident cried out for vengeance. "Yet while crazy and deluded," the *Advertiser* asserted, "their offense is rank and can only be expiated by the most condign punishment."[17]

There was something vaguely primal in the way the social drama of John Brown unfolded. The major actors performed their roles as though they were participating in a carefully choreographed ritual dance. Nervous Republicans attempted at first to distance themselves from Brown. Mesmerized by fear that their 1860 electoral hopes would be dashed if they came to be considered a party of fanatics, many attempted to minimize the incident. "But for the loss of life attending the foray of the crazy Brown among the Virginians," the *Cleveland Leader* editorialized, "the whole thing would be positively ridiculous." Another strategy was to express outrage. Horace Greeley's pro-Republican *New York Tribune* denounced attempts by "the slave Democracy" to connect the Republican party "with Old Brown's mad outbreak." It also called Brown's raid "the work of a madman" but added ominously that "what seems madness to others doubtless wore a different aspect to him." Harpers Ferry, the *Tribune* insisted, resulted from the violence and injustice of "Bleeding Kansas": The real responsibility belonged to those who "sustained the Border Ruffian Pro-Slavery war against Free labor in Kansas." Even William Lloyd Garrison's abolitionist newspaper, *The Liberator*, called Brown's raid on Harpers Ferry "misguided, wild, and apparently insane." The raid was severely condemned as well in Kansas, birthplace of Brown's notoriety. The *Topeka Tribune* termed it "the wild scheme of a bad man who, seeking for personal distinction (not fame) and perhaps plunder, was ready to endanger the lives of thousands," while the *Atchison City Freedom's Champion* thought it "an insane effort to accomplish what none but a madman would attempt."[18]

It was tempting for both Democrats and Republicans to use the affair for partisan advantage, and few Democrats or Republicans resisted the temptation. Some Democrats found in the crisis an especially convenient opportunity to smear their Republican rivals, portraying the raid as part of some dark Republican plot. Others professed outrage that Republicans failed to show sufficient indignation over the raid. James Gordon Bennett's anti-abolitionist *New York Herald* asserted that Brown had been "rendered daring, reckless, and an abolition monomaniac by the scenes of violence through which he had passed." Old Brown deserved his fate, the *Herald* asserted, "but his death and the punishment of his criminal associates will be as a feather in the balance against the mischievous consequences which will probably follow from the rekindling of the slavery excitement in the South." According to Northern Democrats, talk of "the higher law" and of "the irrepressible conflict" would inevitably lead to violence. Brown may have been a "madman," but irresponsible orators were no less than "traitors."[19]

But there were Northern radicals equally eager to express their approval of Brown's efforts. One of the first prominent Northerners to speak out in behalf of John Brown was Concord's Henry David Thoreau. Within two weeks of the Harpers Ferry raid, the man who had eschewed the company of his neighbors for a winter at Walden Pond called a public meeting to plead the prisoner's cause. Thoreau polished his prose by careful rewriting, tailoring it to his audience. He began as though recounting informal memories of a close friend but became increasingly poetic as he depicted John Brown as "an angel of light." Poets, painters, and historians, he predicted, would one day compare Brown's action on behalf of the slaves to the signing of the Declaration of Independence or to the Pilgrims' landing at Plymouth Rock.[20]

Thoreau's friend and sometime mentor, Ralph Waldo Emerson, took longer to formulate his position. Shortly after the raid he wrote to his brother that Brown had "lost his head" at Harpers Ferry. Nevertheless, he confided a few days later, he hoped for Brown's escape "to the last moment." By November 8, however, all of Emerson's doubts had been dispelled. In a Boston address he referred to Brown as "the Saint whose martyrdom, if it shall be perfected, will make the gallows as glorious as the cross." He wished, he said, that men had "health enough to know virtue" when they saw it and "not cry with the fools, 'madman,' when a hero passes."[21]

In this historical moment individual instability and social instability increasingly came together. And they did so in such dramatic fashion that, under the sway of the root paradigm, the two dramas became increasingly coordinated in tragic counterpoint.

Act II: The Crisis

The initial breach of social relations was followed by a menacing phase in which the breach widened into a major cleavage. The increasingly threatening crisis took its place in the public forum, daring the custodians of order to deal with it. No longer was it possible to pretend that nothing was wrong; no longer could the crisis be ignored or wished away. At such a critical impasse some grasp at straws. John Brown seized roots. The root paradigm of martyrdom now claimed his attention and directed his actions. "Christ the great Captain of *liberty*," he wrote to a supporter, "saw fit to take from me a sword of steel after I had carried it for a time but he has put another in my hand: 'The sword of the Spirit.'" Writing to his wife following the failure of his insurrection, Brown declared: "I have been *whip[p]ed* as the saying *is*, but am sure I can recover all the lost capital occasioned by that disaster by only hanging a few moments by the neck; & I feel quite determined to make the utmost possible out of a defeat." Brown's personal crisis marked a turning point, a threshold between stable phases.[22]

As slaveholders and abolitionists alike now began to realize the terrible implications of the social drama into which they had been thrust, they confirmed that thrust by their very realization. Thus the *Boston Journal*, for example, assured its readers that Brown's actions had "loosened the roots of the slave system." But as the crisis deepened, attitudes hardened. Those not previously activated by the issues more and more took sides; neutrality seemed less and less viable. Some in the North tried to draw fine distinctions between Brown's motives and Brown's means, between what he tried to do and how he tried to do it. But in the critical phase of the social drama motives and means were no longer easily separable. Now one either condemned slavery or tacitly supported it. Now those who detested slavery demonized slaveholders, for unless one wished to be seen as standing shoulder-to-shoulder with slaveholders, one was now constrained to support John Brown. Horace Greeley spoke for many when he wrote in the *New York Tribune* that he would not "by one reproachful word disturb the bloody shrouds wherein John Brown and his compatriots lie sleeping. They dared and died for what they felt to be right." Greeley left little doubt that he sympathized with "what they felt to be right" or that he regarded Brown as a hero for having the courage to do what lesser men wanted to see done but were afraid to do themselves. "Let their epitaphs remain unwritten," he wrote, "until the not distant day when no slave shall clank his chains in the shades of Monticello or the graves of Mount Vernon." Greeley went on to praise John Brown for what he called the "disinterestedness and consistent devotion to the rights of human nature" that had impelled his "desperate undertaking."[23]

As might be expected, the Harpers Ferry foray stirred Southern sensibilities even more deeply than Northern ones. The Brown crisis seemed to touch something dark, something archetypal, in the Southern psyche. Physical invasion and servile insurrection were not, of course, matters to be taken lightly under any circumstances. But under attack men who had once called slavery a necessary evil now defended it as a positive good. It was a dubious measure of abolitionist effectiveness that slaveholders became more defensive than ever in the late 1850s. Widespread agitation to reopen the African slave trade led to a bill to that effect actually being introduced in the South Carolina legislature in 1859, although it was eventually tabled after bitter debate. But the autumn of 1859 clearly polarized proslavery and antislavery positions, as the most ardent agitators on both sides spoke out with increased confidence. How long could they be kept from each other's throats?[24]

In the ritualized rhetoric of the social drama, the philippic—a style of rhetoric abounding in acrimony—became the discourse of choice on each side. The philippic is not a form of rhetoric intended to convert the skeptics. Rather, its purpose is to rally the faithful, to intensify the feelings of those already persuaded. The inevitable effect was further to polarize the estranged sections. As Southern opinion solidified, a salvo of invective blasted forth from editors and politicians below the Mason-Dixon line. In Georgia the *Savannah Republican* joined in the blood chorus. "Like the neighboring population," it said, "we go in for a summary vengeance. A terrible example should be made." Secessionist sentiment was growing as well. "The Harpers Ferry tragedy," the *Mobile Daily Register* declared, "is like a meteor disclosing in its lurid flash the width and depth of that abyss which rends asunder two nations, apparently one." The *Richmond Enquirer* asserted that "the Harpers Ferry invasion has advanced the cause of disunion more than any other event," noting ominously that "the people of the North sustain the outrage!" After all, who was behind the insurrection? Who gave Brown the money to buy guns and ammunition? The fact that only a handful in the North had actually voiced approval of Brown and his actions made little difference: precision was sacrificed to polemic. Earlier references to the "harebrained" character of the undertaking "by a pack of crazy fanatics and poor deluded slaves" and "the impregnable safety of the South" in no way lessened the symbolic significance of John Brown's raid. John Brown had become the overarching symbol of sectional conflict.[25]

The widespread Southern fear of physical invasion and servile insurrection was not limited to fire-eaters. In Salisbury, North Carolina, J. J. Bruner, an old-line Whig and a persistent Unionist, was both owner and editor of the *Carolina Watchman*. In the inflamed and apprehensive autumn of 1859, however, Bruner praised the rapid deployment of Virginia and Maryland troops in the Harpers Ferry crisis. They had, he said, "reported themselves ready to march in the almost inconceivable space of one hour." Their readiness was evidence of "the temper of the people who will be called upon, some day, to defend their institutions, their homes, and their families." He further acknowledged that John Brown's raid gave the secessionists new propaganda with which to foster their cause. "Ah! Should it come, there will have been few such in the history of the world," he wrote, "for nothing short of extermination of millions of brave spirits would end a strife urged forward by madness on the one side and outraged rights on the other." He did not, however, say which side was which.[26]

Virginia's decision to prosecute John Brown for treason prompted South Carolina's elegant conservative William Henry Trescot toward constitutional speculation. Trescot had long maintained that the only real question was, Can the Union and slavery exist together? Despite his doubts that they could, he hoped that some kind of guarantee might grow out of this crisis that could hold the Union together, at least for a while longer. "Do you not think that it would have been better to have given the prisoner[s] to the United States?" he wrote to James Henry Hammond. "As it is, Virginia, if I understand correctly, will try them for not just murder. What I wanted was a decision *that the attempt to execute a servile insurrection is high treason against the United States and [is] to be punished with death by the Federal Government.*"[27]

As the antagonists fell more and more under the sway of the root paradigm, then, the passion of John Brown was no longer individual but generic. And as the social drama unfolded, the ritualized nature of its discourse was more and more striking.

Act III: The Trial

In the third phase of a social drama, representative members of the disturbed social system make an effort to limit the spread of crisis by some attempt at redress or reconciliation. Among other possibilities, the attempt may entail the performance of a public ritual in a formal juridical setting, as in the trial of John Brown. This attempt at redress is the critical phase of the social drama. Are the means of redress adequate? Are they capable, for example, of restoring the status quo ante? Are they even capable of restoring relative calm among the contending parties? If so, how? If not, why not? Clearly, the trial of John Brown failed to restore the previous status quo—and just as clearly that restoration would have been unsatisfactory to either side. As he reflected on his own impotence in the face of the power wielded by the slaveholding states, such considerations must surely have passed through John Brown's mind.[28]

Brown's contemporaries declared him "sane" or "mad" as it suited their mood or their purpose. Brown's court-appointed attorney accordingly questioned the prisoner's ability to stand trial: "Insanity is hereditary in that family. His mother and sister died with it, and a daughter of that sister has been two years in the Lunatic Asylum. A son and daughter of his mother's brother have also been confined," he told the court, "and another son of that brother is now insane and under close restraint." Brown, for his part, rejected a plea of insanity on his behalf. "I look upon it," he said, "as a miserable artifice and pretext of those who ought to take a different course in regard to me." Governor Wise likewise declared Brown sane. "He is a man of clear head, of courage, fortitude, and simple ingenuousness," the governor said. "He is cool, collected, and indomitable." (At the same time, Brown declared Wise to be mad.) But "insanity" is a concept much more clearly defined in legal statutes than in actual human life. The issue demands a more sophisticated formulation. John Brown became a powerful symbol not because he was "sane" or "insane" but because he represented a coincidence of opposites, expressing a tension between opposite poles of meaning, at once proud and meek, lion and lamb. While formally he suffered the fate of the lamb, in the social drama he played the role of the lion. Shrewd yet bold, humble yet angry, Brown's character may have seemed contradictory, but it was curiously consistent.[29]

Like a neophyte in an initiation ritual, John Brown went through an ordeal at the hands of the court. He was made to experience a ritual humiliation, a loss of honor, a form of "social death" not unlike that of the slaves on whose behalf he had attempted to act. He was isolated from secular society in his jail cell, in what some anthropologists have called a "liminal interlude." But in this interlude Brown was also able to stand aside from social conventions, to review past patterns of thought and action, to reconsider all previous standards and models, to interpret experience in fresh ways, and to formulate new courses of action. When he returned to society for his date with the hangman, he underwent what anthropologists call "a ritual of reaggregation," publicly confirming his new status as an initiated champion of freedom. This ritual of reaggregation was a necessary prelude to the rites of apotheosis that followed his execution.[30]

Northern response to the trial was mixed. Most Northern papers castigated Virginia for moving with such unseemly haste to bring Brown to trial. But it was impossible to conceal the unhappy choice faced by those Northerners who sympathized with Brown's antislavery ends but shrank from his bloody means. As Brown himself increasingly became a unified symbol, as sympathy for his ends consequently seemed less and less compatible with disdain for his means, men and women found themselves forced to choose between neither or both. It was an agonizing dilemma, from which many found their escape in the very root paradigm chosen by John Brown—in the symbolic image of a martyr for freedom, slain by the savage slaveholders. Writing from Rome, Theodore Parker defended Brown's actions on logical cum philosophical grounds. Since slavery itself depended on the use of force and terror against the slaves, Parker reasoned, the use of force and terror was justified to achieve freedom. If Brown had succeeded at Harpers Ferry, he contended, "the majority of men in New England would have rejoiced, not only in the end, but also in the means." As long as slavery endured, Parker predicted, insurrections would not only continue but would become more frequent and more powerful.[31]

Such pronouncements only further inflamed anxieties of the slave South, causing some Southern editors to become increasingly vociferous in calling for Brown's execution. But others in the slaveholding states warned of the consequences of creating a martyr. "If old John Brown is executed," Kentucky's *Frankfort Yeoman* noted, "there will be thousands to dip their handkerchiefs in his blood; relics of the martyr will be paraded throughout the North." Virginia's Governor Wise, however, disdained such fears. Hanging, he contended, "would be no more martyrdom than to incarcerate the fanatic. The sympathetic would have asked on and on for liberation and to nurse and soothe him while life lasted, in prison." Retrospect has not been kind to the governor's reasoning. Doubtless groups of diehards would have continued to agitate for the prisoner's release, but nothing solidified Northern opinion so powerfully as the image of John Brown on the gallows. Nothing inspired soldiers in blue so strongly as the mighty hymn by which John Brown's soul marched on with them into battle.[32]

Revelations that prominent Northerners had financed Brown's forays proved especially incendiary in the South. Until Harpers Ferry, most slaveholders had regarded the pronouncements of what Georgia's *Daily Enquirer* called "the raving of Northern fanatics" as no more than "pecuniary Speculation." But now they learned that John Brown had not confined his fanaticism to rhetoric. Now they learned that the so-called "Secret Six"—Thomas Wentworth Higginson, Samuel Gridley Howe, Theodore Parker, Franklin B. Sanborn, Gerrit Smith, and George Luther Stearns—had been hiring thugs to stir up slave revolts in the South. How could Southern rights possibly be secure if the Republicans came to power? The *Charleston Daily Courier* had made up its mind that the continued existence of

Southern security was impossible within the Union. To those who shared that conviction, the Harpers Ferry foray made plain "the destiny which awaits them in the Union, under the control of a sectional anti-slavery party in the free states." It was the Union itself "by which domestic disquietude is created and the mightiest dangers impend over the South," the *Charleston Mercury* contended. "Our connection with the North is a standing instigation of insurrection in the South." The conflict, as the *Mercury* saw it, was irrepressible and so must be waged to its bitter end.[33]

Unionist response in the South was only slightly milder than that of the disunionists. Charlotte's *North Carolina Whig* and other newspapers gave significant space to the Brown story under such headlines as "A NUT to be CRACKED," and "HARPERS FERRY AFFAIR." According to the *Whig*, Brown's attack on Harpers Ferry was more than an attack on the state of Virginia; it was an attack on the entire South. "The affair at Harpers Ferry was a deeply laid scheme by some of the abolitionists," the *Whig* argued, designed "to aid in murdering the people of the South by causing an insurrection of the Negroes." The movements and actions of abolitionists commanded front-page attention as well in Salisbury's *Carolina Watchman*, its banner headline proclaiming, "ABOLITIONISTS RUN MAD." The once moderately unionist *Lancaster Ledger* now took a giant step toward disunion: "Let us endeavor to move in concert, set our houses in order, looking to the grand event which has been mooted for years and which circumstances now indicate as affording the only haven of security, *viz.*, a dissolution of the Union."[34]

In the frontier southwest, where the Harpers Ferry raid seemed distant and Brown's threat far away, the *Arkansas Gazette* might believe that "too much importance has been attached to this matter." But across most of the South the reaction of the North inflamed opinion as much as the raid itself. The *Charleston Mercury* regarded the affair at Harpers Ferry as no more and no less than "a sign of the times and of the temper and intentions of the northern majority." The more extreme Northern opinions were the most widely quoted, on the grounds that for every Yankee who voiced such views there were thousands who applauded or gave silent assent. Governor Wise's *Richmond Enquirer* warned that the large throngs who gathered to cheer Wendell Phillips and other abolitionist orators were "fanning the flame of civil discord, which, in an unlooked for hour, will burst forth into a consuming conflagration." But the *Enquirer* was more inclined to help spread the fire than to extinguish it. "We shall feed the now smoldering embers with every particle of fuel furnished by the

Northern fanatics," it proclaimed. "As long as conservatism sits silent, and listens coward-like to such treason, we shall inform our readers of public sentiment in the North, and if the information *inflames*, why let the consequence fall upon the authors and abettors." Conservatives in the South, it said, could expect no help from their Northern counterparts, who "are cowed and trampled under foot by the impudent, blatant Abolitionism."[35]

There is no greater illustration of the critical significance of the redress stage than its impact on James Henry Hammond, a leading Southern politician. One admirer likened Hammond's election to the United States Senate two years earlier to an event in ancient Rome, when "Cincinnatus was called from his Farm to the head of the nation." Hammond took his seat on January 6, 1858, but did not deliver a speech on the Senate floor for nearly two months. When he finally spoke on March 4, however, he created a sensation with his ringing philosophical defense of slavery. "In all social systems there must be a class to do the menial duties, to perform the drudgeries of life," he argued, "a class requiring but a low order of intellect and but little skill." Such a class he described as "the very mud-sill of society." Without it, he said, there could not be "the other class which leads progress, civilization, and refinement." The strength of the South's social system, he further asserted, was matched by the strength of its economy. "You dare not make war on cotton," he warned the North. "No power on earth dares make war on it. Cotton is king."[36]

Hammond nevertheless shrank from disunion. He maintained that Southern strength would guarantee the protection of Southern rights within the Union. Given his radical background—for more than two decades he had been an ardent disunionist—James Henry Hammond made an unlikely spokesman for conditional unionism. But in a speech on Beech Island in the summer of 1858, his lack of enthusiasm for secession was unmistakable. He told his fellow slaveholders that he desired not disunion, but for "the South to *rule* the Union." In a speech in Barnwell in October he elaborated on his doctrine of Southern dominance, declaring that the South was made up of "the most powerful people who now flourish on the globe." It was "not yet" time for secession; "no measure has yet been strong enough to stand against the South when united." A united South, he insisted, could look forward to "a magnificent future" within the Union. His old fire-eating comrades-in-arms were incensed: they felt he had betrayed them. For his part, Hammond seemed hurt and genuinely bewildered by the hostility his speech aroused in South Carolina.[37]

Perhaps Hammond's nouveau unionism was just political posturing, designed to gain time to unify the South in preparation for the inevitable separation. After all, he did not always voice such optimistic unionism in private letters. "How can any sane man have any hope of saving ourselves from the fate of Jamaica," he had written to the implacable disunionist Edmund Ruffin, "but by cutting ourselves loose . . . as speedily as possible?" But after the heady social whirl of Washington, Hammond seems seriously to have entertained the idea that he might become president, thus ensuring both protection of Southern rights and preservation of the Union. The response to his Barnwell speech north of the Mason-Dixon line had clearly fueled his fantasies. "This speech of mine produced an immense sensation throughout the Country," he exulted in his diary. "It was published in every leading paper North and South. It was read publicly in the streets of the great Northern Cities to immense crowds." What excited him even more, though, was that "I was nominated at once for the Presidency by an hundred newspapers on all sides." He wrote William Gilmore Simms that he had now attained a reputation in the North as an "honest, disinterested, & fearless" statesman "not without a fair share of talent." He was certain that "the thinking & patriotic men want just such a man for the next Presidency."[38]

Whatever hopes there might have been in the autumn of 1859 for Hammond's ambitions both to secure Southern rights and to save the Union by becoming president of the United States—indeed, whatever hopes remained for any peaceful resolution of the sectional conflict within the Union—they were fatally undercut by John Brown's raid and its aftermath. James Henry Hammond's individual instability became implicated in the general social instability. As John Brown's story had become generic, an overarching summation of the sectional conflict, so James Henry Hammond saw his story now taken away from him, saw it translated into another motif of the John Brown social drama. The failure of the redress phase here was especially critical. Unfortunately, whenever Hammond was faced with great opportunities or great challenges—such as the present test of his unionist convictions—he came down with real or imagined ailments that prevented his rising to the occasion. "Any great and severe mental labor," he had already confided to his diary, "prostrates me for months and months with my feeble health." He was certain his health would "not permit my assuming such a toil, and I gave a cold shoulder to it and political intrigue." He wrote to Simms that he was "ready to throw up my hands and retire." But supporters insisted that in this crisis he was needed more than ever. "This Harpers Ferry affair will bring up the slavery question in all its importance to the great interests of the South," wrote George P. Elliott. "The South needs her ablest men in council and South Carolina has a right to claim the talent of her every son. Your post of duty for the present is in the Senate."[39]

If James Henry Hammond wished to withdraw from the crisis he had spent most of his adult life trying to foment, another son of South Carolina could hardly wait to enter the fray. Francis W. Pickens had been appointed minister to Russia by President James Buchanan. Although fears that Russia might enter the Franco-Austrian war kept him at his post until August of 1860, Pickens correctly perceived in the social drama of John Brown a crisis of the Union. Hammond remained sullenly in his Senate seat until the presidential election of 1860, refusing after John Brown's raid to offer any leadership. But Pickens was impatient to return home and "take responsibility in the great events and in whatever may occur," although he disclaimed any plans to seek public office. A moderate by South Carolina standards, Francis Pickens had been radicalized by recent events. He believed the political response to this crisis would determine the fate of the nation. As their state stumbled toward secession, Pickens became more and more a leader, while the social drama increasingly cast Hammond in the role of bystander.[40]

The failure of reconciliation brought a deepening of the crisis. Since no verdict in the John Brown trial could have satisfied both sides, Northerners and Southerners resumed their elaborately choreographed pas de deux. Rumors of an attempt to rescue Brown spread rapidly. "Last night," a supporter wrote Hammond, "startling information was rec'd by Gov. [William Henry] Gist [of South Carolina]—from Gov. Wise advising South Carolina to *arm*." According to the *North Carolina Whig*, Gist offered Wise "any amount of military aid" he felt he needed to repel an attempt to free Brown. On the eve of the alleged rescue attempt a Colonel Elliott was reported to have told the troops guarding Brown that they "might have to undergo arduous and perilous duty," as the *Carolina Watchman* put it, but "if the venerable Commonwealth should be invaded . . . they would effectively wipe out the stain."[41]

An anonymous letter circulated through the South, warning of dire consequences if John Brown were harmed. The letter was also said to have been sent to Governor Wise. "You had better caution your authorities to be careful about what you do with Ossawatamie Brown," it read. "So sure as you hurt one hair of his head, mark my word—the following day, you will see every city, town, and village south of the Mason-Dixon line in flames." However prophetic of times to come, the threat contained in the letter was almost certainly a bluff. All the same, the *North Carolina Whig* was only one of many Southern newspapers to fan the flames by publishing the letter, nor did the *Whig* let the threat go unanswered. "If any of the abolitionists desire to liberate Brown and his accomplices," it responded in an editorial, "let them come and they will be met—force with force." In a similar vein the editor of the *Lancaster Ledger*, a South Carolina paper, wrote, "A few of our most zealous statesmen warned us time and again of the probability of such a condition of affairs being experienced in the South at some time in the future, if the tide of abolition fury was not checked. Many of us hooted at the idea and thought that the danger existed in the imagination of some of our fire-eating politicians; but the prophecy does not now seem so absurd." Battle lines were beginning to form.[42]

The essence of the doomed reconciliation stage was, however, perhaps best expressed in the pious optimism of President James Buchanan. Indeed, the president played his ritually prescribed role in the social drama to perfection. He correctly estimated both the impact of John Brown's raid and the reason for the extreme Southern reaction. "In the already excited condition of public feeling throughout the South," he noted, "this raid of John Brown's made a deeper impression on the Southern mind against the Union than all former events." Although he thought "it would have had no lasting effect" had it been "considered merely as the isolated act of a desperate fanatic," what spread apprehension and alarm across the South, he surmised, was "the enthusiastic and permanent approbation of the expedition by the abolitionists of the North." But if Buchanan had some insight into the cause of the crisis, he lacked the vision to imagine a solution. Like Pontius Pilate, he washed his hands of responsibility, as though no solution were necessary. "The events at Harpers Ferry, by causing the people to pause and reflect upon the possible peril to their cherished institutions, will be the means, under Providence, of allaying the existing excitement," he wrote optimistically, and "will resolve that the Constitution and the Union shall not be endangered." His optimism was, alas, misplaced.[43]

As the crisis deepened, the proslavery press in fact focused much of its outrage on the luckless head of James Buchanan, editors depicting the president embraced in the arms of "his abolitionist friends." The *Caroli-*

na Watchman put the total blame for the crisis on the president "and his wishy-washy men he had around him." In Alabama the *Selma Watchman and Democrat* accused him of refusing to heed "the warning and advice" allegedly given him by "Government officers at Harpers Ferry." By doing so, it was claimed, Buchanan assisted Brown's raiders in "murdering innocent women and children and peaceable citizens and destroying their property." He had, the *Watchman* charged, turned "a deaf ear to their warnings and allowed the Rebels to carry out their hellish plans."[44]

In the opinion of the *North Carolina Whig*, since John Brown had threatened one of the institutions of the South, all Southern institutions (and thus a way of life) were at risk. According to the *Mississippi Free Trader*, if Brown's slave insurrection had succeeded, "out of the ashes of our fair Republic would have risen another Saint Domingo." Virginia's "soil would have reeked with human gore," the *Free Trader* declared melodramatically, "and the torch applied" across "the entire South." The *Whig* called on its readers "to organize a Volunteer Company at, or in the vicinity of, Pineland, North Carolina, that we may be better able to defend our homes and firesides from the incendiary and murderous attacks of Northern Abolitionists." Around the South, military companies were forming in response to the raid. But civilians responded with equal vigor, forming "voluntary associations throughout the South" that pledged "not to eat, or use, or wear, any articles from the North."[45]

In South Carolina the period following the failure of redress was marked by formerly moderate newspapers' embracing disunion. In the town of Pickens the editor of the *Keowee Courier* declared that if "the cut throats at Harpers Ferry are to be sustained, then the sooner we get out of the Union the better." Support for the upcoming Democratic national convention in Charleston was accordingly weakened by Brown's raid and rising disunion sentiment. As the editor of Spartanburg's *Carolina Spartan* boasted, "We do not care a fig about the Convention or election of another President, as we are convinced the safety of the South lies only outside the present Union and this we believe to be the judgment of a large majority of our people." A moderate position, even by South Carolina standards, was becoming increasingly difficult to maintain.[46]

The major actors in the social drama were few, but each symbolized many persons, many relationships, many aims, many interests. Not surprisingly, then, there were many constraints on them to ponder carefully their courses of action, to weigh their words carefully, perhaps even to prefer judicious silence to well-chosen words. Is it not all the more remarkable, then, how melodramatic the social drama of John Brown became? Such intemperance in the face of such constraints merely underscores the ritual quality that a naked confrontation of this sort can acquire when it lacks any adequate means of mediation.[47]

Act IV: The Outcome

The fourth phase of a social drama, Turner suggests, provides an opportunity for the actors to take stock, to compare the situation that preceded the breach with the situation following the attempt at redress.[48] In the case of John Brown the immediate outcome was the creation of a hero; but there was also an intermediate outcome in the election of Lincoln and a long-range outcome in war and emancipation. In the long run the structure of the whole society was changed, and with it the nature and intensity of relations between its parts. Old power relations changed, for example, as former authority was diluted or replaced and a new party system replaced an older one.

The passion of John Brown was not a drama of one man's martyrdom; it was not a soliloquy but a drama of social relations. And every sacrifice in social drama requires a sacrificer as well as a victim. In the case of John Brown the sacrificer was Henry Wise, governor of Virginia. There was in fact a curious complicity between Brown and Wise, in which the governor at crucial moments virtually dared the prisoner to commit himself to the way of the cross. Wise apparently realized, at least subliminally, that Brown was archetypally controlled by the root paradigm of martyrdom. But Wise does not appear to have realized that he could only hang John Brown and give him the martyr's crown he sought at the expense of strengthening the antislavery cause. Thus, the hour of Brown's execution was the hour of Brown's triumph. In the ultimate act of what Brown and other Christian Yankees would denote as *conscience* he forced the South to become his hangman, forced the South to inflict the ultimate act of *shaming* upon him. In doing so he also forced the South to degrade itself, at least in the eyes of outside observers. Ultimately, by shifting the South so decisively toward secession, John Brown made slavery rather than himself the lost cause.[49]

As the day of John Brown's execution approached, the actors continued to perform their roles with ritual precision. On December 2, 1859, supporters in various Northern cities held meetings of sympathy. In Concord, Massachusetts, Louisa May Alcott described the gathering there in her journal. "The execution of Saint John the Just took place on the second," she wrote. "A meeting at the hall, and all Concord was there. Emerson, Thoreau, Father [Bronson Alcott] and [Franklin B.] Sanborn spoke, and all were full of reverence and admiration for the martyr." Her father even composed a sonnet for the occasion:

> Bold Saint, thou firm believer in the Cross,
> Again made glorious by self-sacrifice,—
> Love's free atonement given without love's loss,—
> That martyrdom to thee was lighter pain,
> Since thus a race its liberties should gain;
> . . . .
> O Patriot true! O Christian meek and brave!
> Throned in the martyrs' seat henceforth shalt sit;
> Prophet of God! Messiah of the Slave!

The transfiguration of John Brown, as portrayed by Bronson Alcott, was little short of miraculous. Given the centrality of the crucifixion in Western iconography, one might suppose that Brown had carried his own gallows up the hill at Charleston, where he was hanged between two thieves, while cadets from the Virginia Military Institute threw dice for his garments. Brown's embrace of the root paradigm had not been in vain.[50]

The final step in the process of deification occurred with the translation of Brown's death into the miracle of Christ's resurrection. In Boston's Tremont Temple, William Lloyd Garrison addressed a large gathering assembled under the auspices of the American Anti-Slavery Society. They had come, he told them, to witness John Brown's resurrection. "As a peace man—an 'ultra' peace man—I am prepared to say: 'Success to every slave insurrection at the South,'" he declared. On the following day the *New York Daily Tribune* asserted that Americans ought to be "reverently grateful for the privilege of living in a world rendered noble by the daring of heroes, the suffering of martyrs,—among whom let none doubt that History will accord an honored niche to Old John Brown."[51]

In Philadelphia friends of John Brown staged a public prayer meeting at the hour of Brown's execution. The large hall was crowded with his supporters, both black and white, who were interrupted frequently by heckling from a group of Southern medical students enrolled at the University of Pennsylvania. The principal address was delivered by Theodore Tilton, managing editor of the *New York Independent*. "Today the nation puts to death its noblest citizen!" Tilton declared. "What was his crime? Guilty of what? Guilty of loving his fellow men too well." Cheers and jeers mingled as he commended the soul of John Brown "to that impartial history which vindicates the martyrs and turns their martyrdom into glory," going on to predict that "the deed of this day will not die! It will live in history as long as there shall be a history for heroes." Antiphonal choirs of applauders and hissers accompanied Tilton's closing prayer that "at this solemn and awful moment of death, this nation may be struck down upon its knees, by the sudden glory of God bursting out of heaven—and that it may be humbled in the dust until it shall rise repentant, and the scales shall fall from its eyes, and the whole nation shall stand at last in the light and liberty of the sons of God."[52]

In Cincinnati the Reverend Moncure Daniel Conway, a Virginia-born Unitarian, delivered a guest sermon the following Sunday at the First Congregational Church. Depicting John Brown as "a man dying for a religious principle," Conway urged the parishioners to "set aside the question of the abstract rectitude of the method. The stature of the hero dwarfs such considerations." John Brown, he preached, "summed up a century's work" and "sealed with his blood the death warrant of slavery." As the organ intoned the invitational hymn, Conway delivered a sacred charge to the assembled congregation: "Out of the ashes of our martyr a Revolution must come." It would come, he assured them, "and it will rise up to brood over this land, until the progeny of Freemen arise to crown America's destiny." He urged them all to be "baptized afresh to the cause Of LIBERTY, HUMANITY, and GOD!"[53]

Like others in the grip of the root paradigm, the Grimké sisters of South Carolina regarded Brown's execution as the martyrdom of a man of profound and noble convictions. Although daughters of a prominent slaveholder, Sarah and Angelina Grimké had left their native state to become abolitionist activists as early as the 1830s. On the eve of Brown's hanging, Sarah wrote that she had gone "in spirit to the martyr. It was my privilege to enter into sympathy with him; to go down, according to my measure, into the depths where he has travailed and feel his past exercises, his present sublime position." She regarded Brown as "the John Huss of the United States" and wrote that he now stood ready "to seal his testimony with his life's blood." Devout Quakers and ardent abolitionists, the Grimké sisters were deeply moved by the passion of John Brown.[54]

Virginia's trial and execution of John Brown also convinced Abraham Lincoln's law partner, William H. Herndon, that disunion and war were inevitable, an opinion he expressed in almost equally passionate terms. "I am thoroughly convinced," he wrote to Charles Sumner, "that two such civilizations as the North and the South cannot co-exist on the same soil and be co-equal in the Federal brotherhood. To expect otherwise would be to expect the Absolute to sleep with and tolerate 'hell.' . . . Let this natural war—let this inevitable struggle proceed—go on, till slavery is *dead—dead—dead!*"⁵⁵

By no means, however, was all Northern response sympathetic to the condemned man. On the day John Brown was hanged, Abraham Lincoln told an audience in Troy, Kansas: "We cannot object, even though he agreed with us in thinking slavery wrong. That cannot excuse violence, bloodshed, and treason." The racist *New York Weekly Day Book* went a good deal further. It openly praised Brown's execution and expressed distaste for "Negro equality," claiming that Brown and his followers made up only a small segment of the population and that "the great masses, the laboring class, are as uncorrupted with Negro equality doctrines as ever!" Moreover, the *Day Book* added, the South could be certain that the "North will rejoice when the old wretch gets his due."⁵⁶

Other Northern Democrats, seriously alarmed at the widening sectional rift, held a series of "Union Meetings" throughout the region. On December 8 a large gathering of Democrats filled Faneuil Hall in Boston to pass resolutions condemning John Brown and his admirers. The venerable Levi Lincoln came out of retirement to preside. George Peabody, former president Franklin Pierce, and several former governors of Massachusetts sent letters of greetings that were read aloud. Among the speakers were former United States attorney general Caleb Cushing and the noted orator Edward Everett.⁵⁷

The assembled Democrats listened attentively as Everett proclaimed his conviction that the nation was "on the very verge of a convulsion, which will shake the Union to its foundation." He feared that continuation of violent speech and action would "bring us to the catastrophe," and he called on patriots to forgo political issues for the time being. Everett then asked his New England audience to try to see John Brown's raid and its aftermath through Southern eyes. He asked them to imagine that "a party of desperate, misguided men, under a resolved and fearless leader, had been organized in Virginia, to come and establish themselves by stealth in Springfield in this state, intending there, after possessing themselves, at the unguarded hour of midnight, of the National Armory, to take advantage of some local cause of disaffection, say the feud between Protestants and Catholics—which led to a very deplorable occurrence in this vicinity a few years ago—to stir up a social revolution." Everett next asked those present to suppose that "pikes and rifles to arm 2500 men had been procured by funds raised by extensive subscriptions throughout the South." Then, what if "at the dead of a Sunday night, the work of destruction had begun, by shooting down an unarmed man, who had refused to join the invading force; that citizens of the first standing were seized and imprisoned—three or four others killed."[58]

But, Everett continued, the conspiracy failed, and its leader, having received a fair trial, had been convicted and executed. Everett then asked his New England audience to imagine how they would feel if "throughout Virginia, which sent him forth on his fatal errand, and the South generally, funeral bells should be tolled, meetings of sympathy held, as at the death of some great public benefactor." Imagine how they would feel if "the person who had plotted to put a pike or a rifle in the hands of 2500 men, to be used against their fellows, inhabitants of the same town, inmates of the same houses, with an ulterior intention and purpose of wrapping a whole community in a civil war of the deadliest and bloodiest type, in which a man's foe should be those of his own household," a man who had actually "taken the lives of several fellow-beings, should be extolled, canonized, placed on a level with the great heroes of humanity, nay, assimilated to the Saviour of mankind; and all this not the effect of a solitary individual impulse, but the ripe fruit of a systematic agitation pursued in the South, unrebuked, for years!" What, he asked his audience, did they believe they might "feel, think, say, under such a state of things?"

In his address Caleb Cushing bitterly attacked the abolitionist supporters of John Brown. "By constant brooding upon one single idea—that idea, if you please, a right one abstractedly," he said, the abolitionists had "come to be monomaniacs of that idea, and so have become utterly lost to the moral relations of right and wrong." Cushing asked his audience of New England Democrats to repudiate those whom he called a "band of drunken mutineers" who were about to drive the ship of state onto the shoals. Cushing had expressed similar views in a letter to the chairman of the Massachusetts Democratic party. There were two sets of Northern sympathizers for "this traitor and murderer," he charged, "one set who say that his plans and arts were so stupidly criminal, and so criminally stupid, that he must have been crazy, and should therefore go unpunished—and another set who, moved by their own crazy false estimation of the moral quality of his acts, proceed to proclaim and honor him as a hero, a saint, and a god."[59]

Cushing further charged that the abolitionists were conducting what he called "a systematic *war in disguise*" against the South. The federal government, in his opinion, should give Virginia "at least as much security from invasion by Ohio or any other state of the Union as she has from invasion by England or France." Without such protection, Cushing declared it to be the right, "nay it is the duty, of the Southern States to separate from the Northern States and to form a confederation of their own." By Christmas of 1859 Cushing had come to the conclusion that a separation of some kind was inevitable. Of course John Brown's nineteen-man "invasion" of Virginia had been quickly crushed, not by Virginia but by the federal government, and yet the federal government had made no effort to interfere with Virginia's conduct of Brown's trial. But Cushing believed that the nation's problems had already passed beyond the nation's ability to handle them, and he feared that separation might now be the only solution to the sectional controversy. "The late murderous foray of Northern abolitionists into Virginia," he wrote, "and the endorsement, the canonization, the heroization, the apotheosis, of their head murderer, by so many of both clergy and laity at the North, have at length brought all these questions to a practice issue. The Southern States cannot meekly lie down to be trodden upon by the Northern." No fire-eater could have said it better.[60]

Thus did Northerners and Southerners increasingly play parts ritually prescribed by the root paradigm: ritual adulation of the martyr prompted a ritual backlash. Complexity and ambiguity became less and less tenable. The social drama accordingly seemed to unite much of the white South behind a common cause, in which loyalty to "the South" came to be defined in terms of loyalty to a single institution. In an address to the Virginia state legislature, Governor Wise charged that "the motive of the North is to see whether we will face a danger now sealed in blood," a danger he believed was now inevitable. "We must face it, and have a settlement at once," Wise declared, "the sooner the better."[61]

Fear manifested itself to the point of direct violence against anyone who dared to say a harsh word against slavery or a kind word in favor of John Brown. In North Carolina a man was arrested and held simply for "having uttered abolition and incendiary sentiments." In South Carolina another man dared to "utter antislavery sentiments and sympathy with old John Brown . . . upon the Capitol building at Columbia." After being warned to leave he was taken "to the depot, where [his abductors] first gave him thirty-nine lashes and then tarred and feathered him [before] placing him on a train."[62] In Georgia a Savannah vigilance committee undertook to tar and feather "a resident Yankee" who had "made himself obnoxious by distributing incendiary pamphlets among the negroes who can read, and *reading* them to those who cannot." The alleged agitator was "carried beyond the city limits, stripped to the buff—tarred and feathered and cotton overlaid." Five or six other individuals were given a deadline to leave the city. A correspondent reported Savannah to be "somewhat excited and the women are particularly scared—where will all this end!"[63]

In Louisiana the *New Orleans Daily Picayune* declared that "the action of Brown and his men was nothing compared with the fanaticism of hatred against slavery which the event had shown to exist throughout the North." The Northern response constituted what the *Picayune* called "Brown's treason without his courage, his frenzy without his nerve, with even greater malice, because safe from the penalties he was daring enough to brave in his own person—for we have no statutes against moral treason, the treason of disloyalty in the heart, to the peace and union of the confederacy." Word of the execution spread quickly through the slave quarters on hundreds of plantations, passed on by slaves who had learned to read. Just one day after the *Picayune's* report, seventy-five miles up the Mississippi River from New Orleans a slave who worked in the sugarhouse on a large plantation told a free mulatto Creole all about the hanging of John Brown. His master had given him a newspaper to wipe the machinery with. He had read the newspaper and then spread the news of Brown's execution to the whole slave community.[64]

A train from Philadelphia arrived in Richmond just before Christmas, carrying more than two hundred medical students who had withdrawn from schools in Philadelphia in protest over the Northern response to John Brown's execution. "Let Virginia call home her children!" Governor Wise declared to the large crowd that gathered to welcome them. Indeed, many Southerners had come to feel that the North's true motives were finally unmasked by the response to John Brown. "The South wants and has a constitutional right to demand that slaves not be stolen," the *Carolina Watchman* declared, adding that Southerners also had "a right to demand that all interferences with the institution of the South by the North" such as "Brown's invitation" ought to be "put down by the North." The *Watchman* implied that such acts as the Harpers Ferry raid were backed and promoted by "the North" rather than by certain Northerners in particular. "Is this the Government of two people," the Mississippi *Free Trader* wanted to know, "as different in our sentiments of right and wrong as we are in our institutions?" In Salisbury, North Carolina, citizens were urged to "enroll once more your names, enter the school of the soldier, and han-

dle the old Kentucky rifle." Tarheels not only encouraged military preparedness so that Southerners could defend themselves from outside
threats but also preparedness "to maintain [their] rank among the nations
and to defend [to] the utmost the institution transmitted to us by our
ancestors."[65]

The tempo of events increased, and, as the social drama gained momentum, even longtime South Carolina unionists dutifully embraced their mis-
cast secessionist roles. Christopher G. Memminger, whose unionist creden-
tials dated back to the nullification controversy, was outraged by what he
considered Northern deification of John Brown. "Every [Yankee] village
bell which tolled its solemn note at the execution of Brown," he wrote,
"proclaims to the South the approbation of that village of insurrection and
servile war." Memminger and other former unionists now embraced disunion as the only solution. In the South Carolina legislature "a rank Union
man" was overheard to say that although he had "never expected to live
to see the day when he would come to regard the Union as a nuisance . . . he
was ready for Disunion now." Benjamin F. Perry, perhaps South Carolina's
leading unionist, presented a resolution threatening secession, while Memminger wrote to a friend that "all of us are persuaded that in the Union
there is no security—and either there must be new terms established or a
Southern Confederacy is our only hope of safety."[66]

South Carolina's most ardent voice of secession, the *Charleston Mercury*, exulted that "the staunchest Union men, heretofore, are becoming the
sternest in the vindication of the rights of the South." The *Edgefield Advertiser* seemed to have moved from conditional unionism to a kind of
conditional Southern nationalism. "Neither justice nor patriotism requires that she [the South] forbear longer," the *Advertiser* declared, "unless a change of Northern sentiment and policy be shown by the Presidential election of the coming year." Likewise, Governor William Henry Gist,
in his message to the South Carolina legislature on the eve of John Brown's
execution, said: "It is unbecoming a free people to stake their liberties
upon the successful jugglery of party politicians and interested office seekers, rather than a bold and determined resolution to maintain them at
every hazard."[67] Privately, Gist had confided to William Porcher Miles, the
secessionist congressman from Charleston District, his preference that
South Carolina move in concert with other Southern states rather than
undertaking any unilateral disunion. "I have not the least doubt," he wrote,
"that South Carolina would sustain her [Congressional] members in almost anything they might do in concerted action with the Southern mem-

bers, or any considerable portion of them." A resolution was accordingly introduced into the South Carolina Senate "that South Carolina, still deferring to her Southern sisters, nevertheless respectfully announce to them that, in her judgment, the safety and honor of the slaveholding states imperatively demand a speedy separation from other states of the Confederacy, and earnestly invite the slave-holding states to inaugurate the movement of Southern separation, in which she pledge herself promptly to unite." The resolution passed by an extremely close vote of twenty-two to nineteen. A stronger resolution for unilateral action was then introduced in the House, to the effect that "the Constitution of the United States, ordained and established to 'insure domestic tranquility,' has proven a failure, and the union of these States, so far as the fraternal relations are concerned, is dissolved; and, whereas, the highest intents of the slaveholding states demand that this dissolution shall in form be consummated, which consummation will probably involve the necessity of a resort to arms." This motion, however, was tabled by a vote of sixty-six to forty-four: not even the hotspur state was ready yet to face the possibility of war with the United States. W. S. Mullins of Marion District next introduced a less bellicose resolution "that the State of South Carolina is now ready to act with the slaveholding States of this Confederacy, or with such of them as desire present action in the formation of a Southern Confederacy." An effort to table the Mullins resolution on December 15 failed by a vote of fifty-one to sixty-one, but Mullins withdrew his resolution in deference to Christopher Memminger's resolution, which became part of the resolution finally adopted.[68]

The John Brown affair gave the fire-eaters hope that they could revive the secessionist spirit that had swept the state during the nullification crisis of 1833 and the secession crisis of 1850. South Carolina responded to the excitement of the John Brown affair by appropriating $100,000 for military preparedness; by sending invitations to other Southern states for a conference "to concert measures for united action" in order to obtain new terms as the price of remaining in the Union; and by dispatching Christopher G. Memminger as a special commissioner to Virginia "to express to the authorities of that state, the cordial sympathy of the people of South Carolina with the people of Virginia, and their earnest desire to unite with them in measures of common defense." W. W. Boyce wrote to Memminger proposing that he entice the Virginians into disunion while "letting them suppose that they are leading." Memminger should castigate the Harpers Ferry raid as an "outrage," an attack not only

on Virginia but on South Carolina as well. He should assure the Virginians that "we stand with Virginia in this fray and all its consequences."
The fire-eaters clearly found Virginia's lack of enthusiasm for disunion
disheartening. Even so, by a "conservative estimate" almost half of South
Carolina's House and more than half of its Senate were ready to secede
in 1859. Not quite ready to go it alone, the state nevertheless took a decisive step toward disunion.[69]

There were still a few voices of moderation in the Palmetto state. "John
Brown was only a symptom not more alarming . . . than many others,"
William Henry Trescot wrote to Senator James Henry Hammond. "I don't
relish the idea of being frightened from our propriety by such a vagabond."
Hammond began to draft a Constitutional Amendment, which he hoped
to offer as a means by which slavery might be preserved within the context of the Union:

> All the rights to and of property of any kind which existed under the Consti-
> tution or laws or customs of each or any State, before the adoption of this and
> which were not surrendered by it, shall be fully recognized by this government
> in all its branches: shall be in no wise impaired by any act of any Department
> of it: shall be thoroughly protected in each and all of the Public Territories until
> a Territory by being admitted into this Union as a Sovereign State, shall be-
> come authorized and enabled to protect whatever is [illegible].

Surely he must have known, however, that such an amendment had no
chance of passing in the polarized political atmosphere following the John
Brown episode. How many in the North would support an amendment
to guarantee slavery? And how many in the South believed that there was
any longer a place for the South in the Union? Hammond's longtime
friend Isaac Hayne wrote him that "the masses of this State would, you
may be assured, rejoice in any movement tending to disunion, either on
the part of Virginia or Georgia, and would be glad to move *pari passo* with
either, and run the hazard of any further cooperation." Dispirited, Hammond confessed to William Gilmore Simms that he returned to Washington "more reluctantly than John Brown did to the gallows." The self-cen-
tered Hammond could never have comprehended Brown's embrace of
self-sacrifice; he could only understand that Brown's actions had put additional burdens on his own shoulders. "But for Brown's raid I should have
resigned certainly. I had my letter written and was holding for the meeting of the legislature."[70]

More and more South Carolina "moderates" were wavering. Writing to a friend about the fate of the Union, James McCarty concluded that "the only chance of saving it is to bring about some collision, which will show us the strength of the conservative element in the North. This element I have always considered as large enough to keep the Democratic Party in power with the aid of the South. If I am mistaken in this, my hope is gone." But "moderate" wavering was not enough for the fire-eaters. "So long as the Democratic party is a 'National' organization," Robert Barnwell Rhett, editor of the fire-eating *Charleston Mercury*, declared, "and so long as our public men trim their sails with an eye to either its favor or enmity, just so long need we hope for no Southern action."[71]

All the same, the new year brought renewed attacks on slavery in the name of John Brown. Ralph Waldo Emerson told a Salem audience in January that abolitionism was simply an inevitable response to slavery. "Who makes the abolitionist? The slaveholder. The sentiment of mercy is the natural recoil which the laws of the universe provide to protect mankind from destruction by savage passions." It was impossible, the transcendentalist maintained, not to sympathize with John Brown's "courage, and disinterestedness, and the love that casts out fear." Those who failed to sympathize with the martyr were lacking in "sensibility and self-respect." To those of "savage passions," however, Emerson's deification of John Brown as the "disinterested" champion of "mercy" transcended both evidence and common sense.[72]

In June, Charles Sumner, the senator from Massachusetts, returned to the Senate to deliver an address castigating slavery. In 1856, after his "Crime against Kansas" speech had "insulted" South Carolina Senator Andrew Pickens Butler, Sumner had been brutally beaten in the Senate chamber by Butler's cousin, South Carolina Congressman Preston S. Brooks. Having selected a gutta-percha cane as his weapon, Brooks had approached the seated Sumner from behind and struck him repeatedly over the head. Trying in vain to stand, Sumner had wrenched his bolted desk from the floor while other senators grabbed the enraged Brooks. It was three years before Sumner again occupied his Senate seat, but Massachusetts reelected him, keeping his seat vacant until his return. Now Sumner stood in the Senate chamber to declare that "American Slavery, as defined by existing law, stands forth as the greatest organized Barbarism on which the sun now looks."[73]

On Independence Day Henry David Thoreau spoke at Brown's burial place. "The North, I mean the LIVING North, was suddenly all transcendental," he noted. "It went beyond the human law, it went behind the

apparent failure, and recognized eternal justice and glory." Thoreau echoed Emerson's disparagement of those who failed to see Brown's nobility. "When a noble deed is done, who is likely to appreciate it? Those who
are noble themselves," he declared. "How can a man behold the light who
has no inward light?" Thoreau asked. Brown's detractors, he charged,
could not even *recite* poetry, let alone write it. "Show me a man who feels
bitterly towards John Brown, and let me hear what noble verse he can
repeat. He'll be as dumb as if his lips were stone."[74]

The renewed Northern approbation of John Brown really rankled
Southern honor. The Southern press voiced complaints against what they
considered the North's "pharisaical boast of 'holier than thou,' which they
are constantly uttering as a reproach to the South." John Brown in fact
became a major issue in North Carolina's 1860 gubernatorial election. In
an address to the Democratic State Convention in Raleigh, incumbent
governor John W. Ellis attacked what he called the "unlawful acts" of the
North. "How can the South expect protection to property from those who
aid and abet the assassin and murder as this party did in the case of John
Brown?" he asked. "We had two parties, Democrats and Whigs, but now
democracy is surrounded by antagonists known as Black Republicans."
Ellis's speech dramatized both the climate of fear resulting from Brown's
raid and the general identification of abolitionism with the Republican
party in the South.[75]

Republicans opposed slavery; therefore, reasoned myopic slaveholders,
Republicans endorsed John Brown, treason, insurrection, and murder.
Such subtlety as distinguishing between ends and means was viewed as
mere caviling. In an effort to combat such thinking, Abraham Lincoln
rejected any basis for identifying the Republican party with John Brown.
"You charge that we stir up insurrections among your slaves. We deny it,"
he declared in February. "And what is your proof? Harpers Ferry? John
Brown? John Brown was no Republican, and you have failed to implicate
a single Republican in his Harpers Ferry enterprise." But slaveholders
continued to fear a Republican victory in November. The Republicans
would not be satisfied merely with such acts as those John Brown had
committed; they would "aid and abet" the complete destruction of the
South.[76]

When the Democratic National Convention met in April in Charleston, South Carolina, the presence of John Brown was as palpable as that
of Banquo's ghost. Delegates from South Carolina were instructed "to re-
quire of that body the adoption of a platform of principles which will fully

and clearly recognize the rights of slaveholders to their persons and property in slaves, not in the states [alone] but also in the common Territo-
ries of the United States." If such a platform failed to carry the convention, the South Carolina delegates were instructed "to withdraw from such
convention." In a relatively close vote, the convention rejected such a platform in favor of Stephen A. Douglas's "popular sovereignty" position.
Forty-nine delegates from eight Southern states walked out. After fifty-
seven ballots failed to yield any agreement on a candidate, the remaining
Democrats adjourned. Six weeks later the Northern Democrats nominated Douglas as their candidate. The Southern Democrats, meeting separately, nominated Vice-President John C. Breckinridge as their candidate.[77]

The Republicans held their national convention in May in Chicago.
There they not only nominated Abraham Lincoln as their presidential
candidate but also passed a resolution declaring "that the maintenance
inviolate of the rights of the States, and especially the right of each State
to order and control its own domestic institutions according to its own
judgment exclusively, is essential to that balance of powers on which the
perfection and endurance of our political fabric depends." That sounded
like the kind of commitment Southern moderates had been looking for.
But the Republicans went further. They made their repudiation of John
Brown explicit in a resolution denouncing "the lawless invasion by armed
force of the soil of any state or territory, no matter under what pretext,
as among the gravest of crimes." The resolution passed unanimously.[78]

But slaveholders and their spokesmen persisted in listening only to
their own myths. In the months following John Brown's raid fire-eaters
used the event as an excuse to heap more fuel on their secessionist
bonfires. William Gilmore Simms "wondered how the North could coun-
tenance the actions of John Brown and other zealots who would not rest
until slavery had been abolished." Warning that "the irrepressible conflict
must come," Simms called on his state to defend slavery by force of arms.[79]

As the John Brown social drama unfolded during the presidential campaign of 1860, a curious series of events began to occur in North Carolina, almost as though the moderates finally saw the abyss of disunion ahead
and were trying desperately to revive the unionism of the Old North State.
Until May 15 Salisbury's *Carolina Watchman* used the North Carolina state
seal, bearing the words "Constitution and Law," as its emblem. After May
22, however, the paper adopted a new emblem, an eagle clutching in his
claws a ribbon upon which the words "Pluribus Unum" were imprinted.
In the background was an American flag. This is but one of a series of

symbolic changes that helped build a unionist movement in North Carolina in 1860. What is most significant about the *Carolina Watchman*, however, is that a newspaper with considerable influence in Rowan and surrounding counties switched the focus of its attention from state and local
problems to matters of national interest, in which it showed an overwhelming concern for preserving the Union. Democratic threats of resistance in the event of a Republican victory were met with editorials urging, "Wake Up! Union men of Rowan."[80]

In the presidential campaign the *Watchman* endorsed the Constitutional Union Party's candidate, the "Hon. John Bell of Tennessee." Bell had
considerable strength throughout North Carolina, due in part to a hasti-
ly organized effort by Whigs after John Brown's raid to elect congressmen
and other public officials who were friendly to the Union. Bell supporters launched vigorous attacks against Breckinridge, warning that "treason
is abroad in North Carolina." The *Watchman* reported that "one of Breckinridge's electors in this state came out on the stump and distinctly declared that in the event of Lincoln's election he would vote for resistance
at once and before Lincoln was installed in office." There was a genuine
movement for disunion in North Carolina, but it was a small one, pushed
by a few fire-eaters and propagandists. There was little love for Lincoln
in the Old North State, but most Tarheels believed that if he were elected
he could be checked by the Congress. "Let all good men in every section
do all in their power to defeat Lincoln," the *Watchman* urged, "but if he is
elected let us show him that we have a Senate that detests his abomina-
ble heretics and that we will compel him to fill the important part of the
government with good conservative men." But after John Brown's raid,
not even North Carolina, a state once overwhelmingly unionist, was able
to reunite Union forces. After the election, even North Carolina disintegrated into the final, fatal secession.[81]

The slaveholding South was outraged at the Republican electoral victory, depicting it as a victory for the spirit of John Brown. "They have invaded our States and killed our citizens," thundered the *New Orleans Daily
Crescent*, "and finally they have capped the mighty pyramid of unfraternal
enormities by electing Abraham Lincoln to the Chief Magistracy." In
Charleston, South Carolina, Mary Boykin Chesnut overheard someone ex-
claim, upon hearing of Lincoln's election, "Now that the black radical Republicans have the power I suppose they will Brown us all." As she noted
in her journal what she had heard, Chesnut added, "No doubt of it."[82]
Amidst this crisis, the *Richmond Enquirer* declared, "the public mind" of

the South was tossed "like the storm-whipped billows of an enraged sea." After Lincoln's victory, it was fatally easy for many Southerners to believe the entire North had become abolitionist. Since no Northern intellectuals had sympathized with the South after John Brown's raid, declared William Gilmore Simms, the South had no choice but secession.[83]

Lincoln's election completed the radicalization of Francis W. Pickens that the social drama following the raid had initiated. On November 30 the former moderate addressed the South Carolina General Assembly: "I would be willing to appeal to the God of battles," he declared defiantly, "if need be, cover the state with ruin, conflagration, and blood rather than submit." On December 12 the legislature elected him governor, and on December 20 South Carolina seceded from the Union, once again invoking John Brown when they declared that the free states "have encouraged and assisted thousands of our slaves to leave their homes; and those who remain, have been incited by emissaries, books, and pictures, to servile insurrection." Before it was over, South Carolina would indeed be covered with ruin, conflagration, and blood. But in the end the state would submit anyway.[84]

The passion of John Brown resonates with the stylized character of an initiation ceremony, an initiation into the status of martyr. In this rite of passage Brown was propelled by the root paradigm of martyrdom, embossed upon the actual events of history by a social drama governed partly by judicial edict and partly by its own inner logic. It brought before Brown's consciousness a crown to be won not so much by a meritorious life as by a painful death. Ritual seems often to achieve genuinely cathartic effects in societies, seems to bring about real transformations of individual character and of social relationships. One of the functions of ritual is to induce people to want to do what has to be done, to transform the necessary into the desirable. There is thus a sense in which the symbolic actions of ritual actually create society. It is in this sense that John Brown's martyrdom made the election of 1860 into a referendum on the future of slavery. And it certainly made the Civil War a war against slavery, regardless of Lincoln's initial position that it was only a war to save the Union, nothing more.[85]

The root paradigm of martyrdom—with its rich symbolism of blood and paradise—fortified John Brown for the final trial of will. "I am yet too young to understand that God is any respector of persons," he declared at his trial. "I believe that to have interfered as I have done—as I have always freely admitted that I have done—in behalf of His despised poor, was not wrong, but right. Now, if it is deemed necessary that I should forfeit my life for the furtherance of the ends of justice, and mingle my blood further with the blood of my children and with the blood of millions in this slave country whose rights are disregarded by wicked, cruel, and unjust enactments,—I submit; so let it be done!" John Brown had come to perceive that if he would be a winner then he must first become a loser. Once he understood that, once he understood he would have to die to set slaves free, he achieved a serenity of mind that never failed him, not even upon the scaffold. Under the control of the root paradigm, convinced that his death could accomplish what his life could not, Brown declined aid or escape. The shadow of death merely confirmed him all the more in his purpose.[86]

Such nearly inexplicable behavior provokes in some cultures the notion of fate or destiny to account for it. In Greek tragedy, which John Brown's passion closely parallels, the hero appears both freely to choose his behavior and at the same time to be helpless before the Fates, before the drama ultimately resolves through a catharsis inspired by pity and terror. In the case of John Brown, "the Fates" lay at the intersection of history and social drama. Sophocles could have written the plot.

PART TWO

Three Historiographical Forays

6

The South as a Folk Culture
David Potter and the Southern Enigma

David Potter was right, as usual. He had keen insights into his native South, especially regarding the secession crisis and the sectional conflict that led to it. But his most insightful essay was not about either the sectional conflict or the secession crisis. It was called "The Enigma of the South," and it was about the question of southern distinctiveness. Potter insisted that "to identify and investigate the distinctive features of Southern society" should rank high on the agenda for southern historians. As late as 1967, he noted that historians were still "far from agreeing about so basic a question as the nature of ante-bellum society."[1]

Historians and other scholars had, of course, pondered the singular personality of the South long before Potter, calling attention to its agrarianism, its backwardness, its conservatism, its individualism, its localism, its paternalism, its racism, its religious piety, and its violence. Since Potter's call to study southern distinctiveness, however, scholars have increasingly concerned themselves not merely with the search for distinctive qualities but also with efforts to analyze the significance of those qualities. Over the decades the debate has become sharper, more spirited, and more theoretically sophisticated. In particular, comparative studies of southern slave society with Brazilian, Caribbean, and other slave societies made it clear that the South's "Peculiar Institution" was all too common. While some commentators continued to maintain that differences between antebellum North and South were sufficient to justify regarding them as separate cultures (and thus inevitable adversaries on the battlefield), Potter was pointedly not one of them. But granting that there is good reason to doubt the region's vaunted "uniqueness," and conceding the futility of insisting upon its singularity, one might still question Drew Gilpin Faust's comment that Potter's call for the study of southern distinctiveness "now seems obsolete."[2]

§

To comprehend the southern paradox is to isolate both the authentic and the distinctive elements of southern culture. It is in the historical experience of the region that C. Vann Woodward finds the South's claims to a distinctive heritage. From a cosmopolitan perspective (as distinguished from a national perspective), it is the United States—not the South—that is peculiar among the peoples of the world. The South's historical experience set southerners apart from the rest of the country. That historical experience left southerners more observers than participants in the irony of American history. As Woodward notes, southern participation in the American myth of irresistible progress, success, and victory could—after all—"only be vicarious at best."[3]

But that heritage will remain an enigma unless we comprehend the culture within which that history was experienced. In his perceptive 1961 essay, "The Enigma of the South," Potter finds the South's essential distinctiveness embodied in what he calls "the culture of the folk," a culture that has withstood all the homogenizing onslaughts of commercial popular culture. He considers the relation between land and people "more direct and more primal" in the South than elsewhere in the nation. And he believes that "the relation of people to one another imparted a distinctive texture as well as a distinctive tempo" to southern folk culture.[4]

Potter never explores, in "The Enigma of the South" or in other writings, the implications of that insight, nor does he even describe what he means by the "folk culture" of the South. He would seem to have been influenced by Robert Redfield's conception of folk culture as "an organization or integration of conventional understandings" in a folk society in which behavior is "traditional, spontaneous, and uncritical" and in which "the patterns of conduct are clear and remain constant throughout the generations." But Redfield's characterization of the folk society as "small, isolated, nonliterate, and homogeneous" is hardly an apt description of the South in either its old or its new incarnations. In fact, it is even more applicable to anthropology's "ideal type" of truly primitive society than to the folk societies in which Redfield conducted his own fieldwork.[5]

Potter would appear also to have been influenced by the arguments of the southern sociologist Howard Odum that "the biography of the South is essentially the story of the folk." Acknowledging the significance of social stratification and social change in the South, Odum nevertheless insists that "the folk society of the South is well nigh all inclusive and is reflected on many levels of time and class." But despite class differentiation Odum finds southern folk culture "strangely unified in its complex fabric of many weavings." He marvels at "how timeless and resistless are the processes and products of folk society" despite social change.[6]

If Odum's concept of folk society is more complex and more convincing than that of Redfield, especially when it is applied to the eighteenth- and nineteenth-century South, it still remains more focused on the rural and quasipeasant experience than one might wish. Southern distinctiveness may have been embodied in a folk culture when the South was overwhelmingly agricultural; but if folk culture exists only in rural societies, is the concept of any value in analyzing the twentieth-century South? Is there a folk in Atlanta, in Charlotte, in Birmingham, in Dallas, in Miami, in Memphis, in Richmond, in New Orleans?

It is surely no derogation of the achievements of Potter, Redfield, and Odum to suggest that their concept of folk culture depends on an equation of "folk" with "rural" and "static" that is not supported by modern folklorists, who accept neither such a priori limitations as Redfield's insistence on isolation, illiteracy, and homogeneity nor Odum's and Potter's dichotomy of folk *versus* urban-industrial as the hallmarks of folk culture. The assimilation of cultural patterns through cultural contact has been basic to all the folk cultures, rural and urban, past and present, that folklorists have ever studied. And folklorists have found folk tradition to be dynamic, not static, changing slowly but inexorably. Folklorists who have studied the folk in cities have found a dynamic mutual interaction between oral traditions and literate traditions.[7]

Neither Redfield, Odum, nor Potter is as specific as one would wish in distinguishing between folk *culture* and folk *society*. The anthropologist Clifford Geertz views culture as the mental rules governing behavior, while society is the field of action in which behavior takes place. Culture, he claims, "denotes an historically transmitted pattern of meanings embodied in symbols, a system of inherited conceptions expressed in symbolic forms by means of which men communicate, perpetuate, and develop their knowledge about and attitudes toward life." For example, the concept of royalty is cultural, but the embodiment of that concept in monarchies and courts is social. "Culture is not a power, something to which social events, behaviors, institutions or processes can be causally attributed," notes Geertz, "it is a context, something within which they can be intelligibly—that is, thickly—described."[8]

To penetrate the southern paradox, then, one must penetrate its context—the folk culture of the South. If culture is context rather than cause, then clearly the relation between culture and society is not one-to-one. Culture—because it exists in people's heads—may change at a different rate than society. Culture may forge ahead of social realities or lag behind. For instance, the idea of independence may have attained cultural legitimacy for American colonists or southern secessionists before independence was a social reality. In much the same way, African rulers and African deities may have retained a cultural legitimacy among enslaved Africans in the New World society in which they no longer possessed social power.[9]

Since historians customarily regard the study of change over time as a disciplinary commitment, folk culture—regarded as intrinsically static—seemed to be of little relevance to history. By ignoring folk culture, however, historians often succumbed to what Eric Hobsbawm calls "the temptation to isolate the phenomenon of overt crisis from the wider context of a society undergoing transformation." Anthropologists, for their part, typically concentrate on particular elements of culture in a single time frame. There has been a pervasively static quality in anthropological scholarship that misses the dynamic relationship between past and present that is inherent in the term "tradition." Folk culture and historical change are inextricably related. As E. P. Thompson notes, both "resistance to change and assent to change arise from the whole culture."[10]

Two major approaches to the study of past folk cultures have emerged among historians, each synthesizing (in various ways) theories and methods from both history and anthropology. One approach, called for convenience "historical ethnography," draws (in varying proportions) on the "symbolic anthropology" of Clifford Geertz, Mary Douglas, and Victor Turner, and on the *Annales* school of French social historians.[11]

The *Annales* historians, so called after the journal founded by Marc Bloch and Lucien Febvre in 1929, pioneered "a new kind of history" concerned with the social and cultural past of human beings previously considered "inarticulate." Emphasizing the structures of social, cultural, and technological life in a given geographic environment over long time periods, they asked new kinds of questions of new kinds of evidence, questions about the material basis of human existence and about the relationships of human beings to their environment in the past. Rather than wars, treaties, and monarchs, they stressed the importance of geography, ecology, and demography. Their achievement is impressive, but it has not been accomplished without loss. In *Annales* scholarship the formerly inarticulate masses do achieve equal representation: Everyone is rendered equally inarticulate. But one need share neither the structural determinism bias of the *Annales* "school" nor the semiotic bias of "historical ethnography" to recognize in the synthesis of the two an important new approach to the history of the folk.[12]

Perhaps this *mentalité* is what W. J. Cash meant by "mind" when he wrote *The Mind of the South*. He was writing neither of rational capability nor of intellectual expression but rather of what he called a "fairly definite mental pattern, associated with a fairly definite social pattern—a complex of established relationships and habits of thought, sentiments, prejudices, standards and values, and associations of ideas, which, if it is not common strictly to every group of white people in the South, is still common in one appreciable measure or another." Cash's southern "mind" is an essentially literary device, as much a Weberian ideal type as is his "Man at the Center." Sociologists regard an ideal type as testable, but perhaps it is sufficient to ask whether or not it makes sense of actual facts.[13]

As historians began to make efforts to uncover the past "from the bottom up," students of the South, like their counterparts in other fields, turned to anthropology as a source of new conceptual tools with which to make fresh appraisals of old evidence. A pioneer in this effort was Bertram Wyatt-Brown, who in a stimulating essay describes the Old South in terms much like Odum's folk society. In "The Ideal Typology and Antebellum Southern History," he points out that the southern folk, "stressing oral over literate means of expression," developed "a family centered, particularistic, ascriptive culture" that honored "qualities related to gender, age, racial appearance, bloodlines."[14]

A decade later, influenced by Julian Pitt-Rivers's anthropological studies of honor in Mediterranean societies, Wyatt-Brown builds on this "ideal typology" in his books *Southern Honor* and *Yankee Saints and Southern Sinners*. The southern honor ethic, he maintains, provided a "structure to life and meaning to valor, hierarchy, and family protection." The concept of honor taught conformity to tradition and community consensus; self-respect depended on the opinion of others. Southern honor had more to do with being honored than with behaving honorably. Since one's inner worth was determined by one's public reputation, one had to maintain an image at all times. A man had to be willing to lay his life on the line for his own reputation as well as that of his family and community. An insult to a man's mother, sister, or wife was an insult to the man himself. To lose one's reputation was to lose one's self-esteem. Nothing could be more painful.[15]

There were corollaries to the code of honor. It was "an essential component of personality, family, identity, and moral position" to own as many possessions as possible, especially human possessions. And when the law came in conflict with the code of honor, honor generally took precedence. Political rhetoric was especially volatile because honor was at stake. Words like "defamed" and "persecuted" were prevalent, along with almost constant reference to "manliness" and "nobility." Death in defense of the community was a path to glory and remembrance, while servile submission was disgrace. Thus even counsels of patience were apt to be considered cowardice.[16]

In his study of the political culture of the Old South, Kenneth Greenberg follows Wyatt-Brown's lead in one direction. Conjoining Wyatt-Brown's concept of southern honor to Clifford Geertz's conception of ideology as "a part of the process of symbolic formulation—a template or blueprint for the organization of social and psychological processes, like a genetic system," Greenberg contends in his *Masters and Statesmen* that slavery created a unique political culture that fused honor (the need to exercise power over others) and republicanism (the fear of being subjected to the power of others). That combination of honor and republicanism shaped not only the public life of the South but also the region's response to sectional conflict. Republican fears of enslavement combined with honor's demand that inferiority be spurned and insult be punished to make disunion seem a rational imperative. Southern political figures, intellectually trapped by the "never submit" rhetoric of the duel, found compromise culturally alien.[17]

Edward Ayers follows Wyatt-Brown's lead in another direction in his *Vengeance and Justice*, extending the concept of honor into the postbellum period and analyzing its impact on the criminal justice system. Like Greenberg, Ayers roots honor in slavery. "Slavery," he notes, "generated honor." And in a society of hard-drinking men, a society in which only "one standard of worth can reign" (that is, an "overweening concern with the opinions of others"), "alcohol and honor combined to create a volatile mixture" in which violence was both more prevalent and more harshly punished than in the North. Men when insulted were required to react in violent defiance or face the loss of honor. "Any man living in the South had trouble if he chose not to respect honor's dictates," Ayers suggests. "He might find it difficult to convince other men his stance was not mere cowardice."[18]

Throughout her career Drew Gilpin Faust has used a variety of anthropological concepts with great intelligence and with great perception. She acknowledges the "enormous influence" of Geertz's analysis of belief systems, with his attention to language and his representation of culture as "models for" and "models of" behavior. "In his commitment to reading all the world as a text," Faust writes, "Geertz gave historians a means of moving beyond the formal written legacies of an elite few; he made thought an integral part of all social action; he helped transform the study of ideas in history from the rather narrow analysis of intellectuals to a much broader investigation of people thinking." From her first book, *A Sacred Circle* and her influential essay "The Rhetoric and Ritual of Agriculture in Antebellum South Carolina," through her *James Henry Hammond and the Old South* and *The Creation of Confederate Nationalism* to her magisterial *Mothers of Invention*, she has revealed, whether explicitly or implicitly, the significance of anthropological analysis to southern history.[19]

Another approach to the study of past folk cultures has been developed by Australian anthropologists and historians and has come to be known as *ethnographic history*. For scholars of the South it is perhaps best exemplified in Rhys Isaac's *The Transformation of Virginia*, his prize-winning study of religious revival and political revolution in eighteenth-century Virginia. Strongly influenced by the anthropologist-turned-historian Greg Dening, Isaac both broadens and deepens our understanding of the effects of that transformation on the slave quarters as well as on the "common planter's place" and in the "gentleman's seat," on the parson as well as on the squire, on cock fights as well as on court days, on folk culture as well as on the College of William and Mary.[20]

Ethnographic history makes heavy demands on its practitioners, who must begin with what Greg Dening calls "the most difficult thing of all to see: the experience of past actors as they experienced it, and not that experience as we in hindsight experience it for them." Every document, every piece of evidence, every "text," had its origins as a cultural action, as a presentation-of-self, as a "performance." Thus at the heart of ethnographic history is the requirement that historians or ethnographers remain "conscious of their *own* enculturated nature," conscious that the past they discover is inseparable from the mode and the occasion of their own discovery. In normative history the past is no more likely to recognize itself than

natives are to recognize themselves in ethnography. But history, in Dening's words, is "both a metaphor of the past and a metonymy of the
present." "Be wary," he warns us, "of the history that claims to be separate
from the circumstances of its telling or to have only one meaning."[21]

Ethnographic history seeks not merely to delineate the surface of events
but also to comprehend the skeletal substructure beneath the tough hide
of behavior and expression—the attitudes and emotions of the historical
actors expressed in events. Not readily apparent in everyday life, this skeletal substructure can only be glimpsed through the interaction of people
within the boundaries they place around their own cultural categories.
These boundaries and categories are constantly shifting like sands on a
beach, now piled up around the bulkheads of social structure, now eroded by the riptides of historical events. The effort to comprehend these
underlying attitudes and emotions is what makes ethnographic history
ethnographic. The effort to comprehend this constant negotiation is what
makes ethnographic history historical.[22]

By converging many narratives, by blending metaphors and models,
and by letting the historical actors speak for themselves, ethnographic
history attempts to allow meanings to become more visible, to generate
not proofs but possibilities. By converging *texts* with the *context* of power
and resistance on the slave plantations, ethnographic history hopes to
reveal something about the emotional *texture* of life within an institution
that—however humanized it may have been by occasional human kind-
nesses—rested ultimately upon violence and the threat of violence. To
come to grips with the events and "texts" of *particular* human history is
to contend also with the broader dynamics of universal human history.[23]

The scholar who would undertake ethnography of the southern folk in
past time is confronted by numerous problems. One must begin with
careful ethnographic description, but merely to recognize the importance
of ethnographic description hardly guarantees its attainment. The first
problem is cultural comprehension. When trying to understand folk culture, we must do more than merely interpret our subjects—their customs
and shared beliefs—in terms of our own culture and priorities. This has
led to such nonsense as the establishment of cultural genres by scholarly
fiat. Our problem is to comprehend how the folk make sense for themselves out of their culture. Indeed, we should do well to remember that
culture itself—in most scholarly usage—is actually a logical construct

created in the mind of the observer, who derives the construct from the behavior of the cultural actors. The problem for us is just how much a logical construct can convey an accurate picture of the culture we are trying to understand, a culture in the past, no longer available for *in situ* study. Obviously the qualifications for ethnography of past folk cultures are not easily come by. The closer we are culturally to the group we are trying to interpret, the more difficult it is for us to explain it to others; the closer we are culturally to our audience, the greater our difficulty in understanding our subject. It may be easier for southern scholars to comprehend the culture than to make it comprehensible to outsiders. If, on the other hand, the scholar is from outside the region, communication with an outside audience may be easier than comprehending the folk culture itself.[24]

The scholar of folk culture in past time has much to learn from the folklorist's emphasis on context and on the relation of parts to wholes in culture. From the earliest anthropological studies of isolated and self-contained primitive communities came the characteristic anthropological tendency toward holism. The student of southern folk culture would do well to bear in mind, however, that the relation of parts to wholes in folk culture is more complex than in primitive cultures. The South has never been a land of isolated, self-sufficient subsistence farmers, lacking contact with the centers of commerce and intellect, but rather a region that has produced staples for the world economy. In fact Immanuel Wallerstein views southern culture as itself a product of the region's place in the nineteenth-century capitalist world-system. "To pursue their interests," he argues, "the dominant economic forces" in this agricultural export region had "to create a cultural entity known as the South."[25]

The syncretic relationship between folk tradition and the centers of commerce and intellect has been an important element in the development of southern folk culture; but the most significant syncretic relationship has been that between the African and British components of that culture. The central theme of southern folk history might well be described as the achievement of cultural integration. Cultural integration generally went unrecognized, partly because the South spent a great deal of energy in an effort to create a society that was racially segregated and partly because early students of the culture attributed British origins to many African elements in the culture and African origins to many British elements. As Winthrop Jordan notes in another connection, "many absurd assertions" have been advanced by scholars who tried to compare two things "about one or both of which they were ignorant."[26]

Southern folk culture developed out of a communicative process among the various folk cultures of uprooted Africans and uprooted Britons, commencing with the arrival of the first settlers and their attempts to adjust inherited cultural meanings to one another and to a new environment. Neither African nor British traditions were unaffected by the other, and the influence was often reciprocal. Since people neither remember nor forget without reason, conscious or unconscious, one of the major influences upon the development of southern folk culture was the similarity of any given element of Old World folk culture to elements in the tradition of the other race. Elements of the culture had to be meaningful, memorable, in fact unforgettable, or they suffered the fate of forgettable things. They were forgotten. In the South, and only in the South, a genuinely biracial folk culture was created. African Americans in the North were immigrants into a preexisting culture; in the South they were settlers.

David Potter was correct when he stated the South's best claim to historical distinctiveness can be found in its folk culture, despite his failure to explore its implications or even to indicate very clearly what he meant by the term. He certainly noted that folk culture has the advantage, missing in other purported explanations of the southern paradox, of resting upon the common folk culture of all southerners rather than upon a definition of the southern experience in terms of whites alone. And folk culture shows signs of greater longevity than other explanations. For instance southerners, regardless of race, tend to retain the essential elements of folk culture—to be religious, to embrace the private use of force, and to be rooted in their home place—to a greater degree than people from other regions.[27] Thus to understand southern folk culture in all its complexity is to understand something very fundamental—the essential character of southerners.

7

The Bold Fischer Man

David Hackett Fischer and the British Sources of American Folk Culture

David Hackett Fischer is nothing if not audacious. Out of folklife, he develops a model for the way American culture constructed itself. Skillfully weaving the tapestry of American regional folklife in impressive scope and detail, Fischer places folklife at the very center of American history. Seldom if ever has a historian genuflected so deeply to the power of folk culture. It is Fischer's bold thesis that the major dialects of American speech, the major regional patterns of American life, the continuing conflicts between customary ways of thinking about order, power, and freedom, and the complex dynamics of American politics all derive principally from British folkways brought to America between 1629 and 1775.

In *Albion's Seed*, the first book of a series intended to comprise a cultural history of the United States, Fischer takes on the problems of cultural origins and cultural meaning.[1] Earlier scholars saw cultural origins and cultural meaning as separate issues, but in the poststructural age they are necessarily intertwined. Each modifies the other. Fischer does not share the elitist fallacy of the Guardians of the Temple of Conservative Values.[2] He knows that American culture is more than their received canon of names, events, places, and dates. He knows that any real history of American culture, therefore, must be more than a narrative of that received canon. And thus Fischer writes not narrative history but problem history.

The emerging regional cultures of America, Fischer contends, were especially influenced by four large waves of British immigration: English Royalists and indentured servants from the south and west of England to the Chesapeake; settlers from the borderlands of north Britain and Ireland to the southern backcountry; English Quakers from the midlands to the Delaware Valley; and English Puritans from East Anglia to New England. Folk from each of these British regions spoke distinctive dialects of English, had distinctive folkways by which they conducted their everyday lives, and had distinctive customs and conceptions of order, power, and freedom. To the folklorist's longstanding concern for folk speech, vernacular architecture, onomastics, death customs, folk religion and magic, foodways, folk costume, and labor lore, Fischer adds consideration of what he calls family ways, marriage ways, gender ways, sex ways, child-rearing ways, age ways, learning ways, logic ways, sport ways, time ways, land ways, rank ways, wealth ways, order ways, and freedom ways. He does not consider such folkloric staples as riddles, proverbs, and legends, except in relation to death customs and folk belief. Nor does he concern himself with folk tales, folk music, ballads, or folksongs, folk dance, folk drama, folk gestures, or folk crafts.

Although today, Fischer notes, fewer than 20 percent of the American population have *any* British ancestors at all, he sets out to demonstrate (folkway by folkway) his contention that these four British regional cultures continue to exercise a decisive influence on American life.[3]

In speech ways Fischer traces the Virginia accent to seventeenth-century rural dialects in the south and west of England, overlaid with a veneer of London speech. Border English, he notes, was the progenitor of a family of American dialects called southern highland speech. The Delaware Valley dialect developed from the language of England's north midlands, while the distinctive nasal New England twang derives from an English regional dialect called the Norfolk whine.[4]

The vernacular architecture of Virginia rested upon a foundation drawn mainly from the south of England. The backcountry, in the meantime, developed a distinctive style of cabin architecture related to vernacular traditions inherited from the borderlands of north Britain. Building ways in the Delaware Valley were jointly shaped by the values of Quakers and Pietists and a vocabulary of vernacular forms from England's north midlands, while New England developed a vernacular architecture tradition of wood-framed, box-built, clapboarded cottages built upon East Anglian and Kentish models.[5]

The patriarchal and hierarchical nature of Virginia family ways was reflected in household structure as well as in naming, inheritance, and burial patterns. Backcountry family ways were marked by the persistence of the clan—a large number of mutually supportive nuclear households who shared a common name and the memory of a common origin. Delaware Valley family ways emphasized socialization and spiritual support more than patriarchal family politics. A distinctive feature of the New England family was the idea of the covenanted family, characterized by unique patterns of household composition and family size.[6]

In the southern backcountry, marriage ways often involved rituals of bridal abduction, but actual abductions—sometimes voluntary, sometimes not—were common. In the backcountry, men and women married much younger than in the other regions. Virginia Anglicans considered marriage a sacred bond, a bond not to be sundered by humans. For eighty years Virginia allowed but one separation and no divorces. New England Yankees, on the other hand, regarded marriage as a civil contract, rather than a sacred bond, and distinctive marriage ways were reflected in courtship customs, in rituals of contract and precontract, and in the ages and seasons of marriage. The Delaware Valley concept of marriage as a loving agreement rather than either civil contract or sacred bond reflected the distinctive marriage ways of England's north midlands. Men and women wed later in the Delaware Valley than in the other regions.[7]

A deep and highly explosive sense of inequality pervaded gender ways in Virginia, featuring male insistence upon the primacy of patriarchy while females asserted a strong sense of English liberty. In the backcountry, custom made men into soldiers and women into workers, and gender relations were regulated by complex rituals of love and violence. A popular Quaker proverb in the Delaware Valley proclaimed that "in souls there is no sex." Gender ways were more nearly equal than those of any other section, but there as elsewhere gender relations remained far from equal. Gender ways in New England were organized into a system of delicate complexity, characterized by the idea of a covenant between unequals.[8]

Distinctive sex ways in Virginia promoted a double standard of high intensity. "Virginia gentlemen" were socialized into predatory sexual roles. The backcountry's more open expressions of sexuality, on the other hand, could be seen in dress ways, in living arrangements, and in higher rates of prenuptial pregnancy. In the Delaware Valley, sexual relations even *within* marriage were condemned by some Quakers except for procreation. Sex ways were characterized by a spirit of sexual asceticism, evident in a cultivated prudery and low rates of prenuptial pregnancy. Quakers severely punished what they considered sexual deviance. In New England a strong sexual bond prevailed within marriage, but Yankee sex ways strongly repressed premarital and extramarital sexual activity.[9]

Child-rearing customs in New England were characterized by "will breaking" in early childhood and "sending out" in youth. The child's will was not broken in Virginia but "severely bent against itself" in complex rituals of socialization and stoic ideas of proper conduct. Delaware Valley child rearing featured neither will breaking nor will bending but will bracing in processes of "guarded education." Instead of being sent out, Quaker youths were kept at home for prolonged periods. Backcountry child rearing, at least for males, was positive will building, as a means of instilling a sense of courage and manly honor. Female child rearing, on the other hand, concentrated on patience, sacrifice, obedience, and other "domestic virtues."[10]

The regions even named children in different ways. In Virginia's unique onomastics, eldest children were named for grandparents more often than for parents, and for European warriors and kings more often than for biblical figures. Backcountry onomastics exhibited distinctive forename frequencies, producing large numbers of Andrews, Patricks, and Davids. Fischer notes that, by contrast, Harvard College admitted no Patrick to its student body for two hundred years. First-born children in New England were normally named for their parents. Nearly all (90 percent) New England forenames were biblical. In the Delaware Valley, Fischer points to a three-generation, bilateral gender-reversing pattern in which first sons were named for the wife's father, first daughters for the father's mother. Delaware Valley names ran to a mix of biblical and plain north-midland names.[11]

Patriarchal respect for seniority rather than for old age itself characterized Virginia age ways. In the backcountry, some of the elderly were exalted and others were degraded, depending upon their strength, cunning, and courage. From the Calvinist concept of old age as a "sign," New England age ways fostered ideals of veneration for elders and condescension toward the young. The elderly were held in high respect as elder-teachers in the Delaware Valley rather than as elder-saints as in New England or as elder-patriarchs as in Virginia. Fischer says their busy roles made the word *elder* into an active verb in the Delaware Valley.[12]

Death ways in all four regions featured variations on the universal fatalism of the age. New England's distinctive death ways took the Puritan form of instrumental fatalism, quickening the pulse of life and creating unique death customs. Virginia's stoic fatalism was very different from Puritan fatalism. Delaware Valley death ways featured an optimistic fatalism quite unlike that of either New England or Virginia. Backcountry death ways were also fatalistic in yet another way. There death was seen as a cruel destroyer—purposeless, random, illegitimate, unknowable, and meaningless.[13]

There were more differences than similarities in the religious ways of the four regions. Virginians' worship services centered on a liturgical style in their Anglican churches, while the camp meetings of backcountry Christians drew upon the "new light" theology and field meetings of British border Christianity. New Englanders leaned toward more austere rituals of meeting and lecture, marked by special forms of prayer and preaching. In the Delaware Valley, on the other hand, rituals of worship among English Quakers and German Pietists emphasized the movement of the spirit rather than lecture or liturgy.[14]

Differences in religious ways in America were paralleled by differences in what Fischer calls magic ways. New Englanders, obsessed with witchcraft, held periodic purges. There were similar witch-hunts in Britain that were especially strong in East Anglia. For their part, Virginians worried little about witchcraft, but they tested fortune with gambling and games of chance. And they seemed virtually obsessed with fortune-books and astrology. Delaware Valley Quakers, like the Virginians, cared little for witchcraft. But they were also hostile to gambling and games of chance. Quakers, on the other hand, were quite uniquely obsessed with spiritualism, resurrection, and reincarnation. Fischer describes backcountry magic ways as exhibiting some interest in witchcraft and pragmatic superstition, but without the urgency that existed in New England.[15]

Learning ways varied widely among the four regions. Backcountry settlers distrusted both higher learning and education in general. While the backcountry exhibited low levels of literacy and cultivated a contempt for writing, it also manifested a highly developed oral tradition. Vernacular logic in the backcountry stressed empirical reasoning and experience. According to Fischer, backcountry proverbs strongly resembled formal north British systems of empirical and inductive logic in their epistemology. Virginia exhibited great inequalities in literacy and total education rates. The Virginia elite showed scant interest in common schooling but supported higher learning and the education of gentlemen. In New England, high rates of literacy, total education, and cultural achievement prevailed. New Englanders strongly supported both common schools and higher learning. New England produced the greatest proportion of cultural leaders in the *Dictionary of American Biography*, just as East Anglia produced the greatest proportion of cultural leaders in the *Dictionary of National Biography*. Distinctive forms of vernacular logic appeared in New England—such as the Yankee proverb, "Some folks are weatherwise; some folks are otherwise"—and in disjunctive reasoning in formal logical systems. Delaware Valley Quakers, on the other hand, supported common education (if it was controlled by the family and the meeting rather than the state) but were skeptical of higher learning. They considered reason as an inner light rather than a learned system and thought of reason as common sense. For them logical argument was a matter of reference to self-evident truths.[16]

Virginia food ways derived from southern England, while New England styles of cooking came from the customs of East Anglia. Virginians, even in modest homes, considered dining an important daily ritual, while New Englanders merely ate. Delaware Valley Quakers subscribed to a simple, ascetic cuisine called "Quaker food"—for example, dumplings and boiled puddings. Such classic Quaker dishes as cream cheese and dried beef were produced by slow heating and drying, techniques of preservation drawn from the north midlands. By changing the ingredients of British border cooking from oats and mutton to corn and pork, while retaining traditional border cooking methods of potboiling, panfrying, and hearth baking, the backcountry developed a distinctive cuisine.[17]

In the unique dress ways of the backcountry, gender distinctions were exaggerated both in male and female clothing. Horizontal seams across the chest and shoulders displayed the masculinity of the men, while loose bodices, tight waists, and short skirts proclaimed the women's femininity. These patterns, rooted in the British borderlands, continue to survive in the backcountry. Virginia dress ways stressed the sartorial display of rank and wealth. In the Delaware Valley, however, the plain style was elaborated in rules of fantastic complexity. Quakers especially preferred a neutral color known as Hodden gray after its north midland origin. New England dress ways required simple clothes and sad colors.[18]

Backcountry sport ways stressed martial arts—wrestling, fighting, running, leaping, weapon throwing, and shooting. Such contests were later organized as "Highland Games" and are considered by Fischer to be ancestors of modern track and field events. But blood sports were the favorite amusements of the Virginians. There, blood sports were organized into a hierarchy in which the size of the prey was proportionate to the social rank of the hunter. New England encouraged such "lawful recreation" as rule-bound communal games, but New Englanders disliked blood sports and games of chance. Fischer considers "the Boston Game" to be the origin of American football and "the town game" or "the New England game" to be the ancestor of baseball. Delaware Valley Quakers favored exercise for fitness—such as walking, skating, and swimming—and such "needful" recreation as gardening while exhibiting a hostility to both blood sports and the kinds of "needless" games favored by New Englanders.[19]

Backcountry work ways were reminiscent of British borderland work ways not only in the structure of a herding and farming economy but also in customary attitudes toward work. New England work ways, on the other hand, were noted for their Puritan work ethic, with a unique mix of commerce and agriculture like that of East Anglia. Virginia work ways exhibited a classic cultural ambivalence, scorning "base getting and unworthy penurious saving," while at the same time attempting to build up an estate to leave one's children. Quakers in the Delaware Valley displayed a distinctive worldly asceticism in their work ethic. As Fischer puts it, Quakers made play into work and made work into worship.[20]

New England Puritans held that time was money, and New England time ways were characterized by efforts to improve time, such as the invention of such things as the alarm clock and daylight saving time. Delaware Valley Quakers condemned haste. They sought not to improve time but to redeem it, to sanctify it and make it less worldly. Virginians sought neither to improve time nor to redeem it, but to kill it. They developed the unique idea of killing time. Time was hierarchy in Virginia. A servant's time was not his own, but a Virginia gentleman put his declaration of temporal independence on public display. If New Englanders improved time, if Quakers redeemed it, if Virginians killed it, backcountry settlers placed great value on passing the time as they had passed the time in the British borderlands.[21]

Unique land ways in the backcountry were based on a deep commitment to residential privacy (Fischer notes that Andrew Jackson called his house the Hermitage) combined with a deep sense of impermanence (expressed in high rates of internal migration). As in the British borderlands, the characteristic backcountry settlement was the isolated farmstead. New England patterns of land use featured an instrumental ecology that both preserved and exploited the land. Following East Anglian models, land went to yeoman proprietors in average holdings of sixty acres. Settlement patterns were characterized by compact towns with high persistence rates.

Virginia ecological attitudes were less communal, less instrumental, and less preservationist than in New England. Virginia land was parceled out to individual planters in grants ten times the size of New England land holdings. There was a moral ecology of great intensity and a strong tradition of stewardship in the Delaware Valley. Quakers favored living on middling-sized family farms rather than on either plantations as in Virginia or in towns as in New England.[22]

In rank ways, Virginia extended and deepened the upper and lower British social orders while at the same time reducing the middling ranks and degrading servants and slaves. New Englanders, on the other hand, truncated upper and lower British social orders. Invidious distinctions were carefully observed in the middling ranks, however. Neither Virginia's extended ranks nor New England's truncated ranks found favor in the Delaware Valley. Instead, Quaker rank ways displayed a system of stratification within a single order. In the southern backcountry, rank ways were characterized by a system of stratification without orders. There an obsession with equality of esteem coexisted with extreme inequalities of wealth.[23]

In wealth ways, the wealthiest 10 percent of the population in New England held 20 to 30 percent of the taxable property and 30 to 40 percent of estates in probate. This pattern was reminiscent of that among East Anglian villagers. Virginia's wealth ways reflected much greater inequalities, with the richest 10 percent owning 50 to 60 percent of the wealth. In the Delaware Valley, Philadelphia was more egalitarian than the towns of any other region, while the rural counties (where the richest 10 percent of the population owned 25 percent of the wealth) exhibited the most egalitarian patterns in the Western world before 1750. Fischer is surprised to find the highest levels of inequality in eighteenth-century America in the backcountry.[24]

Backcountry power ways—the politics of personal loyalty—seemed incomprehensible to other American regions, but they reflected the power ways of the north British borderlands. Power in Virginia, on the other hand, was oligarchical. Control was vested in a few county families. Voter turnout was high and stable, but elections were infrequent and irregular. New England's power ways favored a polity of town meetings and selectmen reminiscent of local government in East Anglia. Turnout was usually low in New England, but elections were frequent. And some elections did elicit high surges of voter turnout. Voting patterns in the Delaware Valley were also characterized by frequent elections and low voter turnout. The Quakers invented a county commission form of government there that still survives. Commissioners were considered cultural referees.[25]

Concepts of order varied widely among the four regions. Order meant *hierarchy* in Virginia, with its unique concepts of social disorder, means of keeping order, and treatment of the disorderly. Virginia developed a concept of everyone in the proper ranks, even if it was necessary to hold them there by force. Order meant *unity* in New England. As in Virginia, New Englanders developed distinctive means of keeping order and distinctive treatment of the disorderly. In the Delaware Valley, order meant *peace*, an unusual idea in the seventeenth century. Quakers punished few crimes against order itself, but they rigorously kept the peace between contending individuals and among contending groups. They appointed special officers called peacemakers. A novel feature of Quaker order ways was that they directed treatment of the disorderly toward rehabilitation. Order in the southern backcountry rested upon the vital border principle of justice as *retribution*. "Never go to court about slander or assault," Fischer quotes the advice of Andrew Jackson's mother. "Always settle them cases yourself." Punishment of disorder derived its force from the importance of reputation in backcountry culture. Order ways were thus characterized by lynch law and blood feuds.[26]

Concepts of freedom varied as widely among the four regions as concepts of order. In the backcountry, freedom meant *personal sovereignty*, a quasi-anarchist tradition that asserted a natural right to be let alone, to be as nearly free from government as possible. But right implied responsibility. The right of individual freedom *from* government implied the responsibility of individuals to protect their own property, as epitomized in the backcountry proverb, "Every man is sheriff on his own hearth." Freedom in Virginia meant *hegemonic freedom*, a form of status for a small elite, a condition of mastery over themselves and over others. Virginia gentlemen had a great deal of freedom, but Virginia's large underclass had little or none. Fischer sees hegemonic freedom as a powerful and genuine libertarian idea, even though it coexisted with slavery. As hegemonic freedom developed into antebellum republicanism, the slavery of some came to be considered necessary to the freedom of others. Freedom in New England meant *ordered freedom*. New Englanders had a strong sense of fundamental laws and liberties and envisioned an active role for the state. But their distinctive concept of ordered freedom did not allow for toleration of "error" or radical dissent. Freedom meant *reciprocal freedom* in the Delaware Valley, emphasizing a reciprocity of rights based on the golden rule. This unique Quaker idea was very different from either New England's ordered freedom or Virginia's hegemonic freedom.[27]

Together these bundles of folkways, emanating from four British regional cultures, constitute what Fischer calls "the determinants of a voluntary society." Together they explain the origins and stability of an American system he pronounces "democratic in its polity, capitalist in its economy, individualist in its society, libertarian in its laws, and pluralist in its culture."[28]

Given the complexity of the task David Hackett Fischer sets for himself and the sophistication with which he pursues it, it is impossible to do full justice to his insights here. At 898 pages of text, *Albion's Seed* is a long book; but perhaps it is not long enough. It has been most often criticized for its sins of omission. Some have criticized the absence of any systematic discussion of race, class, and gender. Others have criticized what they consider insufficient attention to either structural or functional relations among the various folkways in Fischer's long litany. Virtually everyone has asked "Where are the *other* Americans?" Fischer's four waves of British immigrants settled in only a small part of the area that is now the United States. Other areas early received significant numbers of French and Spanish immigrants, and smaller numbers of Scottish, German, Dutch, and Russian immigrants (not to mention the sons and daughters of the so-called "New Immigration" of the nineteenth and twentieth centuries). Africans in varying numbers came to all regions where the Europeans settled. And they all settled on land already populated by native Americans. *Albion's Seed* devotes only two pages to immigration and race and gives not quite three pages to other colonial cultures.[29]

To be fair, some of these groups have their own volumes forthcoming in the series. Nevertheless, that *Albion's Seed* purports to explain the origins and meaning of American culture, and that it purports to explain "the determinants of a voluntary society," without acknowledging much influence from either native American residents or from African or continental European immigrants, has led some to suggest that perhaps *Albion's Seed* is overly Anglocentric and that it perhaps tends to exaggerate the role of its four British regional cultures in a very complex pattern of multiethnic interaction. Fischer acknowledges that eventually "African folkways also began to transform the language and culture of Europeans, and the 'peculiar institution' of slavery created new folkways of its own." Nonetheless, it is a "major conclusion" of *Albion's Seed* that "race slavery did not create the culture of the southern colonies; that culture created slavery."[30] Nearly thirty years ago a perceptive historian of philosophical bent hazarded firm warnings to historians against "the idea that Anglo-American . . . cultural characteristics are the cultural norm." Some have suggested that perhaps the author of *Albion's Seed* might have paid more heed to his own earlier advice.[31]

It is perhaps inevitable that the author of *Historians' Fallacies* should have his logic in *Albion's Seed* scrutinized. Does he improperly lump diverse peoples who inhabit the same geographic area into a single group? Does he treat geographical groups as though they were in fact cultural groups? Does he improperly construct his profiles of the four British regions by reasoning from folkways characteristic of *some* members of the group to folkways characteristic of the group itself? For example, although Fischer attributes a set of common folkways to his borderers, present-day English, Irish, and Scottish borderers certainly do not consider *themselves* to be one people. And historically their greatest shared characteristic has been a long tradition of warfare with one another. Does he exaggerate *some* similarities between East Anglia and New England, between the English midlands and the Delaware Valley, between southwest England and the Chesapeake, and between the north British borderlands and the American backcountry into a more perfect correspondence? "'Culture,'" a wise historian wrote nearly a generation ago, "is an abstraction, and an exceedingly dangerous one, but historians are tending to graft this abstraction called culture upon the root of national history." That wise historian was David Hackett Fischer.[32]

Fischer describes *Albion's Seed* as a search for "the determinants of a voluntary society."[33] But is his "voluntary society" not more assumed than demonstrated? Membership in this society has not been entirely voluntary, for instance, for either black or white southerners. When Fischer's Virginians and other white southerners attempted in the mid-nineteenth century to dissolve the political bonds that had connected them to American society and attempted to assume a separate and equal station among the powers of the earth, they were forced at the point of a bayonet to remain part of the United States. For black southerners, the very experience of coming to America was involuntary. To these and other "involuntary Americans," Fischer would seem to be rather begging the question of a "voluntary society."[34]

Among the great strengths of *Albion's Seed* is its interdisciplinary approach. In trying to comprehend the regional patterns of American folk culture, Fischer has relied on the writings of scholars in several disciplines and has interpreted their data for his own purposes. Here he runs into the inevitable problem common to all scholars who undertake interdisciplinary studies. Unless they are omnicompetent, they cannot explore the validity of their evidence as specialists trained in the theoretical and methodological principles of their own fields would analyze the same data. They are inevitably captive to the quality of their sources and to the amount of data they provide. In *Albion's Seed* Fischer relies heavily upon the *data* of linguists, folklorists, and anthropologists; but he makes less use of linguistic, folkloristic, and anthropological *analysis* than one would wish.

In particular one wishes Fischer had rested his analysis upon a firmer theoretical base, upon a more modern conceptualization of folk culture, a conceptualization more firmly grounded in the studies of contemporary folklorists. His effort to revive and update the old myths of Herbert Baxter Adams and William Graham Sumner has not served him well. According to Adams, the American system evolved monogenetically from the "Teutonic germs" of free institutions, spreading from the black forest of medieval Germany first to Britain and then to America. Sumner coined the term "folkways" to describe habitual "usages, manners, customs, mores, and morals."[35] Wisely, Fischer does not attempt to trace American folkways further back than Britain; and he repudiates Sumner's assertion that folkways arose from biological instincts. But since Fischer's sense of "folkways" appears more nearly analogous to the "folklife" of contemporary folklorists, I believe he might better have drawn on such folklife theorists as Richard Weiss, Sigurd Erixon, Iorwerth Peate, or Don Yoder.

Fischer rarely draws upon folklorists' studies except when folklorists have been specifically interested in colonial New England, the Delaware Valley, the Chesapeake, or the backcountry. For example, he does draw upon Henry Glassie's studies of Virginia folk architecture. But he eschews folkloristic scholarship on analogous problems, such as Glassie's classic study of folklife in a small community in Northern Ireland, *Passing the Time in Ballymenone*. And his discussion of what he calls "magic ways," might well have benefited from a consideration of the implications of, say, David Hufford's sophisticated study of folk beliefs, or "superstitions," in Newfoundland.[36]

The problem can perhaps best be illustrated by looking at Fischer's treatment of what he calls "speech ways." It is in *Albion's Seed* that he relates the distinctive nasal New England twang to the Norfolk whine, and the Delaware Valley dialect to the language of England's north midlands. The sources of the Virginia accent he posits in a cluster of seventeenth-century rural dialects in the south and west of England, with an overlay of London speech, while he anoints border English the ancestor of a family of American dialects called southern highland speech.

In making these pronouncements, he draws upon evidence that is weak on several counts. While geographers, folklorists, and historians have written a great deal about the *general* cultural patterns of colonial whites, linguists (with the notable exception of Michael Montgomery) have written almost nothing about the *speech* patterns of colonial whites.[37] Considerable scholarly attention has been paid in recent years to African-American creole languages such as Gullah, but the question of how Anglo-Americans used their native tongue in the seventeenth and eighteenth centuries has thus far held little appeal for linguists. Thus, in the absence of stronger evidence, Fischer is forced to rest his analysis mainly on descriptions of twentieth-century speech patterns. He has to assume that twentieth-century examples are reliable indicators of seventeenth- and eighteenth-century speech. Furthermore, such early data as he has available consists mainly of anecdotal evidence from nonlinguists. It is less systematic, less reliable, and less useful for comparative purposes than one would wish. Finally, support for Fischer's thesis rests most heavily upon the comparison of word forms, the least stable area of language. Vocabulary is the area of language most easily borrowed and spread across social, ethnic, and geographical boundaries. The available sources reveal much too little about grammar, the area of language least susceptible to change from contact with other languages or dialects.

In dealing with other disciplines, Fischer is perhaps too ready to yield to their claims of authority. In particular, he treats some hotly contested issues as though they were settled. For instance, linguistic geographers, especially those engaged in the various long-term linguistic atlas projects, have long sought to prove connections between regional American dialects and regional English dialects. Even major figures such as Hans Kurath and Raven McDavid, however, based such pronouncements mainly on inferences from historical accounts of immigration and settlement pat-

terns. Here Fischer would simply seem to be completing the circle of reasoning.[38] *Albion's Seed* highlights how very little basic linguistic research
has actually been done.

Perhaps the deepest problem with *Albion's Seed* is the curiously static
quality of the folk culture that it portrays. Despite Fischer's insistence that
folkways (though highly persistent) are never static,[39] he tends to treat
them as though they are. The problem is inherent in the Sumnerian model
of folkways, which Sumner proclaimed to be unchangeable. While Fischer
does not share Sumner's dismissal of culture change, he does not seem to
feel any need to build a mechanism for change into his own adaptation
of Sumner's model. The sense of stasis is reinforced by the influence of
the *Annales* paradigm. Fernand Braudel promoted the study of human
interaction with forces that changed so slowly as to be almost imperceptible except when seen over very long periods of time, what he called the
longue durée.[40] In some *Annaliste* scholarship, however, it was men and
women that became imperceptible and change became nonexistent
(*l'histoire immobile?*). Fischer's history is certainly not imperceptible; but
by segregating various native and immigrant cultural groups who occupied the same geographic space into separate volumes (and thus separate
cultural space), he has painted in *Albion's Seed* a portrait of American folk
culture that minimizes cultural interaction.

Despite a two-page treatment of "Rhythms and Regional Development," *Albion's Seed* might have profited from a deeper consideration of
the nature of culture change. The creolization model of linguistic change
has been applied to broader cultural patterns in attempting to explain the
emergence of African-American culture. But Fischer need not necessarily look beyond his own discipline. Jack Greene elaborates a model of "convergence" in the American colonies. According to Greene, this process
facilitated the emergence of a distinctive American culture very much like
the one described by Fischer, albeit without its American regional variations or its British regional sources.[41]

To overemphasize reservations is to demean a remarkable achievement. *Albion's Seed* remains one of the very few truly seminal works in
American history. It is a book of astonishing depth, power, and feeling,
filled with stimulating insights. The brilliance of Fischer's analysis lies in
the extraordinary erudition he brings to his task, his elegant writing, and
his bold thesis. Fischer's incisive analysis, his rich and fascinating stories
of the men and women who embodied the folkways of these four British
and four American regions, and above all the sheer creativity with which

he teases out sources and meaning make *Albion's Seed* an indispensable volume for an understanding of American culture.

Now the Bold Fischer Man threatens to bring folklorists, linguists, anthropologists, and historians together for good or ill, either to restate, refine, revise, or refute his contentions. *Albion's Seed* seems likely to shape discussion of American culture for a long time to come. One can only hope that other parties to the debate will proceed with the same care and civility that David Hackett Fischer brings to *Albion's Seed,* and with the same fidelity to the evidence.

Fischer has elsewhere written of the historian's craft: "The monographs do not commonly come first and the general interpretations second. Instead some master architect . . . draws a rough sketch of a pyramid in the sand, and many laborers begin to hew their stones to fit."[42] Perhaps in these few lines, written a generation ago, Fischer best summed up his own achievement in *Albion's Seed:* he has become the master architect of American cultural history.

8

The Narrowing Gyre

Henry Glassie, Irish Folk Culture, and the American South

I came up from the coast where I had been measuring the remains of slave cabins on miasmic rice plantations. Henry and Kathy came down to South Carolina from Philadelphia to give a Saturday talk on southern folk art. On Sunday we piled into my aging station wagon and drove past the incongruous New England salt-boxes of Olympia Mill village, leaving behind the enthralling bustle of Columbia. Out beyond Fort Jackson we turned right off Highway 378, eschewing paved surfaces for stretches of gravel road, the dry, dust-laden air rising rapidly in thin clouds behind us. It was 1980. A region of memories stretched before us between the Congaree and the Wateree. We paused to photograph the fading majesty of an antebellum church, then moved dustily on. Off to our right, at the head of an avenue of oaks, stood a once-stately mansion, now abandoned to kudzu. Disused plows rusted among the weeds beneath the ramshackle shed of a broken barn. Here and there people waved to us from the shabby elegance of unpainted, tin-roofed shacks tied to the road by rutted lanes, surrounded by patches of cotton stalks stretching almost to the woods.

We spoke of the South—the South where, twenty years earlier, Henry had drifted around the backcountry with Paul Worthington and young Bobby Zimmerman, coaxing Blue Ridge tradition-bearers to sing ballads into his tape recorder. (Zimmerman has since become better known under his stage name—Bob Dylan.) We dreamed again the future we had each envisioned in those idealistic years, a future of the beloved community, a future that would embrace both tradition and innovation, ethics and aesthetics, art and justice. Now that future, once a dream, had become history, in all its magnificent failures and all its flawed successes, in its ironies and in its tragedies.

Henry spoke, too, of his forthcoming book on Ulster—Ulster, where the sacred heart of the community had been split by political terror. I myself had known Ulster. I had done fieldwork in County Armagh a decade earlier, driving country lanes marked by roadblocks and ambushes that murdered mothers and soldiers alike, mental milestones, festering memories of the immoderate past. As we talked, in the Indian summer of a Carolina September, the similarities between Ulster and our native South were inescapable. How, we had wondered, do people keep their balance when they are so mastered by the brute blood of the air, when people peacefully at work on their farms are suddenly, brutally murdered, when innocent men are cut down in crossfire? How can they live there? How can they remain good people? How can the divided heart be reconciled? That, in an important sense, is what his book *Passing the Time in Ballymenone* is about. And that, in an important sense, is what folklore is about as well.[1]

Throughout his career, Henry Glassie has been concerned with what the historian Eric Hobsbawm calls "societies under the impact of social transformation."[2] In this concern, as in their mutual fondness for the Irish, his work has been much like that of the great film director John Ford. Both Ford in his films and Glassie in his books have been drawn to the study of cultural dislocations caused by cultural convergence or by rapid social change within a single culture, or both. Frequently, internal culture change is the result of *kulturkampf*—the clash of different cultures—as more "advanced" technological societies work out their will upon traditional peoples, forcing drastic perceptual changes upon them. Caught in the sensual music of conquest, the "advanced" societies neither understand nor value the traditions of their victims.

Unlike Glassie, John Ford was a conservative who celebrated the triumph of "progress"—white conquest over "primitive" and "backward" Indians—in his early films, such as *The Iron Horse*, (1924), *Drums along the Mohawk* (1939), *Stagecoach* (1939), and *My Darling Clementine* (1946). In his later films, however, he vividly expressed his growing disillusionment with cultural imperialism. In such films as *The Searchers* (1956) and *The Man Who Shot Liberty Valance* (1962), and especially in *Cheyenne Autumn* (1964), he explored the cultural dislocations inflicted upon the Indians by

the coming of the whites, with their technology and with their "civilization." Throughout his post–World War II career Ford explored the interaction of different modes of cultural perception in a cross-cultural and
often biracial context. Again and again he returned to the theme of drastic perceptual changes required by new cultural configurations, never
more trenchantly than in his *The Quiet Man* (1952), filmed in Ireland, in
which an American must learn to understand and appreciate traditional
Irish ways. Ford's repeatedly evidenced concern with larger forces of history and culture thus raised his conservative emphasis on traditional cultural values above the level of sentimentality and transcended his earlier
racism and cultural nationalism.[3]

A more modern figure than Ford, Glassie from the beginning of his
career was free of the archaic racism and imperialism that marred the
early work of the director. Like Ford, however, he has sought liberation
from the burden of modern history by probing the plight of traditional
societies under the impact of cultural dislocation. But where Ford lamented the relentless destruction of traditional culture by the forces of modernization, Glassie extols traditional culture as a source of strength that
enables people to survive the hail and upheaval of modern life. In *Pattern
in the Material Folk Culture of the Eastern United States* (1968), he surveyed
relationships between geographic regions and their cultural implications
over the *longue durée*. In *Folk Housing in Middle Virginia* (1975), he explored
technological and architectural changes in the eighteenth century and
probed the changing modes of cultural perception that accompanied
them. In *All Silver and No Brass* (1975), he studied human beings under the
impact of the woebegone pyre of violent change and the significance of
obsolescent mumming traditions in helping them to cope with such
changes.[4]

Unlike Ford, Glassie has—with one exception—eschewed study of the
racial context of social upheaval. The exception was a piece written early
in his career, a sensitive and sympathetic study of a man whose inherited
racist attitudes—once virtually universal among white Americans—were
themselves suffering the impact of social transformation. One may sympathize with such a person's plight, and perceive the humanity beyond the
racism, without sharing the racist views. Because it offended the man he
wrote about and lost the author a friend, Glassie has disowned the piece.
"Friends," he writes, "are more important than books." One suspects he
lost a friend not because he betrayed the friendship, but because he could
not betray his own better nature and thus could not share the friend's

racism. In any event, the effect upon the young folklorist—and upon his own cultural perceptions—was profound. He turned from the direct study of human beings to the study of artifacts, a turn that led him to history and to the rapprochement of history with folklore. Even now, as he returns to the direct treatment of human beings, the trauma of that lost friendship still lies close to the surface of his consciousness; he writes with the explicit desire to harm no one, to cause no pain.[5]

Passing the Time in Ballymenone tells of pain, but surely causes none. It tells of the history and culture of a County Fermanagh community, beneath the mountains of Benaughlin and Cuilcagh, and the people who inhabit the cottages along the Arney and Sillees Rivers. We have already met them in Glassie's *All Silver and No Brass*. P Flanagan, the community's great musician—master of the fiddle, flute, and tinwhistle—perches on a stool before a turf fire. Dressed in his work clothes, curls falling across his forehead, he fingers upon a fiddle string. Michael Boyle, thin and drawn, looks up from his hospital bed with deep, piercing eyes. As he lies dying, he spends his last days talking into Glassie's tape recorder, dredging up the hopes of time onto the surface of consciousness, bequeathing a community's history to posterity, his experience surviving in the act of its telling. Ellen Cutler smiles her lovely smile, her hair plaited down her back, her body bent above a sinking fire, placing a new stick across the coals, telling a tale in the gray twilight of fingers tightening on triggers, of men armed with guns and children armed with rocks, a tale that finds the tragedy of trivial things. And the community's oldest man, Hugh Nolan, the great historian of Ballymenone, nods by the fire with the kettle on the hob like some scholarly old monk from Ireland's golden age, his head falling forward, his body fatigued at evening. His history was learned not from books but from "listenin to the old people talkin," he says. "I'd hear the old people talkin and I'd learn that and I'd put in the details along with what I was taught be the Master." Hugh Nolan's politics were as Green as Ellen Cutler's were Orange.

With seventy or more winters upon each head, and with a twinkling of ancient eyes, they are revealed as monuments of unaging intellect, both wise and merry of tongue. "Their lack of education and poorness in the things of the world," Glassie writes, "tell nothing about their good minds." But Henry Glassie tells us of their good minds. They become, in these pages, our teachers and friends, the singing-masters of our souls, sharing with us their moments of glad grace, their tea and tales, drawing us away from the grim and scary present to the sacred drama of a more dream-heavy land, where time and the world, ever in flight, brood upon high lonely mysteries.

In clear, flowing, flutelike prose, Glassie presents his stylistic arrangement of their experience. He writes with the grace of an Irish musician. Like his friend P Flanagan, he "soars in melodic runs, in loping long sentences that descend to short, punctuating statements." Here, devoid of cowardly jargon, are marvelous descriptions of his meeting informants and developing rapport, of false starts and mistakes, and of deepening friendships. Like his friends, Glassie "puts wit in service to courage, and makes the self a gift to the community." Describing their world in Kelly green, bittersweet tones, he measures out their lives in vast quantities of tea and talk—chat, crack, bid, and story—allowing the meaning to glimmer just beneath the surface of his prose, as if it were a Yeatsian trout gliding through the shallow clear waters of an Irish stream. It is an approach that occasionally gives the reader the impression of eavesdropping on his dreams.

In his desire not to offend, not to inflict pain, Glassie may be too innocent. He wants people to be good, and in his neoromantic vision they are. He shies away from the heart of darkness in conflict with itself. And yet, as Ulster's shadows deepen and thicken into darkness, it is easy enough to believe that the whole land is cursed, and all whom it ever suckled, Orange and Green alike, lie under the curse, not malevolent but just doomed; where bombs rock the towns, conveying horror to hearers, and barricades block the roads; where even the route to the pub is a corridor of marching armed men and gunfire; where the madmen's love is felt in the suffering of the poor, and the dreadful martyrdom of dead men is felt in the guts of the living, in the nightmare of the dark, in the prison of their days, attacking the very sanity of those who experience them; not so much because of the brooding ugliness of the land, the wet winds howling cold in the streets, or the fanatic piety and profanity of its people, or of the measured and sonorous imbecility of the mind or the unquiet dreams and the baseless hopes of the heart; nor because of the arrogance and the anxiety, the isolation and the fear, the self-destructive drive to recall a fatal past rather than look forward toward the quicksand and terror of the future; nor because they have inherited a long legend of irrational brutality, of wreckage and destruction, a barbaric past out of an old dead time, merged with a flawed and cherished past melting into one desolation, one hopelessness, an elusive banality that looms and towers in their dreams, an anachronism indomitable and invincible, paradoxically both the tragic flaw of their social order and their most valued possession; and not because of the people's boundless bitter courage, their sense of being doomed survivors and victims of history, for history is more fantastic than any myth, and doom darker and deeper; nor even because they have endured, for no degree of razor-edge endurance can reverse the fragmentation of modern times in Ulster. These years, it is said, have seen a boom in sorrow; and now it has no innocence at all.

This, too, is Irish folk history. Southerners such as Glassie find it all-too-familiar. And yet he is surely correct to emphasize history's redemptive power rather than its curse. He knows the land is full of weeping; he melts our bones with pity. He is aware that Northern Ireland has her madness and her weather still. But if winter nights are black and bleak, he writes, it "is a time to sit by the fire, safe in the family's circle, waiting for the days to lengthen and warm." Henry Glassie loves the sorrows of Ulster's aging faces, and raises instead of doom the image of the reconciler. His message is unity; in unity the loneliness of heart is withered away. In trust and tale he fathoms sense in Ballymenone; in trust and tale he promotes the meeting of sense and spirit. Though Ulster appear mad, yet he finds sanity in a sense of continuity with generations gone before, a precious lifeline to courageous ancestors who survived the wars and had the additional and even greater courage and endurance to resist and survive centuries of poverty and occupation and so preserved a heritage of memories to hold in trust.

The folk history of the Irish—their heritage of memories—may be as crucial to our sanity and survival as to theirs. Nowhere has Glassie expressed its importance more eloquently or more directly than in *All Silver and No Brass:* "I may be of some use when I reinforce their traditions with my interest, but they don't need me. I need them. I need their memories, for without them, an authentic history cannot be written, and I need history to understand how we have come to this pass and to consider alternatives for the future. I need their presence because they face the modern absurdity with good humor and great strength. I need their wisdom because they know and can explain a more sane social ethic than that of my own society."[6] Such memories are the most fragile and delicate of the human gifts, the most unfathomable in their elusive retrospect, and the most precious.

§

Just as Glassie finds unity in the divided heart of Ballymenone, so does he find unity in the divided mind of his academic discipline. Yeats asked, "How can we know the dancer from the dance?" Here are reconciled dancer, dance, and dancing. Like the modern folklorist he is, Glassie wishes "to understand acts and arts in their own terms—the terms of their performers, their audience's traditions, and conditions." While reconciling—and drawing upon—traditions of scholarship in history, geography, and anthropology, his approach is fundamentally folkloristic, for, as he says, "I begin with texts, at forms created by the people themselves, and move through them to the culture and the environment, and swing from the culture and the environment back to the texts, while feeling toward the meanings in works of art and attempting to gain some understanding of the world as viewed from Ballymenone." He begins with texts, then weaves contexts around them to make them meaningful. Context, he says, is neither in the eye of the beholder nor in the ear of the behearer, but in the mind of the performer. "Some of the context is drawn in from the immediate situation, but more is drawn from memory. It is present, but invisible, inaudible."

To say that *Passing the Time in Ballymenone* is about ceilis, about songs and stories—and about the ethnography of speaking, and work patterns, and foodways, and folk religion—is inadequate. It may be more helpful to say that it synthesizes Dan Ben-Amos's theories of genre; and Robert Plant Armstrong's theories of the affecting presence of art; and Linda Degh's interest in the connections between people, their narratives, and their communities; and Richard Dorson's commitment to the historical dimension of folklore; and Dell Hymes's "breakthrough into performance"; and the ethnopoetics of Dennis Tedlock; and the historical archaeology of James Deetz; and the cultural geography of Estyn Evans and Fred Kniffen.[7] Such a catalog may be more helpful, but it still falls far short of describing the achievement of Glassie's monumental book.

Passing the Time in Ballymenone synthesizes the advances of a generation of work in folkloristics. If it accomplished no more than that it would have to be proclaimed a landmark accomplishment. But over and above that it is an extraordinary work of original, empirical scholarship, a thick ethnographic description of a community and its tradition-bearers, and of their friendship with a young American who came into their midst. It is syndetic as well as synthetic. It is also a collection of peerless narrative texts, set out on the page in such a way as to assault our complacency into "seeing" the poetic elements in the stories. These tales are available separately in the companion volume, *Irish Folk History: Texts from the North*, as well as in the larger book.[8]

But over and above its value as a collection or as a work of scholarship, *Passing the Time in Ballymenone* refutes the idea that useful things cannot be art, for it is a work of art in its own right. Glassie's pen-and-ink sketches—independent, affecting statements of delighted observation, of feelings and impressions—transcend mere illustration. Using the accidents of individuality to reveal the inner dignity of the community, he makes in these sketches a passionate, forceful impact that could not be conveyed with words. Not merely the sketches, however, but the whole book is a work of art. In its epic scope and humane themes, in its breadth of sympathy and depth of perception, in its vividness of characterization, its richness of description, and its felicity of expression, it moves us and affects us in precisely the way that great literature moves us and affects us.

Passing the Time in Ballymenone is a masterpiece, a watershed in the history of our discipline. "Turning and turning in the widening gyre, the falcon cannot hear the falconer," wrote William Butler Yeats. "Things fall apart; the center cannot hold. Mere anarchy is loosed upon the world." And yet the center, that liminal space between the pages on either side (Archie Green calls it "the margins between"), may be the only thing that does hold, or will, or should hold. Here, in *Passing the Time in Ballymenone*, social science joins the humanities; art and culture and history merge; time and space connect; and theoretical and empirical studies fuse. Glassie reconciles the "new" folkloristics with the "old," reconciles text and context, etic and emic, folklore and folklife, Penn and Indiana (not to mention LSU, Cooperstown, and the Irish Folklore Commission), even Orange and Green. Yeats would have liked it. Things come together: the gyre is narrowing.

PART THREE

The New South

9

A Community of Memory

Assimilation and Identity among the Jews of Georgetown

Tell ye your children of it,
and let your children tell their children,
and their children another generation.
— Joel 1:3

To be a Jew is to be part of a community woven by memory.
— Daniel Bell

Jews were not aliens in the promised land but blood-and-bones part
of the South itself—Jewish Southerners.
— Eli Evans

Yizkor Elohim nishmas aboh more . . .
[May God remember the name of . . .]

At dusk on a Friday evening, a hush fell over Front Street as the business district of Georgetown seemed to stop breathing. Friday was the day of the eve of the Sabbath, *Erev Shabbes,* and the Jews of Georgetown prepared themselves to celebrate another engagement with their God. They would hurry to reach home before sunset, in time to greet the Sabbath with their own families. As the sun disappeared over the treetops, the Sabbath entered Georgetown, met with the traditional Sabbath greeting, "*Gut Shabbes!*" The table would be spread, and the candles would give off a festive light. Meals during the week might be hurried or irregular, might be eaten alone or on the job. But this was the Sabbath. After prayers of gratitude for God's blessings, the family sat down together to the Sabbath meal.

As the Sabbath candles burned low, the Jews of Georgetown remembered the commandment to put aside not only weekday acts but weekday thoughts—thoughts of business, of money, of family problems. It was the Sabbath; it was time for the People of the Book to turn their thoughts to God. They knew that the other Jewish families of Georgetown shared their

Sabbath experience. But even beyond that, in celebrating the Sabbath they felt a community with all the millions of Jews around the world. Undismayed by perils past, they felt a sense of identification with the ancestors, with a tradition, with a proud and joyous past, with all the Jewish world living or dead. Far more than the Jewish *people* had kept the Sabbath, they realized, the *Sabbath* had kept the Jewish people. Then they would smile, and thank God for being Jewish.

The southern Jewish experience has been both unique and ironic. To be a Jew in the South is both to affect and to be affected by the culture of the region. Jews did not come to the South as immigrants into the Promised Land; they were among the earliest settlers who helped to make the South what it is. The legacy of Jews in the South has been and remains distinctive, a contribution that has deeply enriched the politics, economics, philanthropy, and culture of the region. Jews have undergone a historical experience in the South that has made them different not only from other Jews but also from other southerners. There is deep irony in inheriting the Jewish longing for a homeland while growing up with the southerner's sense of home. As *Jewish southerners*, they made a special contribution to the region they helped to found and to shape. As *southern Jews*, they made a special contribution to Jews everywhere, playing a distinctive part in a living testimony to the Jewish presence in the world that not even the ultimate horrors of our century were able to eliminate.[1]

At the dawn of the new nation more Jews lived in South Carolina than in any other state of the United States, according to America's first two censuses, in 1790 and 1800. Charleston's Kahal Kadosh Beth Elohim (the Holy Congregation of the House of God) was the nation's largest synagogue, and Charleston's Jewish community was the nation's foremost. The Jews of South Carolina achieved prominence early—partly because of their own energetic efforts, partly because South Carolina had been more receptive to Jews than other colonies had been. According to Abram Vossen Goodman, the dean of Jewish historians, "South Carolina's record has been outstanding, with its treatment of the Jews more uniformly favorable than that of any other colony where they settled in numbers. . . . The rights enjoyed by the Jews establishes South Carolina as the first community in the modern world where Jews might vote. It was also the first government where a Jew was elected to office by his Christian neighbors." It is true that Jewish enfranchisement was revoked in South Carolina in 1716 and was not reinstated until 1790. Even then, however, it would still be a half-century before Jews were allowed to vote in England. Furthermore, the revocation was not uniformly enforced in South Carolina, and Jews continued to hold elective office in the interim.[2]

At the dawn of the nineteenth century the largest group of Jews in South Carolina outside of Charleston was in the state's second-oldest Hebrew community—Georgetown. The great pioneers of Georgetown Jewry were Mordecai Myers and Abraham and Solomon Cohen. The Cohens had come to Charleston from London in 1750 with their father—Charleston's first *Haham*, Moses Cohen. By 1761, scarcely a decade after organizing a congregation there, they moved northward up the coast to Georgetown. Myers and the Cohen brothers became founding fathers of the Georgetown mercantile community in the eighteenth century.[3]

Through their commercial relations with the outside world and through the consumer goods available in their shops, Mordecai Myers and Abraham and Solomon Cohen helped to bring a more comfortable life to the people of Georgetown and the surrounding rice plantations. They found economic opportunity and economic success in Georgetown, but they also contributed to making Georgetown successful. From the beginning Myers and the Cohens actively participated in community affairs.[4]

By 1800 a strong Jewish contingent virtually dominated the civic life of Georgetown. Although numerically small—approximately eighty persons—at 10 percent of the white population of Georgetown they exemplified one of the highest concentrations of Jews in any community in America. The Cohen and Myers families held many local offices at the turn of the century, establishing an especially notable record of community leadership.[5]

The mercantile business established by Abraham Cohen early in the 1760s furnished supplies to the Continental Army during the Revolution. One of the founders of the Georgetown Library Society and the Georgetown Fire Company, Cohen was one of the prominent Georgetonians who successfully petitioned the South Carolina legislature to authorize the election of three commissioners (town councilmen) in 1785. He became a member of the prestigious Winyah Indigo Society in 1786 and was elected the society's secretary in 1798. He served as commissioner of streets and markets in 1799 and as postmaster from 1797 until his death at sixty-one in December 1800.[6] Abraham Cohen's brother Solomon served as postmaster, as treasurer of the Georgetown Library Society, and as a member of the Winyah Indigo Society. He also held the position of tax collector of Georgetown at the turn of the century and was first sergeant of the Winyah Light Dragoons. Solomon Cohen's long and illustrious career was climaxed by his election as intendant (mayor) of Georgetown in 1818 and director of the Bank of the State of South Carolina in 1819.[7]

Thus from early times the leaders of Georgetown Jewry were the leaders of Georgetown. They served on all sorts of boards and committees, and they were elected by their Gentile neighbors to the highest political offices in the town. In addition Jews were members of various lodges and social organizations in Georgetown. It was probably through the local Masonic order that Jews first came into political leadership in Georgetown. A committee of Freemasons, including Abraham Cohen, met with President George Washington when he visited Georgetown on his southern tour in 1791.[8] And Georgetown's most prestigious social organizations welcomed Jewish members.[9]

In the second generation, the four sons of Mordecai Myers established distinguished records. Moses Myers was the first Jewish attorney in South Carolina. He was admitted to the bar in 1793 at the age of twenty-one. Like the Cohens, he was a member of the Georgetown Library Society and the Winyah Indigo Society. He also served as Clerk of Court of General Sessions and Common Pleas from 1798 until 1817. Jacob Myers took over Abraham Cohen's blacksmith business in 1800. He became a member of the Georgetown Library Society, postmaster, and a captain in the Winyah Artillery Company. Abraham Myers was admitted to the bar of South Carolina in 1796. He was twice elected intendant of Georgetown, in 1826 and 1827. Levi Myers received his medical degree from the University of Glasgow in 1787 and was the first Jewish doctor to belong to the Medical Society of South Carolina. He enjoyed a distinguished medical practice in Georgetown and later in Charleston. In 1822 a hurricane struck the South Carolina coast and swept Dr. Myers's house out to sea, drowning the entire family.[10]

Solomon Cohen Jr. was born in Georgetown in 1802. His was the first Jewish birth recorded in Georgetown County. He was educated at the South Carolina College (now the University of South Carolina) where he became friends with Joshua John Ward, later to become lieutenant-governor of South Carolina and the foremost rice planter of his day. After being admitted to the bar Cohen undertook a law practice in Georgetown. Rising rapidly in public affairs, he served as director of the Bank of South Carolina from 1819 to 1826. A leader of the Nullification faction in state politics, Cohen was elected to represent Prince George's Parish in the

South Carolina legislature in 1831, a post he held until 1836. In 1837 he was elected intendant of Georgetown. Solomon Cohen Jr. was as prominent in Georgetown's social life as in its political life. Like his father, he was a member of the Winyah Indigo Society. And when the Planters Club—the most prestigious social organization of antebellum Georgetown—was organized, Cohen was a charter member, along with the wealthy rice planters of the Waccamaw, the Pee Dee, the Black, the Sampit, and the Santee Rivers. In 1836 he married Miriam Gratz Moses of the prominent Gratz family, thus uniting a leading Georgetown Jewish family with a leading Philadelphia one. At the end of 1838 Solomon and Miriam Cohen moved to Savannah, where he embarked on an illustrious legal career.[11]

The third generation of the Cohen and Myers families continued the family traditions of service, but sought new arenas in which to serve. Sarah Henrietta Cohen, the daughter of Solomon Cohen Sr., married the son of Mordecai Myers. Their son, Julian Myers, was named a midshipman in the United States Navy in 1839 and rose to command his own ship by 1854. Abraham C. Myers, the son of Abraham Myers, was nominated to the United States Military Academy by the prominent rice planter John Ashe Alston, who wrote of him that he was "from one of the best families of our state and is the only son of the Hon. Abraham Myers Intendant of this town and a gentleman of weight and influence here. . . . The abilities and understanding of [the young] Mr. Myers are eminently conspicuous. His moral character is a pattern highly worthy of imitation." Abraham C. Myers later became quartermaster general of the Confederacy.[12]

According to Bertram Wallace Korn, the leading historian of Jews in the Old South, southern Jews either supported slavery or kept quiet. After the Nat Turner insurrection, a great wave of enforced conformity stifled what had previously been a lively debate on the issue. Jews, no less than other southerners, were constrained to support the region's "Peculiar Institution," whatever their true feelings. Before the mid-1830s, however, the true feelings of Georgetown Jewry were divided on the issue. In the Nullification controversy, at bottom a sectional clash over slavery, the Jews of Georgetown did not merely support the nullifiers or the unionists but provided conspicuous leadership to each side. Dr. Aaron Lopez, a leader of the Nullification faction, was one of five delegates selected to represent Georgetown at the 1832 Nullification Convention in Charleston. And Solomon Cohen Jr. was elected to the state legislature in 1831 as a Nullification candidate. He ran second in a field of six, only one vote behind the front runner (and ahead of Robert F. W. Allston, one of the most prominent nullificationists). At the same time, his nephew, Mordecai Cohen Myers, was a leader of the Unionist faction in Georgetown.[13]

Some of the Georgetown Jews were themselves slaveholders. Abraham Cohen, Lizar Joseph, and Levy Solomon engaged in the slave trade at the beginning of the century, as did Jacob Sampson in the 1850s. Solomon Cohen Jr., the largest Jewish slaveowner, held title to more than twenty human beings. That did not make him a large slaveholder by the standards of Georgetown District's immense rice plantations, but few of the Jewish slaveholders of Georgetown owned nearly so many slaves. As the years passed more and more Georgetown Jews owned slaves, but rarely did anyone own more than two adults and a few children—a single slave family.[14]

The Jews of Georgetown did not take as conspicuous a role in the secession movement as they had in the Nullification controversy. Nevertheless, once the Southern Confederacy was established, they supported it with considerable devotion. Georgetown Jewry contributed a disproportionately large share of men to Confederate service during the Civil War. Five Jewish casualties of that war are buried in the Georgetown Jewish cemetery. Nathan Emanuel lost two of his sons. Sgt. Edwin Emanuel died in 1862 in Oxford, Mississippi, at the age of twenty-nine. Pvt. Washington Emanuel was barely twenty years old when he was killed in the battle of Atlanta in 1864. Maj. W. P. Emanuel was in command of the Georgetown Military District during 1862 and 1863. His command was controversial. Henry Middleton, a rice planter, complained in 1862 that Emanuel was "so feeble a man that—command going by elections—he does not dare give an order." Middleton felt that, as an aristocrat and therefore a "natural" leader, he should have been given the command. While Emanuel did not enjoy Middleton's confidence, most of the troops placed sufficient trust in him to elect him to command. It was marked by neither outstanding success nor conspicuous failure.[15]

Sol Emanuel lost two brothers in the war. Afterward, writing to his fiancée, Esther Alexander, he gave poignant voice to the depth of feeling some of Georgetown's Jews felt for the lost Confederate cause. He praised its "blood stained Banner—unto whom a united nation looked with reverence and love—as the chosen symbol of a people for adherence to the cause they espoused as just and holy." He praised the "gallantry of its Sons" and the "heroic devotion of the Daughters whom History will delight to honor in song and story." That gallantry and that devotion, he declared, had "no parallel not even in the annals of the Spartan days of old." That gallantry and that devotion were "all that is left save memory alone to marke the Glorious record of a once happy and prosperous but now prostrate and powerless People." He hoped that posterity might "accord justice to the Heroes who offered up their lives, sacrificed on the altar of the sacred but lost cause of Liberty, upon whose noble brows Heaven itself will entwine wreaths of our dying Glory."[16]

The Jews played a major part in the new leadership of Georgetown during Reconstruction. Some of the older Jewish families continued to move up the economic scale. The Sampsons and the Emanuels, for example, built their little shops into thriving mercantile businesses. They also continued the earlier Jewish tradition of active involvement in the civic affairs of Georgetown. Both Samuel Sampson and Nathan Emanuel served as wardens of Georgetown.[17]

But increasingly taking the lead among Georgetown Jewry were new men, self-made men, such as Marcus Moses, Elkan Baum, and Heiman Kaminski, all recently arrived from Eastern Europe. In 1875, Marcus Moses disappeared, leaving behind frustrated creditors and a reputation as a "great rascal."[18] But Elkan Baum was a businessman of another type altogether. He had first come to Georgetown in the early 1850s and opened a little shop, E. and H. Baum, with his wife, Hannah. They experienced financial difficulty from the very beginning, and their effort to establish themselves in Georgetown in the early 1850s was unsuccessful. In 1856 Baum and his family removed to Conwayboro, in South Carolina's Horry District. He returned to Georgetown after the war, however, and within a decade he had become a prosperous and respected businessman. In 1877 he purchased Willbrook, one of the fabled rice plantations on the Waccamaw River north of Georgetown.[19]

Heiman Kaminski was born in Posen (then part of Prussia) in 1839. He came to South Carolina at the age of fifteen. When the Civil War broke out he was a clerk in Elkan Baum's store in Conwayboro. He fought in the Tenth South Carolina Regiment and was mustered out after Appomattox as a sergeant. Heiman Kaminski arrived in Georgetown at the age of twenty-six with two silver dollars in his pocket, destined to become not merely the most important man in Georgetown Jewry in the late nineteenth century, but perhaps the most important man in all of Georgetown. First opening a dry-goods store in partnership with Sol Emanuel and W. W. Taylor, Kaminski soon expanded his business enterprises to include a hardware store, a medical dispensary, a boat and oar company, and a steamship line. He served as agent for Clyde Line ships and was also co-owner of the three-masted schooner the *Linah C. Kaminski,* named after his mother. He also served as vice-president of the Bank of Georgetown. And he was director of the Georgetown Rice Milling Company, a collaboration between the Georgetown merchants and the rice planters that successfully forestalled the collapse of the rice industry until the beginning of the twentieth century. The rise of Heiman Kaminski is nicely summarized in the terse credit reports of the R. G. Dun Company (predecessor of Dun and Bradstreet) in the Baker Library of the Harvard Business School. In 1867, the Dun reporter described Kaminski as "prompt." By 1870 he pronounced Kaminski's credit "excellent." In 1871 he described him as being of "excellent character & credit." The following year he wrote that Kaminski was "believed to be getting rich." By 1875 his report only said "rich."[20]

In 1867 Heiman Kaminski married Charlotte Virginia Emanuel, the daughter of Nathan Emanuel, thus uniting his fortune with that of an older Georgetown Jewish family. The couple had four children—Edwin, Linah, Nathan, and Joseph. After Charlotte's death, Heiman married Rose Baum, member of a prominent Charleston Jewish family.[21]

Heiman Kaminski and other Georgetown Jews participated eagerly in the Reconstruction revival of the Georgetown Rifle Guards as "a club for self defense." Kaminski secured uniforms and rifles for the organization. Sol Emanuel, Kaminski's brother-in-law, was elected second vice-president. The Georgetown Rifle Guards were active in Wade Hampton's campaign to wrest control of state government from the Republicans and return it to white Democratic domination in 1877.[22]

Sol Emanuel, the son of Nathan Emanuel, inherited his father's business in 1869, but by 1877 he discontinued the family business to concentrate on his partnership in the various business enterprises of his brother-in-law, Heiman Kaminski. Sol Emanuel's position of leadership in the Georgetown Rifle Guards and his staunch support of the Hampton campaign were warmly received by the white voters of Georgetown in the critical election year of 1876. Upholding his father's tradition of involvement in public life, he was elected to the first of his two terms as intendant of Georgetown.[23]

Kaminski's leading rival in postwar Georgetown was Joseph Sampson, agent for New York steamship lines and partner in a mercantile firm with his brother Samuel. While the Sampsons had endured a near-bankruptcy at the end of the war, they managed to rebuild their business by extending credit to the hard-pressed rice planters. Taking liens on rice crops, the Sampsons accumulated capital while the fortunes of the once-mighty planters declined.[24]

Joseph Sampson's daughter Cornelia married young Louis S. Ehrich, who became a partner in Joseph Sampson and Company. Ehrich, described as an "active and energetic young man," enjoyed a meteoric career in Georgetown's economic and political life. In 1880, at the age of twenty-five, he became the superintendent of the Georgetown Rice Milling Company. By 1886 he was a director of the Georgetown Telegraph Company and the Georgetown and Lanes Railroad Company, and was secretary-treasurer of the Board of Pilot Commissioners. (His brother-in-law, Joseph Sampson Jr., was a riverboat pilot.) As director of the Georgetown Land Association, Ehrich was also involved in developing subdivisions out of old rice plantations. In 1886 he was elected to the first of his three consecutive terms as intendant of Georgetown.[25]

The dawn of a new century was accompanied by two important events in the life of Georgetown's Jews. The noted financier Bernard M. Baruch, a relative of both of the major Jewish factions in Georgetown (the Kaminskis and the Sampsons), became a part-time member of the community when he purchased virtually all of the plantations at the base of Waccamaw Neck that had once been the rice empire of the mighty Alston family. Here Baruch attempted to re-create the old king's grant of Hobcaw Barony (although in actuality his re-creation was rather larger than the original). It was at Hobcaw that Baruch entertained such world notables as Winston Churchill, Franklin Delano Roosevelt, George C. Marshall, and the widow of Woodrow Wilson.[26]

An event of much more importance to most of Georgetown's Jews was the organization of a formal congregation on October 30, 1904. Congregation Beth Elohim (House of God), comprising more than one hundred persons, was served by Barnet A. Elzas, rabbi of K. K. Beth Elohim in Charleston. Thus the old century ended and the new century began with a new religious life for the Jews of Georgetown and a new affirmation of their Judaism. Over more than a century they had planted deep roots in this little patch of ground.

This much we know for certain. These are facts, not inferences. These facts spell out the apparent "success" of a southern Jewish community in business, in politics, and in social assimilation. These Jews left their imprint on Georgetown's culture, politics, philanthropy, and business. Theirs was a community marked by economic success, actively involved in the world around it, determined to gain acceptance into the mainstream but not at the cost of abandoning Judaism itself. If this history of Georgetown's Jews appears more southern than Jewish, if their fortunes seem flushed with success and conformity, that emphasis has not been dictated by any desire on my part to minimize controversial or unpleasant experiences but by the lack of controversial or unpleasant evidence.[27]

While common sense and experience suggest the universal occurrence of discrimination—whatever their comparative proportions—common sense is not the same thing as evidence. There was discrimination in the South, to be sure, sometimes carried to excesses that shocked the conscience of the nation. But it was not usually directed against Jews. Still, few periods in modern history either in America or in Europe have been so charged with overt anti-Semitism as the closing years of the nineteenth century—the era of the Dreyfus affair. Even the Jews of Georgetown must have lived in the shadows of its flames.[28]

In Georgetown there were occasional expressions in private correspondence that can be taken to indicate distaste for Jews. The rice planter Charles P. Allston, for instance, found himself unable to meet his financial obligations in the wake of the devastating hurricane of 1893. "The effect," he lamented, "is to kill the credit of the [rice] industry." Allston worried how he might "prevent any grab game on the part of the G[eorgetown] Jews." It is clear that Allston preferred not to let his plantation fall into their hands. And his characterization of the motives of Jewish creditors as a "grab game" hardly testifies to his own liberality of spirit. If such comments were common they might suggest an underlying anti-Semitic attitude. But standing alone as an expression in private correspondence, Allston's comment does not clearly indicate anything more than frustration on the part of a man unable to pay his debts and fearful that his creditors will foreclose on him.[29]

A few stereotypical expressions regarding the Georgetown Jews were indulged in by the anonymous credit reporters for the R. G. Dun Company. The comment about Heiman Kaminski that he "is a Jew, but I always found him prompt" is certainly patronizing.[30] The description of Marcus Moses as an "active little fellow" may be a stereotypical description. For some strange reason (despite the imposing girth of such Jews as Harry Golden and Ariel Sharon) Jewish men or women are often stereotypically described as "little." In the absence of any other description of Marcus Moses one cannot be certain whether or not the description is physically apt, but one can note that physical size is not normally considered relevant to a credit evaluation. In any event, patronizing descriptions seem to be the limit. No evidence has yet surfaced of any stronger expression of anti-Semitism in Georgetown.

Certainly Jews faced economic, political, and social problems in the South as well as in the North, problems they learned either to overcome or to accept. Rank-and-file Confederates shared the prevalent Yankee suspicions that Jewish merchants were war profiteers, a suspicion that led not only to General Ulysses S. Grant's 1863 order expelling Jews from the Union-occupied Department of the Tennessee but also an earlier Confederate order in 1862 expelling German Jews from Thomasville, Georgia. The first Jewish professor at the University of Virginia was hounded from his job in 1842 within a few months of his appointment. In North Carolina restrictions on Jewish voting and office-holding were not lifted until the Reconstruction Constitution of 1868. Georgia witnessed the most dramatic expression of southern anti-Semitism in the 1915 lynching of Leo Frank for the alleged murder of little Mary Phagan.[31]

But the Jews of Georgetown—so far as surviving evidence reveals— experienced none of the expulsions, dismissals, restrictions, or lynchings that characterized Jewish life elsewhere; experienced no *de facto* social and economic discrimination; experienced no demands for any kind of limitation on either Jewish immigration or Jewish influence; experienced no violence or even calls for violence against any individual Jew or Jews in general. Indeed, all the evidence points toward the "success" of the Jews of Georgetown in business, in politics, and in social assimilation.

The marriage of Heiman and Rose Kaminski's son Harold to Julia Pyatt marked the first intermarriage between Georgetown's Jewish community and Georgetown's old plantation aristocracy. There is today no way to ascertain whether the two families supported or opposed the young people's choice. But there is a way to tell what Georgetonians in general thought of it. Shortly thereafter, they elected Harold Kaminski to be their mayor.[32]

Harry Golden, the famous editor of Charlotte's *Carolina Israelite*, contended that "there is little real anti-Semitism in the South." He added that "there is even a solid core of philo-Semitism, the explanation of which lies in the very character of southern Protestantism itself—in the Anglo-Calvinist devotion to the Old Testament and the Hebrew prophets." Jews have often found greater acceptance in such small southern towns as Georgetown than in northern industrial cities.[33] Whatever the explanation, the Jews of Georgetown accomplished extraordinary economic, political, and social success in the nineteenth century. Their Gentile neighbors elected them to high public office, entered into business partnerships with them, and welcomed them into their most prestigious social clubs. This brief account may make their achievement seem easier than it was. But that accomplishment is not an interpretation. It is a fact.

Still, to limit the story of Georgetown Jewry to what can be known with certainty may, in fact, distort the Jewish past. Southern pressures for conformity affected those who feared the consequences of living, thinking, and worshipping differently. To be sure, the region's demands for conformity operated on both Jew and Gentile; but it affected Jews differently, because it led to a minimizing of Jewish life and tradition and thus struck at the very roots of Jewish identity.[34]

From their first appearance in South Carolina, Jews were confronted with a crisis of identity. A *persecuted* minority's sense of identity may be heightened by being singled out for oppression, but how does one remain a Jew while becoming a southerner? Could the religion of their ancestors, which had survived centuries of persecutions and pogroms in the Old World, survive the journey from a closed society to an open one? The Israelites of the early Diaspora feared that their children might grow up ignorant of the Torah or might even become skeptics who abandoned their faith, who ignored the commandments and rituals, who lost their sense of the past.[35] If asked the classic question of identity, "Who are you?" would such a child give the traditional answer, "I am Isaac Ben Abraham" (I am the son of my father), or would he merely reply, "I am Isaac Moses of Georgetown"?

These are questions I wish I could answer. The history of Georgetown Jewry is not merely the outside, or public, history that can be documented by evidence. Without an understanding of the emotional texture of interior life we cannot pretend to have understood the history of Georgetown's Jews—or anyone else. How did they perceive the political, economic, and social world in which they lived? How did that world affect their emotional reality? How did they deal with what Eli Evans calls "the loneliness that plagues small-town Jews throughout the South?"[36]

In particular I wish it were possible to answer more questions about the religious life of Georgetown's Jews. The simplest means of sustaining Jewish identity is orthodoxy, to keep at least the ritual if not always to keep the faith. Nevertheless, there was a drift toward a lower level of religious observance during the nineteenth century, even to the extent of secularism and nonobservance. The Mishnah (the basic part of the Talmud consisting of the codified oral law) may still have rested next to the Hebrew scriptures in the Jewish household, but neither was consulted as often as it might have been. Many of the Jews of Georgetown were members of Beth Elohim in Charleston, the second-oldest synagogue in North America. But the trip to Charleston was too long and difficult to attempt weekly. On most Sabbath mornings, religious meetings were held in someone's home, where a *minyan* (or quorum) of ten adult male Jews could be assembled. The Winyah Indigo society offered the use of its hall for High Holy Days. Some evidence survives of the religious ritual of circumcision performed under adverse conditions during the Civil War. I wish it were possible to reconstruct the extent to which the Jews of Georgetown may have kept kosher kitchens, for food served symbolic as well as nutritional functions. Food was a way of expressing and maintaining basic commitments of Jewish identity. Perhaps the Jews of Georgetown were more like the Jewish family in Anniston, Alabama, who recalled their "favorite Shabbas meal" at the dawn of the twentieth century as "oyster stew; steak, ham, or fried chicken; Mama's homemade biscuits and corn bread, too; hoppin' john . . . and sweet potato pie for dessert."[37]

Each spring the Hebrew community of Georgetown, like Jews the world over, gathered to celebrate Passover with the ritual of the Seder, commemorating their ancestors' escape from slavery in ancient Egypt. In a ceremonial yet joyous observance family and friends gathered around the dinner table to teach the children the story of the Exodus, the story of how the Jews—after forty years of wandering in the wilderness—triumphed over despair and returned to the Promised Land. The biblical events were related within the structure of the Haggadah, with hymns, prayers, and stories, and through the eating of symbolic foods. The traditional Seder meal included matzos, salt water, and bitter herbs to recall the Egyptian bondage, and a mixture of apples, nuts, spices, and wine to symbolize the mortar made by the ancient Jews for Pharaoh's bricks. The Seder thus presented history through symbolic action that explained the present by explaining the past, symbolic action that gave meaning and value to daily life. Some came to the Seder for religious reasons: tradition holds that God ordained the Passover rites as an enduring reminder of his deliverance of the Jews from slavery. No doubt others came because of family ties, friendship, good food, and wine. Even in a time when ritual observance among Jews was waning, the ancient ritual of the Seder remained vital, part of the way in which the Jews of Georgetown defined themselves as Jewish. No other festival was so influential upon Jewish thought and ritual as Passover. As the Jews of Georgetown brought into it their historical traditions, it became a ceremony that not only allowed them individual sacrifices of redemption, but also reminded them of the fragility of freedom and the necessity of vigilance.[38]

Similarly, Hanukkah—the Festival of Lights—brightened the dark of winter for Georgetown's Jews with a joyous celebration of fun and feasting among family and friends, a celebration punctuated with jest and song. They were celebrating a miracle that occurred in 165 B.C.E. when Judah the Maccabee and his Jewish army had driven the invaders from Judea. In gratitude to God, they attempted to rededicate their Temple. Miraculously, their single container of oil burned for eight days and became a basis for the eight-day celebration of Hanukkah. Each night the Jews of Georgetown, like Jews elsewhere, would carefully place the festive candles in the menorah from right to left, according to tradition, and would light them from left to right. The Shammah, or lead candle, was used to light the other eight candles and was placed in the center above the rest. Each night one candle would be added until, on the eighth night, all the candles glowed from the menorah. Once the candles were lit, thoughts turned inevitably to food. While the Seder meal was governed by law and ritual, Hanukkah foods were derived from legend and folk custom. By tradition it must be hearty fare, bringing warmth to the cold winter. In this celebration, so joyous and festive, the Jews of Georgetown were reminded not only of the world's first great victory for religious freedom, but also of the many obstacles their ancestors had overcome to maintain their beliefs. Thus Hanukkah strengthened their sense of Jewish identity, both as a religion and as a people.[39]

In modern times, Jews have been pushed and pulled across numerous linguistic, cultural, and political boundaries. I wish it were possible to explore more closely the emotional texture of relationships between Sephardic and Ashkenazic Jews in early Georgetown. The formation in 1824 of the Reformed Society of Israelites in Charleston—the beginnings of Reform Judaism in America—strongly affected Georgetown Jewry, some of whom were members of the Reformed Society. Reform Judaism, which has been called "the folk religion of the German-American Jew," represented a crisis in the longstanding linguistic and religious differences dividing Sephardim and Ashkanazim. Throughout the nineteenth century, Sephardim were increasingly supplanted in Georgetown by Ashkenazim. But what were the relations between older German Ashkenazim in

Georgetown and the Eastern European Ashkenazim—such as Heiman Kaminski and the Baums—who came into the community after the Civil War? What did they think of one another?[40]

Millions of Polish, Russian, and Lithuanian Jews immigrated to America at the turn of the century. In the North, they complained of what they considered the worst features of the older German-Jewish community and of the treatment they received at their hands. They considered the older American Jews to be socially aloof and prejudiced against Eastern Europeans, and they viewed their assimilation with suspicion. They were not, to be sure, entirely mistaken in all of this. Many American Jews did distance themselves from the newcomers. After their arrival, the historian Moses Rischin writes of New York, "to be identified as a Jew became more and more irksome. Hosts of uncouth strangers seemed to cast a pall upon all Jews." Many American Jews doubted the potential of the new Ashkenazim to succeed.[41]

In Georgetown the relationship between old and new Ashkenazim appears to have been more open and more positive than in New York, at least on the surface. Heiman Kaminski and other Eastern European Jews seem to have met easy acceptance not only from the older Jews of Georgetown but also from other Georgetonians. But we would do well to remember that all that survives is not all there was.

These conclusions are more tentative and more speculative than I would wish, but it cannot be helped. Inevitably they must rest on inference and assumption as well as on evidence. In the absence of more personal documents, many of the questions I pose must remain not merely unanswered but unanswerable. Fortunately, sufficient evidence exists to justify confidence in speaking of the achievement of the Jews of Georgetown and to elevate speculation about their sense of Jewish identity from guesswork at least to inference. Even as they assimilated into the larger community of Georgetown, by preserving a heritage of cultural tradition they were able to remain Jews as they became southerners.

In 1980 I interviewed Judge Phil Ringel, a retired federal judge living in Daytona Beach, Florida. His father had come to Georgetown from Austria as a young man, and he himself was born in Georgetown in the last decade of the nineteenth century. Judge Ringel reached into his wallet and showed me a photograph he carried there of the Ringel Heights Baptist Church. He proudly informed me that Georgetown had the world's only Baptist church named after a Jew. Judge Ringel told me that in Georgetown it was always best to be an Episcopalian. But if you weren't an Episcopalian, it didn't matter whether you were a Baptist or a Jew. Or even a Presbyterian.[42]

To comprehend the Jewish experience in Georgetown, it is necessary to comprehend the community's delicate balance of continuity and adaptation. Perhaps that balance is best illustrated in a Jewish parable. A holy man knew a certain prayer that had to be said at a certain time over a fire lit in a certain way at a certain place in the middle of a certain forest. If the ritual were properly followed, God would hear the prayer and a great calamity would be averted. But in the next generation the holy man's son no longer knew the prayer. He knew only the time and place and how to light the fire. Still God heard the prayer of the heart, and that was enough. Once again the calamity was averted. In the next generation the holy man's grandson no longer knew the prayer or the time or the place in the forest. But there was still a prayer in his heart, and that was enough. God heard the prayer of the heart, and again the calamity was averted.[43]

To lose a cultural heritage, to lose the prayer of the heart, is to lose something precious to any people—but perhaps something crucial to Jews. The break with the past is not uniquely Jewish; it is part of the modern condition. But to be a Jew is to be part of a community woven of memory, an enclave of eternity. To lose the past, to lose tradition and continuity, to lose the prayer of the heart, may be to lose a future as well.

A Little Music on the Slave Plantation. Drawing by Charles Joyner, from a detail of an anonymous folk painting, *The Old Plantation*, c. 1800, in the Abby Aldrich Rockefeller Collection, Colonial Williamsburg. (Unless noted otherwise, all illustrations were drawn by Charles Joyner.)

John Brown. Drawing based on photo in the Library of Congress taken at Brown's trial in 1859.

Ben Owen, Master Potter

Pottery from Author's Collection. Clockwise from left: nineteenth-century Edge-field (S.C.) jug; candlestick by Ben Owen III, at age 15; covered pot by Ben Owen; pitcher by Waymon Cole, Jugtown, N.C. Photo by Michael A. Black.

Sweetgrass Baskets from Author's Collection. Clockwise from left: Senegalese basket; three baskets by South Carolina basketmakers, Marie Manigault, Laurie Ann Dumas (age 8, adopted daughter of the great basketmaker Edna Rouse), and Elizabeth German. Photo by Michael A. Black.

Basket Woman. Drawing based on turn-of-the-century photo in the South Caroliniana Library, University of South Carolina, Columbia.

Philip Simmons, Blacksmith. Drawing based on photo in John Vlach's book *Charleston Blacksmith* (University of Georgia Press).

Hank Williams. Drawing based on photo in the Alabama Department of Archives and History, Montgomery.

Bessie Smith. Drawing based on
photo by Carl van Vechten in the
Beinecke Library, Yale University.

Elvis Presley. Drawing based
on photo in the Michael
Ochs Archives, Venice, Calif.

Dizzy Gillespie. Drawing
based on photo taken by
Lee Tanner at the New-
port Jazz Festival, 1963,
courtesy Lee Tanner.

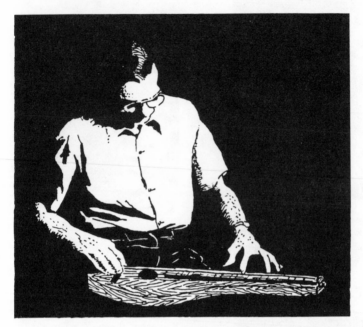

Homer Ledford, Kentucky Dulcimer Maker and Player. Drawing
based on photo in Gerald Alvey's book *Homer Ledford, Dulcimer
Maker* (University of Kentucky Press).

Dulcimer Made by Homer Ledford. Photo
by Charles Joyner.

THE DULCIMER MAKER

Edd Presnell, North Carolina Dulcimer Maker. Needlework picture designed by Charles Joyner.

Dulcimer Made by Edd Presnell, 1987. Photo by Michael A. Black.

Grave of Alice Flagg, All Saints Church (Episcopal), Waccamaw, Pawleys Island, S.C. Inset: detail, inscription on grave marker. Photos by Michael A. Black.

"Alice of the Hermitage." Needlework picture designed by Charles Joyner.

10

The Sounds of Southern Culture
Blues, Country, Jazz, and Rock

In 1928 the Georgia-born historian Ulrich B. Phillips attempted to define the essence of "Southernness" when he declared that the "central theme of Southern history" was "a common resolve, indomitably maintained—that it shall be and remain a white man's country." He insisted that white determination to maintain white supremacy, "whether expressed with the frenzy of a demagogue or maintained with a patrician's quietude," constituted "the cardinal test of a Southerner and the central theme of Southern history." Phillips's own genteel racism, expressed with the quietude of an academic patrician, did not blind him to a realistic recognition of the potency of racism as a factor in southern life. Since then, few have doubted that white racism was *a* central theme; many have doubted that it was *the* central theme. But most have recognized that Phillips was on to a good thing with this "central theme" business, and over the past two generations, one might say that the central theme of southern historians has been the search for a central theme.[1]

Phillips's student David M. Potter wrote in a perceptive 1961 essay that the "essential distinctiveness" of the South was embodied in what he called a folk culture. "In the folk culture of the South," he noted, "the relation of people to one another imparted a distinctive texture as well as a distinctive tempo to their lives." Potter never pursued the implications of that insight, nor did he even describe what he meant by the "folk culture" of the South. But his insight was sound nevertheless.[2]

Southern folk culture is multicultural, the product of the intermingling of Europeans of various ethnic backgrounds with Africans of various ethnic backgrounds and Native Americans of various ethnic backgrounds in one of the world's great epics of cultural transformation. That cultural transformation is perhaps best revealed in southern music, from the fusing of musical and textual elements in the great slave spirituals and the parallel tradition of white spirituals, in the stirring work songs and the blues, and especially in the development and continuing cross-fertilization of musical influences in jazz, blues, rock, and country music.

Black and white southerners worshipped and made music together almost from their colonial beginnings, and they have continued to do so throughout the region's history. Underlying and informing every style of music performed in the South, religious music has been the bedrock of southern vernacular music—both black and white. From the "Dr. Watts" hymns of the eighteenth century through the camp-meeting hymns and shape-note hymnals as well as the black and white spiritual traditions of the nineteenth, to the exciting expressions of gospel music in the twentieth, the performance of worship through music has mutually influenced southerners of both races. Its power was perhaps best expressed by Mahalia Jackson, who chose to devote her musical career exclusively to gospel songs. Growing up in New Orleans, surrounded by jazz bands and blues singers, she recalled that "I loved best to sing in the congregation of our church—the Mount Moriah Baptist Church. All around me I could hear the foot-tapping and hand-clapping. That gave me bounce." She was influenced not only by the music of her own denomination but also by "the Sanctified or Holiness Churches we had in the South." Accompanying themselves on drums, cymbals, tambourines, and triangles, "everybody in there sang and they clapped and stomped their feet and sang with their whole bodies." They sang to "a rhythm we held on to from slavery days, and their music was so strong and expressive it used to bring the tears to my eyes." Virtually all the major southern grassroots musicians—whether country, jazz, bluegrass, rock, or even blues—have testified to the influence of church music on their early musical orientations.[3]

In the closing decades of the nineteenth century, itinerant musicians began to improvise a new musical and poetic form that came to be known as the blues. A black Mississippian recalled that on a Saturday afternoon in the Delta, "everybody would go into town and those fellows like Charley Patton, Robert Johnson, and Howlin' Wolf would be playin' on the streets, standin' by the railroad tracks, people pitchin' 'em nickels and dimes, white and black people both." The blues inevitably reflected the southern soil from which they sprang and to which they belonged. "That's where the blues start from," explained the great Mississippi Delta blues singer Bukka White, "back across them fields . . . right behind one of them mules."[4]

Richard Wright described the blues as "starkly brutal, haunting folk songs created by millions of nameless and illiterate American Negroes." The creators of the blues were marginal individuals even among a marginal people—rural, lower-class black southerners. Yet out of the formless field hollers of southern cotton fields they fashioned a cultural response to the disappointing experience of being "free" in a New South in which however hard they worked they found themselves unable to succeed. Robert Johnson sang:

> I got to keep moving, I got to keep moving
> > blues falling down like hail
> > blues falling down like hail
> Uumh, blues falling down like hail
> > blues falling down like hail
>
> And the days keeps on 'minding me
> > there's a hellhound on my trail,
> > hellhound on my trail,
> > hellhound on my trail.

The blues were "secular spirituals," representing a postemancipation extension of the sorrow songs of the slaves. The blues have been considered *secular*, the devil songs of the convict, the pimp, and the prostitute. But the blues may also be considered *spiritual* in the agonized poetry of their representation of ultimate concern in the African-American experience.[5]

The blues, according to Ralph Ellison, resulted from "an impulse to keep the painful details and episodes of a brutal experience alive in one's aching consciousness, to finger its jagged grain, and to transcend it, not by the consolation of philosophy but by squeezing from it a near-tragic, near-comic lyricism." It is difficult to imagine any more starkly brutal or haunting testimony to the bleakness and bitter frustration of African-American life, to the loneliness and lack of hope in the early twentieth-century South, than the 1926 recording of "Two Nineteen Train" by the Charleston blues singer Bertha "Chippie" Hill: "I'm gonna lay my head on some lonesome railroad line, / Let the two nineteen train pacify my mind."[6]

As a vocal music, the blues found their greatest interpreters in such "classic" female blues singers as Ma Rainey, "Chippie" Hill, Alberta Hunter, and above all, Bessie Smith. According to Alberta Hunter, "Bessie Smith was the greatest of them all. . . . Even though she was raucous and loud, she had a sort of a tear—no, not a tear, but there was a *misery* in what she did."[7]

As the blues were developing in the Deep South, black southerners were developing other new musical forms, drawing not only upon folk tradition but also upon European instruments and methods of playing them. Ragtime was most commonly played on a piano, marked by syncopation in the treble juxtaposed to a steady rhythm in the bass. The first published rag was composed in 1897 by a white musician, but the acknowledged "King of Ragtime" was a black southerner—Scott Joplin. Growing up in a musical family in Texarkana, Texas, he not only absorbed African-American folk music, but he also studied European classics with a German piano teacher. The interplay of African and European musical influences was crucial in Joplin's artistic development.[8]

§

New Orleans at the turn of the century was the crossroads of an exciting mélange of musical traditions. Patterns of separating and mixing in New Orleans were always complex, even more complex than in the rest of the South. But while new legal codes sought to keep the races apart, other activities brought creative and racially diverse people together in New Orleans, where spirituals and blues from the plantations rubbed shoulders with opera and concert music, ragtime and brass bands with French, Spanish, and Caribbean folksongs and dances. It was, as they say in New Orleans, a rich gumbo.[9]

The early jazz musicians learned to play their European instruments using European-style march music as a model, but the sounds they blew through their horns were anything but European. They were sounds African Americans had been evolving in the South for more than two centuries, out of pain, poverty, and injustice. Adopting the blues timbre and the blues spirit, they eschewed the tonal "purity" pursued by European horn players in favor of a more expressive emulation of the human voice. Jazz was rooted in the blues.[10]

Another important element in the emergence of jazz was the New Orleans brass band tradition. Brass band funeral marches had originated among antebellum whites but were well entrenched in New Orleans by the turn of the century, where they absorbed the musical traditions of slave funerals. George Lewis, a clarinetist, recalled, "I knew the spirituals, I always did know the spirituals. . . . Even when I was a kid, I heard 'The Saints Go Marchin' In.'. . . I heard it in the churches; I heard it at wakes. . . . When I first heard 'Closer Walk with Thee,' I heard it slow. . . . First time I played it was with, ah, I played it with the Eureka Band. . . . A woman asked us to play for a funeral, and we played it without any music." There was also a parallel New Orleans tradition in which white bands played for funerals. Papa Jack Laine, leader of the fabled Reliance Band, recalled the New Orleans tradition of funerals with marching bands. "That's the time it was a rage for a colored band, you know, played funerals, for colored." White bands played for funerals, too, Laine recalled. Nick LaRocca, leader of the Original Dixieland Jazz Band, also recalled having played funerals in New Orleans between 1908 and 1916. Laine denied that he ever went to any black funerals as a youngster. He said he did not really know what kind of music blacks were playing as he grew up. Both men denied that they were influenced by black tradition.[11]

The first individual to emerge from the misty bayous of jazz prehistory was a cornetist, "Buddy" Bolden. In the absence of any known recordings (despite rumors of a lost Buddy Bolden cylinder), he has become a larger-than-life figure more nearly comparable to John Henry than to any known musician. "On a still day," Louis Armstrong maintained, "you could hear him a mile away." Perhaps because of such legends, Buddy Bolden became the first "King of Jazz."[12]

The career of "King" Buddy Bolden was cut short by mental illness, and his crown passed to Freddie Keppard, leader of the famous Olympia Band. Keppard's style was incandescent, indelible, and erratic. He was famed for his power and drive. "He became to be the greatest hot trumpeter in existence," Jelly Roll Morton contended. "He hit the highest and the lowest notes on a trumpet that anybody outside of Gabriel ever did." But Keppard "spent every dime he ever made on whiskey," Morton added. "A quart a day? That was at the beginning," recalled the veteran New Orleans banjoist Johnny St. Cyr. "Freddie Keppard graduated from that."[13]

As Keppard's career disintegrated, he was succeeded by another cornetist, Joe Oliver, who was destined to become the next King and the most influential of the early jazz musicians. If Freddie Keppard was known for his power and drive, King Joe Oliver was famed for his subtlety and imagination. His cornet was lyrical and melancholy, with a dark sound and laid-back attack that seemed to disappear almost before it registered, drifting away like smoke.[14] As a youth Louis Armstrong had a job driving a coal cart. He was always happy to be sent to Storeyville, the city's legalized red-light district, where King Oliver was playing. Once he delivered "an or-der of stone coal to the prostitute who used to hustle in her crib right next to Pete Lala's cabaret. Just so's I could hear King Oliver play. I was too young to go into Pete Lala's at the time. And I'd just stand there in that lady's crib listening to King Oliver beat out one of those good ole good-ones like *Panama* or *High Society.* All of a sudden it would dawn on the lady that I was still in her crib and she'd say—'What's the matter with you, boy? Why are you still there standing so quiet?' And there I'd have to explain to her that I was being inspired by *the* King Oliver and his orchestra. And then she handed me a cute one by saying—'Well, this is no place to day-dream. I've got my work to do.'"[15]

There were some mixed jazz bands in early New Orleans, even after 1902, when, as Jelly Roll Morton put it, "they began that segregation out-fit." For example, Papa Jack Laine, who led the earliest of the New Orleans white bands to play the new music, insisted that he never had black play-ers in his band. But when Laine was interviewed for the Jazz Archive at Tulane, his wife, Blanche, told Richard Allen that despite what her hus-band claimed, "they had some bands were pretty good mixed up" at the turn of the century. Laine was defensive; speaking of one musician, he said, "When I found out he was a colored boy, I stopped hiring him." In New Orleans racial lines were somewhat more fluid than elsewhere, and race was often a matter of context.[16]

Laine veteran Tom Brown was strongly influenced by black musicians in New Orleans. When he and his brother Steve organized their own band around 1913, they hired an African-American bass player. Tom Brown re-called, "He was a light complected Creole sort of a fella. He played a good bass. I used to admire him with the colored bands." Steve Brown added, "He played a good bass." But there were no black faces in "Tom Brown's Band from Dixieland" when it became the first to carry New Orleans jazz beyond the Crescent City. People whispered that Brown's Band was play-ing "jazz" when it opened in Chicago in 1915. Recognizing the titillating potential of the word (which had not theretofore been associated with music), the club's manager billed the group as "Brown's Dixieland Jass Band, Direct from New Orleans." The band's success stimulated a north-ern search for more of this exciting music from the South.[17]

The year 1917 was a pivotal one in jazz history for three reasons: First, the general public began to hear about jazz with the release of the first recordings of the music. Second, Secretary of the Navy Josephus Daniels made New Orleans brothels off-limits to the navy. Deprived of its main patrons, Storeyville closed down, forcing many musicians to seek employment elsewhere. Among the New Orleans musicians joining the Great Migration was King Oliver, who set out for Chicago, where there was a ready-made audience of black southerners thirsty for the kind of music they had left behind. Third, a child was born in Cheraw, South Carolina, who was given the name John Birks Gillespie.[18]

It is not the least of the ironies of southern history that the first jazz recordings were made by a white band. They were fresh from the exciting New Orleans music scene, they played without scores, they played "hotter" than their audiences had ever heard white musicians play before, and they called themselves the Original Dixieland Jass Band. Both the songs and the styles of the five Papa Jack Laine alumni were staples of the New Orleans jazz tradition as it had been developing for nearly two decades. The ODJB succeeded in playing jazz as something more than mere imitation, not only reproducing something of the legitimate feeling of an Oliver performance, but also making separate and valid emotional statements within their adopted musical tradition. In both Chicago and New York they stunned musicians, white and black, who had never heard anything like the new music from New Orleans.[19]

Inspired by the pioneer black jazz musicians of New Orleans, the New Orleans Rhythm Kings soon became even more prominent. "We did our best to copy the colored music we'd heard at home," the trumpeter Paul Mares acknowledged. "We did the best we could, but naturally we couldn't play real colored style." In an extraordinary flouting of southern racial mores, the African-American artist Jelly Roll Morton served as musical director to oversee recording sessions of the NORK in 1923. Morton even played piano with them on his famous composition "Milenburg Joys" and several other pieces.[20]

By the 1920s jazz had become a national fad, and the so-called Jazz Age was underway. The historian Eric Hobsbawm marveled at what he called the "extraordinary expansion" of jazz, which, he wrote, "has practically no cultural parallel for speed and scope except the early expansion of [Islam]."[21]

By 1922, King Oliver sent for Louis Armstrong, then twenty-two years old, to come to Chicago and join his famous Creole Band at the Lincoln Gardens as second cornet. In the Oliver band, the young cornetist developed rapidly. His tone, his range, his speed, and his creativity were like nothing jazz had known before. In his elegant and fearless solos, the melody disappeared and reappeared like facets of a dark jewel, each phrase sweeping away the silence before it in a kind of controlled ecstasy. Once Louis Armstrong hit his stride, jazz was never again quite the same.[22]

Armstrong's hegira from New Orleans to Chicago had a powerful impact on northern audiences, especially on other musicians. Hoagy Carmichael and Bix Beiderbecke went to hear Oliver and Armstrong at the Lincoln Gardens in 1923. As Carmichael recalled, they

> took two quarts of bathtub gin, a package of muggles [marijuana], and headed for the black-and-tan joint where King Oliver's band was playing. The King featured two trumpets, a piano, a bass fiddle, and a clarinet. As I sat down to light my first muggle, a big black fellow, playing second trumpet for Oliver . . . slashed into *Bugle Call Rag.* I dropped my cigarette and gulped my drink. Bix was on his feet, his eyes popping. For taking the first chorus was that second trumpet, Louis Armstrong. Louis was taking it fast. . . . Then the muggles took effect and my body got light. Every note Louis hit was perfection.

For Eddie Condon, Bud Freeman, and Jimmy McPartland, hearing King Oliver's Creole Jazz Band was little short of a religious conversion experience. "Oliver lifted his horn," Condon recalled, "and the first blast of Canal Street Blues hit me. It was hypnosis at first hearing." To these young white musicians, jazz was like "a new religion just come from Jerusalem."[23]

In the interracial jam sessions of the exiled southerners in Chicago, racial lines were loosened and cultural sharing began to occur. The white New Orleans bassist Steve Brown recalled that he played in Chicago with another New Orleans expatriate: "I played alongside of Armstrong there, see. . . . The cornet player, Armstrong." Away from the constraints of southern racial conventions, "we used to have more fun with Louie than enough, see."[24]

By 1924, Louis Armstrong was gracing the brass section of Fletcher Henderson's band in New York and was developing a unique voice in his improvisations, a distinctively African-American voice that asserted an empowering creativity that amounted to the musical component of the Harlem Renaissance. In his dramatic and lyrical improvisations he not only impelled the jazz world's first big band to prominence but also thrust the field of jazz into a new era—the era of the star soloist.[25]

While Armstrong was revolutionizing jazz cornet and later trumpet with his improvisations, other musicians were pioneering new approaches to other instruments. Among the most significant were three southerners. The emergence of the New Orleans–born tenor saxophonist Lester

("Pres") Young signaled the emergence of the saxophone as an autono-
mous instrument challenging the trumpet's previous dominance of the
jazz scene. With his gentle and downy tone and his subtly beautiful improvisations, Young showed that "sometimes one single deeply expressed
note could say more than a hundred skillfully executed others." The self-
taught Jack Teagarden, a white Texan, almost singlehandedly transformed
the trombone, with his warm tone, his bluesy lyricism, and his logically
constructed solos, from a novelty instrument for imitating barnyard
sounds to a real solo instrument ranking only slightly behind trumpet and
saxophone. And the Georgia-born bandleader and arranger Fletcher
Henderson adapted the African and African-American antiphonal response of the spirituals and work songs into the soloist-riff structure of
his arrangements, making those arrangements the catalyst for transforming the big band into a swinging vehicle for jazz improvisation. In the
process he transformed jazz itself from a music limited to small groups
into music for big bands.[26]

It was 1940, and the Great Depression still lay heavy upon Harlem. The
young musician was not quite twenty-three. They had named him John
Birks Gillespie when he was born down in South Carolina, but somewhere
along the way he had acquired the nickname "Dizzy." He was developing
an individual trumpet style in keeping with the harmonies he heard in his
head, when he began to meet at a place called Minton's Playhouse in Harlem to make informal music with a small group of fellow expatriates from
the South, such as the North Carolinian Thelonious Monk and the Texan
Charlie Christian. Monk was only twenty, but he was already playing
many of the challenging harmonic sequences, jagged but oddly logical
melodic contours, and expressive rhythmic accents that would make him
a major jazz pianist and composer. Charlie Christian, born in Dallas but
raised in Oklahoma City, had just turned twenty-one and had a steady job
with Benny Goodman. Although his playing on electric guitar clearly revealed the influence of western swing (a new fusion of jazz, blues, and
string band idioms developed by white country musicians in Texas and
Oklahoma), he was already developing a mature personal style. Christian
typically substituted new chords into the progression, suggesting different keys. He would start a solo with a placid legato, snake up the middle
register, then suddenly erupt into a series of speedy double-time phrases
that delighted and stimulated Dizzy. So did the boldness of Thelonious

Monk's harmonies and his complex compositional probings in which each phrase evolved from its predecessor. Monk favored unusual harmonic progressions and a calculated use of dissonance in his solos, punctuating his serpentine mixture of strange intervals and off-course flurries of oblique, flyaway arpeggios with sudden rhythmic downward jabs.[27]

But the stimulation did not all flow one way. "Dizzy was everywhere at the time," recalled the bassist Milt Hinton. "Charlie Parker was never there." In fact it was some months later, in 1941, before Parker became part of the Minton scene. Parker was an original and fertile musician, and obviously a kindred spirit; but by then the Minton dissidents were already well on their way to creating a new form of jazz. Gillespie was the essential catalyst: he would blow a promissory note, then let slip a sly, epigrammatic phrase, allowing several beats to sneak by almost unnoticed; then, with quick feints to right and left, he would trampoline into the stratosphere with a series of upper-octave choruses played at blistering speeds, exhilarating combinations of long asymmetric lines punctuated by brief rhythmic ejaculations, sometimes giving the impression that he was playing two solos at once. He extended the trumpet's range beyond gravity; and he not only hit climactic high notes, he played complex chromatic phrases up there, as though engaging in some postmodern poetic discourse of his own. His improvisations embraced all sorts of crisscrossing, reversal, implied polyphony, irony, allusion, whimsy, and parody. At the same time he created logical (but playful) improvisations over the most bewildering of Monk's harmonic progressions. As he incorporated his own advanced harmonies into a complex melodic line played with dazzling technical facility, he stimulated higher achievements among his colleagues as well. A synthesis began to take place; a new kind of jazz began to crystallize. It came to be called bebop, after a characteristic Gillespie trumpet phrase.[28]

Dizzy Gillespie and his fellow southern expatriates knew they were creating a new jazz at Minton's, and they disdained sharing their innovations with unhip spirits who, as Gillespie put it, "walked in . . . and tried to sit in with us. . . . There were always some cats showing up there who couldn't blow at all but would take six or seven choruses to prove it." When the musical dissidents began to play the different changes they had created, "the no-talent guys" would "become discouraged after the first chorus and slowly walk away." Some musicians, like the drummer Dave Tough of the Woody Herman band, recognized that something important was taking place. "As we walked in," he remembered, "these cats snatched up their horns and blew crazy stuff. One would stop all of a sudden and another would start for no reason at all. We never could tell when a solo was supposed to begin or end. Then they all quit at once and walked off the stand. It scared us."[29]

Nearly four years went by before the music created by the Minton dissidents was heard by very many people, in part because a recording ban was in effect at the time. But somehow the word got around. The success of bebop coincided with the end of World War II. By 1944 Gillespie and Monk were recording the new music and finding employment in Fifty-second Street clubs, where they could bring modernist ideas to a broader jazz audience. Their music, as Gillespie would later note without hyperbole, "laid a foundation for all the music that is being played now."[30]

Not only were the blues at the heart of the jazz of black southerners, they influenced the music of white southerners as well, lending chords and color to the emerging new musical form known as country. Charlie Parker, the great jazz saxophonist, was a great fan of country music. When asked why, Parker exclaimed, "The stories, man! Listen to the stories!" The lyrics of country music express an understanding of the peaks and valleys of everyday life, of continuity and change in an industrializing South, portrayed in down-to-earth terms. Like the great blues singers, the most enduring legends of country music have been those who have put an autobiographical stamp on their songs, who have been able to convince their audiences that they have *lived* the songs they sing. Over the generations the songs have captivated listeners with their apparent sincerity. Country music lyrics explore the same themes that have preoccupied the region's greatest writers: the struggle of working-class folk to survive in a world in which the economic odds seem stacked against them, the warm appeal of home and fireside and the lonesome trainwhistle call to forsake such an existence in search of new experiences, and the persistent spiritual travail of being torn between such conflicting values, the travail of what William Faulkner calls "the problem of the human heart divided against itself."[31]

Country music was ostensibly the purest expression of what might be called "white soul," but it was heavily influenced by the music of black southerners. The blues and country music were cousins. Country music is rooted in the music of the early settlers, deriving its forms and styles not only from the culture of the British Isles but also from that of Germany,

Spain, France, Mexico, Africa, and the Caribbean. One can find in country music not only tastes of the old ballad styles of singing, of bagpipes
and fiddle sounds, of minstrel show songs and sentimental songs of the
nineteenth century, but also large helpings of the blues.[32]

When guitars first became an integral part of southern folk music in
the early 1920s, black and white musical interaction accelerated. African-
American melodic, textual, and instrumental styles influenced white
musicians, as social, economic, and racial barriers that separated southerners were bypassed by music and converted into positive forces of
mutual appreciation. In the 1920s Jimmie Rodgers, a white Mississippian, fused the twelve-bar country blues of his black neighbors with the
Swiss yodels (or "tyrolean warbling") of popular vaudeville entertainers,
to become the first great star of country music. As a youth Jimmie Rodgers learned to play the banjo from black gandy dancers in the Meridian
railyards, and heard the songs and slang. Soon he picked up the guitar and
the blues from black musicians on Meridian's Tenth Street. The founders
of the intense Delta blues style were Mississippians, and the singer who
brought the blues into country music was a Mississippian, too.[33]

The 1927 sessions in Bristol, Tennessee, when Jimmie Rodgers and the
Carter Family made their first recordings, are generally regarded as seminal in the history of country music. They created a transition in public
taste away from the older Appalachian style of string band with vocal
associated with musicians such as Charlie Poole, Riley Puckett, Ernest
Stoneman, and Henry Whitter to the newer black-influenced style of
Rodgers.[34]

Another important country musician decisively influenced by the
music of black southerners was Bob Wills. He grew up in Texas with his
musician father's old-time fiddle and banjo music ringing in his ears. But
he also lived and worked among black southerners from whom he absorbed the blues and jazz. Since skin color mattered less to musicians than
did music, the young white fiddler and his black musician friends borrowed freely from one another, sharing musical concepts and, in the process, creating new musical styles. Not only did Wills learn black music
directly from black musicians but also indirectly from radio and phonograph recordings. Fusing elements of both black and white traditions, he
created a unique musical hybrid of big band and string band—a complex
and exciting musical form that became known as Western swing. Many
of his band, the Texas Playboys, had begun as jazz performers, and they
immersed themselves in both the style and repertory of blues and jazz.

There is a story that Wills while drunk once hired a black trumpet player. Skin color may not have mattered to musicians, but it certainly did to audiences, who were unwilling to accept a black trumpeter playing jazz in an otherwise white band. Wills emerged as a major innovator in country music during the 1930s.[35]

Other important country musicians were also decisively influenced by the music of black southerners. The Carter Family of Virginia learned such songs as "Coal Miner's Blues" and "Cannon Ball Blues" from Leslie Riddles, a black neighbor who sang and played guitar. At about the age of twelve, Bill Monroe, the future "father of bluegrass," received instrumental training from a black musician named Arnold Shultz, for whom Monroe then served as guitar accompanist. "Arnold and myself," Monroe recollected, "we played for a lot of square dances back in those days." Monroe's early exposure to Shultz and other local black musicians instilled in him an enduring fondness for the blues. When he formed his famous band, the Blue Grass Boys, he blended the blues with Anglo-American folk music to create an exciting new kind of country music containing elements of each. Hank Williams grew up in Greenville, Alabama, his repertoire and singing style strongly affected by the black music he had heard. When he was about twelve years old, he began to follow a black street singer known locally as Tee-Tot (Rufus Payne), who played for nickels and pennies on the streets of Greenville. Tee-Tot liked the little white boy and taught him songs and guitar chords.[36]

Country music recording sessions were integrated almost as early (and as rarely) as those of jazz musicians. A few white country performers included black musicians on their recordings, as when Jimmie Rodgers recorded "Waiting for a Train" with an Atlanta jazz band in 1928. In 1930 Rodgers featured Louis Armstrong and his then wife, Lillian Hardin Armstrong, on his celebrated recording of "Blue Yodel No. 9." Another country performer, Jimmie Davis, recorded with black blues singers, by whom he was much influenced. His early associations with black southerners, both personally and professionally, contrast strikingly with his later posture as an ultrasegregationist governor of Louisiana.[37]

The recorded blues of the 1920s became the urban, electrified, and aggressive "rhythm-and-blues" of the 1950s, mainly produced for blacks by blacks. But the fences between musical forms were not high enough to keep musical styles from "crossing over." Black and white southerners had long engaged in a vigorous musical interchange, and it was probably inevitable that country and rhythm-and-blues would fuse their cultural traditions and musical chemistries. When they did, they set off a musical explosion called rock 'n' roll that still reverberates in its latter-day form of rock.[38]

The performer who most personifies the musical mixing of black and white southerners, of rhythm-and-blues with country, was Elvis Aron Presley of Tupelo, Mississippi, a working-class white country kid who fused the black sounds of urban blues and the white sounds of country music, along with large doses of both black and white gospel music, into the sound that made him a galvanizing cultural force as the first great star of rock 'n' roll. His first disc, recorded in 1954, featured "That's All Right, Mama," an old rhythm-and-blues tune first recorded by the bluesman Arthur "Big Boy" Crudup, on one side, and a supercharged version of Bill Monroe's bluegrass classic, "Blue Moon of Kentucky," on the other. Elvis and such kindred spirits at Memphis's Sun Records as Carl Perkins, Jerry Lee Lewis, Johnny Cash, and Roy Orbison, soon created the musical form known as "rockabilly" music. Not only in his music, but in his accent, his diet, his manners, and his hedonistic but pious religiosity, Elvis exemplified a characteristically southern blend of African and British cultures. "The colored folk been singin' it and playin' it just the way I'm doin' now, man, for more years than I know," Elvis explained. "Nobody paid it no mind 'til I goosed it up."[39]

But black southerners also left their mark on country music more directly, as country music performers. Some, like Louis Armstrong and Lillian Hardin Armstrong on the early Jimmie Rodgers recording sessions, or Ray Charles on his highly popular recordings of country music in the 1960s, made their contributions in their usual African-American style. DeFord Bailey was another story. Bailey was a popular and frequently scheduled performer on the Grand Ole Opry from 1925 to 1941, playing harmonica and occasionally banjo. The first black superstar identified with country music, however, was Charley Pride. His first records were accompanied by neither photographs nor any mention in the promotional material that he was black. His singing was so country that people hearing it on the radio or buying his records did not suspect his racial identity. By the time they saw his photograph or saw him in concert, his singing had already won them over.[40]

Music is not, of course, the only element of southern culture. But the transformation of southern music may serve as a model for explaining other elements of culture change across the South. As E. P. Thompson notes, both "resistance to change and assent to change arise from the whole culture." On the folk level, black and white traditions in the South were similar enough to permit growth and continued cultural exchange, but different enough to keep those cultural exchanges exciting.[41]

Thus it may be seen that the central theme of southern culture is an unconscious resolve, subliminally maintained, that the South has been and will remain a multicultural mix of European and African elements. Whether expressed with the virtuosic frenzy of a Dizzy Gillespie or an Elvis Presley, or with the laid-back quietude of a Lester Young or a Willie Nelson, whether stubbornly denied or acknowledged with pride, every black southerner has a European heritage as well as an African one, and every white southerner has an African heritage as well as a European one. *That* shared heritage, I submit, constitutes the cardinal test of southern identity and the central theme of southern culture.

11

Sweet Music

Tradition, Creativity, and the Appalachian Dulcimer

It was an evening in Knoxville, Tennessee, in the summer of 1965 when I first met Homer Ledford. A group of people were crowded around one of the booths at the craft fair, listening to a strange, sweet music. The sign said, "Fine homemade crafts from the shop of Homer Ledford." The music was quiet. The listeners had silenced their children and were listening intently to the music, its drones echoing as though coming from inside a deep mountain cavern. As I joined the group, I saw within the booth a thin, tall man—lithe as a mountain poplar—hunched over the graceful instrument in his lap. He pressed the melody string against the frets with the fingers of one large hand and strummed the strings with a worn felt pick held in the other. He did not sing but played simply and quietly, at first, beginning with the ancient, stately phrases of "Amazing Grace" and following with the modal melodic inflections of "Old Joe Clark," climbing nimbly up and down the fretboard, as lively as a mountain square dance. He punctuated "Wildwood Flower" with sudden agile sprays of melody in the upper register and climaxed with the dazzling runs of "Little Liza Jane," his sprightly clusters of notes—slippery as a mountain trout—just on the verge of darting away. The sound of his dulcimer was a remarkable convergence of lyricism and raucousness, melancholy and high rambunctious humor. He let the sound die slowly, echoing in the summer evening. After a little he put his instrument down, letting his audience hang at that intoxicating point somewhere between satisfaction and wanting more.

What was most singular, however, was that the same hands that had just brought music to life on the dulcimer had also brought the instrument to life—had carved and sawed and glued and sanded and polished it.

Homer Ledford—for it was he—had taken a bit of wood and his native genius and from them had created a thing of beauty, a cultural artifact, a work of art to delight the eye and the ear.

The plucked dulcimer, often called the Appalachian dulcimer, is a southern mountain folk instrument. Dulcimers usually have three or four strings (although they may have as many as eight) running over a fretboard. The diatonic scale of the fretboard makes the dulcimer an ideal instrument to accompany songs in the various modes. Mountain people have used them for generations to accompany the tragic English and Scottish ballads as well as for sprightly instrumental pieces.[1]

Unfortunately, the instrument has also become a symbol for a certain stereotype of Appalachian mountaineers as "yesterday's people" in a land where time stood still. Modernization did not pass Appalachia by.[2] Still, the region continues to be perceived as a "vanishing frontier," an anachronistic throwback in twentieth-century America. On the surface, the dulcimer would seem to symbolize just how hopelessly backward Appalachia—with its quaint folkways, folksongs, and folk instruments—really is. But a closer look at the dulcimer and dulcimer making reveals an Appalachian culture that is dynamic and creative, not static and anachronistic—a tradition still of value to today's people in Appalachia.

The folk music revival of the 1960s, and especially the prominence attained in that revival by two dulcimer players from the southern highlands, Jean Ritchie of Kentucky and Frank Proffitt of North Carolina, sparked what eventually came to be known as the "dulcimer revival." Dulcimers were produced in greater quantities than ever before in the southern mountains to serve a growing urban interest in the instrument. The dulcimer revival not only created markets for native southern folk artists but also sparked renewed interest in the art of dulcimer making among disaffected young urbanites in all sections of the country.[3]

During the 1960s and 1970s I came to know several traditional dulcimer makers in the southern Appalachians. They were all highly conscious of their part in preserving a great tradition. They shared my sense of dulcimer making as a precious but endangered art, although they did not share my sense of irony that the dulcimer revival was a direct outgrowth of popular culture's interest in the instrument nor my worry that popular culture's interest is rarely long lasting. But we were all optimistic that both the physical and aural beauty of the dulcimer and the relative ease with which one can learn to play it might help to renew interest in the instrument from generation to generation.[4] We even dreamed that a compensating side effect of the international energy crisis at that time might be a return to acoustic music, or at least a decline in the amperage of popular music, either of which could increase interest in the dulcimer.

These dulcimer makers became my teachers and my friends. They found themselves busier than ever during the dulcimer revival, all of them deriving the greater part of their income from making the instruments. None of them were strangers to power tools, television, or Sears and Roebuck catalogs, and most of them were acquainted with a wide range of other traditional artists through craft fairs. Most of them knew one another's work. And, despite the pervasive influence of various forms of popular culture, they remained traditional folk artists. Folk culture is not defined by its lack of contact with popular culture. Indeed Robert Redfield stresses such contact as the crucial distinction between folk and primitive culture. And folk culture is only partially defined by its cultural conservatism, its tendency to preserve the past with the present and its resistance to change. Folk culture is also partially defined by cultural innovation, by change and variation. The lack of variation in a given item signals to folklorists that the item has not been governed in its development by traditional processes, in other words that it is not folk.[5]

In my interviews with these artists I was particularly interested in how they saw their place within the folk tradition they had inherited. Without slavishly following any questionnaire, our conversations often concentrated on four major questions: 1) How did the artist acquire his or her *competence* in the art? 2) What changes had taken place in the *means* of craftsmanship in his or her lifetime? 3) What was the relationship of craftsmanship to society when he or she was acquiring competence? 4) How had that relationship changed as the society changed? Was dulcimer making a tradition that should be kept alive in today's society, and if so, why? I found the answers deep in the value structures of the artists themselves, in the very personal ways in which they responded to the twin pressures to conform and to be different, to preserve and to create—in short, how they related to the polarities of tradition and innovation.[6]

The relation of Homer Ledford's dulcimer making to the tradition was complex and revealing. "My whole life has been music and making things," Homer Ledford says. That life began on September 26, 1927,

among the misty coves and cliffs of the Tennessee mountains, before the
WPA built roads across the ridges into the valleys. His youth was spent
on the steep hillsides of his parents' farm, surrounded by an Appalachian
folk culture rich in custom, oral tradition, and music.[7]

"When I was a boy," he recalled, "there was a very good fiddler and a
guitar player who traveled all over the country, and they came to our house
every year." The musicians "played for their food and lodging; they might
even stay a week; and we would have people come in and they would play
for everyone, and some of the local people would play, too." Neighbors
also "congregated at our house for play parties; we had fiddles, banjos, and
guitars, and sometimes even a mandolin; we had singing and buck-wing
dancing, too." Nearly everyone in the community knew folk hymns, and
religious music especially appealed to him. At the age of seven or eight
he attended a weeklong shape-note singing-school led by one of his un-
cles in the community's one-room schoolhouse. He did not know anyone
whom folklorists might call a traditional ballad singer, nor did he see or
hear a dulcimer.[8]

The young mountain boy first heard "what is called folk music" in high
school. "The principal introduced some folk songs into the chapel programs by way of a little songbook. At that time, as a teenager, I really didn't
enjoy them very much because I wasn't familiar with them; that is, I had
not heard them in my own community." But he heard music more nearly
like that of his own community from new media in popular culture. His
childhood coincided with "the great hillbilly watershed," when recordings of performances by folk artists were bought and played by the folk
themselves, and recorded songs began to enter tradition—to become "folk
songs"—much as broadsides had entered tradition in the eighteenth and
nineteenth centuries. "Of course I shouldn't leave out the influence of the
old spring-wound phonograph," Ledford says. "Every family tried to have
one, would even trade to get one, say trade a hog for a phonograph. I listened to music on the wax records; I remember that I especially enjoyed
Buell Kazee's recordings of banjo-picking in the real old style." And the
radio was also entering the mountains. "My family bought a battery-pow-
ered radio—we didn't have electricity in those days—and I started listening to station WSM and the Grand Ole Opry; that influenced me a lot
because it was the only well-played music I could hear on a regular basis."
Radio spread localized folk styles over a broader region. "Many of the
performers simply wanted to play the music they grew up with for others who also appreciated it, and if some 'sponsor' wanted to pay them for

it, then so much the better." The emerging blend of local folk music styles for popular consumption came to be called *country* music. "We never listened to classical music 'cause there wasn't any classical music, not even on the radio," he explains. "It was all country music. And so that's all I knew and that's what I wanted, and of course not being able to buy musical instruments, my biggest aim was . . . to make a fiddle and a guitar out of birch bark."[9]

He learned to play an instrument before he was able to make one. His first opportunity came when an uncle taught him five chords on the guitar. A woman who owned a Stella guitar, which she used to accompany her hymn singing, taught him a bit more; and he incorporated licks he learned from local and itinerant musicians.[10]

He could not afford to buy an instrument; but the self-reliant temper of the Appalachians, instilled by hard necessity, was strong within him. "I got my first pocketknife for Christmas at age twelve," he recalled. "I just seemed to have to try to make a musical instrument." He remembered as a child "sitting out on that old woodpile more than once—would nearly all be cedar, *beautiful* red cedar Dad cut up, or I would, to burn in the cookstove. It burned good and of course it whittled good. So I sat there and whittled, and I wanted to be a great carver." He began to learn woodworking. "My uncle lived right across the pasture field from us, and he was a carpenter and also a blacksmith, and he began to show me some stuff when he saw I was interested." Another local carpenter helped him to refine his techniques. "He was a fine carpenter. I learned a lot from him because he was so good at it, and he would show me, he didn't mind showing me." By the age of fifteen he had built his first playable instrument— a fiddle. "I made the top and back from dynamite boxes, but the sides were made by setting matchsticks side by side on end and gluing them together to join the top and back. I carved the neck out of a piece of maple which I chopped out of my dad's old maple tree. Well, that fiddle played." The following year he made another. "I did a much better job, and I still have it and even play it occasionally. It's no Stradivarius, but it does play, and it stays glued together."[11]

At the age of eighteen Homer Ledford was stricken with rheumatic fever. As recuperation he spent three months at the John C. Campbell Folk School at Brasstown, North Carolina. It was to be a crucial three months in his life. There he met people who recognized and encouraged his talent in music and woodworking. And there he saw his first dulcimers: "There were two hanging on the wall behind the piano; one was made by

John Jacob Niles while he was there working a great deal with music, and the other was made by Park Fisher, who used to be in charge of the craft program at the school." He met Edna Ritchie, one of the famous dulcimer-playing and singing family of the Cumberlands, who was then working at the school. "She knew how to play the dulcimer and how to sing, using it as an accompaniment," he recalls. "I really enjoyed the sound of it."[12]

While he was at school, he was given the task of repairing a damaged dulcimer. "This is really where I gained some knowledge of the construction of the instrument," he says. At the same time, a New York craft shop was seeking "someone to make two dulcimers, to fill two orders they had received. . . . Well, the school asked me if I would make those two for the crafts shop in New York, and I did." The instruments were successful. "When they saw those two dulcimers I made, they just went wild, and I got eight more orders." Homer Ledford was launched on what would become his career. "That started it all; those people advertised to others, and I have been getting orders ever since."[13]

When Ledford returned home from Brasstown, his grandmother showed him pictures of dulcimers in family photographs and "told me stories about people who used to have them and play them; she knew a lot about them. Several of her stories dealt with two troubadours who had dulcimers and who used to travel through our area playing for their keep, but none of my family ever owned any." He associated dulcimers with the past, with the era of his grandmother's youth.[14]

In 1949 Homer Ledford enrolled in Kentucky's Berea College under a grant from the Vocational Rehabilitation Administration, seeking to become an industrial arts teacher. There he studied both woodworking and folk music from an academic perspective. In 1952 he left Berea to enter Eastern Kentucky State Teachers College, where he received a B.S. in industrial arts in 1954. After teaching for a year in Louisville, he became an industrial arts teacher in Winchester, Kentucky (some forty miles from Berea), and made dulcimers on the side. In 1963 he resigned his teaching job to devote himself to his craft full time. Over the next quarter-century he would build nearly five thousand dulcimers and assorted banjos, guitars, mandolins, fiddles, and ukeleles.[15]

Like his Appalachian ancestors, Homer Ledford worked within a folk tradition that encouraged creativity. The Appalachian tradition was not anachronistic but timeless, not a pattern to be imitated but a heritage to be developed. Homer Ledford found tradition to be not an ill-fitting garment that inhibited his growth as an artist but a source of both continuity and innovation. "When I started making [dulcimers] in increased numbers, I made a few changes in the basic design," he explained. "I broadened the width of the body slightly and made the body a little deeper to improve the sound; broadened the fingerboard some in order to make noting easier, and redesigned the pegbox to suit my own aesthetic notions." He also standardized as many parts as he could. Even the ends of his pegs are now shaped by a tool that he invented: "Any peg I make will fit any of my dulcimers." His undercut fingerboard was an innovation, as was his use of a double string (two strings close together, tuned as one and played as one—as on a mandolin) on the four-string dulcimer. Until the 1960s, however, he refused to make four-string dulcimers. "I had this crazy idea that it wasn't a traditional dulcimer. But that was wrong; I was just hard-headed." His innovations extended beyond the dulcimer into such hybrid instruments as his dulcitar—"you can play it like a guitar and a dulcimer both"—and his dulcibro, a dulcimer with a dobro resonator. His dulcitar is in the Smithsonian Institution's permanent collection and has been displayed in a Smithsonian traveling exhibition illustrating innovation within traditional crafts.[16]

But there was an integrity in tradition that Homer Ledford would not violate. "You have to be careful not to let the machinery entice you into taking the skill out of your work," he said. "I still always put the handmade touch to all parts of each instrument." A member of the Southern Highland Handicrafts Guild and the Kentucky Guild of Artists and Craftsmen, he served two terms on the latter's board of directors. "Experience, and a lot of it, over several years," he insisted, "is needed to be able to produce a really fine dulcimer." Homer Ledford's dulcimers were built only by Homer Ledford. "I have always insisted that each and every dulcimer has only my personal attention, and I intend always to remain a one-man shop."[17]

Folk, popular, and elite cultural influences intersected in Homer Ledford's craft. His earliest music influences were folk, reinforced by formal study of folk music. Similarly, he first learned woodworking from the folk process, from kin and neighbors; but his skills were honed by formal study. If his dulcitar and dulcibro exemplify Ledford at his most innovative, his dulcimer surely exemplifies him at his most traditional. Ironically, by marketing his dulcimers through commercial outlets to an urban public with different values needing fulfillment, Homer Ledford helped to keep alive a traditional craft that might otherwise have disappeared.[18]

§

The other dulcimer makers that I knew in the 1960s and 1970s lived in the Blue Ridge Mountains of North Carolina. Stanley Hicks learned to make dulcimers and fretless five-string banjos from his father, Roby Monroe Hicks, who learned in turn from *his* father, Samuel Hicks. As a child Stanley helped his father to make dulcimers, but he was not interested in learning to play them. It was not until about 1970, when he began in earnest to make dulcimers for sale, that he learned to play the instrument. He felt that playing it would be a help in demonstrating how it worked and might increase sales. He just sort of picked it up on his own, he said, although "Dad would have helped when I was little." Stanley's repertoire was made up of songs he had remembered since childhood.[19]

Samuel Hicks made his own patterns, which he passed on to his son and grandson. Roby Hicks made dulcimers of poplar, a soft wood. His basic tools were a drawing knife (which he made himself) and a keyhole saw. He also used an old-time crosscut saw blade.[20] When I first visited Stanley, he was still using hand tools—a hand sander and a wood rasp. But he soon built himself a workshed in his yard and bought a bench saw and an electric sander, both of them second-hand. He continued to make dulcimers out of local woods, but by the early 1970s he was no longer able to supply wood for himself and had to purchase it in Boone.

Roby Hicks sold his dulcimers for three dollars each, banjos for two dollars and a half. Stanley Hicks sold his dulcimers and banjos for sixty-five dollars each in 1974. By comparison, overalls were thirty-nine cents a pair in Roby Hicks's day, five dollars a pair in Stanley's. But, Stanley noted carefully, "you can get five dollars now easier than thirty-nine cents back then." There were not any jobs. "WPA was the first work to come to this country," he says, referring to the Blue Ridge area. It paid fifty cents a day. Stanley can remember during the 1930s walking six miles each way to work daily and working ten hours a day for seventy-five cents. But he also farmed and "didn't have to buy nothing."

Stanley Hicks believed that people used to have more fun back then than they do now. "People were happier then than they are now," he said. They used to whistle or sing these old songs and ballads in the fields. And "if you didn't have nothing to eat and another man had it they would divide it up." A major part of the life of the people, he recalled, was looking forward to such festivities as corn shuckings. People would gather not only to shuck corn but also to play games, especially kissing games. "Sometimes they kissed too long," he mused, somewhat wistfully. They had a good time, of that he was certain. Sometimes they would stay all night, drinking moonshine whiskey from stone jugs. "Dad used to make it." And there was always music, banjos and fiddles mostly. There were only a few dulcimers when Stanley was growing up. His daddy was the only one making dulcimers then, he says, and there were only about two dozen dulcimers in the area.

Stanley Hicks believed strongly, perhaps romantically, in tradition. "Whatever you grow up with, that's what you like," he noted. "I think it should keep the old tunes, the old songs the same as they always was. . . . If they keep a'changing and keep a'changing the first thing you know they h'aint got none of the old. It's all gone, we don't have it. We won't have none of the old-time songs, we won't have none of the old patterns, or nothing like that. . . . You ain't got nothing but just the new."

While it is difficult to imagine a more eloquent defense of tradition, Stanley Hicks had himself made some innovations and not merely in his technology. His dulcimers were somewhat smaller than those of his father and grandfather because he did not lap the edges of the top and bottom over the sides, as they did. But he was quick to point out that "the *box* is just as big."

Nonetheless Stanley did not think the old ways should be changed lightly. He regarded the dulcimer as the oldest instrument there was, mentioned in the Bible. He was certain it went back at least three hundred years in the mountains. He especially lamented the proliferation of strings among some modern dulcimer makers. Four strings, six strings. "Three strings. That's the only real dulcimore is three strings."

Was tradition dying in the mountains? It *was* almost gone, he believed, but was picking up again now. Stanley's devotion to the dulcimer was just barely short of religious. Among other things, he believed it could be part of a solution to the problem of youthful *anomie*. "Young people don't have anything to do. They get to messing with that old dope. They git where they don't care. And hit's gittin' worse. But if they just had music. Even if they couldn't play it they could beat on it."

Making dulcimers was a means of making a living to Stanley Hicks. He made more at his craftsmanship than he ever did at farming or odd jobs. In the winter of 1972–73 he did not fare so well, however. "I been messing around here and I cut my finger off and it shore stuck me behind," he says laconically. To make matters worse it was "the main one I did my work with." Some neighbors told him he would never play the dulcimer again. He told them he would play it with his feet if he had to. "I'd take my toes and play it before I'd give up and quit."

§

Edd Presnell had made dulcimers for a long time when I first met him. In his lifetime he received considerable recognition for his instruments. In November of 1973 the North Carolina Folklore Society honored him with the presentation of its Brown-Hudson Folklore Award, the highest award it can give for contributions to folklore and folk art in North Carolina.[21] Presnell began making dulcimers in the mid-1930s. He said he learned how from his father-in-law. He already had some woodworking experience before that, mainly helping his brother to make chairs. "The price was ridiculously high back then," he recalled. "I got three dollars for my first dulcimer." He calculated that the rate of return for effort had not really changed very much. Wages then were a dollar a day. In the 1970s, he said, a dulcimer still only brought about three days' wages.

According to Edd, his father-in-law got the pattern from his brother, who saw a man named Millard Oliver who came through the area with a dulcimer. "I don't know whether he got a pattern off of it or just looked at it good and *imagined* a pattern off it," he said. In any event, according to Edd, he was "the first in these parts" to make a dulcimer.[22]

For Edd Presnell the process changed over the years, although the number of hours involved remained about the same. By the 1970s he used more power tools and put a better finish on his dulcimers. Up until 1948 or 1949 there was no electricity in the mountains, and the dulcimers were all made with hand tools—hand planes, hand saws, and axes. The earliest ones were, in his opinion, "pretty crude."

Edd made from fifty to a hundred dulcimers a year, roughly one or two a week. But averages could be misleading, because he sometimes worked on as many as twenty-eight dulcimers at a time. "You can't just make one at a time if you want to keep busy working," he said. It is necessary to wait to let the glue dry at various stages, and while he was waiting he could be working on other stages of other dulcimers.

Presnell's boiling of the sides to bend them was "the only way we ever saw one made around here." Boiling helped the process along. That way the sides took less time to set. He did not think their thickness affects the sound much one way or the other. The sound mostly comes from the back, he believed. He never used nails. He stapled his fretboards to the top of the dulcimer; otherwise everything was joined with glue.

The scroll and fretboard on a Presnell dulcimer were all one piece. This was not Edd's innovation, however, but a feature he inherited from his father-in-law, who in turn got it from his brother. "It's not any stronger, I don't think. I just kinda like it a little better." As for what woods he used, he just gave the customer what the customer wanted. He said he had no preference in woods, although 75 percent of his dulcimers are walnut. He did acknowledge that he did not like a rosewood dulcimer with a spruce top.

He did change the old patterns somewhat. The old dulcimers were the same width at each end. He thought they would look better if he narrowed one end. He did not think it would affect the sound much, but he acknowledged that it might make different vibrations at each end.

Edd Presnell expressed his attitude toward the old days succinctly: "When I grew up, I had a picnic compared to my parents; they had a picnic compared to their parents, and my children had a picnic compared to me, and their children's got a picnic compared to them." He remembered the corn shuckings, when they would bury a half-gallon of liquor halfway down the cornpile. It got the corn shucked faster. Music and square dances were the source of entertainment then, before movies, radio, and television. "Don't have time for music and square dances. Is that a loss?"

I asked him if he made dulcimers just to make a living, or did he attach some sort of cultural significance to it. "Well," he considered, lighting his pipe for the thirtieth time, "it'd be a part of the culture, but naturally you're going to have to have money out of it to make a living, so the two go together. You could do it just as a culture if you had an income of something else and just give the things away. I'd like to do that. . . . It's not as easy a'making it in crafts as people think it is."

And tradition? "Well, you more or less have got to keep up with the times. In a way, I guess you could go back and live like they did fifty, a hundred years ago. It would seem awful darn hard." Most people, he believed, are motivated by a spirit of innovation. "Everybody will do the same thing, but do it a little bit different." As for himself and his dulcimers, "You try to do each one a little bit better than the other, even if it doesn't always turn out like that."

Jim Sams had been making dulcimers about twelve years at the time of the last visit. He usually worked on twenty-five to thirty dulcimers at a time, but he once had ninety started at one time because he had the services of an apprentice from a nearby college. He did not *finish* twenty-five or thirty before starting another, of course. He sold roughly a hundred and twenty-five dulcimers a year, a little over two a week on the average. Some years were better than others. In 1972, for example, he got tired of working at it and did not sell as much.

He had worked at the Enka plant for twenty-seven years as an "expediter," which, he said, meant he mainly wrote requisitions and got parts. He started making dulcimers because he had been a woodworker most of his life. He happened to see a dulcimer one day and decided to try to make one. He made three, then did not make another for three or four years. But when there was a market for them he began making them again and eventually quit his job at the Enka plant to make dulcimers full time.

Did he make more money now as a dulcimer maker? "My yearly salary wouldn't be, hit likes, well taking everything into consideration, hit likes three or four thousand dollars being as much" as he would have been making in the plant. But his children were all grown and it did not take as much to live on. "I just try to make a living and that's all." He thought he could make more if he "managed better" and worked longer hours. "I just work when I want to, and when I need to, and most of the time I get to wanting to before I get to needing to, you know what I mean."

He got his first pattern from a magazine, one of those designed for home workshop enthusiasts. There was an article on how to make a dulcimer, with a diagram, but no full-size pattern. Jim made the pattern himself. What about his ram's horn scroll? Where did that come from? "You're familiar with Edsel Martin, Well, now, he was the man that I saw carving that scroll and making that first dulcimer that gave me the bug to want to make one. In other words he had a display at the fair." But Martin's scrolls are bigger than Sams's. "And I like his scrolls, but I didn't want to make mine just exactly like his. I wanted more of an original, if you can call it an original. In other words one that I made instead of one that he made, you see." To get what Sams wanted was not easy. "I don't know how many of these things I made trying to get that scroll. I couldn't get it worked out. I finally bought a book on violin making and it had the layout for—to get that particular scroll and shape." He made at least a hundred before he got it the way he liked it. Of course, he did not throw those others away.

As for the dulcimer pattern he made then, "I just kept changing" until "I got it down to where it looked good, the way I wanted it, and it worked easy, and just stayed with it after I finally got it worked down to where— the shape that I liked. Easy to work. In other words, if you've got too sharp a bend in it, you know, on the curves, why your wood is too hard to bend around the sides. I kept doing that till I got it on down to where it'd do what I wanted." He sawed his sides "real thin" and sanded them "to where they'll bend just right." He started out that way. It was easier, he says. Quicker. Made a better tone. He did not play the dulcimer. In fact he could not even tune it. He thought he could learn, but he just did not have time.

Sams believed in tradition, and he believed it was important for the tradition to continue. His apprentice at the time of one of the visits was the tenth or twelfth he had tried to get started in making dulcimers. He felt that this was important in keeping the traditions alive. Sams also felt some need to reconcile the way he made dulcimers with his sense of tradition. For instance, he used power tools. But even if you used *hand* tools now, he noted, it was not like the original, because they were more advanced than they were years ago. There was probably more artistic satisfaction in hand work, he thought, but that was "more in the craftsman's mind than any other thing." He believed there were still enough things in his dulcimer making that had to be done by hand "to class it as a hand-made instrument." Then he added, "I don't want this to be a production line too much, but you've got to cut as many corners as you can if you're gonna establish any kind of income out of it. . . . If I did this every bit by hand, why, hell, I'd starve to death, I guess." He admitted that "well, you turn right around and look at this and this would be a small factory, if you wanted to break it right down to that."

It would be too easy to dismiss Sams as a commercializer, mass producing dulcimers in his "factory," experimenting with new ways to cut corners, and concerned not at all with what folklorists call "tradition." But when one reflects that he left a job that paid, at his seniority level, nearly double his income from making dulcimers, such an idea falls of its own weight. Furthermore, he could have cut more corners, could have turned out more dulcimers more cheaply. He just did not want to. He had worked out his own compromise between economic necessity, his desire to participate in the tradition of making dulcimers, and his desire to work out innovations that were aesthetically satisfying to his creativity. It would certainly have been less time consuming to produce a plainer scroll. To consider such a man merely a popularizer would be to miss the fundamental complexity of the interplay of tradition and innovation in his aesthetic. He realized that his aesthetic was shaped by a mixture of factors. For instance, he liked a slick finish on his dulcimers, rather than leaving the knife marks to show, as his inspiration Edsel Martin did. "If I knew as much about wood-carving as Edsel did, well, I might have an entirely different opinion," he said, "but I'll never live long enough to do work like Martin does."

B. F. Robison started making dulcimers about 1970. He had helped Sams for three or four weeks before that for free in order to learn how. Sams helped him with his first one. He retired from the Enka plant in 1967, after thirty-eight years as a lead-burner (something like a welder, he explained). He had always been interested in woodworking and had his own woodworking shop. Since learning the specifics from Sams, Robison had made more than two hundred dulcimers. Like Sams he had changed his patterns over time. Why? "Well, I'd just think about it, you know, and it seemed to be better and look better, you know." He had made a few of the four-string dulcimers, in a larger size, but did not think they looked as good or sounded as good as the smaller three-string. He did not see anything wrong with changing the dulcimer to suit yourself. "What you've got now is an instrument that people like and will enjoy it, see? But now, I don't know what, I don't have any idea what the old dulcimer in the old Bible days was, but what you git now is something pretty and something people enjoy. It's a nice instrument."

He could make about two dulcimers a week, he said, and still have time to do something else. He wished he knew what had happened to each one that he had made. He had shipped them all over the United States, to Canada, and to the Philippines. He could play the dulcimer a little, "not much," he said with the mountain man's typical modesty. I never heard him play. He had always been a North Carolina mountain man except for three years in Michigan during the Depression. The Depression was rough in the mountains, he recalled. "You can't hardly imagine how rough it was without you was old enough to go through it."

For Robison the most important thing about the dulcimer, or at least about *making* dulcimers, was that it gives you "something to do when you haven't anything *to* do." He believes it is important to keep the art alive for that reason. "I've worked hard all my life. I can't just sit and loaf."

Two of my students, Allen Papp and Tim Rand, made a documentary film about Hicks, Presnell, Sams, and Robison as a class project in 1972. The film was entitled *The Most Important Thing about a Dad-burned Dulcimore*, and it received its "world premiere" on Beech Mountain, North Carolina, in 1972. Stanley Hicks pronounced it "the greatest movie ever made, even better than *Gone with the Wind.*" The film also received a national screening at an annual meeting of the American Folklore Society in Nashville, Tennessee, in 1973.

These artists and their dulcimers offer persuasive evidence of the veritable explosion of creativity among Appalachian dulcimer makers in the nineteenth and twentieth centuries. Tradition and creativity are not opposites: tradition is dynamic, always growing, always adding new creation. Properly understood, folk tradition is a society's lifeline to its collective identity.[23] Now that modernization is using the profits made exploiting Appalachian mines and miners to construct condominium complexes atop majestic Appalachian peaks, it may be time for mountain people to ask, "What kind of modernization? According to whose standards? For whose benefit?" Will it be the kind of modernization that will help today's people in Appalachia to realize their own goals in accordance with their own identities and their own cultural traditions, or will it be the kind of modernization that will destroy their identity and obliterate the kind of beauty and creativity that the Appalachian dulcimer symbolizes?

The Appalachian dulcimer was once considered an original American creation; but it is more often regarded now as a variant of a northern European instrument such as the Norwegian *langeleik,* the Swedish *hummel,* or the German zither, presumably brought into the Appalachian mountains by Pennsylvania Germans.[24]

In the mid-1970s, L. Allen Smith, his curiosity piqued "as to whether we could actually find something about the Appalachian dulcimer from surviving instruments," set out to take a census. In six months of fieldwork in 1974 and 1975 and another month in 1976–77, he searched through eastern Kentucky, southern Ohio, West Virginia, eastern Tennessee, western North Carolina, western Virginia, and southeastern Pennsylvania. "Local inquiries," he notes, "yielded more instruments than did institutions." From that research he compiled a photographic record of 191 dulcimers that he was able to examine or that were to be found in published sources. He published the results of his research in 1983 as *A Catalogue of Pre-Revival Appalachian Dulcimers.*[25]

Smith's data support the generally held conclusion that the Appalachian dulcimer evolved from the Pennsylvania German zither. But from his collection he boldly challenged prevailing beliefs that the evolution of the dulcimer took place in Kentucky, that it did so no earlier than the last quarter of the nineteenth century, and that the characteristic dulcimer shape was the "hourglass" shape, with double bouts, or two curves per side.

First, Smith classified the dulcimers he found into three basic shapes: dulcimers with straight sides (his type C), dulcimers with a single bout (his type D), and dulcimers with double bouts (his type E). "The evidence in the *Catalogue* certainly suggests that the Appalachian dulcimer did not originate in Kentucky," he maintains, although those with double bouts may have done so. His chief evidence was dulcimer D5, attributed and "dated reliably," he says, to John Scales Jr., of Floyd County, Virginia, in 1832. He adds that "there is reason to believe this instrument represents a tradition of dulcimers before 1800."[26] There is no evidence in the census records, however, that anyone named Scales lived in Floyd County before 1900.

The absence of any census record is not to be taken as evidence that Scales did not live there. By the same reasoning, however, neither is the absence of a dulcimer from Smith's *Catalogue* to be taken as evidence that it never existed. Time and again Smith treats his collection as though it were a substantially complete record. In fact it represents less than one percent of the known production of only three craftsmen—J. Edward Thomas, S. F. Russell, and Jethro Amburgy—out of a list of known pre-1940 dulcimer makers extended by Smith from thirteen to sixty-nine. Since their products were sold widely, the distribution of dulcimers may have been quite different from the picture suggested by Smith's research. For example, Jean Ritchie argues (in her foreword to Smith's book) that dulcimers were more numerous in eastern Kentucky in 1917–21 than Cecil Sharp noted. Sharp and his assistant, Maud Karpeles, did not find many because they were looking for ballads and songs, not dulcimers.[27]

Regarding the relation of the dulcimer to the Pennsylvania German zither, Smith sensibly distinguishes between the zither and the dulcimer by the position of the noted strings, rather than by the shape of the soundbox. He acknowledges that "the fretted zither probably did accompany the Pennsylvania Germans into the upland South," although he is unable to authenticate more than a few of the zithers in his *Catalogue* as to location.[28]

Smith limits his *Catalogue* to instruments made before 1940 in order to avoid influences from what he calls "the folk-song revival since 1940." Here he has stepped into a perennial controversy. Some scholars date the folksong revival to the 1917 field trip of Sharp and Karpeles. A. L. Lloyd always insisted that it dated from the dawn of the twentieth century. There are even those who trace the revival to the eighteenth century, when Sir Walter Scott elicited ballads from living singers. Many scholars speak not of a single folksong revival but of a series of related revivals. Smith can, of course, end his study where he chooses. To choose 1940, however, is to exclude the dulcimers of such later traditional craftsmen as Frank Proffitt, Homer Ledford, Stanley Hicks, Edd Presnell, Jim Sams, and B. F. Robison, while including the untraditional 1930s dulcimers of John Jacob Niles.[29]

No one has attempted to explain why the dulcimer should more often be found in the southern mountains than in the upper Midwest, where there are larger concentrations of Americans of German and Scandinavian ancestry. The Appalachian majority was heavily English and Scots in ancestry, although the ethnic composition of the southern mountains was always more diverse than those who wrote about the region's "pure Anglo-Saxon stock" assumed. One view is that the *sound* of the dulcimer was especially congenial to British settlers, since its diatonic scale and heavy drones make it sound like a gentler version of bagpipes. The main problem with this explanation is that the bagpipe is the hallmark of Scottish highlanders, rather than lowlanders; and highlanders immigrating to America settled predominantly in the southern lowlands, while the southern highlands were populated with Scots lowlanders—usually called Scotch-Irish.[30]

The Appalachian dulcimer carries within its body not only sweet music, but also a story that reveals a great deal about how folk cultures become symbolically embodied in particular objects of folk art, objects that become often more important in their message than in their actual origin or function. Throughout history there would seem to have been a creative tension between satisfaction and dissatisfaction, between pressures to keep things as they are and pressures to seek a newer way. This tension has functioned to provide both sufficient continuity for the creation and maintenance of a culture and sufficient innovation to keep that culture from stagnating. In folk culture a certain continuity has been ensured by the fact that its elements developed to serve certain basic human wants and needs. Moreover, perfecting certain traditional techniques and methods of production—which are then passed on to succeeding generations—ensures that folk artists do not have to invent everything anew. Thus there is a sense in which tradition frees the artist's creativity to operate selectively, to make what are perceived to be *improvements*, rather than having to invent both method and artifact anew each time. Over the centuries folk artists have continually made new demands on their own originality, on their knowledge and skills, on their sensibilities, and on their experience in their efforts to enhance their hand-made objects with special practical or aesthetic value.[31]

The psychiatrist Erik H. Erikson speaks of a national sense in which "identity is derived from the ways in which history has, as it were, counterpointed certain opposite potentialities: the ways in which it lifts this counterpoint to a unique style of civilization, or lets it disintegrate into mere contradiction." One who would understand the role of creativity in a traditional culture must understand the operation of polarized potentialities upon the aesthetics of the individual, the inherited culture, and the changing society.[32] Cultural values themselves, being subject to the historical process, are also molded by the interplay of opposing forces. For southern folk artists, then, to be involved in a tension between creativity and tradition is itself traditional.

In his study of artists in tribal societies, the anthropologist Edmund R. Leach muses over the irony of trying to examine the role of innovation and creativity in an art form in which imitation and adherence to tradition are the standards. "The paradox here," he writes, "is that although, in a sense, originality is ruled out and although, in a sense, the productions are . . . tied down to rigid conventions, they nevertheless appear to us to have strong vitality." In the southern mountains, folk artists have not only preserved traditional forms and patterns, they have also adapted traditional methods to new materials and new techniques to old materials to create new forms and patterns of their own. Not all innovation can be considered creative, of course (although all creativity is innovation), but the changes wrought in dulcimer design by southern folk artists often exemplify creativity of an high order.[33]

Interaction of the aesthetic of the individual with the aesthetics of the group—each judging the other—is especially complex in a tradition-centered community. The role of individual creativity in a traditional art form must be measured against the range of choices for the expression of individuality open to an artist within the tradition. It is always, as the folklorist Roger Abrahams puts it, a matter of "how far the individual is allowed to go in introducing new features or items of performance" into the community's shared traditions.[34] Similarly, the folklorist Henry Glassie notes "the qualitative divisions in creativity" that are related to "the newness of the product and the uncertainty of its acceptance." The *extent* of community acceptance is emphasized by the anthropologist H. G. Barnett, who distinguishes between active and passive acceptance. If being taken up by tradition may be regarded as a very strong form of active acceptance, then Edsel Martin's ram's horn scroll may be considered actively accepted, while his carvings of women's heads or birds on dulcimer scrolls are only passively accepted. That is, it is considered all right in the community for him to carve women's heads on dulcimer scrolls, but not everyone can do it. None of the innovations of the dulcimer makers under study falls outside the range of *safe* innovation, in that none has been actively rejected by the community.

The recognition beyond the community gained by the highly traditionalist Frank Proffitt and the highly innovative Edsel Martin seems to exert an influence on the amount of innovation considered acceptable in the Avery-Watauga area and the Buncombe area, respectively. All the dulcimer makers studied profess an orientation toward tradition in varying intensities. While an open advocate of novelty might risk his status within a traditional society, there is no reason to reject the makers' protestations as hypocritical. It is important to note, however, that they do not look upon tradition as a static set of binding restrictions, but as an evolving, growing set of experiences that function as guides for how to operate in varying contexts. It is considered appropriate to make a certain kind of dulcimer for this customer, but not for that one.[35]

Tradition functions for them in the manner described by the folklorist Kay L. Cothran as the means by which "a given context is made sensible, by means of which further contexts are made possible." She calls this "the context of context." Thus tradition to these dulcimer makers does not refer merely to the past but to a sense of the past still alive in the present. They cannot simply throw away the past and begin anew. In one of the most famous passages in American literature, William Faulkner reminds us that "the past is never dead. It's not even past." A misunderstood tradition can, of course, seem ill-fitting and uncomfortable. As T. S. Eliot notes, "if the only form of tradition, of handing down, consisted in following the ways of the immediate generation before us in a blind or timid adherence to its successes, 'tradition' should positively be discouraged." For the dulcimer makers of western North Carolina, however, understanding of the relation of the past to the present serves as a source of strength and as a guide to present and future conduct. People who know where they come from have a better sense of direction, a better sense of where they are going and how to get there. Tradition is not merely a matter of Time Past or of Time Present, or even of both, but of Timelessness.[36]

Tradition stretches back to the recesses of prehistory, but it has neither ceased to evolve nor has it abandoned anything along the way. Thus it would seem that the concept of tradition shared by these folk artists—as dynamic rather than static, as reference point rather than restriction— mediates between the Eriksonian polarities of continuity and innovation; and the creativity of these artists would seem to draw vitality from both. It is not innovation alone that is the source of creativity, but the creative tension between innovation and continuity as cultural polarities.

12

Sea Island Legacy
Folk Tradition and the Civil Rights Movement

The traffic on River Road was heavy. When I first came to this part of Johns Island in 1964, it was a quiet rural black community. Now, over twenty years later, expensive cars cruise past on their way to Kiawah and Seabrook Islands. These resort islands can be reached only by driving across Johns Island and meeting the approval of a guard at a security gate. Beyond the guarded gates are plush hotels and upscale shopping facilities, beachfront houses and condominiums. Those who are waved through the checkpoint are mainly affluent visitors from afar. But some natives are allowed to pass through the gates. After all, the resort rich need maids, cooks, waiters, and yard men. The traditional and the modern coexist eerily on Johns Island now. I notice the incongruity at once in Wesley United Methodist Church, a handsome structure with elegant pews, a robed choir, and a fine organ. The congregation sings staid old hymns from the Methodist hymnal, but they sing them in the traditional African polyrhythmic style of the Sea Islands, almost as though they were ancient spirituals. The present organist accompanies the hymns in a jazz-influenced modern gospel style that dominates the singers and sometimes drowns them out. The result is exciting, but I miss the special kind of excitement of the old a capella shouting style that Johns Island is famous for. Someone tells me that the four-square, God-fearing cadences of a former organist deadened the complex, God-praising rhythms of the congregation's singing; but the Lord had mercifully called her to greater service somewhere in Virginia.[1]

I have come to Johns Island with Candie Carawan; Albert Raboteau, a noted scholar of slave religion; and a couple of filmmakers who hope to produce a documentary about the culture of the Sea Islands. Candie's husband, Guy, is flying in from a folksong concert and is to join us this afternoon at Janie Hunter's house.

I had known Guy and Candie since 1964, when my wife, Jeannie, and I came to a folk festival on Johns Island. It was there also that we met Janie Hunter, a talented storyteller and quilter and one of the principal singers in the Moving Star Hall Singers. I had been able to bring Mrs. Hunter and the Moving Star Hall Singers to perform at St. Andrews Presbyterian College, where I was then teaching. In 1984, the National Endowment for the Arts recognized Mrs. Hunter as a National Heritage Fellow. According to her citation, "The music heard in Moving Star Hall is joyous, a music in celebration of life, freedom, and a deeply felt religious optimism, the dawning of a better world."[2]

Al Raboteau was a black Catholic Mississippian who was chair of the Department of Religion at Princeton. I had first met him at Berkeley in 1980, but I came to know him better later when we were both involved in a Ford Foundation program at the University of Mississippi.

In the 1960s Guy and Candie lived and worked among these black people on Johns Island for two years. They wrote a book about the people of Johns Island—*Ain't You Got a Right to the Tree of Life?* But they are more than just the chroniclers of the story. They are an important part of the story too. They came to Johns Island to learn about Gullah culture; but they also made a great contribution to the people of Johns Island, and through them, to the civil rights movement and to all of us. They arranged for Janie Hunter and the Moving Star Hall Singers to perform at the Newport Folk Festival and elsewhere, they helped the islanders produce a series of Sea Island Folk Festivals, and they produced two record albums of Johns Island spirituals, folktales, and children's game songs.

After the services at Wesley our little group visits the grave of Esau Jenkins; and we stand in the churchyard with his family, friends, and neighbors as we recall some of his achievements. Esau Jenkins was one of the most effective community leaders to emerge in the twentieth-century South. The remarkable impact of his work was felt not only on his native Johns Island, but all across the South.

A short distance down River Road is a small wooden structure named Moving Star Hall. In the 1960s it served as a health care and burial society, a meeting place, and a praise house where worshippers could express themselves more actively than in the formal church services at Wesley. Now a Pentecostal congregation worships here. Their pastor is the Reverend David Hunter, the son of Janie Hunter. Moving Star Hall exemplifies the incongruous mixture of old and new, of traditional and modern, that is found everywhere on Johns Island. Ancient and complex African poly-rhythms are still part of the worship service. In the 1960s the polyrhythms were clapped and stomped by hands and feet in the "shouting" style. To-day in Moving Star Hall the ancient polyrhythms are beaten out on a modern snare drum.

The story of Johns Island is a story of a community's efforts to devel-op its economic and social resources in accordance with its own needs while at the same time preserving its incredibly rich folk cultural heritage. Balancing development and preservation is a difficult task under any cir-cumstance. When one considers the formidable obstacles against which the people of Johns Island had to contend—the old hard legacy of slavery and segregation, the burdens of poverty and lack of education, the pres-sures of economic survival—the fact that they have maintained that pre-carious balance for more than a generation seems little short of miracu-lous. It is not a story of inevitable or easy success, and it is not over yet. But enough has happened to command our attention and our admiration. And enough remains in doubt to command our concern.

When Guy Carawan first came to Johns Island in 1959, skin and hair seemed to matter more than anything else. It seems unbelievable in ret-rospect, but the statute books in South Carolina were filled with laws reg-ulating skin and hair. It was the official policy of my native state to sepa-rate South Carolinians from one another on the basis of skin and hair. Blacks and whites could not legally associate except in the sanctioned roles of subordinate and superior. Not only were most black citizens disfran-chised at the polls, blacks were systematically separated from whites in schools, in jobs, and in public accommodations. The policy was called segregation, or Jim Crow, and it was quite thoroughgoing. Behind the mask of civility, our harsh racial caste system branded all black South Carolinians as inferiors.

Segregation was characterized by two sets of almost everything: there was one set of churches, stores, funeral homes, and drinking fountains for black Carolinians. There was another set for white Carolinians. Black stu-dents were relegated to Jim Crow schools, black travelers to the back of the Jim Crow bus, and black moviegoers to the Jim Crow balcony. And there were separate neighborhoods for blacks and whites. It was not difficult to tell which were which: the pavement ended where the black neighborhoods began. But not everything came in pairs. Some things—such as parks, libraries, and swimming pools—were rarely available to black Carolinians at all.

There was only a four-month elementary school on Johns Island when Septima Clark first came over from Charleston to teach as a young teen-ager in 1916. But few of the island children attended all four months. During harvest season, farmers came and took the children out to help work in the fields. There was no high school for blacks on the island. Some islanders who were fortunate enough to have relatives in Charleston might send their children over to try to get an education there. Nor were there any medical facilities on the island. Islanders had to go to the Jim Crow emergency room in Charleston, where, as one islander recalls, "the peo-ple were treated so badly by the nurses and sometimes the physicians. It was segregated there. And many people died trying to get to medical care." The islanders carried their peas, corn, potatoes, and rice across to Charles-ton by rowboat. "They had a hard time, living and raising their children," Alice Wine recalled. "Those old time foreparents was something else, I tell you."[3]

In 1955 the South Carolina legislature passed a law forbidding any city or state employee to belong to the NAACP. Septima Clark, a longtime member of the organization, was dismissed from her elementary school teaching position. Although she had taught in the Charleston County school system for almost forty years, the Charleston County School Board denied her retirement pay when she was fired. She then took a job with Highlander Folk School.[4]

One of Septima Clark's students on Johns Island had been a lad named Esau Jenkins. "I knew Esau Jenkins when he was a boy of fourteen and came to my school to learn to read," she recalled. "All his life Esau devot-ed himself to improving conditions on Johns Island."[5] Jenkins was unable to complete his high school education until after he was married. He spoke in the unmistakable accents of Gullah, the creole language that his black ancestors had created in the South Carolina lowcountry. Some educated blacks urged him to try to change the way he talked, to abandon his down-home Gullah speech. But he spoke the language of the people. People lis-tened when he spoke, and people understood what he was saying.

Jenkins took the lead in persuading some of the poorest people on the island to pool their resources to establish a number of institutions to improve conditions: the Charleston County Citizens' Committee, a coun-tywide credit union, and the Comprehensive Health Center on Johns Island. Perhaps the most unusual and modern institution on Johns Island was a consumer's cooperative named the Progressive Club, containing a grocery store and recreation center.[6]

By the 1950s Esau Jenkins had a bus. Each morning he drove a busload of tobacco workers and longshoremen to work in Charleston. Each evening he drove them back to Johns Island. One morning one of his passengers, Alice Wine, asked him to help her learn to read and write in order to register to vote. "I don't have much schooling, Esau," Alice Wine said. "I wasn't even able to get through the third grade. But I would like to be somebody. I'd like to hold up my head with other people. I'd like to be able to vote." She asked him to help her. "I'll be glad to learn the laws and get qualified to vote. If I do, I promise you I'll register and I'll vote." Her request appealed to Esau Jenkins, who had lost a race for the school board in 1954 because there were not enough blacks registered on the island to elect him. He ran fourth for three school board seats. All of his passengers understood the importance of getting registered to vote. An idea was born. Jenkins distributed typed copies of the South Carolina laws pertaining to voter registration to the passengers on his bus. Many of them could not read, however. Others were unable to understand the arcane legal terminology. Whenever he arrived in town a few minutes early, Jenkins patiently discussed the laws and explained the requirements for voting to his passengers. Alice Wine soon memorized the whole section of the constitution that they were studying. When she went to register, she recited every word perfectly from memory and received her registration certificate. But she was not satisfied. She asked Jenkins if there was any kind of school where she could really learn to read and write.[7]

At Septima Clark's urging, Jenkins went to a Highlander Folk School workshop in 1955 and asked for help. At Jenkins's invitation, Myles Horton, director of Highlander, went down to Johns Island with his children and spent Christmas with the Jenkins family, walking around the island and meeting with people. In this manner, he learned the islanders' problems. They suffered from poverty and lack of education, yet they possessed a folk wisdom about life that he found inspiring.[8]

With support from Highlander, Septima Clark and Esau Jenkins began Johns Island's first citizenship education school in 1957. They chose Bernice Robinson to be the first teacher, partly because, having had no teaching experience, she was more likely to be experimental and nonjudgmental. "They did not want a professional teacher to do it," Robinson recalled, "because they adhere to too strict a curriculum and they wouldn't listen to what the people were saying." Robinson expected to learn as much from the Johns Islanders as they would learn from her.[9]

The curriculum was developed day by day. Islanders wanted to learn how to write letters to distant relatives and read letters from them, how to fill out money orders, how to order from catalogs. They learned to read the South Carolina constitution, which was required for voter registration, and learned to fill out the voter registration forms. But, as Robinson noted, "Our classes didn't just stick to reading and writing to register to vote. We talked about the power that was in the hands of the people if they know the set-up of the government. So we talked about the set-up and who you go to for what." A major function of the citizenship school was to make the islanders aware of their rights as citizens and aware of how to achieve them. By 1960 they had added nearly six hundred registered black voters to the rolls in Charleston county.[10]

Guy Carawan first arrived on Johns Island on Christmas Eve of 1959, and Esau Jenkins took him to the all-night Christmas Watch Meeting in Moving Star Hall. There he encountered African cultural continuities and what he called "the oldest form of Negro folk life still alive today in the United States." He had come to Johns Island from Highlander Folk School to learn about Sea Island culture and to serve as a chauffeur for Septima Clark, who did not drive. A native Californian with family roots in South Carolina, he had a master's degree in sociology and some training in folklore when he came to live with Esau Jenkins on Johns Island. Jenkins and Septima Clark took Guy to community meetings and church services, where he met and sang with various members of the black community. "With these two beloved leaders to vouch for me," he noted at the time, "I've had the inside track in getting to know people who under different circumstances might be suspicious and unfriendly." He was inspired by the islanders' Afro-Christianity and their "praise house" form of worship. He thrilled to the old Sea Island spirituals and the islanders' exciting "shouting" style of singing them. He fell in love with the Sea Island folk tales and folk beliefs. He recognized the importance of the rich folk culture he encountered on Johns Island. It would bring him back to the island year after year.[11]

During his first winter on Johns Island, Guy developed a singing program as a new feature of the citizenship schools. The singing program had two functions. Not only did singing Sea Island folk songs, spirituals, and protest songs help to keep alive the beautiful old singing traditions of the is-landers themselves, but it also, as Myles Horton described it, "helped build the group's consciousness and boosted morale." The singing program proved to have profound inspirational value for the whole enterprise.[12]

One day Guy sang a version of "Keep Your Hand on the Plow," a song he had learned in the 1950s as part of the Peoples' Songs Movement. Al-ice Wine told him she knew "a different echo to that" and sang a Sea Is-land version. She sang "keep your eyes on the prize." Later, at a Freedom Song gathering he organized in Atlanta, Guy passed Alice Wine's version on to the young civil rights workers. Thus it was that her Johns Island version of this spiritual spread across the South as one of the great inspi-rational theme songs of the civil rights movement.[13]

The first citizenship school met twice a week for three months. As word spread about the program, enrollment nearly tripled. A second school was established. Sixty people passed the literacy test required for voter regis-tration in South Carolina. As Myles Horton of Highlander put it, "they 'graduated.'" These enthusiastic alumni not only voted, they also spread the word to neighboring islands. Soon there were citizenship schools on Wadmalaw and Edisto Islands and in the North area of Charleston as well as on Johns Island. Within three more months, half of those students had passed the literacy test and were registered to vote. Some of them began to organize voter registration campaigns.[14]

By the early 1960s the schools had expanded their services from reading and writing, citizenship training, and voter education to include agriculture, arithmetic, driver education, health education, and sewing classes.

In 1961 the citizenship school program was transferred from Highland-er to the Southern Christian Leadership Conference. Septima Clark and Bernice Robinson developed a program to train citizenship school teach-ers. After the training program was transferred to SCLC, thousands of teachers were trained. Andrew Young told Septima Clark that, as she put it, "the citizenship schools were the base on which the whole civil rights movement was built." Graduates of the training programs "went home to teach and to work in voter registration drives," said Clark. "They went home and they didn't take it anymore." The curriculum first developed on Johns Island went all across the South. Participants came from the Carolinas, Georgia, Alabama, Mississippi, and Tennessee. "We recruited the wise leaders of their communities, like Fannie Lou Hamer in Missis-sippi. Hosea Williams started out as a citizenship school supervisor," Clark noted. "From one end of the South to the other, if you look at the black elected officials and the political leaders, you find people who had their first involvement in the training program of the citizenship school."[15]

By 1962, when the major civil rights groups turned their attention to voter registration, they were able to use the approach pioneered in the citizenship schools between 1957 and 1961 because by then it was clear that the approach worked. Thus the citizenship schools developed by Septima Clark, Esau Jenkins, and the people of Johns Island were the foundation for the voting rights movement and played a major role in the overthrow of Jim Crow.

Since 1959 Guy had spent part of each year working with the citizenship school on Johns Island. In 1961, Guy married Candie Anderson; and in 1963 they moved to Johns Island full time with their small son, Evan. During the next two years they shared in the life and fellowship of the black community around Moving Star Hall. Their purpose was to help preserve some of the older black folk culture on the island by bringing honor and recognition to it. As Guy wrote to Pete Seeger in 1965, "These days, you can go to any one of the major folk festivals at Berkeley, UCLA, Chicago, Philadelphia, or Newport and see some of the finest folk talent in the country. But the communities from which these people come have been neglected. Leadbelly and his music are forgotten in Shreveport, Louisiana. I'm hoping our work on Johns Island (South Carolina) will provide an example of what can be done in other areas. It would be a shame to let this music die at the roots." To that end Guy and Candie arranged for the Moving Star Hall Singers to perform across the country, from the Newport Folk Festival to UCLA. The Carawans produced recordings of the Moving Star Hall Singers, and Guy in his own performances told the story of the Sea Islanders and sang some of the songs of the Moving Star Hall Singers. As a result of Guy and Candie's efforts, the Moving Star Hall Singers became widely recognized across the country as outstanding tradition bearers of the oldest layer of African-American cultural expression in living American tradition.[16]

During this period Guy and Candie organized a number of "Sing for Freedom" workshops around the South, cosponsored by Highlander, the Southern Christian Leadership Conference, and the Student Nonviolent Coordinating Committee. At a three-day gathering in Edwards, Mississippi, for example, young civil rights workers from all over the region came together. There they exchanged ideas and shared experiences with the Moving Star Hall singers, the Georgia Sea Island Singers, and traditional singers and instrumentalists from Mississippi. There they swapped

songs and learned new verses. Many Sea Island songs spread around the
South as a result of these freedom song gatherings.[17]

Guy and Candie also worked closely with Esau Jenkins to help the Johns
Island community produce a series of Sea Island Folk Festivals. The folk
festivals took on added meaning from the context of all the things that
were happening in the Sea Islands and across the South. William Saunders, a Johns Islander, described the context: "It was a time in history
when a lot was going on, voter registration, awareness, blacks were about
being black. Everything fit in, and the festival was like the tape that brings
a lot of things together. It really kept people's spirits up, and that is what
was needed at that particular time. We needed to draw on each other." The
festivals did not celebrate a quaint past; they related the past to the
present. The festival became the focal point for "pilgrimages" from leading civil rights workers in the South—Vincent Harding, Julius Lester, Bob
Moses, Willie Peacock, and Bernice Johnson Reagon. The old songs and
the old stories, the old talk and the old tales seemed strikingly new and
fresh. The old traditions had a power to move a generation, a power to
call the youth to the task of achieving democracy.[18]

Shortly before he died in 1972, Esau Jenkins, along with William Saunders and others, helped to put together a health program for the islands.
They began with a small clinic, but it developed to include nutrition programs, environmental health programs, and programs for dealing with
drug abuse. "We had the foresight with the health center to add the nursing home and the home for the elderly," recalls Saunders. "That's the kind
of thing where Esau and others were thinking ahead and did things in
advance."[19]

Many changes have come to Johns Island since Guy and Candie Carawan
first lived and worked there. Some of the changes (such as low-cost housing, a health care facility, and a home for the elderly) have been initiated
by the islanders themselves. "I think the housing, the health care facility,
you have to look at it as an elevation, an improvement," notes William
Saunders. But rapid resort development on Kiawah and Seabrook Islands
have contributed in their own way to the transformation of Johns Island,
bringing new pressures and new challenges to the islanders.[20]

One area of contention is the question of jobs. Resort development
created hundreds of new jobs, but few of them went to native Johns Islanders. "People saw what happened when all that money came in with

Kiawah," according to Esau Jenkins's son Abraham, a retired air force officer. "And yet no one that I know got in any of those administrative positions out there." The jobs that seemed to be set aside for the native islanders were mainly low-paying service jobs—cooks, maids, and yard workers. "Ninety percent of the jobs are in the lowest level," says Jenkins, "and then maybe five to ten percent are in a higher bracket, but not up in the really well-paid bracket. So people don't see that 'big Santa Claus' they once thought of." In the meantime resort development continues to raise the cost of living for the islanders.[21]

Another area of contention is the land question. As resort development continues, land becomes increasingly valuable and property taxes rise accordingly. "At one time you could get an acre of land for less than fifty dollars," Abraham Jenkins recalls a bit wistfully. But now land prices have risen beyond the reach of most islanders. It is essential for the islanders to become more knowledgeable about inheritance and tax laws if they are to hold on to their land. Some developers try to induce the islanders to sell too cheaply. "We got people out here now that come to buy with cash money," says Abraham Jenkins. "This is a way of enticing and influencing people because people have spent all their lives trying to make some money and here this guy walks up to you with rolls of thousand dollar bills circled by hundreds and five hundreds and starts talking." It is understandable that many of the islanders are inclined to sell out. "But you have to let them know that God ain't making no more land," says Jenkins, "and if you got any, you better hold onto it and try to work some other type of arrangement like long-term leasing."[22]

Many changes have come to Johns Island. More changes are coming. "There's no way that the island can stay unchanged. It's already changed," says William Saunders. "The new people can always take advantage of the older people. Hopefully we can control some of the change." He has little faith in either the developers or the environmental groups that often oppose them. "There was a million dollars spent on turtles on Kiawah, because these people were concerned about the turtles," he notes ruefully. "But they were never concerned about the people that live on these islands." Saunders hopes that the people of Johns Island, as they have done in the past, will pool their resources to build the things that need to be built on Johns Island. "It can be done," he says, "but we would have to trust each other."[23]

One part of Esau Jenkins's legacy is a dedication to progress, to building institutions that enable the people of Johns Island to control their own lives. But another part of his legacy is a dedication to preserving the cultural heritage from which the people of Johns Island draw their strength and their distinctiveness. His son Bill has a plaque on his office wall: "No people who are indifferent to their past need hope to make their future great."[24]

Not all Johns Islanders share both parts of Esau Jenkins's legacy. There are some who believe that the magnificent cultural heritage created by the ancestors in the bitter days of slavery and segregation would be better forgotten. "Now some of us," Esau Jenkins once remarked disapprovingly, "forget about the place we came from and some of the songs which help us go on." The past is felt as a burden of shame rather than as a source of strength. "There's a lot of people on this island, older than I am, they know all about the past," says Janie Hunter, "but they feel so embarrassed to explain about it. They figure people are going to look down on them as nothing." But Esau Jenkins's 1963 advice would still seem to hold true: "If we hide those sweet songs and try to get away from what we came from, what will we tell our children about the achievement we have made and the distance we have come?"[25]

That heritage is too much a part of the older people on Johns Island for them ever to lose it. Whether the next generation will recognize and value the strength and beauty of that heritage is another question. "The young people don't know many of the things that happened," says Janie Hunter. "It takes somebody who came out of this experience to teach them and tell them the meaning of it, and what it can do for them." Her brother Benjamin Bligen considers it a mutual responsibility to his ancestors and to his descendants: "We're trying to pass it on to the younger folks so they can carry the old traditions on. Our old folks taught us these songs and they would like for we to carry it on through and they would like for we to pass it on to the young generation so they can keep it up." At least some members of the younger generation are drawing strength from the old traditions. "I don't know how other young people feel, but I get my strength from the older people on these islands," says Esau Jenkins's daughter Elaine, now a young lawyer involved in the effort to help the islanders preserve their land ownership. "The songs at Wesley [United Methodist Church], I mean the songs that the older people raise from the floor, those things do something for me."[26]

There is considerable wisdom in William Saunders's complaint, "if somebody is sitting around hungry and you're gonna tell them about some damn culture, it don't make any American sense." Saunders is convinced that if the health care, the housing, and the education of the islanders can be improved, "then they themselves begin to look at their own history." Still, it would seem that those on Johns Island who are moving most vitally and most confidently into the future are those who know where they come from. They are at home in the present because they are oriented in time as well as in space. Without a sense of where they came from, how else can people know whether they are going forward or backward?[27]

Johns Island has come a long way since Alice Wine first asked Esau Jenkins to help her learn to read and write so that she could vote. Some complain that there has been no progress, for in their ignorance of the past they do not know how far their ancestors have brought them. Some are satisfied to stop here, for in their blindness they cannot see how far they have to go. If Esau Jenkins were still alive, Bernice Robinson believes, he would draw strength from the past, but he would still look to the future. "He would be very disappointed about how far we still have to go, but he wouldn't be bitter about it," she says. "He would be saying that we haven't accomplished yet what we need to accomplish. And he would see in what way he could work to bring it about." But other Johns Islanders are drawing from that cultural heritage as Esau Jenkins did: as strength to look to the future, to see what contribution they can make, to summon their friends to work together to do what still needs to be done.[28]

PART FOUR

Folklore and History: A Dialogue

13

"Alice of the Hermitage"

A Study in Legend, Belief, and History

Alice, according to legend, is a beautiful young girl of sixteen who lives at Murrells Inlet in All Saints Parish in the mid-nineteenth century, when rice culture by slave labor is at its peak.[1] One summer Alice meets a famous artist from the North, a friend of her brother, who completely captures her heart. In some versions of the tale, the famous artist from the North is a cousin. In others he is described as a turpentine man (perhaps indicating that he is of a lower social class than the plantation aristocracy, or perhaps simply a euphemism for artist or painter). In any event, he recognizes that he would not be considered an acceptable suitor for Alice, either because of his profession or because of his kinship. He and Alice secretly pledge their love to each other but are unable to make their feelings public.

Before returning to the North, the suitor gives Alice a beautiful ring as a token of his love, vowing to come back the following year to claim her as his wife. She wears the ring, her most cherished possession, on a gold chain about her neck. One day the authoritative father-figure of the legend (in some versions he is her father, in others her uncle, in yet others her brother) comes into her room unexpectedly while she is admiring the ring and takes it from her. In some versions he throws it into the creek. Alice begs and pleads for the ring, and often searches his room from top to bottom looking for it.

Shortly afterward Alice is dispatched to Charleston to an exclusive finishing school for young ladies, where she is the belle of the season, her mysteriously melancholy beauty radiant in a flowing white dress. Sometime during the school year she comes down with an illness that is taken to be malaria. Since the father-figure is a doctor, she is sent home; but the long ride so weakens her that she is in critical condition by the time she reaches the Hermitage, her family's summer home at Murrells Inlet. As Alice lies dying, she calls her lover's name over and over and pleads in vain for her ring. After her death, she is dressed in the beautiful white gown she had worn in Charleston and placed in a glass casket in her room, while the family awaits her mother's return from a visit to Flat Rock in North Carolina. A few days later, Alice is buried temporarily in a bed of oyster shells near the house. Upon the mother's return, Alice is reinterred in the family plot at All Saints Church, Waccamaw.

Soon afterward, as various versions of the legend would have it, servants begin to hear strange noises from the room where the casket had been (E402.1.8). Many years later a visitor's son reports having seen a lady in white during the night. When he describes her to the mistress of the house, she realizes that he is speaking of Alice (E422.3, E425.1.1). Many times Alice appears to members of the family outside near the oyster bed where she was temporarily buried (E334.2)and is seen walking around the grounds and in the room where she died (E334). Years after Alice died, a resident of the Hermitage is alone in the house, upstairs reading. She has her hand behind her head, and feels a cold, clammy finger tugging at her ring. Turning around, she catches a glimpse of a girl in white fading through the door (E422.4.3, E425.1.1). Noises such as the opening and closing of drawers are heard in the Hermitage. The rocking chair in Alice's room rocks back and forth unoccupied. Alice is seen near her grave in All Saints churchyard. It is said that if one walks around her grave backward thirteen times after midnight and calls her name, Alice will appear (E333, E386.4).[2]

Modern scholars of legendry offer a refreshing vision of the nature and development of legends and their relationship to folk belief. Such major scholars as Max Luthi, Linda Degh, and Lauri Honko have made important contributions to our comprehension of legendry. Still, in their hands the legend remains a fragmentized form of folk narrative, less creative and less valued than its more highly polished and more highly esteemed contrast genre, the *märchen*.[3] The legend's more fragmentary and less creative quality is depicted as being directly related to what Degh pertinently calls the legend's "collective nature."[4] In turn, the legend's "collective nature" is a function of its close relationship to folk belief. Belief in the legend is no longer seen by all as a defining criterion; however, belief remains a central issue in legend scholarship.[5] Honko describes an evolution in legend formation from folk belief to memorate to full legend.[6] Finally, Herbert Halpert emphasizes the influence of print in curbing the excesses of oral tradition by standardizing legends.[7]

Unquestionably these scholars offer a more realistic assessment of legendry than did their predecessors. However, they have shown, as a group, a surprising disinclination to analyze the historical or communicative contexts of legendry. Closer attention to the historical context of folklore—perhaps legendry in particular—may in fact emphasize the importance of folklore as artistic communicative event.[8]

The theoretical implications of historical context in the comprehension of folklore as artistic communication may be illustrated by an examination of "Alice of the Hermitage," a legend that I collected numerous times in the 1960s and 1970s in All Saints Parish, along the Waccamaw River just north of Georgetown, South Carolina.

A basic question is that of the classification of "Alice of the Hermitage." Is it simply a localized version of a migratory revenant legend—of Eliade's "eternal return"?[9] Or is it a memorate? Certainly many variants tell of personal encounters with the revenant of Alice.[10] Still other accounts are just statements of belief (that the Hermitage and All Saints churchyard are "haunted" by Alice), what Carl von Sydow terms simply a *dite*.[11] Attempts to classify "Alice of the Hermitage" in a single pigeonhole inevitably oversimplify. The key to legendry is to be found in strategies. Legends have strategies as surely as do proverbs, and the fact that any given legend may be performed in a variety of ways (*dite*, memorate, full legend, etc.) is basic to the legend's strategy.[12]

My summary of the Alice legend is "pieced together"[13] from a number of oral versions in wide circulation in All Saints Parish, ranging from lengthy narratives to memorates of personal encounters with Alice, to simple statements of knowledge of the Alice legend. None of them is complete in content or polished in style; however, the fragmentary quality of the legend is often considered the most reliable means of distinguishing legends from other forms of prose narratives and thus a key to its definition (or perhaps a defining criterion). Max Luthi distinguishes legend from *märchen* by the polished consistent structure of the latter. The *märchen* is a compositional whole, the legend a fragment.[14] But, we must ask, what is "*the* legend"?[15] Have I just presented a conflation of several related legends or a summary of "*the* legend"? In fact, does "*the* legend" exist, outside of the collector's conflated version? Acknowledging that each storytelling event is unique,[16] we still must ask, Is each storytelling event a separate legend? Does the legend actually exist in the mind of the performer before it is performed, and in between performances? Does it exist in the community repertory, with each performer performing a fragment of the full legend? In other words, does existence precede performance, or does performance precede existence?

"Alice of the Hermitage" is a historical legend, in that it purports to describe events in the lives of actual people. Like most such legends, it includes a number of historical congruities. There is little doubt that the historical Alice from whom the legendary Alice is derived is Alice Belin Flagg (1833–49). Her brother owned the Hermitage, and her stone lies in the Flagg family plot at All Saints Church, Waccamaw. In 1784 her grandfather, Dr. Henry Collins Flagg (1742–1801), of Rhode Island, had married Rachel Moore Allston, the widow of Colonel William Allston of Brookgreen, a wealthy rice planter. Their son, Dr. Ebenezer Flagg (1795–1838), married Margaret Elizabeth Belin (1801–85) in 1817. This marriage produced nine children, but only three lived to maturity—Dr. Arthur Flagg, Dr. Allard Flagg, and Alice Flagg. Allard was established as a rice planter when his uncle, the Reverend James Belin, gave him Wachesaw plantation, along with its summer home—the Hermitage.[17]

There were other notable historical congruities. Alice Flagg *did* have a close relative who was a famous artist from the North. Washington Allston, considered the most important artist of the early romantic period in America, was her father's half-brother.[18] Furthermore, the prevalent danger of malaria in the lush swamps of the South Carolina lowcountry are well attested in the travel literature of the antebellum period.[19] Elizabeth W. Allston Pringle (Alice's second cousin) wrote in her memoirs, "No white person could remain on the plantation without danger of the most virulent fever, always spoken of as 'country fever.'"[20] So the planters and their families fled the malarial swamps en masse for the seashore, for the mountains (Flat Rock was a favorite resort), for such northern resorts as Saratoga and Newport, and for Europe.[21]

If such tantalizing historical congruities give the legend a ring of authenticity, there remain puzzling incongruities as well. One set of problems is raised, for instance, by the suitor's unsuitability, whether on occupational or kinship grounds. The profession of art was, in fact, highly regarded by the rice planters, who numbered among their ranks such notable patrons as Ambassador John Izard Middleton; Secretary of War

Joel R. Poinsett; Washington Allston's cousin, Governor Robert F. W. Allston (a patron of Thomas Sully); and John Ashe Alston, a leading supporter of contemporary artists who was considered "the most astute connoisseur of art" of his day.[22] The question of the suitor's kinship (in some versions of the legend) is not, as it would seem, an explanation of his unsuitability but another incongruity. Kinship should have rendered him more, not less, eligible among the highly endogamous plantation aristocracy. The historian Chalmers Davidson observed that "they were amazingly interwed, the marriage of cousins being almost the rule rather than the exception."[23]

There is a surviving oil painting of Alice Flagg, said to have been painted by her suitor; but it bears little relation to the controlled luminosity, deep resonances of tone, and visions of the magical that characterized Washington Allston's style. More likely the painting is the work of another artist cousin, George Whiting Flagg (1816–1897), who was much closer to Alice's age. Connecticut born, he became a pupil of Allston; and, while he never attained the master's fame, he enjoyed a successful career as a portrait painter in Charleston.[24] In any event Washington Allston could hardly have been the legendary suitor, since he died in 1843—when he was sixty-four and Alice was ten.[25]

The prevalence of malaria raises another set of problems of historical congruity. The "sickly season" was from late spring until early autumn, but the vestry records for All Saints show the date of Alice's burial to have been January 25, 1849. Furthermore, planters and their families left their plantations for such places as Charleston in order to avoid malaria, not the other way around. Dr. Flagg's day book for 1848 and 1849 shows that Alice was frequently sick throughout the year. During her illness in late March and early April of 1848 Dr. Flagg prescribed opium. During her final illness, which began in December of 1848, he also prescribed opium. But Alice's medication and dosages were frequently, one might even guess frantically, changed until the last entry on January 16. There are no further entries in Dr. Flagg's day book until February 24.[26] The church records also show Alice's age to have been fifteen years and four months at death, not sixteen as in the legend.[27]

Neither Alice's precise age nor her precise illness are crucial to the legend (although they tend to be remarkably consistent in the various oral versions); nor are the occupations and kin-connections of her suitor (which vary from version to version anyway). A much more intriguing, and a much more important, historical incongruity arises in relation to the Hermitage itself. It is not possible to determine with certainty when the Hermitage was built, since the Georgetown County public records were destroyed by fire during the Civil War. Practically every published source that lists a date, however, indicates that the Hermitage was built in 1849.[28] Since the historical Alice was buried on January 25 of that year, it is extraordinarily unlikely that she ever lived in the Hermitage.[29] These incongruities are not surprising. Such incongruities are common in European and American legendry.

An even more intriguing question of historical perspective has to do with the historical origins of the legend itself. While the Alice legend is widely found in All Saints Parish today, it does not appear to have been common in oral tradition before the 1950s. I have been unable to find informants who can specifically remember having heard it before that decade. At least two lifelong residents of the area (since 1910 and 1920, respectively) specifically recall that they heard it for the first time about then. It was not reported in the volume on South Carolina in the Federal Writers Project State Guide Series in 1941, even though the author of the portion of the volume treating All Saints Parish was Genevieve Willcox Chandler, an experienced and energetic folklore collector and an associate of John A. Lomax. Furthermore, Genevieve Chandler's parents had purchased the Hermitage in 1910, and she had lived in the Hermitage since childhood. Since she wrote about "The Gray Man" and other Waccamaw folk legends, and since she collected a great deal of Waccamaw folklore for the Federal Writers Project, why did she not report the Alice legend if it existed in tradition at the time?[30]

"The process of legend formation," notes Linda Degh, "is of major concern to scholars interested in the definition, description, and classification of the legend genre."[31] The Alice legend is particularly important for the light it sheds on the process of legend formation. According to Genevieve Willcox Chandler, it was created by her older brother, Allston Moore Willcox (Bubba Dick), shortly after their father purchased the Hermitage. For the four rambunctious Willcox children, growing up in a stately antebellum structure, making up stories about a ghost who had once lived there was a great deal of fun, especially when it so scared their cousins from Marion. Years later, when Genevieve was a grown-up folklore collector, she knew that folklore was something that circulated in oral tradition, not just stories made up when one was a child. She would not have considered including such material among the authentic folk narratives that she collected in oral tradition.[32]

The legend of "Alice of the Hermitage" does not appear to have circulated in oral tradition until after it had first circulated in print. The influence of printed texts in standardizing legends, as with standardizing ballads, has been noted in an important essay by Herbert Halpert.[33] What has not been noted, however, is the dynamic and creative role played by print in legend formation itself.

Julian Stevenson Bolick learned of the Alice story from members of the Willcox family while doing research for what he intended to be a factual book on the plantations of the Waccamaw. Fascinated, he included the legend in his *Waccamaw Plantations* in 1946 and returned to the story with two elaborate versions in a collection of "ghost stories" from the region in 1956. Bolick's books were circulated mainly in All Saints Parish, especially to summer tourists in the Pawleys Island area.[34] Bruce and Nancy Roberts included the story of Alice in their *Ghosts of the Carolinas* in 1971, a book that enjoyed intensive circulation throughout the two Carolinas.[35] The Georgetown Rice Museum put out a leaflet in 1975, in its Historic Georgetown County series, recounting the Alice story with other ghostly legends of the area.[36] Various newspapers and magazines have picked up the story from time to time as well.[37]

Perhaps the most important force in the transmission of the Alice legend—both orally and in print—was Clarke A. Willcox, younger brother of Bubba Dick and Genevieve. In 1956, the same year that Bolick published his first collection of ghost stories, Willcox retired from the grocery business in Marion, South Carolina, and returned to his boyhood home at the Hermitage. Developing some of the Hermitage grounds into a nursery, where he sold plants and shrubs to natives and tourists alike, he soon found that his visitors were even more enthralled with his stories about Alice. In return he nurtured and cultivated the Alice legend as carefully as he did his plants. He erected a marker on the spot that he believed to have been her temporary grave, and restored "Alice's room" to reflect its appearance during her lifetime. He even had a copy made of the painting of Alice, the original of which belongs to a Flagg descendant. He delighted in leading constant streams of visitors to the Hermitage on tours of the house and grounds and in telling them how Alice's rocking chair in the parlor sometimes rocked unoccupied. Linda Degh notes that in modern society "individuals usually do not accumulate a large body of legends nor do they have an audience to honor their knowledge."[38] Clarke Willcox, with his one legend, drew audiences large enough for anyone.

While Clarke Willcox was highly regarded as a raconteur during his lifetime, he also nurtured the Alice legend through his writing. In 1966 he published *Musings of a Hermit,* a memoir and an anthology of his own poetry as well as poems by other members of his family, with historical and folkloristic sketches and illustrations by his sister. The volume enjoyed extraordinary success, selling out four editions. The story of Alice is featured in each edition, rather more elaborately in the fourth.[39]

Despite Linda Degh's cogent insight that "the fragmentary character of the modern legend is closely related to its collective nature,"[40] we must distinguish between collective transmission and collective composition. It is clear that the Alice legend had individual composition, that the widespread oral tradition is deeply and continually influenced by printed versions (with reciprocal oral influence on print), and that each of the principal printed versions has been affected by direct contact with one or another of the surviving siblings of the legend's creator. Finally it is clear that there was a continuing influence, both orally and in print, by one of these siblings.

The active participation of Clarke Willcox in the transmission of the legend would seem to beg the questions of whether tellers believe legends. Linda Degh and Andrew Vazsonyi in a seminal essay have suggested how complex the question of belief can be, ranging from full belief through nonbelief to antibelief.[41] Elsewhere they raise basic questions about that part of the definition of the legend having to do with belief.[42] Clarke Willcox, in other words, does not have to believe his story for it to be a legend. The attitudes of individual narrators do not change the essential qualities of the genre.

But the essential qualities of the genre are very much bound up with the appearance of telling the truth—that is to say, with the strategy or rhetorical intention of the narrator. The narrator knows that no hearer's attitudes can be taken for granted (least of all when discussing ghosts); they must be rhetorically established. If the teller wishes to make an audience respond to the story in a desired way, he or she must employ communicative means to do so. Thus the rhetorical strategy of a legend is different from the rhetorical strategy of a *märchen.* Degh contends that "legends are not as dependent on creativity as tales are."[43] But many legends, for all their apparently fragmented quality, are skillfully structured to present witnesses and evidence in a convincing way. Like a good lawyer, the good narrator knows the audience does not always believe the speaker who is the most polished, the slickest. The art of the legend is to appear artless.[44]

Lauri Honko has devised an intriguing model showing a smooth flow from folk belief to memorate to full legend formation.[45] While Honko's flowchart seems to oversimplify both the complexities of legend formation and the ambiguities of active and passive belief-responses, who can doubt that there is a close and reciprocal relationship between legend and folk belief?[46] Without that relationship the Alice story would have been narrated in a different style, would have developed in a different structure, or would (more likely) have been forgotten. Degh noted that in Europe legends "are generally carried on by mature or elderly people, whereas the village youths reject and ridicule them."[47] In the Age of Aquarius, youths adopted them and added to them. Adolescent enthusiasm for cemetery ghosts became widespread and well documented.

No one has yet discovered precisely what belief-levels are necessary and sufficient for legend formation. But clearly it is possible to disavow the legend itself and still maintain belief in Alice's spirit. One informant who is aware that the legend was created by Allston Moore Willcox nevertheless reports having seen Alice's revenant and having felt mysterious tugs at her ring. Furthermore, her son told her he had seen a lady in a flowing white dress vanish into thin air while he was an overnight guest at the Hermitage, even though she says he had never before heard the legend of Alice.

Such personal experiences add to the main body of the legend and keep it alive and growing in oral tradition. I happened to be present at one such event in January 1972, with a group of college students who were studying Georgetown County folklife. The group had permission from All Saints Church, Waccamaw, to visit the churchyard at midnight in hopes of raising the ghost. As we drove down the dark road, festooned with long gray beards of Spanish moss, our mood was jovial. Students joked with one another about what they might do if they actually saw Alice.

The lighthearted mood faded quickly once we entered the churchyard. We did not know the exact location of Alice's grave, so we proceeded systematically by flashlight from gravestone to gravestone, noting the elaborate obelisks, headstones, and above-ground vaults, each featuring appropriate epitaphs. At length we had worked our way back to the Flagg family plot. As we examined each grave, our flashlight beam fell upon a simple slab, flat upon the ground, with a single word inscribed upon it— ALICE—and the ground around it trodden bare for several feet in each direction.

After backing around the slab thirteen times at midnight and calling Alice's name—to no avail—the party of students split up. Some went to dark corners of the graveyard and set up sinister howls and moans for the benefit of others, some went home (in fright or disgust), some explored other headstones. Two students—Katrina Nesbit and Beth Stalder—kept a vigil by Alice's stone. Beth later recalled: "Katrina and I settled down by the grave to wait for Alice to appear. We speculated upon our possible reactions to the possible sudden appearance of Alice. Katrina was writing comments about the whole experience in her notebook. She then decided to see how tall Alice was by lying down next to the grave." When Katrina stood up to brush herself off, the large class ring on her right hand dropped off. Beth added: "I laughed at this, making some mention of how Alice was after the ring. However, in the next instant as she continued to brush herself off, the ring on her other hand flew off. The situation was no longer funny." According to Katrina:

> As I stood up, I brushed my coat off. First the class ring fell off, but this was not unexpected as it was a bit too large. I picked it up and in the next moment I noticed that my other ring was gone. I had no sensation of its falling off, only the realization that the ring was gone. I was even more shaken when I remembered that Alice's unfinished task was to find her lost ring. I can truthfully say that I consciously did nothing to cause the ring to come off. It was not a particularly cold night so the ring's falling off due to cold hands does not fit. The ring itself fit rather tightly and could not be shaken off by the most vigorous of hand shakings.

The ring, which had once been Katrina's grandmother's, looked a great deal like an old-fashioned engagement ring. All of us searched by flashlight for the next two hours, without success. The group was not at all certain that this was not Katrina's practical joke, anyway (although she was not at all given to such trickery). They were not convinced that she was serious until the following morning, when she awoke Beth at daybreak to help her start her ailing automobile (it had to be pushed) and return to the graveyard. According to Katrina: "After about fifteen minutes of searching, my hand brushed some leaves aside and there with only a few centimeters of the band showing was the ring. It was almost as if Alice, on seeing that the ring was not hers, had dropped the ring in her retreat from the grave."

Katrina's experience has now become part of the still growing legend. I have even collected *dites* that say if one backs around Alice's grave thirteen times at midnight and then lies down upon the grave, she will appear.

The fact that the slab bearing the word ALICE is a commemorative marker rather than a gravestone is not well known, even among the communicants of All Saints. But the records of All Saints show that Alice was buried at Cedar Hill, in Murrells Inlet, not at All Saints. There is no record of re-interment in the family plot.

Because we are able to reconstruct with such accuracy both the history of Alice Flagg and the history of the legend that has developed about her, "Alice of the Hermitage" is an extremely important legend with profound implications for folklore theory. Careful analysis of the Alice legend reveals that 1) the legend does exist in the community repertory, and that individual performances are related to the legend as parts to wholes; 2) legend formation is collective, but legend creation is individual; 3) legends develop by the accretion of memorates rather than evolving smoothly from *dite* or memorate to full legend; 4) the relationships of print and oral tradition in legend development are dynamic and creative, not merely stabilizing, and call into question the conception of print as inevitably "fakelore"; 5) the question of the narrator's or the audience's belief in the legend is a non sequitur; 6) what is more important is the relationship of the legend to folk belief systems; and finally, 7) the historical context of folklore—whether item, genre, or performance—is not merely an ornamentation on folkloristic inquiry, but is of its very essence.

14

A Model for the Analysis of
Folklore Performance in Historical Context

In 1959 Richard M. Dorson called on folklorists to study American folklore in the context of "the great dramatic movements of American history,"[1] and in a distinguished career he continued to insist upon the primary relationship between folklore and history. As director of the Folklore Institute at Indiana University, author or editor of a score of books and nearly two hundred articles and essays, and supervisor of innumerable doctoral theses in folklore, he was in a position to impress his views indelibly upon folklorists.[2] Nevertheless, judging from published output, the Dorsonian concept of the importance of historical context to folkloristic studies is shared by only a tiny minority of folklorists. For most folklorists the notion of historical context must be considered part of their passive repertory.

This essay is about folklore and history, but I should make clear at the outset what aspects of the subject it is not about. I am not here concerned with the "historical-geographical method," which attempts to trace the history of the folklore item or genre across time and space (although I would not agree with Américo Paredes that such studies "teach us little except to show once again that folk tales do travel").[3] Nor do I intend to deal with the historical-reconstructional method, which attempts to recreate past societies through studying their folklore; nor with the historical validity of the oral traditions of the "inarticulate"; nor with time-interval studies of the type exemplified by Daniel J. Crowley in his Bahamian research[4] (although I employ all three approaches in my own work). Nor is this essay intended to be a jeremiad against the communications orientation of the "new folkloristics." I share that orientation. I merely seek to emphasize the importance of *historical* context to that orientation.

With the shift in the focus of folkloristic study from "folklore as a collection of things" to folklore as a "communicative process,"[5] younger folklorists have emphasized what Richard Bauman calls "performance as an organizing principle that comprehends within a single conceptual framework artistic act, expressive form, and esthetic response, and that does so in terms of locally defined, culture-specific categories and contexts."[6] One notes in Bauman's imposing list the omission of that sense of relationship between past and present that is usually represented by the word "tradition." Robert Jerome Smith has contrasted the historical sophistication of Latin American folklorists with their North American counterparts "who forgo diachronic studies in favor of synchronic, who would rather do away with the concept of tradition altogether."[7] One of the leading theorists of the "new folkloristics," Dan Ben-Amos, specifically de-emphasizes tradition as a defining criterion of folklore in order to concentrate on folklore in terms of communicative process, as "artistic communication in small groups."[8]

The focus on communicative process in a context of social interaction has had important reciprocal consequences for folklore and linguistic studies.[9] Roger Abrahams contends that individual folklore performers are "understandable only in terms of the social matrix in which they rise," and he insists on probing "the relationship of form and attitude and performance."[10] A considerable sociological richness has been achieved in the "new folkloristics" through borrowing from the social sciences, but that achievement has been at the expense of historical richness. "Ahistorical social science is as often narrow and superficial as sociologically primitive history," Stephan Thernstrom observes, "and it is certainly no less common."[11] In fact an influential school of social anthropologists, following A. R. Radcliffe-Brown and Edmund R. Leach, takes great pride in proclaiming what Leach himself has called "the irrelevance of history for an understanding of social organization."[12] One can be provincial in time as easily as in space.

One finds over and over in the writings of communications folklorists descriptions of events lying on a single time-plane and of the microdynamics of folklore performance at a particular moment in time, rather than concern with the ongoing dynamics of tradition. The pervasively static quality of such writings is the result of what M. G. Smith calls "the fallacy of the ethnographic present."[13] We know that culture is dynamic, that culture changes. Why, one wonders, should it not be studied in its historical dimension as well as in its social dimension? Why should folklorists not concern themselves with culture change? Should not folklorists be concerned with how people respond to new influences? What elements of tradition do they discard? What elements do they modify? What elements of tradition do they retain? In what proportions? Why?[14]

If we are really interested in folklore as an aspect of human behavior, why do we neglect longitudinal research and causal analysis? If we are serious about developing locally defined, culture-specific categories and contexts, longitudinal data would seem to be not merely relevant but essential.[15] Any society has a lifespan extending beyond the lifespan of any of its members. The members at any given time cannot by themselves define the boundaries of social experience. So long as new generations are being born into the society, social context will remain a dynamic process, not a static setting. "Events," such as folklore performance, if studied apart from their historical context, will remain only partially comprehended.[16]

I applaud the emphasis on performance in contemporary folklore studies as a good and proper turning in the right direction. Performance can be studied as process as well as event; and such an approach could be potentially far more historically dynamic than an exclusive concentration upon text or artifact could be. Nevertheless, I must lament the lack in contemporary performance studies of an adequate historical context. It is a lack that needs to be liquidated.

Since the folklore item—be it proverb, tale, ballad, or carnival—comes alive only when performed, it is appropriate that the study of folklore should focus at those points at which it comes alive. It is widely accepted that communicative events are not comprehensible apart from social interaction,[17] but it is not generally recognized that society is itself "a human process and not simply a static system of external constraints."[18] Since the event is the crucial variable in the study of society, and social context the crucial variable in the study of communicative event, it can be seen that the study of folklore performance without reference to the historical dimension involves a certain amount of circular reasoning. The "relationship of form and attitude and performance" (or artifact, mentifact, and sociofact) is intimately bound up with the changing values and institutions of a changing society.[19]

The folklorist, after collecting the relevant data and describing the communicative event, must organize the various interrelationships involved into a conceptual unity; thus the folklorist, like the historian, is faced necessarily with the problem of parts and wholes. One means of attempting to organize these relationships is the construction of models. A model is based on the concept of "a whole that could be understood as a system of functionally interrelated parts."[20] It is constructed by the observer; it does not purport to describe any particular folklore performance or other event.[21]

A model for the analysis of folklore performance should not only draw upon precise ethnographic description and the various kinds of folklore data but should encompass all the variables that are involved in folklore performance as a human behavioral activity, including social, psychological, cultural, and environmental variables. And it should permit sufficient complexity in the interaction of personality, society, and culture to reflect the complexity one encounters in field work.

Perhaps the diagram (fig. 1) will help visualize the complex system of variables affecting folklore performance. In the oval at the bottom of the

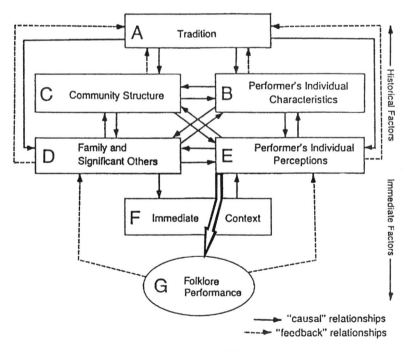

Figure 1. Classes of variables affecting folklore performance

diagram is the dependent variable, folklore performance. The lettered boxes in the diagram represent different types of independent variables. The solid lines represent flows of influence, or "causation." The different types of variables are arranged along two lines: individual characteristics appear on the right side of the diagram and social characteristics on the left. Historical factors are arranged at the top of the diagram and immediate factors toward the bottom. The variables affecting folklore performance may be grouped into four major classifications: the performer's individual characteristics (B); the structure of the community in which the performer lives (C); the relationship of the performer to family and significant others (D); and the performer's individual perceptions (E).

The aggregate of the performer's individual characteristics (B), what one might call the personality or "identity" of the performer, is strongly associated with the character and level of that individual's performance of folklore. Identity is itself a process, however, not a static quality. Personality development continues throughout the life-cycle of the individual and is indelibly shaped by memories and past experiences.[22] Such characteristics as age, sex, ancestry, education, and occupation stand in a major affective relationship to the performer's folkloric competence.[23]

The structure of the community in which an individual lives (C) has an effect on whether or not that individual engages actively in folklore performance. Such "vertical" divisions within a community as households, neighborhoods, and the like, and such "horizontal" divisions, transcending the community but existing within it, as class, caste, race, or special interest, interact with such formal institutions of the community as local government, economic institutions, churches, and schools, to produce the community value system—a "system of value-orientations held in common by the members of the social system"[24]—which in turn decisively affects the folkloric repertory available to the performer.[25] Thus community characteristics have an effect on the individual's folklore performance regardless of the individual's own personal attributes. But the community value system, like the performer's individual characteristics, cannot be adequately described apart from its historical dimension; it is a product of the "memories and past experiences of the system."[26]

Out of the multitude of variables that in one way or another affect human behavior, those that really count are the expectations and estimations of what Harry Stack Sullivan called "significant others"—those persons most important in an individual's life (D). The list begins in infancy with the family but tends to expand with the life-cycle.[27] The individual experiences and memories of the family and significant others are shared with one another; thus any individual is affected by a variety of historical experiences in which he has not directly participated, simply because they have affected the personalities and expectations of persons important in his life. Therefore the approval or disapproval of "significant others" powerfully affects how, and how much, individuals engage in folklore performance and has an impact on performers that is independent of individual or community characteristics.

The performer's individual perceptions (E) have a crucial impact on folklore performance. Changes in perception, in attitudes and cognitions, bring about changes in performance even when other variables remain unchanged. The artifacts, mentifacts, and sociofacts of folklore are all products of ideation. The folklorist must become increasingly aware of the ideational concepts of performers. What attitudes and cognitions underlie their aesthetic? What is the taxonomy of their generic and performance categories? What is their sense of the structure of the material they perform? What are their psychological and social reactions to their materials? A folk-centered aesthetic must be a constituent of any model of folklore performance.[28] The problem is just how much the folklorist's cultural description conveys an accurate picture of the performer's ideation. The folklorist's description is, after all, only an observer's explicit construction of the actor's implicit ideation, derived by the observer from the actor's behavior.[29] The task of the folklorist is not made easier by the realization that the attitudes and cognitions of folklore performers are partly shaped by traditions that extend back to before the performers were born or by the realization that, paradoxically, changes in the continuing tradition are influenced by the attitudes and cognitions of performers.[30]

These four classes of independent variables are related not only to folklore performances but also to one another. Thus, for example, the extent of an individual's interest in folklore performance (attitudes and cognitions) is probably shaped by the extent of his or her exposure to traditional expressive culture; providing exposure is partly accomplished by the family and significant others[31] and partly by the community structure, or the "generalized other."[32] The folkloric resources available to a performer are decisively affected by the folkloric repertory of the community and especially of the performer's significant others.[33] A greater use of role theory might serve folklorists well in distinguishing between the performer's sociocultural environment and the performer's personality, since the roles a performer plays represent "the organism's more or less integrated way of adapting to *all* the influences that come its way."[34]

This analytical scheme (model) includes several other features that lead to a full explanation. First the variables thus far considered were all shaped by events that occurred, conditions that arose, and processes that began decades or even centuries before any performance we might apply them to. Thus a fifth category of independent variable appears at the top of the diagram; this is tradition (A), which includes (but is not limited to) handed-down forms of expressive behavior. Dan Ben-Amos has effectively disposed of the static concept of tradition that allowed for no innovation or creativity in folklore.[35] But innovation without tradition is no more satisfactory an explanation of folklore performance than tradition without innovation. Folklore performers do not look upon each context as existing in isolation from all others. A mediating set of what might be called "understood social rules" inherited from the past transcend any given social interaction, telling the performer and the audience what is appropriate in any given context. It is tradition, then, that relates any given context to other contexts and distinguishes it from yet others.[36] Tradition, then, may be understood as "the rules by means of which a given context is made sensible, by means of which further contexts are made possible."[37] Tradition should be seen neither as environment nor as technique but as ways and means, not as something people have, but as something people participate in, willy-nilly, because they are social beings.[38]

The influence of tradition on the performance of folklore is thus felt all the more strongly because every variable affecting folklore performance is directly affected by participation in tradition. It is important to note that the relationship between tradition and the other variables—that is to say between past and present—is not one-sided but reciprocal. The folklorist's task is made much more complex by the fact that tradition is itself always changing under the influence of new ideas, technology, and especially the increasingly wider dissemination of popular culture influences by mass communications media.[39] Not only does the past affect the present, but the present affects the past. Jan Vansina points out that "each type of society has in fact chosen to preserve the kind of historical traditions suited to its particular type of structure."[40] Thus our model indicates a "feedback" relationship, represented by dotted lines, as well as a "causal" relationship between tradition and the other variables.

Finally, a sixth box, labeled "immediate context" (F) intervenes between the other variables and folklore performance (G). A situational approach is useful to the student of performance at this point.[41] The response of the immediate audience may affect the performer in a number of specific ways,[42] but the immediate context is less likely to *produce* performance than it is to *inhibit* or reshape performance—to cause a performer to bowdlerize or otherwise select from his folkloristic repertory.[43] Therefore it is represented in the diagram as a broad arrow that redirects the influence flowing from E to G, rather than as one of the multiple "causes" of folklore performance.

All the independent variables must be filtered through individual perception (E) before they can affect folklore performance. The model therefore includes no direct "causal" links between the dependent variable, folklore performance (G), and any of the classes of independent variables. While it is true that all folklore performance takes place in some specific immediate context (F), or situation, it should be remembered that the performer responds to the situation in terms of his or her perception of the situation.[44] We have taken the standard model of a situation with the independent and dependent variable that comprise it, and we have added to them the concept of postulated intervening variables (the actor's perceptions) and postulated causal connections between the types of variables.[45] Thus we may say that folklore performance, like all human behavior, takes place in situations in which the response or responses to the situational stimuli happen in terms of the actor's perception or "interpretation" of the situation. Folklore performance, then, is not to be seen as a direct reaction to the situation but as a response made in accord with ideational mediation.

Folklorists and historians still have much to learn from one another. The development of a historical perspective on folklore performance may have the effect of restoring tradition to the central place in folkloristic theory it once enjoyed. The development of such a perspective is contingent upon understanding the relationship between internal change within a tradition and external change in the social context.[46] Achieving such an understanding is important for both folklorists and historians. I agree with Richard Dorson that the more folkloristic historians become and the more historical folklorists become, the better for both.

15

Folklore and Social Transformation
Historians and Folklorists in the Modern World

In the flickering light of a slave-cabin fireplace in All Saints Parish, South Carolina, little Sabe Rutledge listened in wide-eyed wonder to the endlessly fascinating tales of Buh Rabbit. "How come I know all these Buh Rabbit story, Mudder spin, you know," he would recall. "Mudder and Father tell you story to keep you eye open." He and the other slave children delighted in Buh Rabbit's struggle with Buh Bear. The symbolic struggle fostered a sense of identification with the ever-resourceful Buh Rabbit, who seemed so much like Sabe's grandfather, Rodrick, while the powerful but foolish Buh Bear seemed so much like Ole Mossa. These narratives redefined the harsh realities of life in bondage into a realm more attractive. They made a virtue of necessity and gave a voluntary color to an involuntary plight.[1]

About ninety miles upcountry from All Saints Parish, at Plane Hill near the village of Stateburg in the high hills of Santee, little Mary Miller learned from her grandmother to sing the old Scottish ballads "Lord Lovel" and "Barbara Allen." In "Lord Lovel" a rich young aristocrat rides off on his steed, "strange countries for to see." He returns in a year and a day, only to find that his neglected sweetheart has died. He has lost his most cherished desire while away engaging in quixotic adventures. In "Barbara Allen" a young woman is summoned to the sickbed of her sweetheart, who had earlier slighted her by toasting another woman at a local tavern. He tries to arouse her pity ("Yes, I'm surely dying"), but his stratagem fails and she rejects his explanation of the tavern incident. In both ballads, as in so many others, the actions of the hero appear futile. The hero and heroine are united only in the grave. These ballads take place in a strongly patriarchal world, one that both reflected and gave shape to the real world in which little Mary lived. Although the father-figure appears but briefly as a faceless symbol of power in "Barbara Allen," he makes his presence strongly felt ("Oh father, oh father, come dig my grave, come dig it long and narrow"). Sung without the intrusion of sentiment, sentimentality, or didacticism, the stark actions of the ballads approached tragic stature. To recognize the impersonality of Mary Miller's ballads is not to deny their drama. It is only to point out that singing of such misfortunes, unrelieved by comment, promoted a sense of ironic detachment—perhaps the ultimate taking for granted.[2]

Later, as the grown-up Mary Boykin Chesnut, she sat at the death bed of the Old South, victim of its own quixotic adventures. Vividly recording its final agonies in her famous "diaries," she was as aloof and coldhearted as Barbara Allen. From the heedlessness of the Lord Lovels and the helplessness of the Sweet Williams (as well as the tyranny of the arbitrary patriarchs) she encountered in ballads, she developed a detached skepticism toward the male dominance and female subordination of the patriarchal society in which she was bred. From the stark but understated lost causes of the ballads, she absorbed an awareness that human life is filled with little ironies and that large disasters from time to time shape the course of historical events.[3]

It would appear, then, that oral traditions served as sources of ethical inspiration not merely in the slave cabins of Rodrick Rutledge and his family, but in the Big House of United States Senator Stephen Decatur Miller and his family as well. Just as Sabe Rutledge's ancestors brought African traditions with them and reshaped those traditions on southern slave plantations into an African-American folk culture marked by strong African continuities, so Mary Boykin Miller Chesnut's ancestors brought with them British and Celtic folk traditions that helped to shape her worldview and ethical dynamics in significant but imperceptible ways.

In every age creative thought has been at least partly shaped by the swirl of historic events. Just as wars, holocausts, and mushroom clouds haunt the pages of twentieth-century writers, so the social alterations of the industrial revolution affected European thinkers of the nineteenth century. A feudal society, once ordered by ranks and ruled by absolutism, was replaced by a new, capitalist society with new notions of cultural patterning as well as new notions of social hierarchy. This transformation changed cultural styles as well as living conditions. Emancipation from the chains of the old regime meant new conceptions of aesthetic norms and symbolic forms as well as political, economic, and social reforms. Social transformation contributed to a new awareness and a new analysis of social realities and cultural differences.[4]

The relationship between folklore and history has been long and tangled. It has engaged the attention and divided the opinion of several generations of scholars. In their hands the relationship has assumed as many shapes as Tam Lyn. Scarcely anything asserted by one scholar has not been called into question by another. Earlier efforts focused upon whether or not folklore was, as George Lawrence Gomme proclaimed in 1908, "an historical science." The most conspicuous disputes clustered around the question of whether folklore *itself* came from actual historical events. Gomme contended that all folk customs and folk beliefs were rooted in concrete historical reality. His contemporaries Hector and Nora Chadwick added that heroic oral tradition grew out of historical actuality and that historical elements could be separated from fictional elements by careful scholarship. Their antagonists responded, sometimes calmly and sometimes not. An especially vociferous criticism was voiced by Lord Raglan, whose readings in comparative folklore convinced him that such folk narratives as epics, sagas, heroic legends, and ballads originated not in historical fact but in ritual. From a historical perspective, the differences between these antagonists seem less striking than their similarities. The debate, whether pursued with civility or shrillness, was conducted within an accepted and clearly defined framework. The participants in this difficult and profitless discussion shared a persistent delusion that if folklore did not arise from actual historical situations then clearly folklore was unreliable for the study of history, and history was irrelevant to the study of folklore.[5]

Eschewing involvement in such intramural and enfeebling theoretical debates, a small number of American folklorists and historians made some concrete use of folklore texts as historical documents in attempts to study the history of one or another folk group. The Kentucky historian Thomas D. Clark mined humorous and legendary traditions in antebellum newspapers as part of his 1938 study, *The Rampaging Frontier*. A Minnesota historian, Theodore R. Blegen, followed in Clark's footsteps in the following decade, attempting to move historians away from the history of the elite to the history of the folk, toward what he called "grass roots history." In his studies of Norwegian-Americans in the upper Mississippi Valley, Blegen told the stories of individual immigrants—homesteaders, farmers, laborers, and merchants. In the 1950s the Texas folklorist Américo Paredes used *corridos* of such outlaw heroes as Gregorio Cortez and Jacinto Trevino as a means of probing esoteric-exoteric attitudes and folk stereotypes along the Texas-Mexico border.[6]

The old preoccupation with the historical origins of folklore yielded in the 1950s to a concern for the historical *context* of folklore. Richard M. Dorson, in a seminal 1959 essay, called upon his fellow folklorists to study American folklore in the light of what he called "the great dramatic movements of American history: Exploration and colonization, Revolution and the establishment of a democratic republic, the Westward surge, the tides of immigration, the slavery debate that erupted in Civil War, and the triumph of technology and industrialization." At the same time he urged historians to study the history of the American folk in terms of *folk* themes, not merely in relation to the "*great* themes" derived from the history of the elite. Transcending his earlier concern with the historical *reliability* of various American hero legends, Dorson launched upon a remarkable career in which virtually all his writings reflected his interest in the relationships between folklore and history. But history remained bitter medicine to most folklorists, and few were disposed to swallow it.[7]

During the 1960s and 1970s a revolutionary series of studies fundamentally altered historians' understanding of the nature of their discipline. Into the grave and dignified company of powerful individuals and powerful institutions came collective portraits of ordinary folk, especially of people previously considered "inarticulate." Historians sought to write history—as the phrase had it—"from the bottom up." They became as concerned with the marriages, fertility, and infant mortality of the many as their predecessors had been with the philosophy, statecraft, or military prowess of the few. The new social history, as the revolution came to be called, was at first received as a kind of intellectual *treif* by orthodox historians, but eventually became the *nouvelle cuisine* of the profession. With smiles and scalpels, scholars applied themselves ever more assiduously to loving dissections of New England and Chesapeake communities, to slavery in Brazil, the Caribbean, and the American South, and to the preindustrial consciousness of European and American working classes. New and ever more sophisticated quantitative techniques seemed to promise a degree of accuracy never previously attained in historical study. Some of those who followed carried the revolutionary spirit further and further and determined to outdo the achievements of all who preceded them by the ingenuity of their enterprise.[8]

Part of the inspiration for the new social history came from a group of French social historians loosely associated with the journal *Annales*—founded by Marc Bloch and Lucien Febvre. Caustic in their condemnation of traditional historians' preoccupation with elites and events (which they dismissed contemptuously as *l'histoire événementielle*), *les annalistes* promoted studies of how people lived and worked together. They pored over new kinds of evidence in census returns, court records, deed registries, parish records, ancient tools, old maps, and folklore to produce what they called "a new kind of history." There was no single approach to what came to be called the *Annales* "school," but most *annalistes* agreed on a few central themes. First, human behavior could not be understood apart from human interaction with the "structures" of history, forces that changed so slowly as to be almost imperceptible except when seen over long periods of time—*la longue durée*. Second, the *annalistes* shared a passionate espousal of quantitative analysis. Things that *could* be counted, such as price series and birth rates, even tithes and annual rainfall, *should* be counted. Third, they wished to grasp history holistically. According to Peter Burke, Febvre "did not believe that there was such a thing as diplomatic history or the history of ideas or even social history: there was only history, total history, without compartments." Perhaps the grandest work of *l'histoire totale* was Fernand Braudel's magisterial synthesis, *The Mediterranean and the Mediterranean World in the Age of Philip II*, but most of Braudel's intellectual progeny explored the structures of everyday life on a smaller and more provincial scale.[9]

At the same time the folklife studies movement attempted to awaken folklorists to a more holistic approach to their discipline. While most folklorists were preoccupied with *lore*—manifested in the collection, classification, and analysis of *texts*—European scholars of *volkskunde*, or regional ethnology, were more interested in the folk themselves. They embraced not merely the oral traditions of the folk, but also their customs and material culture. According to Don Yoder, "not only does the researcher study the verbal arts of folksong, folktale, riddle, etc.—which the folklorist has long ago made his province—but also agriculture and agrarian history, settlement patterns, dialectology or folk speech, folk architecture, folk cookery, folk costume, the folk year, arts and crafts." Yoder used the term *folklife* to describe the "total range of folk-cultural phenomena." Despite the impressive achievements of Richard Weiss and Henry Glassie, however, most folklife scholars in America seemed attracted exclusively to material culture. They eschewed analyzing what Yoder called "this

exciting totality of the verbal, spiritual, and material aspects of a culture."
Still, it was an attractive idea, a possibility not to be casually dismissed.
Perhaps here was the long-sought means through which the study of his-
tory and the study of folk culture might be reconciled.[10]

Whatever opportunities there might have been for a *rapprochement*
between the new social history and the folklife studies movement, they
were swept away in a new revolution, one which in its own way altered
the discipline of the folklorist as fundamentally as the new social history
altered that of the historian. At an international conference in Helsinki
in 1974, Lauri Honko hailed the victory of the revolutionists and proclaimed an international shift in folklore scholarship from concern with
traditional genres to the study of oral communication. Scholars of the new
folkloristics, as the revolution was called, tended to go beyond questions
of text, beyond questions of origins and diffusion, to stress the primary
importance of performance. The significant element in the new folkloristics was its emphasis on the communicative event, not the text, as the
analytical focus. The new paradigm, calling for the micro-analysis of contemporary communicative events, would seem to offer little promise of
rapprochement with the new social history.[11]

Even revolutions run their course, however. In his *Thinking Back*, the
historian C. Vann Woodward approvingly quotes Henrik Ibsen that "a
normally constituted truth lives . . . as a rule, seventeen or eighteen years;
at the outside twenty, seldom longer. And truths so stricken in years are
always shockingly thin." By the late 1980s both the new social history and
the new folkloristics had grown gaunt. Both appeared to be on their way
to retirement. In the uncovering and exposure of errors of fact and fudg-
ing, of flaws in research and fallacies in reasoning, scholars have come to
rely upon a certain assistance from critical colleagues. In the case of neither paradigm were those expectations to be disappointed. Regarding the
new social history, one distinguished historian expressed a feeling that
"historical scholarship has gotten out of control," although he did not say
whose control. Another complained that writers and readers of social history were "drawn to studies of ordinary folk, rather than to those of central institutions and established power." The annual presidential addresses
at the American Historical Association were performances of an old folklore genre—the jeremiad. One president lamented that the focus on communities and small groups had caused "an intellectual splintering that has
been going on for decades." Another president declared that "the greatest challenge that will face historians in the years ahead . . . is not how to

deepen and further sophisticate their technical probes of life in the past, but how to put the story together again." Storytelling became the code-word for the counterrevolution. A prize-winning scholar proclaimed, "Our job is to tell a good story." Even pioneers of the new social history defected to the other side, warning darkly of "widespread disillusionment" with the movement and decrying its imminent "collapse into trivia." Be-mused observers thought they detected in such posturing a rather disin-genuous flight from earlier commitments.[12]

These magnificent tantrums were the products of various incentives and were prompted by a variety of intentions. Some of the peevish reac-tion was identified with methodologically traditional or politically con-servative skepticism about social history and its putative radical politics. It would be a mistake, however, to dismiss all of such criticism as politi-cally or methodologically motivated, for some of it was deeply principled and carefully reasoned. Still, much of it was prompted by motivations less worthy than the pursuit of historical truth.

It would be difficult to withhold respect and admiration for the many achievements of the new social history, but there is no denying a certain justification for reservations. Despite its richness and strength, some of the new scholarship remained more static, more abstract, and less read-able than one might wish. Some scholars found an entirely adequate key to social history in quantification alone. Dazzled by the apparent preci-sion of multiple-regression and multivariate analysis, some scholars con-fused means with ends. Some of them succumbed to the temptation of reducing diverse and complex human beings to simple abstract catego-ries—workers, immigrants, women—and of manipulating them as math-ematical constructs rather than as flesh-and-blood humans. To do much of this work took patience, and so one may understand the great forbear-ance of those who sat at computer terminals, wholly absorbed in long-term demographic and economic trends, beset with too many method-ological and theoretical considerations to give much attention to the role of accident, of motivation, and of the individual. One fears that such sim-plifications do less than full justice to historical reality. These complaints certainly do not apply to all efforts of the new social history, but they are applicable to an embarrassingly high proportion.[13]

Not even the great Fernand Braudel, *doyen* of *les annalistes*, was immune to the lures of oversimplification. To criticize the legacy of a historian uni-versally regarded as one of the craft's greatest practitioners is not a task to be undertaken lightly, especially by one who remains in his intellectual debt. Braudel boasted of having achieved "a history whose passage is almost imperceptible, that of man in his relationship to the environment, a history in which all change is slow." In some *annaliste* scholarship, change became nonexistent and people became imperceptible, buried under layers of "structures" that "incumber history," according to Braudel, "and thus control its flow." In such hands the individual remained anonymous, "imprisoned within a destiny in which he himself has little hand," Braudel said. "All efforts against the prevailing tide of history," he added, "are doomed to failure." For more than seven decades *les annalistes* have offered a pathbreaking, if somewhat problematical, approach to the study of history. Their scholarship has materially enhanced their discipline's understanding of the role of the folk in past time. It would no longer seem possible, after their monumental studies, to maintain that the "lower classes" were either unimportant or inarticulate. It is surely no derogation of their accomplishment, however, to suggest that their "structures" are built upon a notion of historical determinism that is very difficult to accept.[14]

Just as historians were sounding a retreat from social history to narrative, a similar paradigmatic palace revolt was taking place in the field of folklore. Once more it was at an international scholarly conference that the coup was proclaimed. Once more the dissidents scrutinized the deeds of their predecessors and found them wanting. Only this time folklorists manifested a worldwide shift from concern with performance to a renewed preoccupation with texts. At the 1984 Congress of the International Society for Folk Narrative Research in Bergen, Norway, in paper after paper participants from Europe, Asia, Africa, and the Americas stressed structuralist and poststructuralist analysis of texts. As in the case of the new social history, attacks on the new folkloristics were prompted by a variety of motives and characterized by a variety of intentions. There were criticisms that were justifiable and some that were less than that. Some were prompted by the call of ambition and some by the dictates of fashion—the paradigm *du jour*. There were critics who combined candor with civility as well as some of another type altogether. Folklorists—perhaps to a greater degree than other pursuers or purveyors of truth—seem given to occasional lapses of decorum in scholarly discourse. Conceding wryly the great differences of style and substance between the concerns of folklorists and those of historians, it would nevertheless seem unduly myopic to miss the similarity of motifs in this tale of two disciplines: the same jeremiads, the same manifestoes, and the same disingenuous flight by some from earlier intellectual commitments.[15]

If the merits and demerits of the new folkloristics be fairly balanced, it must be acknowledged that the scholars of the new departure showed a sensitive appreciation of the fact that the cultural meaning of folklore is inseparable from performance, that the same proverb, tale, or custom may generate different meanings in different performances. So impressive has been the achievement of the new folkloristics that it ought now to be possible to criticize certain aspects of its scholarship without seeming to impugn the movement's entire contribution. Within its paradigm, scholars went further than any of their predecessors in relating the communicative elements and the social elements of folklore. Nevertheless, they showed a surprising disinclination to conceptualize folklore in holistic terms. Nor did they face the full implications of their emphasis on performance. They studied performance not as fluid process but as static event (one might call it *folklore événementielle*), an approach almost as *immobile* as the old-fashioned emphasis on text or artifact. Seduced by linguistics, they spent their energies in static synchronic analysis and became mired in microstudies of folklore performance in the ethnographic present. In the process, the dimension of time—tradition—was neglected.

In these postmodern times, neither historical nor cultural "meaning" is absolute. "History is natural selection," says Salman Rushdie. "Mutant versions of the past struggle for dominance; new species of fact arise, and old . . . truths go to the wall, blindfolded and smoking last cigarettes." Meaning is the result of a struggle between competing interests to gain power through control of speech or "discourse." "Discourse" has been called the opiate of the postmodernists. Meaning, after all, is created by the manipulation of language, is it not? But language is subversive, eroding the intentions of those who would use it. Meaning is inherent not in the intentions of "authors," but in the multiple and even contradictory "readings" of "readers."[16] Some scholars consider it their function not to "interpret" history or culture but to "deconstruct" it, to reveal it as a linguistic construction.

It is thus a temptation to regard history as no more than a sequence of representations (and not even a causal sequence at that), a temptation to regard history as simply an acrimonious contest among narratives made by historical actors and narratives made by historians. The temptation is acute, and not all scholars have been able to resist it.

The issue is particularly complex and hazardous in the study of folk culture. The performer of a proverb or tale is perforce on one level a "reader" of culture and on another level an "author" for an audience of cultural observers who may or may not be members of the cultural group. Folklore theory needs to be grounded in the deconstructive insight that folklorists no less than other "readers" are implicated in folk culture. Folklorists may perceive cultural "grammars" that are not perceived (or at least not articulated) by the folk. At the same time, they must avoid carrying such insights to the point that it exalts "reader" over "author," observer over actor, folklorist over the folk, as the "true" creator of cultural meaning. To do so would beg the question of cultural authorship, of who is "author-ized" to speak for a cultural group's identity and authenticity. To do so would honor the etic over the emic, the outsider over the insider, the tourist over the native, as the authentic voice of the folk. To do so would be to commit an act of profound cultural arrogance and appalling professional naiveté.

Some of the criticisms of the new social history and of the new folkloristics, then, are too substantive to be casually dismissed. Both paradigms would seem, for the moment, to have reached the limits of their momentum in their present forms. The fields they till have grown narrower and less fertile. Their methods, of course, can be replicated ad infinitum in ever smaller historical and folkloristic contexts, but asking the same questions and getting the same answers in new locations seem less and less likely to advance either discipline. The excesses to which both paradigms are prone, under the intoxicating influence of mathematics in one case and linguistics in the other, would now seem to call for sober thought and stocktaking.

The question remains, however, what prospect exists for retaining and extending the advances that each paradigm has contributed to understanding the culture of the folk. The answer lies neither in repudiating the achievements of the new social history or the new folkloristics nor in building upon their limitations. Critics call for historians to desert analysis of the folk to write the narratives of the elite and for folklorists to desert the performances of the folk to study the texts of the lore. To accept those calls would seem to suggest a nostalgic return to outmoded paradigms and an *alleged* wholeness and equilibrium that were actually delusions of each discipline's intellectual infancy. To accept these calls is to accept the notion that the minds of the next generation of historians and folklorists, like those of young children, should be protected from too early and too intimate acquaintance with the life and lore of "the nether herd." Rather the key would seem to lie in a reconsideration of relationships between history and folklore. Folklorists *need* history to help them understand the process of change in folk culture; social historians *need* folklore to help them understand the role of the folk in history, lest they degenerate into a gaggle of sycophantic yarn spinners.

Granting that each discipline has legitimate scholarly purposes of its own, and conceding that neither discipline exists merely to serve as handmaiden to the other, one cannot help note that neither events nor structures, nor their interactions with one another, can be understood unless analysis is grounded in the attitudes and actions of real men and women, without whom there is neither history nor folklore.

The Ark, the plantation where Sabe Rutledge first learned the fascinating tales of Buh Rabbit, has long since been altered beyond recognition. It is now an oceanfront resort named Surfside Beach, part of South Carolina's famous Grand Strand. Sabe Rutledge's daughter, Mary Burroughs, moved inland across the Waccamaw River to the site of another former plantation near Bucksport. As we drive down Martin Luther King Road to her house, we note indications that her community may itself soon face development. Sewer lines are being installed, and there are rumors of a new highway. "Papa fixin' to tell dem lies, now," she remembers. "Make dem boys laugh. Tell all kind of stories." She smiles to recall his tales of Buh Rabbit. "Dat's all he *would* do! Make us laugh!" She also remembers his stories of hags, haunts, and plat-eyes. "Papa used to scay [scare] me out of goin' to bed. Go to sleep put de cover over yuh head." As she recounts childhood memories of listening to her father tell tales, her own grandchildren are listening to soul music on the radio in the same room. Her daughter Mary Ann is working at a nearby restaurant, serving visitors who come down the Waccamaw on yachts. Outside, wooden surveyors' stakes, their small orange flags fluttering in the warm Carolina breeze, point toward a future that may be as inhospitable to Gullah folk culture as other resort developments have been. Mary Burroughs no longer tells the old stories she learned from her father. But her daughter does.[17]

PART FIVE

The Future of Folk Culture

16

Endangered Traditions
Resort Development and Cultural Conservation on the Sea Islands

The Sea Islands are low and flat, and they have a beauty beyond description. When I was a child growing up in the South Carolina lowcountry, we used to take Sunday afternoon drives. If we went down from Charleston across the Ashley River and Wappoo Creek onto James Island and then across the Stono River onto Johns Island, we saw great live oaks leaning dreamily over the road. I remember (or perhaps I imagine) that their low branches, almost hidden by gloomy gray moss, seemed to enclose the road into long miles of gray tunnel. Here and there we passed through swampy lowlands. I was told that in such places snakes and alligators (and haunts and plat-eyes) were lying in wait for bad little boys and girls. The tangled vines and underbrush had a menacing and sinister beauty. Here and there, too, the oak-lined avenue was broken by fields and pastures. Mules and cows dozed and switched flies under a torrid sun. Rainfall seemed an ancient memory, and in places the grass appeared to have abandoned the effort to be green. Here and there families of black people waved from the porches of small, gray, weather-stained cabins. Shouting children and barking dogs chased one another across neatly swept yards. I can still recall the soft sound of pine needles rustling in the breeze and the fresh clouds of fragrance wafted in from the nearby salt marsh.

Atlantic waves break upon a series of barrier islands all along the coast of Georgia and South Carolina. Tidal streams and inlets, draining an intricate system of shallow, marsh-filled coastal lagoons, separate the islands from the mainland and from one another. From Waties Island in the mouth of Little River near the North and South Carolina line south past the wide beaches and thick dunes of the Grand Strand; past Pawleys and

North Islands to Georgetown; from South, Cedar, and Murphy Islands to Cape Romaine; down past Bull, Capers, and Dewees Islands and the Isle of Palms to Charleston; from James and Johns, past Kiawah, Wadmalaw, and Edisto Islands to Beaufort; down past St. Helena, Hunting, Fripp, and Parris Islands; past Hilton Head and Daufuski to Savannah; from Tybee, Wassaw, Ossabaw, and St. Catherines to Sapelo; past St. Simons and Jekyll Islands to Cumberland on the Georgia-Florida border—the Sea Islands guard the coast. The coastline is intersected not only by Winyah and Bull Bays, Charleston Harbor, and St. Helena, Port Royal, Sapelo, and St. Andrew Sounds, but also by many lesser inlets curling around the Sea Islands. Bounded on one side by the ocean and on the other by the salt marsh, these Sea Islands use the energy of wind and wave to build sand barriers that protect the mainland from storm and surf.

The Sea Islands north of Charleston are often older beach resorts such as Pawleys Island and the Isle of Palms. Their residents and visitors are mainly white. Other islands are wildlife sanctuaries such as the 31,000-acre Cape Romaine National Wildlife Refuge, the 20,000-acre Tom Yawkee Wildlife Center on South Island, and the 17,000-acre Belle W. Baruch research facilities on Hobcaw Barony. They serve as home for such endangered species as the bald eagle, the eastern brown pelican, the short-nosed sturgeon, and the loggerhead turtle. Many islands south of Charleston are populated entirely or primarily by black Carolinians and Georgians, heirs of a venerable folk culture and a vivid creole language. On the coastal mainland adjacent to the Sea Islands are black people who, while they are not—strictly speaking—Sea Islanders, share that folk culture and that creole language.

For two centuries this coastal region has been the home of enslaved Africans and their descendants. Theirs is a sad but inspiring story. They built—in a very literal sense—the plantations, and they tilled the rich fields of rice, indigo, or Sea Island cotton. Some of the slaves were brought to the Sea Islands by Barbadian planters who migrated to the Carolina colony in the seventeenth and eighteenth centuries as a refuge from the overcrowding of Barbados. Many more were imported directly from Africa. By the American Revolution the black majority, from various parts of Africa and from various ethnic and linguistic groups, had already created a distinctive culture. During the Civil War, when white planter families fled the Sea Islands before the invading Union troops, black Sea Islanders began to cultivate the land for themselves. Hundreds of them joined the Union Army in the celebrated First South Carolina Volunteers.

On January 16, 1865, General William Tecumseh Sherman's famous Special Field Order No. 15 set aside for the former slaves "the islands from Charleston [and] the abandoned South fields along the rivers for thirty miles back from the sea." Within weeks black homesteaders were happily farming their own plots on Edisto, Wadmalaw, Johns, and James Islands. By September, President Andrew Johnson had nullified Sherman's order. Many freedmen were dispossessed, but others tenaciously held on to their lands and passed them on to their descendants. Some even managed to buy more land at the end of the nineteenth century as whites again abandoned the islands after years of feeble cotton prices and a series of killer hurricanes. For the first half of the twentieth century blacks continued to be in the majority on the Sea Islands, and land values continued to be low.

For generations the Sea Islanders lived under the same hot sun, surrounded by the same sea and salt marsh, forming a barrier that isolated them from the mainland. For generations fishermen flung their nets into creeks and marshes and ocean for crabs, shrimp, and fish; and they gathered oysters and clams. These supplied both local markets and their own kitchens. For generations islanders cultivated their own little plots of land. Farmers hoed the loamy soil of the islands to produce crops of beans, peas, and cotton. First there was the planting, then the weeding, then the reaping. In the winter women sewed clothes and made quilts; the men looked for work ashore. In the spring they started the cycle over from the beginning—the planting, the weeding, the reaping.

The years passed. The young grew old and the old died. And the planting, weeding, and reaping, and the fishing, shrimping, and crabbing went on. Each year was like the year before. Each generation was like the generation before. Each generation prayed the same prayers and hoped the same hopes, held the same faith and the same fear, worked the same work with the same result. For generations there was the same old, hard legacy of slavery that robbed men and women of their honor, a legacy visited upon the children and the grandchildren and the great-grandchildren, a legacy against which honest hard work seemed useless, a legacy so old it took its place among natural phenomena like the wind and the rain.

It was not an easy life; but it was a self-sufficient life adapted to the environment, a life shaped by a rich folk culture. Cut off from the mainland, generations of Sea Islanders preserved their cultural heritage, reflecting both continuity with Africa and creativity in the New World. Perhaps most important, Gullah continued to be the language in which their folk culture was passed down to posterity. Proverbs, metaphors of social ex-

perience, continued to reflect the African preference for speaking by indirection; and African naming patterns persisted on the Sea Islands. For
generations Sea Island storytellers regaled their listeners with tales of
the animal trickster Buh Rabbit and of the slave trickster John, blending elements of African folk narrative with elements of the Sea Islanders' historical experience. For generations talented Sea Island artisans
created traditional arts and crafts such as coiled sweetgrass baskets and
strip quilts. Out of this tradition one Sea Islander, Philip Simmons of
Daniel Island, became Charleston's preeminent artist in wrought-iron
gates. For generations folk medicine of both the pharmaceutical and the
psychological varieties continued to heal the sick on the Sea Islands, and
natural phenomena continued to serve as signs foretelling the future,
whether changing weather or impending death. Ghosts or haunts—the
spirits of the dead—returned from time to time to trouble the living,
although local conjurers (assisted by various substances held to be magical) helped to ward off their unwelcome visits. For generations, after
the day's work was done, Sea Islanders entertained their children with
play songs and sang them to sleep with lullabies. Their folk version of
Christianity retained the earliest "shouting" styles of singing spirituals,
in which the African religious phenomenon of spirit possession remained vividly linked with prayer, music, and bodily movement. No one
thought this way of life would change. The life of the land and the people seemed fixed in an invisible circle, enclosed by the waters and the
passage of time.

And then something happened. It did not seem revolutionary at the
time. In 1950 a Georgia timber magnate, General Joseph B. Fraser, and his
associates bought large tracts of land on the southern end of Hilton Head
Island. At first they simply cut down the ancient stands of timber. But soon
Fraser's son Charles, a young Yale law school graduate, launched the development of such lavish resort "plantations" as Sea Pines, pioneering the
"resort island" concept. In 1956 the first bridge to Hilton Head Island was
constructed. Feverish land speculation ensued as other developers scur-
ried onto Hilton Head and other Sea Islands to exploit the boom, buying
up land from black islanders and building more resorts.

Hilton Head Island became known as a resort for the affluent. But similar developments have taken place on other Sea Islands. Hilton Head
appears in many ways to have forecast what the future would bring. Its
recent course is worth closer examination. In 1950 nearly all of the residents of Hilton Head were black; by the end of the century they were

overwhelmingly white. According to Charles Fraser, development has been a good thing for black natives of the islands. Resort development "caused black-owned land on Hilton Head Island to increase in value from $100 an acre near the beach or near the marshes to $50,000 or $100,000 an acre today. This flows into the pocket of the blacks who elect to sell," he noted in 1982. "I sold lots at $7,000 which today sell for $350,000. Some blacks have done the same. Some of them, smarter than I was, held onto their land, as I and developers developed our land and pushed up the values. Now they are selling. I am jubilant, positively jubilant, when a black farm family that has held the land for five generations on Hilton Head Island, land that was worth $100 when we arrived here, sells it today for $50,000. I think that's wonderful." Fraser contends that "it is a wise thing, for those who need the money, to elect to sell. Every black family that sells a portion of their heritage that was maintained with great struggle and great effort by their parents and grandparents and great-grandparents, and uses a part of that heritage to send a child to engineering school or to boarding school, is making an investment in the future of that family. I wish more of them would do it." The emergence of Hilton Head Island as a playground for rich white northerners, in the opinion of Charles Fraser, has been beneficial for everyone.[1]

But others are less sanguine. "We have witnessed some changes on Hilton Head over the last twenty-five years," suggests Emory Campbell, a native of the island, "and they have not all been good from the black perspective." Some contend that black landowners were induced to sell their land too cheaply—either through trickery or because they did not know the land's fair market value. Unquestionably some black families made money on the transactions, at least by comparison with the barter-like economy of the predevelopment decades. But even those who received fair prices made money at the cost of selling their birthright. For those who were unwilling to sell, rising land values only meant rising property taxes. Many were forced to sell because they could no longer afford to keep up the additional tax burden. "We have witnessed land being sold because the family no longer wanted to tolerate taxes on land that's doing nothing," Campbell stresses. A money economy has come to Hilton Head and the other Sea Islands. Land is being sold, he points out, "merely because people, families, need the money."

The resort island rich give Beaufort County, which includes Hilton Head and other Sea Islands, the second highest per capita income in South Carolina. But unemployment in the county surpasses the state average with depressing regularity. And half the county's nonagricultural employees work in low-paying service jobs—as caddies, cooks, maids, maintenance workers, waiters, and waitresses. It is certainly true that this generation of islanders is better paid than the generation before them; it is not necessarily true that they are economically better off. But the islanders now live in a money economy. They must earn money to live.

While low-paying service jobs are easily available on the resort islands, higher-paying skilled occupations are rare. And those positions are not normally filled by islanders, who usually lack the requisite education. Incentives to acquire an education for positions that seem to be set aside for outsiders are lacking; incentives to take the low-paying jobs are abundant. The situation "enslaves" young people, says Emory Campbell. "They forget that a job is only a means to an end." Sea Island blacks "are not motivated to go beyond the tenth, eleventh grade because they see the immediacy of the dollar," he notes. But education does not seem to break the cycle on the Sea Islands. "The few that have gone to college, they're motivated to leave rather than to stay. They can't tolerate the situation. We just don't have the kinds of jobs here that would dignify staying. They become overwhelmed by the subservient roles that most blacks are put in here."

Fraser is sensitive to charges that hiring practices are discriminatory. "I get continued crap that we should confine our employment exclusively to people who were born on Hilton Head Island, without regard to their ability or what they do," he complains. "When we had a vice president for personnel, black, college educated, graduate degree in personnel management, we got nothing but hell because he had not been born on Hilton Head Island. This is the sort of crap we get over and over again." Fraser's preference for well-qualified employees to fill upper-echelon positions is understandable. But the fact remains that of all the jobs created by development on the Sea Islands, virtually the only ones that are available to the Sea Islanders themselves are jobs as servants.

Even more striking than the economic consequences of development on the indigenous population of the Sea Islands has been its cultural impact. Modernization has caused severe social dislocations. "Developers just come in and roll over whoever is there," charges Emory Campbell, "move them out or roll over them and change their culture, change their way of life, destroy the environment, and therefore the culture has to be changed." Perhaps the unintentional vanguard of white cultural imperialism has been the school. Campbell calls for a school system "that is in tune with the culture of the black child of this island. That child's heritage," he notes, "is different from a child who came here from Chicago, New York, or Ohio. And that's where a lot of our white kids are coming from; so you put them in a classroom and say you're integrated and you've got a classroom situation at Hilton Head Elementary School that's oriented to those kids who are moving in." Teachers with little understanding of the islands' rich historical and cultural heritage criticize the island children's Gullah speech—as though the children were the outsiders who speak funny. They do not know that Gullah is a creole language with a very regular syntax and phonology of its own. They do not know that other forms of the islanders' cultural expression are parts of an ancient and beautiful tradition with a rich history behind it. It is little wonder that many Sea Island children—in the face of daily assaults on the way they talk and the way they express themselves—see the school as the enemy, taking away more than it gives. With white dominance of the economic and educational systems some Sea Islanders have become ashamed of their culture. Thus the schools, intended to be the agents of cultural enrichment, have become agents of cultural destruction.

There is a story that during the 1930s an aged black man on one of the Sea Islands was asked how he was faring in the Great Depression. "Dat Depression new-come," he replied. "Ah bin-yuh. *New-come* can't beat *bin-yuh*." The Sea Islands survived the Great Depression, but now they suffer from what the historian Eric Hobsbawm calls "the impact of social transformation." The old coexists uneasily with the new, *bin-yuh* with *come-yuh*; but *bin-yuh* is on the defensive. Not even those islands that have thus far eluded the bulldozers have immunity to development. To endure, a community must be able to bequeath its shared traditional expressive culture to the next generation. Without the living context in which that expressive culture arises, cultural endurance is by no means certain. It is not the wildlife of the islands that is the most endangered, says Emory Campbell. "*We* have become the new endangered species."

The old talk and the old tales, the old prayers and the old personal expressiveness are more than just quaint cultural artifacts. They have provided the islanders with a sense of continuity with generations gone before, a precious lifeline to courageous ancestors who survived slavery and endured generations of poverty. That heritage is a source of strength that has enabled them to cope with the hail and upheaval of life. As we drift further and further out upon the sea of modernization, that heritage may be as crucial to our sanity and survival as to theirs. The Sea Islanders and their folk culture have something precious to offer us if we do not destroy them first.

Notes

Introduction

1. C. Vann Woodward, *The Burden of Southern History* (Baton Rouge, 1960), viii.

2. Ulrich B. Phillips, "The Central Theme of Southern History," *American Historical Review* 34 (Oct. 1928): 30–43; rpt. in his *The Course of the South to Secession*, ed. E. Merton Coulter (New York, 1939), quote on 152.

3. Eugene D. Genovese, *The Southern Tradition: The Achievement and Limitations of an American Conservatism* (Cambridge, Mass., 1994), 2, 9, 27.

4. Woodward, *Burden of Southern History*, ix–xi, 167–70.

5. David M. Potter, "The Enigma of the South," *Yale Review* 51 (1961): 142–46.

6. Howard W. Odum, *The Way of the South: Toward the Regional Balance of America* (New York, 1947), 64. See also Howard W. Odum, *Folk, Region, and Society* (Chapel Hill, 1966), 219–38, 293–354; John Shelton Reed, *Southern Folk, Plain and Fancy: Native White Social Types* (Athens, Ga., 1986).

7. James McBride Dabbs, *The Southern Heritage* (New York, 1958), 35.

8. Odum's phrase is quoted from his *Way of the South*, 62. The celebrated northern traveler Frederick Law Olmsted claimed that the South had but three social classes: a planter elite, poor whites, and black slaves, while Daniel R. Hundley listed what he called "some half-dozen other classes possessing different degrees of culture and refinement" on rungs of the southern social ladder below the Southern Gentleman. They included the Middle Class, the Southern Yankee, the Cotton Snob, the Southern Yeoman, the Southern Bully, and the Poor White Trash (not to mention the slaves). See Olmsted's *Slavery and the South, 1852–1857*, vol. 2 of *The Papers of Frederick Law Olmsted*, ed. Charles E. Beveridge and Charles Capen McLaughlin (Baltimore, 1981); and Hundley's *Social Relations in Our Southern States* (1860, rpt., Baton Rouge, 1979), 10.

9. Frank L. Owsley, *Plain Folk of the Old South* (Baton Rouge, 1949); Wayne Flynt, *Dixie's Forgotten People: The South's Poor Whites* (Bloomington, Ind., 1979) and his

Poor but Proud: Alabama's Poor Whites (Tuscaloosa, 1989); Bill Cecil-Fronsman, *Common Whites: Class and Culture in Antebellum North Carolina* (Lexington, Ky., 1992); and Grady McWhiney, *Cracker Culture: Celtic Ways in the Old South* (Tuscaloosa, 1988).

10. David M. Potter, "Depletion and Renewal in Southern History, in *Perspectives on the South: Agenda for Research,* ed. Edgar T. Thompson (Durham, N.C., 1967), 84.

11. Owsley, *Plain Folk of the Old South.* The so-called "Owsley School" included his students Herbert Weaver, Blanche Henry Clark (later Blanche Clark Weaver), and Harriet Chappell Owsley (his wife). See Blanche Henry Clark, *The Tennessee Yeomen, 1840–1860* (Nashville, 1942); Herbert Weaver, *Mississippi Farmers, 1850–1860* (Nashville, 1945); and two articles by Frank L. and Harriet Owsley: "The Economic Basis of Society in the Late Ante-Bellum South," *Journal of Southern History* 6 (1940): 24–45, and "The Economic Structure of Rural Tennessee 1850–1860," *Journal of Southern History* 8 (1942): 161–82. For a memoir of the research and writing of *Plain Folk of the Old South* see Harriet Chappell Owsley, *Frank Lawrence Owsley: Historian of the Old South, with Letters and Writings of Frank Owsley* (Nashville, 1990), 134–51. Other pioneering studies of this white majority include Julia A. Flisch, "The Common People of the Old South," *Annual Report of the American Historical Association* (1909): 133–43; Paul H. Buck, "The Poor Whites of the Antebellum South," *American Historical Review* 31 (1925–26): 41–54; Avery O. Craven, "The Poor Whites and the Negroes in the Antebellum South," *Journal of Negro History* 15 (1930): 14–25; Clement Eaton, "Class Distinctions in the Old South," *Virginia Quarterly Review* 33 (1957): 357–70; and William Best Hesseltine, "Four American Traditions," in *The Pursuit of Southern History,* ed. George B. Tindall (Baton Rouge, 1964), 413–37.

12. Steven Hahn, *The Roots of Southern Populism: Yeoman Farmers and the Transformation of the Georgia Backcountry, 1850–1890* (New York, 1983); Lacy K. Ford Jr., *Origins of Southern Radicalism: The South Carolina Upcountry, 1800–1860* (New York, 1988); Stephanie McCurry, *Masters of Small Worlds: Yeoman Households, Gender Relations, and the Political Culture of the Antebellum South Carolina Low Country* (New York, 1995).

13. Hundley, *Social Relations in Our Southern States,* 193. It is interesting that on the same page Hundley describes the yeomen as "nearly always poor, at least so far as this world's goods are to be taken into account."

14. Owsley, *Plain Folk of the Old South,* 133. See also J. Mills Thornton III, *Politics and Power in a Slave Society: Alabama, 1800–1860* (Baton Rouge, 1978).

15. See Roger W. Shugg, *Origins of the Class Struggle in Louisiana* (Baton Rouge, 1939); Michael P. Johnson, *Toward a Patriarchal Republic* (Baton Rouge, 1977); Flynt, *Dixie's Forgotten People* and *Poor but Proud;* Hahn, *Roots of Southern Populism;* Randolph Campbell, *A Southern Community in Crisis: Harrison County Texas, 1850–1880* (Austin, 1983); J. William Harris, *Plain Folk and Gentry in a Slave Society: White*

Liberty and Black Slavery in Augusta's Hinterlands (Middletown, Conn.: 1985); Fred A. Bailey, *Class and Tennessee's Confederate Generation* (Chapel Hill, 1987); and Cecil-Fronsman, *Common Whites*. See also earlier studies such as A. N. J. Den Holland-er, "The Tradition of 'Poor Whites,'" in *Culture in the South*, ed. William T[erry] Couch (Chapel Hill, 1934); Fabien Linden, "Economic Democracy in the Slave South: An Appraisal of Some Recent Views," *Journal of Negro History* 31 (1946): 140–89; Stephen E. Ambrose, "Yeoman Discontent in the Confederacy," *Civil War History* 8 (1962): 259–68; and Gavin Wright, "'Economic Democracy' and the Concentration of Agricultural Wealth in the Cotton South, 1850–1860," *Agricultural History* 44 (1970): 63–95.

16. Eugene D. Genovese, *The World the Slaveholders Made: Two Essays in Interpretation* (New York, 1969), 16. See also his *Roll, Jordan, Roll: The World the Slaves Made* (New York, 1974), 25–26; his *The Political Economy of Slavery: Studies in the Economy and Society of the Slave South* (New York, 1969); and especially his "Yeomen Farmers in a Slaveholders' Democracy," *Agricultural History* 49 (1975): 331–42.

17. Grady McWhiney, *Cracker Culture: Celtic Ways in the Old South* (Tuscaloosa, 1988), 38, 47, 112, 142–43, 264; Grady McWhiney and Forrest McDonald, "The Antebellum Southern Herdsman: A Reinterpretation," *Journal of Southern History* 42 (1975): 146–66 (quotation on 166). See also McWhiney and McDonald, "The South: From Self-Sufficiency to Peonage: An Interpretation," *American Historical Review* 85 (1980): 1095–1118; idem, "Celtic Origins of Southern Herding Practices," *Journal of Southern History* 51 (1985): 165–82; and Forrest McDonald and Ellen Shapiro McDonald, "The Ethnic Origins of the American People, 1790," *William and Mary Quarterly* 37 (1980): 179–99; as well as the supporting articles by the archaeologist John Solomon Otto, "Southern 'Plain Folk' Agriculture: A Reconsideration," *Plantation Society in the Americas* 2 (1983): 32–34, and "The Migration of the Southern Plain Folk: An Interdisciplinary Synthesis," *Journal of Southern History* 51 (1985): 188–95.

18. David Hackett Fischer, *Albion's Seed: Four British Folkways in America* (New York, 1989), 605–782.

19. See, for example, Henry Glassie, *Pattern in the Material Culture of the Eastern United States* (Philadelphia, 1968); his "The Types of the Southern Mountain Cabin," in Jan Harold Brunvand, *The Study of American Folklore* (New York, 1968), 338–70; and his *Folk Housing in Middle Virginia: A Structural Analysis of Historic Artifacts* (Knoxville, 1975); Charles G. Zug III, ed., *Material Culture in the South*, special issue of *Southern Folklore Quarterly* 39 (1975); Fred Kniffen, "American Cultural Geography and Folklife," in *American Folklife*, ed. Don Yoder (Austin, 1976), 51–70; Ralph Rinzler and Robert Sayers, *The Meaders Family: North Georgia Potters*, Smithsonian Folklife Studies, no. 1 (Washington, D.C., 1977); John A. Burrison, *Brothers in Clay: The Story of Georgia Folk Pottery* (Athens, Ga., 1983); Nancy Sweezy, *Raised in Clay: The Southern Pottery Tradition* (Washington, D.C., 1984); Charles G. Zug III, *Turners and Burners: The Folk Potters of North Carolina* (Chapel Hill, 1986);

and Catherine Wilson Horne, ed., *Crossroads of Clay: The Southern Alkaline-Glazed Stoneware Tradition* (Columbia, S.C., 1990).

Chapter 2: "Let Us Break Bread Together"

1. Nolan Porterfield, *Jimmie Rodgers: The Life and Times of America's Blue Yodeler* (Urbana, 1979); Dave Marsh, *Elvis* (New York, 1982); Colin Escott and Martin Hawkins, *Catalyst: The Sun Records Story* (New York, 1975).

2. Grady McWhiney, *Cracker Culture: Celtic Ways in the Old South* (Tuscaloosa, Ala., 1988), 38, 47, 112, 142–43, 264. Such a hypothesis has, in fact, been put forward in an unpublished paper by John Morgan Dederer.

3. David Hackett Fischer, *Albion's Seed: Four British Folkways in America* (New York, 1989).

4. John Boles writes, in his *Black Southerners*, "In no other aspect of black cultural life than religion, had the values and practices of whites so deeply penetrated." Boles, *Black Southerners, 1619–1869* (Lexington, Ky., 1983), 165. John Blassingame, *The Slave Community: Plantation Life in the Antebellum South*, 2d ed. (New York, 1979), 98 (quote in text). See also John Boles, ed., *Masters and Slaves in the House of the Lord* (Lexington, Ky., 1988).

5. Sterling Stuckey, *Slave Culture: Nationalist Theory and the Foundations of Black America* (New York, 1987), 35–36, 57, 54. See also Molefi Kete Asante, *The Afrocentric Idea* (Philadelphia, 1989); Joseph E. Holloway, ed., *Africanisms in American Culture*, Blacks in the Diaspora series (Bloomington, Ind., 1990).

6. Ralph Ellison, *Shadow and Act* (New York, 1961), 115.

7. Ulrich Bonnell Phillips, *American Negro Slavery* (New York, 1918), 3–5. Occasionally Phillips seemed to believe in African cultural continuity among the slaves. "While produced only in America," he wrote, "the plantation slave was a product of old world forces. His nature was an African's profoundly modified but hardly transformed by the requirements of European civilization. The wrench from Africa and the subjection to the new discipline while uprooting his ancient language and customs had little more effect upon his temperament than upon his complexion." Yet only a few sentences later Phillips emphasized discontinuity between Africa and African Americans. He quoted with approval a saying of the slaveholders that "a negro was what a white man made him." On the slave plantation, Phillips wrote, the slave left Africa behind. "Ceasing to be Foulah, Coramantee, Ebo or Angola, he became instead the American negro." Ibid., 291. For explications of Phillips's life and works see Eugene D. Genovese, "Ulrich Bonnell Phillips and His Critics," foreword to Phillips's *American Negro Slavery* (Baton Rouge, 1966); Eugene D. Genovese, "Race and Class in Southern History: An Appraisal of the Work of Ulrich Bonnell Phillips," *Agricultural History* 41 (1967): 345–58; John Herbert Roper, *U. B. Phillips: A Southern Mind* (Macon, Ga., 1984); Merton L. Dillon, *Ulrich Bonnell Phillips, Historian of the Old South* (Baton Rouge,

1985); and John David Smith, *An Old Creed for the New South: Proslavery Ideology and Historiography, 1865–1918* (Westport, Conn., 1985).

8. According to Park, "the Negro, when he landed in the United States, left behind him almost everything but his dark complexion and his tropical temperament. It is very difficult to find in the South today," he wrote in 1919, "anything that can be traced directly back to Africa." Robert E. Park, "The Conflict and Fusion of Cultures with Special Reference to the Negro," *Journal of Negro History* 4 (1919): 116–18. For an interesting perspective on conservative and radical manifestations of the sociological catastrophist school see Orlando Patterson, "Rethinking Black History," *Harvard Educational Review* 41 (1971): 299–304.

9. E. Franklin Frazier, *The Negro Family in America* (Chicago, 1939), 21–22, 479; E. Franklin Frazier, *The Negro in the United States* (rev. ed., New York, 1957), 680–81. See also his "Traditions and Patterns of Negro Family Life in the United States," in *Race and Culture Contacts*, ed. E. B. Reuter (New York, 1934), 194; and his *The Negro Church in America* (New York, 1963).

10. "The Negro's almost complete loss of African language heritages is startling at first glance," Johnson wrote, "but slavery as practiced in the United States made any other outcome impossible." On the Sea Islands, according to Johnson, "the Negro took over the English of the whites with whom he was associated, and he did it remarkably well." Gullah grammar, he said, "is merely simplified English grammar." As for songs, "the general pattern and many of the particulars of the music developed in slavery were borrowed from white folk music." Even "superstitions," so often regarded as evidence of the primitive African origins of black southerners, Johnson attributed to white sources. "A surprisingly large proportion of the Negro folk beliefs found in the South is of European descent." Guy B. Johnson, *Folk Culture on St. Helena Island, South Carolina*, (Chapel Hill, 1930) 10–11, 128, 171. See also Guion Griffis Johnson, *A Social History of the Sea Islands* (Chapel Hill, 1930); T. J. Woofter Jr., *Black Yeomanry: Life on St. Helena Island* (Chapel Hill, 1930). For a discussion of Guy B. Johnson and his seminal role in the St. Helena project, see Daniel Joseph Singal, *The War Within: From Victorian to Modernist Thought in the South, 1919–1945* (Chapel Hill, 1982), 315–27; see also Johnson's own account, Guy B. Johnson, "Reminiscences about Sea Island Research in 1928," in *Sea and Land: Cultural and Biological Adaptations in the Southern Coastal Plain*, ed. James L. Peacock and James C. Sabella, Southern Anthropological Society Proceedings, no. 21 (Athens, Ga., 1988), 3–12. Some black scholars, such as John Wesley Work (introduction to *Folk Song of the American Negro*, ed. Frederick J. Work [Nashville, Tenn., 1907]), James Weldon Johnson (*The Book of American Negro Spirituals* [New York, 1925], with J. Rosamund Johnson), and N. G. J. Ballanta (*St. Helena Island Spirituals* [New York, 1925]), claimed African origins for the African-American spirituals, although they did so in short introductions that rested their cases more upon rhetoric than upon evidence. The only white scholar who had shared their view was the music critic Edward Krehbiel (*Afro-American Folksongs:*

A Study in Racial and National Music [New York, 1914]). In the 1920s and 1930s a number of white scholars, including Edward M. von Hornbostel ("American Negro Music," *International Review of Missions* 15 [1926]: 748–51), Newman Ivey White (*American Negro Folk Songs* [Cambridge, Mass., 1928]), and George Pullen Jackson (*White and Negro Spirituals* [New York, 1943]), had contended that the African-American spirituals represented selective borrowings from white folk hymnody. For studies of the controversy over the spirituals, see Charles Joyner, "Music: Origins of the Spirituals," in *Encyclopedia of Black America*, ed. W. Augustus Low and Virgil A. Clift (New York, 1981), 591–96; John David Smith, "The Unveiling of Slave Folk Culture, 1865–1920," *Journal of Folklore Research* 21 (1984): 47–62; and D. K. Wilgus, *Anglo-American Folksong Scholarship since 1898* (New Brunswick, N.J., 1959), 345–64.

11. See the following by Elsie Clews Parsons: *Folk Tales from the Sea Islands, South Carolina* (Cambridge, Mass., 1923); *Folk Tales of the Andros Islands* (Cambridge, Mass., 1918); *Folk Lore from the Cape Verde Islands* (Cambridge, Mass., 1923); *Folk Lore of the Antilles, French and English*, vols. 1–3 (Cambridge, Mass., 1933–35, 1943). See also Newbell Niles Puckett, *Folk Beliefs of the Southern Negro* (Chapel Hill, 1926), i–ii; Zora Neale Hurston, *Mules and Men* (Philadelphia, 1935).

12. Zora Neale Hurston, Eau Gallie, Florida, to Franz Boas, New York, Apr. 21, 1929, Zora Neale Hurston Papers, American Philosophical Society Library, Philadelphia, Pa. I am grateful to Amy Horowitz for bringing this letter to my attention. A quilter on Johns Island, South Carolina, explained to the folklorist Mary Arnold Twining in the 1970s that the cross in her quilt pattern was not a Christian cross. Instead, "it represented danger, evil, and bad feelings." See Mary Arnold Twining, "An Examination of African Retentions in the Folk Culture of the South Carolina and Georgia Sea Islands" (Ph.D. diss., Indiana University, 1977), p. 188. The archaeologist Leland Ferguson noted the same African symbolism in crosses marked on Colono Ware in the South Carolina lowcountry, in "'The Cross Is a Magic Sign': Marks on Pottery from Colonial Carolina," paper presented at conference entitled Digging the Afro-American Past: Archaeology and the Black Experience, University of Mississippi, May 17–20, 1989.

13. With the publication of *The Mind of Primitive Man* (New York, 1911), Franz Boas set the tone for all subsequent serious work in anthropology. According to Boas, "The traits of the American Negroes are adequately explained on the basis of his [*sic*] history and social status. The tearing away from the African soil and the consequent complete loss of the old standards of life, which were replaced by the dependency of slavery and by all that it entailed, followed by a period of disorganization and by a severe economic struggle against heavy odds, are sufficient to explain the inferiority of the status of the race, without falling back upon the theory of hereditary inferiority." See also Boas, *Race and Nationality* (New York, 1915), 140. Another Boas student, Ruth Benedict, wrote of African Americans in her book *Race*: "Their patterns of political, economic, and artistic behav-

ior were forgotten—even the languages they had spoken in Africa." She account-
ed for this loss in the same way that E. Franklin Frazier and Guy B. Johnson had:
"Conditions of slavery in America were so drastic that this loss is not to be wondered at." Ruth Benedict, *Race: Science and Politics* (New York, 1940, 1959), 86–87.
See also Boas, *Race and Democratic Society* (New York, 1945).

14. Gunnar Myrdal, *An American Dilemma* (New York, 1944), 928–29.

15. Nathan Glazer and Daniel Patrick Moynihan, *Beyond the Melting Pot* (Cambridge, Mass.: 1963), 53.

16. Melville J. Herskovits, "The Negro in the New World: The Statement of a
Problem," *American Anthropologist* 32 (1930): 141–55. "That they have absorbed the
culture of America," Herskovits wrote in 1925, "is too obvious, almost, to be mentioned." Idem, "The Negro's Americanism," in *The New Negro*, ed. Alain Locke
(New York, 1925), 359–60. As late as 1937, when he published his *Life in a Haitian
Valley*, Herskovits still believed that "going native" (that is, being a participant
observer) was "neither possible nor of benefit among West African Negroes and
their New World descendants." His stated reason was that the failure of the field
researcher to observe the racial etiquette of segregation would embarrass informants and subject the fieldworker to community ridicule. Melville J. Herskovits,
Life in a Haitian Valley (New York, 1937), 326–27.

17. Melville J. Herskovits, *The Myth of the Negro Past* (1941; Boston, 1958), 8, 25,
37, 40, 41, 45, 88, 118, 120n, 126, 127, 304; Savannah Unit, Federal Writers Project,
Drums and Shadows: Survival Studies among the Georgia Coastal Negroes (Athens, Ga.,
1940; rpt. 1987). See Guy B. Johnson's review of Herskovits in *American Sociological Review* 7 (1942): 289. See also John F. Szwed, "An American Anthropological
Dilemma: The Politics of Afro-American Culture," in *Reinventing Anthropology*, ed.
Dell Hymes (New York, 1972), 153–81.

18. Joel Williamson, *The Crucible of Race: Black-White Relations in the American
South Since Emancipation* (New York, 1984); I. A. Newby, *Jim Crow's Defense: Anti-
Negro Thought in America, 1900–1930* (Baton Rouge, 1965).

19. Mechal Sobel, *The World They Made Together: Black and White Values in Eighteenth-Century Virginia* (Princeton, 1987), See esp. 5 (quote), 11, 137, 221, 233. In
many ways her interpretation is similar to that of James McBride Dabbs a generation ago. In *The Southern Heritage*, Dabbs wrote that "not only has the Negro
adopted our culture, he has helped to create it. Witness the Negro folk-tale, the
spirituals, the blues, jazz. It is too late to bother about what a so-called Negro
culture, under desegregation, may do to ours; it's been doing it, and happily, for
a long time. . . . Is there, possibly, a single Southern culture? . . . It is a Southern
culture, born of all our people—the immortal spirituals, the blues, the plaintive
mountain ballads, the hoedowns—binding us together." See his *The Southern Heritage* (New York, 1958), 72, 260–61, 263–64.

20. See Charles Joyner, *Down by the Riverside: A South Carolina Slave Community*
(Urbana, 1984); idem, *Remember Me: Slave Life in Coastal Georgia* (Atlanta, 1989);

Daniel C. Littlefield, *Rice and Slaves: Ethnicity and the Slave Trade in Colonial South Carolina* (Baton Rouge, 1981).

21. See Joyner, *Down by the Riverside*, esp. xx–xxii, 196–240; Ian Hancock, "Componentiality and the Origins of Gullah," in Peacock and Sabella, *Sea and Land*, 13–25; Charles Joyner, "Traditions and Transformations in the Coastal South," in Peacock and Sabella, *Sea and Land*, 159–64.

22. Patricia C. Nichols, "Creoles of the USA," in *Language in the USA*, ed. Charles A. Ferguson and Shirley Bryce Heath (New York, 1981), 77–81; Barry Jean Ancelet, *Cajun Music: Its Origins and Development* (Lafayette, La., 1989), 1; Barry Jean Ancelet and Elenore Morgan Jr., *The Makers of Cajun Music* (Austin, Tex., 1984); Cléoma Falcon, *Blues Nègres*, Decca 17004. The title is translated on the label as "Niggar Blues." The flip side is Joseph Falcon doing "Soucis Quand J'étais Gamin," or "Troubles When I Was a Boy." I am grateful to Richard B. Allen for bringing this record to my attention. *Louisiana Cajun Music* (Arhoolie 5005) and *Cléoma B. Falcon: A Cajun Music Classic* (Jadfel 101) are modern long-playing reissues of early recordings by Cléoma and Joseph Falcon. See also Nicholas R. Spitzer, "Zydeco and Mardi Gras: Creole Identity and Performance Genres in Rural French Louisiana" (Ph.D. diss., University of Texas, 1986).

23. Charles Joyner, "Creolization," *Encyclopedia of Southern Culture*, ed. Charles Reagan Wilson and William Ferris (Chapel Hill, 1989), 147–49.

24. See also Clifford Geertz, *The Interpretation of Cultures* (New York, 1973), 89–90, 119; Darryl Forde, ed., *African Worlds: Studies in the Cosmological Ideas and Social Values of African Peoples* (London, 1954); Meyer Fortes, *Oedipus and Job in West African Religion* (Cambridge, 1959); Geoffrey Parrinder, *African Traditional Religion* (London, 1962); William R. Bascom, *Ifa Divination: Communication between Gods and Men in West Africa* (Bloomington, Ind., 1969); E. E. Evans-Pritchard, *Nuer Religion* (Oxford, 1956), and *Witchcraft, Oracles, and Magic among the Azande* (Oxford, 1936); W. E. Abraham, *The Mind of Africa* (London, 1962), ch. 2; R. S. Rattray, *Religion and Art in Ashanti* (Oxford, 1926); John Mbiti, *African Religions and Philosophy* (Garden City, N.Y., 1969), ch. 3; Melville J. and Frances S. Herskovits, *An Outline of Dahomean Religious Belief* (New York, 1933); Martha Warren Beckwith, *Black Roadways: A Study of Jamaican Folk Life* (Chapel Hill, 1929), chs. 2, 6; Dominique Zahan, *The Religion, Spirituality, and Thought of Traditional Africa*, trans. Kate E. Martin and Lawrence M. Martin (Chicago, 1979); Mechal Sobel, *Trabelin' On: The Slave Journey to an Afro-Baptist Faith* (Westport, Conn., 1979). The importance of a continuing Yoruba and Ashanti influence and declining Bantu religious influence in Afro-American religion, despite Bantu demographic dominance in the New World, is discussed in Roger Bastide, *African Civilisations in the New World*, trans. Peter Green (New York, 1971), 104–15.

25. Frances Anne Kemble, *Journal of a Residence on a Georgian Plantation in 1838–1839* (New York, 1863; Brown Thrasher ed., Athens, Ga., 1984), 141–42, 259–60; Norman Yetman, *Life under the Peculiar Institution* (New York, 1970), 262.

26. Yetman, *Life under the Peculiar Institution*, 190; Benjamin A. Botkin, *Lay My Burden Down: A Folk History of Slavery* (Chicago, 1945; Brown Thrasher ed., Athens, Ga., 1989), 63; Savannah Unit, Federal Writers Project, *Drums and Shadows*, 141, 189,

27. Yetman, *Life under the Peculiar Institution*, 167; Botkin, *Lay My Burden Down*, 146.

28. *Been in the Storm So Long: Spirituals, Folk Tales, and Children's Games from John's Island, South Carolina*, Smithsonian Folkways CFS 40031; Benjamin A. Botkin, ed., *Negro Religious Songs and Services*, AAFS L10; Alan Lomax, ed., *Afro-American Spirituals, Work Songs, and Ballads*, AAFS L3; William F. Allen, Charles P. Ware, and Lucy M. Garrison, *Slave Songs of the United States* (Boston, 1867); Miles Mark Fisher, *Negro Slave Songs in the United States* (Ithaca, 1953); Howard Odum, *The Negro and His Songs* (Chapel Hill, 1925); Locke, *The New Negro*, 199–205.

29. Fredrika Bremer, *The Homes of the New World*, trans. Mary Howitt (New York, 1853; rpt. New York, 1868), vol. 1, 306–7; Jesse Lee, *A Short History of Methodists in the United States of America* (Baltimore, 1810), 42. Mechal Sobel believes that whites may have developed their own styles of singing spirituals "under the subconscious influence of blacks." See her *Trabelin' On*, 140. See also George Pullen Jackson, ed., *Sacred Harp Singing*, AAFS L11; Newman Ivey White, *American Negro Folk Songs* (Cambridge, Mass., 1928); Guy B. Johnson, *Folk Culture on St. Helena Island, South Carolina* (Chapel Hill, 1930); George Pullen Jackson, *White and Negro Spirituals* (New York, 1944).

30. James Weldon Johnson, Notes on spirituals, James Weldon Johnson Papers, Beineke Library, Yale University; W. E. Burghardt Du Bois, "Of the Sorrow Songs," in his *The Souls of Black Folk* (New York, 1903; rpt. 1965), 377–88.

31. Caroline B. Poole Diary, entry for Mar. 16, 1837, in "A Yankee School Teacher in Louisiana, 1835–1837: The Diary of Caroline B. Poole," ed. James A. Padgett, *Louisiana Historical Quarterly* 20 (1937): 677; *Drums and Shadows*, 62; Frederick Law Olmsted, *A Journey in the Seaboard Slave States in the Years 1853–1854* (New York, 1856), vol. 1, 26–29. In New Orleans, the spirituals were easily absorbed into the new jazz music at the end of the century, and the musical tradition of slave funerals became embodied in the New Orleans tradition of funerals with marching bands. George Lewis, interviewed by Richard B. Allen, New Orleans, Nov. 14, 1958, reel 4, Hogan Jazz Archive, Tulane University. Papa Jack Laine, interviewed by Richard B. Allen, New Orleans, Mar. 26, 1957, reel 2, Apr. 25, 1964, reel 2, Hogan Jazz Archive, Tulane University; D. James LaRocca Collection, file 2, Hogan Jazz Archive, Tulane University.

32. Johnson, Notes on spirituals; Dorothy Scarborough, "The 'Blues' as Folksongs," *Publications of the Texas Folklore Society* 2 (1917): 52–66; Benjamin A. Botkin, ed., *Negro Work Songs and Calls*, AAFS L8; Lomax, ed., *Afro-American Spirituals, Work Songs, and Ballads;* Marshall Stearns, ed., *Negro Blues and Hollers*, AAFS L59; Alan Lomax, ed., *Afro-American Blues and Game Songs*, AAFS L4.

33. Robert C. Toll, *Blacking Up: The Minstrel Show in Nineteenth-Century America* (New York, 1974); Hans Nathan, *Dan Emmett and the Rise of Early Negro Minstrelsy* (Norman, Okla., 1962); Marshall Stearns, *The Story of Jazz* (New York, 1956), 82–91; Bill C. Malone, *Country Music, U.S.A.: A Fifty-Year History* (Austin, Tex., 1968). Out of the integration of cultural traditions emerged such songs as "Raise a Ruckus," an antebellum black hoedown with a veneer of minstrel-show influence. The ambiguity of the title epitomized the dual purpose of the song. It was both a carefree blackface minstrel song that delighted unsuspecting white slaveholders and a song of protest that alerted black slaves to the possibility of doing something about their condition. See Howard Odum and Guy B. Johnson, *Negro Workaday Songs* (Chapel Hill, 1926), 73–74.

34. Richard B. Allen to Charles Joyner, Mar. 13, 1970; Louis James, interviewed by Richard B. Allen, New Orleans, Apr. 19, 1965, Hogan Jazz Archive, Tulane University; Reg Hall, liner notes to *Louis James String Band*, Mono Records, MNLP II (1965). There were mixed jazz bands in New Orleans as well. Papa Jack Laine insisted to Richard Allen that his bands were always white. "Gil Rouge was no white man," Laine's wife Blanche interjected. "Baptiste Aucoin neither." Allen asked Laine about Aucoin. Laine explained that he stopped hiring Aucoin when he discovered his race. "I never knew he was colored, but he married a white woman," Laine said. "One fine day I passed on Ursuline Street, where he lived, and I saw his Daddy and that was enough." Papa Jack Laine, interviewed by Richard B. Allen, New Orleans, Apr. 24, 1964, reel 1, Apr. 25, 1964, reel 2, Hogan Jazz Archive, Tulane University.

35. Steve Brown, interviewed by Richard B. Allen, New Orleans, Apr. 22, 1958, reel 4, Hogan Jazz Archive, Tulane University.

36. Bill C. Malone, "Blacks and Whites and the Music of the Old South," in *Black and White: Cultural Interaction in the Antebellum South*, ed. Ted Ownby (Jackson, Miss., 1993), 169.

Chapter 3: "In His Hands"

1. Jacob Stroyer, *My Life in the South*, new and enlarged [3d] ed. (Salem, Mass., 1885), 9–27, in *A Documentary History of Slavery in North America*, ed. Willie Lee Rose (New York, 1976), 401–5.

2. Cato to Charles Colcock Jones, Sept. 3, 1852, in *Blacks in Bondage: Letters of American Slaves*, 2d ed., ed. Robert S. Starobin (New York, 1988), 49.

3. George P. Rawick, Jan Hillegas, and Ken Lawrence, eds., *The American Slave: A Composite Autobiography, Supplement, Series 1*, 12 vols. (Westport, Conn., 1978), vol. 6, pt. 1, 243.

4. Lydia Parrish, *Slave Songs of the Georgia Sea Islands*, (New York, 1942), 245–47.

5. Charles L. Perdue Jr., Thomas E. Barden, and Robert K. Phillips, *Weevils in*

the Wheat: Interviews with Virginia Ex-Slaves (Charlottesville, 1976; rpt., Bloomington, Ind., 1980), 306.

6. Ibid., 281.

7. Ibid., 322.

8. Ibid., 148 (Hunt), 224 (Perry).

9. Evangeline W. Andrews, ed., *Journal of a Lady of Quality: Being the Narrative
of a Journey from Scotland to the West Indies, North Carolina, and Portugal in the Years
1774 to 1776* (New Haven, 1922), 194.

10. Parrish, *Slave Songs*, 225.

11. Ibid., 236.

12. Solomon Northup, *Twelve Years a Slave*, ed. Sue Eakin and Joseph Logsden
(Baton Rouge, 1968), 159–61.

13. J. Carlyle Sitterson, *Sugar Country: The Cane Sugar Industry in the South, 1753–
1950* (Lexington, Ky., 1953), 112–56.

14. Quoted in Rose, *A Documentary History of Slavery*, 400.

15. Frances Anne Kemble, *Journal of a Residence on a Georgian Plantation in 1838–
1839* (New York, 1863; rpt., Athens, Ga., 1984), 99–100.

16. George P. Rawick, ed., *The American Slave: A Composite Autobiography*, 19 vols.
(Westport, Conn., 1972), vol. 7, 301.

17. Ibid., vol. 11, pt. 7, 22 (Walker); ibid., vol. 6, 45 (Bradfield); Rawick, Hillegas, and Lawrence, *American Slave, Supplement, Series 1*, vol. 9, pt. 4, 456 (Matthews).

18. Rawick, *American Slave*, vol. 6, 189.

19. Rawick, Hillegas, and Lawrence, *American Slave, Supplement, Series 1*, vol. 9,
pt. 4, 1465.

20. Rawick, *American Slave*, vol. 7, 89.

21. Ibid.

22. Kemble, *Journal of a Residence*, 256, 363–64.

23. Rawick, *American Slave*, vol. 6, 7 (Abercrombie), 105 (Davis), 321 (Poole),
325 (Rice).

24. Ibid., vol. 7, 69 (Hodges); ibid., vol. 2, pt. 1, 346 (Durant); ibid., vol. 6, 59
(Colbert).

25. Ibid., vol. 11, pt. 7, 22 (Walker); ibid., vol. 6, 36 (Bishop); ibid., vol. 11, 215
(Jones).

26. Rawick, Hillegas, and Lawrence, *American Slave, Supplement, Series 1*, vol. 9,
pt. 4, 1555.

27. Ibid., vol. 7, pt. 2, 601.

28. Ibid., vol. 12, 5.

29. Rawick, *American Slave*, vol. 14, pt. 1, 95–96, 123–24.

30. Ibid., vol. 7, 295.

31. Ibid., vol. 4, pt. 1, 158, 189.

32. Ibid., vol. 6, 104 (Pugh), 120 (Eppes), 430 (Witherspoon).

33. Ibid., vol. 11, pt. 7, 9.

34. Ibid., vol. 2, pt. 1, 28; ibid., vol. 14, pt. 1, 74 (Barbour).

35. Ibid., vol. 11, pt. 7, 29.

36. Ibid., vol. 14, pt. 1, 47 (Arrington), 71 (Baker).

37. Ibid., vol. 6, 191; Norman R. Yetman, *Life under the Peculiar Institution: Selections from the Slave Narrative Collection* (New York, 1970), 299.

38. Perdue, Barden, and Phillips, *Weevils in the Wheat*, 84; Stanley Feldstein, *Once a Slave: The Slaves' View of Slavery* (New York, 1971), 222–23 (Bruce quotation); Catherine Clinton, *The Plantation Mistress: Women's World in the Old South* (New York, 1982), 208–11 (Simms quotation).

39. Robert Manson Myers, ed., *Children of Pride: A True Story of Georgia and the Civil War* (New Haven, 1972), 740–41.

40. Kemble, *Journal of a Residence*, 207; William Kaufman Scarborough, *The Overseer: Plantation Management in the Old South* (Baton Rouge, 1966), 164–66.

41. C. Vann Woodward, ed., *Mary Chesnut's Civil War* (New Haven, 1981), 169.

42. Ibid., 29.

43. Eugene D. Genovese, *Roll, Jordan, Roll: The World the Slaves Made* (New York, 1974), 417–18; Clinton, *Plantation Mistress*, 211–12.

44. Drew Gilpin Faust, *James Henry Hammond and the Old South: A Design for Mastery* (Baton Rouge, 1982), 86–88.

45. George P. Rawick, ed., *The American Slave, Supplement, Series 2*, 10 vols. (Westport, Conn., 1979), vol. 8, pt. 7, 3292–94.

46. Rawick, *American Slave*, vol. 7, 347.

47. Perdue, Barden, and Phillips, *Weevils in the Wheat*, 91.

48. Social Science Institute, Fisk University, *The Unwritten History of Slavery: Autobiographical Accounts of Negro Ex-Slaves* (Nashville, 1945), in Rawick, *American Slave*, vol. 18, 2.

49. Northup, *Twelve Years a Slave*, 41.

50. William Craft, *Running a Thousand Miles for Freedom; or, the Escape of William and Ellen Craft from Slavery* (London, 1860), 16–17, in *Great Slave Narratives*, comp. Arna Bontemps (Boston, 1969), 279.

51. Orville Vernon Burton, *In My Father's House Are Many Mansions: Family and Community in Edgefield, South Carolina* (Chapel Hill, 1985), 185–86.

52. Perdue, Barden, and Phillips, *Weevils in the Wheat*, 84.

53. Fisk University, *Unwritten History of Slavery*, in Rawick, *American Slave*, vol. 18, 2.

54. Frederick Douglass, *Narrative of the Life of Frederick Douglass, an American Slave. Written by Himself* (Boston, 1845), 3–4.

55. Rawick, *American Slave, Supplement, Series 2*, vol. 4, pt. 3, 127.

56. Yetman, *Life under the Peculiar Institution*, 127.

57. Rawick, *American Slave*, vol. 16, 34 (James); ibid., vol. 15, pt. 2, 396–97 (Wil-

liams). For a variant of the Williams quotation, see Yetman, *Life under the Peculiar Institution*, 317.

58. Feldstein, *Once a Slave*, 222–23. Except for the gender of the protagonist, this incident is remarkably similar to the plot of Robert Penn Warren's novel *Band of Angels*, written a half-century later.

59. Charles Colcock Jones, *Suggestions on the Religious Instruction of the Negroes in the Southern States* (1838; rpt., Philadelphia, 1947), quoted in Starobin, *Blacks in Bondage*, 42.

60. Fredrika Bremer, *The Homes of the New World*, trans. Mary Howitt (New York, 1853; rpt., New York, 1868), vol. 2, 491.

61. Quoted in Starobin, *Blacks in Bondage*, 43, 52.

62. Sarah Hodgson Torian, ed., "Antebellum and War Memories of Mrs. Telfair Hodgson," *Georgia Historical Quarterly* 27 (1943): 351; Rawick, *American Slave*, vol. 7, 189 (Logan); ibid., vol. 6, 20, 77 (Clayton); ibid., 155, 237 (Jones).

63. Rawick, *American Slave*, vol. 11, pt. 7, 246; ibid., vol. 14, pt. 1, 193 (Crasson).

64. Rawick, Hillegas, and Lawrence, *American Slave, Supplement, Series 1*, vol. 8, pt. 3, 1146.

65. Ibid., vol. 7, pt. 2, 716.

66. [Zephaniah Kingsley,] *Treatise on the Patriarchal or Cooperative System of Society as It Exists . . . Under the Name of Slavery* (N.p., 1804), 26; Rawick, *American Slave*, vol. 6, 53; ibid., vol. 6, 398 (Van Dyke).

67. Ibid., vol. 14, pt. 1, 143.

68. John G. Williams, *De Ole Plantation* (Charleston, 1895), 40.

69. Rawick, Hillegas, and Lawrence, *American Slave, Supplement, Series 1*, vol. 8, pt. 3, 899.

70. Booker T. Washington, "Christmas Days in Old Virginia," in *The Booker T. Washington Papers*, ed. Louis R. Harlan (Urbana, 1972), vol. 1, 395; Bremer, *Homes of the New World*, vol. 1, 393–94; Woodward, *Mary Chesnut's Civil War*, 214; James Waddell Alexander, "Thoughts on Family Worship," in Jones, *Suggestions on the Religious Instruction of the Negroes*, 56; Booker T. Washington, *Up from Slavery* (1901; New York, 1986), 19–20.

71. Rawick, *American Slave*, Ind., vol. 6, 159 (Richardson), 161; ibid., vol. 14, pt. 1, 143.

72. Yetman, *Life under the Peculiar Institution*, 57.

73. Rawick, Hillegas, and Lawrence, *American Slave, Supplement, Series 1*, vol. 6, pt. 1, 316.

74. Rawick, *American Slave*, vol. 3, pt. 4, 111.

75. Yetman, *Life under the Peculiar Institution*, 63.

76. Ibid., 63, 115–16, 201, 251, 258.

77. Jones, *Suggestions on the Religious Instruction of the Negroes*, 59.

78. Feldstein, *Once a Slave*, 85–86.

79. Peter Randolph, *Sketches of Slave Life: or, Illustrations of the "Peculiar Institution" by Peter Randolph, an Emancipated Slave*, 2d ed. (Boston, 1855), 49.

80. Arthur Singleton [Henry Coggswell Knight], *Letters from the South and West* (Boston, 1824), 352; Savannah Unit, Georgia Writers Project, *Drums and Shadows: Survival Studies Among the Georgia Coastal Negroes* (Athens, Ga., 1940; rpt., 1987), 62.

81. Kemble, *Journal of a Residence*, 146–47.

82. Torian, "Ante Bellum and War Memories," 352.

83. Georgia Bryan Conrad, "Reminiscences of a Southern Woman," *Southern Workman* 30 (1901): 13. The name is transcribed Bi-la-li, Bu Allah, or Ben Ali in various sources.

84. Savannah Unit, Georgia Writers Project, *Drums and Shadows*, 161, 166.

85. Rawick, *American Slave*, vol. 2, pt 2, 304 (Horry); ibid., vol. 4, pt. 1, 149 (Brooks).

86. Yetman, *Life under the Peculiar Institution*, 63; Rawick, *American Slave*, vol. 14, pt. 1, 157 (Burnett); Perdue, Barden, and Phillips, *Weevils in the Wheat*, 97.

87. Benjamin A. Botkin, ed., *Lay My Burden Down: A Folk History of Slavery* (Chicago, 1945; rpt., Athens, Ga., 1989), 238.

88. Yetman, *Life under the Peculiar Institution*, 281.

89. Rawick, *American Slave*, vol. 6, 111–12; Douglass, *Narrative of the Life*, 106–108.

90. Rawick, *American Slave*, vol. 3, pt. 4, 249. For an extraordinary study of the significance of the cornshucking ceremony see Roger D. Abrahams, *Singing the Master: The Emergence of African American Culture in the Plantation South* (New York, 1992).

91. Yetman, *Life under the Peculiar Institution*, 262.

92. Kemble, *Journal of a Residence*, 141–42, 259–60.

93. Rawick, Hillegas, and Lawrence, *American Slave, Supplement, Series 1*, vol. 6, pt. 1, 244.

94. Ibid., vol. 9, pt. 4, 1554.

95. Yetman, *Life under the Peculiar Institution*, 190; Botkin, *Lay My Burden Down*, 63; Savannah Unit, Georgia Writers Project, *Drums and Shadows*, 141, 189.

96. Edmund Kirke [James Roberts Gilmore], *Among the Pines: Or, The South in Secession Time* (New York, 1862), 145–48.

97. Yetman, *Life under the Peculiar Institution*, 56; Perdue, Barden, and Phillips, *Weevils in the Wheat*, 53, 186, 108; Charles Joyner, *Down by the Riverside: A South Carolina Slave Community* (Urbana, 1984), 221–22.

98. For a discussion of the slaves' use of proverbs, see Joyner, *Down by the Riverside*, 209–14.

99. Botkin, *Lay My Burden Down*, 18.

100. Ibid., 13–14.

101. Ibid., 10.

102. Savannah Unit, Georgia Writers Project, *Drums and Shadows*, 111. The plot is exactly like the Ashanti folk tale of the spider and the porcupine, in Robert Southerland Rattray, *Akan-Ashanti Folk-Tales* (Oxford, 1930), 43.

103. Botkin, *Lay My Burden Down*, 3.

104. Rawick, *American Slave*, vol. 2, pt. 1, 26 (Ballard); ibid., vol. 3, pt. 4, 51.

105. Ibid., vol. 7, 188.

106. Kemble, *Journal of a Residence*, 99–100.

107. Rawick, Hillegas, and Lawrence, *American Slave, Supplement, Series 1*, vol. 9, pt. 4, 51.

108. Rawick, *American Slave*, vol. 14, pt. 1, 424.

109. Ibid., vol. 6, 190; Rawick, Hillegas, and Lawrence, *American Slave, Supplement, Series 1*, vol. 9, pt. 4, 1455.

110. Botkin, *Lay My Burden Down*, 66.

111. See, for example, Stacy Gibbons Moore, "'Established and Well Cultivated': Afro-American Foodways in Early Virginia," *Virginia Cavalcade* 39 (1989): 70–83.

112. Rawick, Hillegas, and Phillips, *American Slave, Supplement, Series 1*, vol. 10, pt. 5, 220; Botkin, *Lay My Burden Down*, 89; Rawick, *American Slave*, vol. 7, 76, 233; Yetman, *Life under the Peculiar Institution*, 336.

113. Yetman, *Life under the Peculiar Institution*, 52, 144, 151, 205, 282, 291; Rawick, *American Slave*, vol. 7, 145, 172, 207; Botkin, *Lay My Burden Down*, 89, 307.

114. Botkin, *Lay My Burden Down*, 63; Yetman, *Life under the Peculiar Institution*, 170.

115. Rawick, *American Slave*, vol. 6, 311 (Patton); ibid., vol. 15, pt. 2, 320 (Stewart); ibid., vol. 2, pt. 1, 125 (Brown), pt. 2, 197 (Green).

116. Ibid., vol. 6, 131; Rawick, Hillegas, and Lawrence, *American Slave, Supplement, Series 1*, vol. 9, pt. 4, 1792–93 (Ramsey).

117. Rawick, *American Slave*, vol. 7, 271.

118. Ibid., vol. 14, pt. 1, 95.

119. Work Projects Administration Mss., South Caroliniana Library, University of South Carolina, Columbia; Rawick, Hillegas, and Lawrence, *American Slave, Supplement, Series 1*, vol. 11, 194 (Horry).

120. Perdue, Barden, and Phillips, *Weevils in the Wheat*, 181.

121. Rawick, Hillegas, and Lawrence, *American Slave, Supplement, Series 1*, vol. 6, pt. 1, 314 (Butler); ibid., vol. 10, pt. 5, 2199; Rawick, *American Slave*, vol. 15, pt. 2, 318 (Stewart).

122. Rawick, *American Slave*, vol. 2, pt. 1, 11 (Adams), 15 (Adamson).

123. Rawick, Hillegas, and Lawrence, *American Slave, Supplement, Series 1*, vol. 9, pt. 4, 1550 (Montgomery); Rawick, *American Slave*, vol. 3, pt. 3, 260 (Horry).

124. Rawick, *American Slave*, vol. 2, pt. 2, 317.

125. Kemble, *Journal of a Residence*, 215 (first quotation), 161 (second quotation).

126. Rawick, *American Slave*, vol. 6, 60 (Cheatam), 120 (Mistress), 311 (Patton); ibid., vol. 7, 228 (Montgomery).

127. Charles Ball, *Slavery in the United States: A Narrative of the Life and Adventures of Charles Ball, A Black Man* (1837; rpt., New York, 1937), 348–51.

128. Rawick, *American Slave*, vol. 7, 301, 347 (Wilson); ibid., vol. 6, 62 (Cooper); Yetman, *Life under the Peculiar Institution*, 40 (Branch).

129. Rawick, *American Slave*, vol. 7, 135 (Henry), 166 (King).

130. Yetman, *Life under the Peculiar Institution*, 40 (Branch); Rawick, *American Slave*, vol. 6, 130 (Garlic).

131. Langdon Cheves to Langdon Cheves Jr., May 2, 1864, Cheves Family Papers, South Carolina Historical Society, Charleston; Elizabeth Collins, *Memories of the Southern States* (Taunton, Eng., 1865), 71.

132. Rawick, Hillegas, and Lawrence, *American Slave, Supplement, Series 1*, vol. 9, pt. 4, 1500–1502; ibid., vol. 8, pt. 3, 1132.

133. Philip J. Schwarz, *Twice Condemned: Slaves and the Criminal Laws of Virginia, 1705–1865* (Baton Rouge, 1988).

134. Rawick, *American Slave*, vol. 7, 239 (Petite); ibid., vol. 3, pt. 4, 52–53 (Russell); ibid., vol. 4, pt. 1, 203.

135. Ibid., vol. 12, pt. 2, 59.

136. Botkin, *Lay My Burden Down*, 3; Olmsted, *Journey in the Seaboard Slave States*, I, 116–17.

137. Rawick, Hillegas, and Lawrence, *American Slave, Supplement, Series 1*, vol. 6, pt. 1, 47.

138. Douglass, *Narrative of the Life*, 40; Rawick, *American Slave*, vol. 6, 191.

139. Rawick, Hillegas, and Lawrence, *American Slave, Supplement, Series 1*, vol. 6, pt. 1, 47.

140. See Betty Mitchell, *Edmund Ruffin: A Biography* (Bloomington, Ind., 1981), 30.

141. Rawick, *American Slave, Supplement, Series 2*, vol. 7, pt. 6, 2578; (Marshall); Rawick, Hillegas, and Lawrence, *American Slave, Supplement, Series 1*, vol. 12, 6 (Mose).

142. Rawick, *American Slave*, vol. 6, 171 (Rudd); vol. 8, pt. 2, 42; Yetman, *Life under the Peculiar Institution*, 19.

143. Rawick, *American Slave*, vol. 6, 60.

144. Ibid., vol. 7, 17.

145. Ibid., vol. 3, pt. 3, 130; ibid., vol. 6, 350.

146. Ibid., vol. 3, pt. 4, 113.

147. Jack P. Greene, ed., *The Diary of Colonel Landon Carter of Sabine Hall, 1752–1778* (Charlottesville, 1965; rpt. Richmond, 1987), vol. 1, 286–92. For a brilliant analysis of this series of events, see Rhys Isaac, *The Transformation of Virginia, 1740–1790* (Chapel Hill, 1982), 328–44.

148. Rawick, *American Slave*, vol. 2, pt. 1, 27.

149. Charles T. Haskell to Langdon Cheves, S.C., June 16, 1862, Cheves Family Papers.

150. Harriet Jacobs, *Incidents in the Life of a Slave Girl*, ed. Jean Fagan Yellin (Cambridge, Mass., 1987).

151. Rawick, *American Slave*, vol. 6, 46.

152. Adele Petigru Allston to Col. Francis W. Heriot, May 31, 1864, in *The South Carolina Rice Plantation as Revealed in the Papers of Robert F. W. Allston*, ed. J. Harold Easterby (Chicago, 1945), 199.

153. Rawick, Hillegas, and Lawrence, *American Slave, Supplement, Series 1*, vol. 9, pt. 4, 1500–1501.

154. Rawick, *American Slave*, vol. 6, 418.

155. Petition of John Rose, Richland District, 1831, Slavery Files, South Carolina Archives, Columbia.

156. Rawick, *American Slave*, vol. 15, pt. 2, 132.

157. Thomas G. Allen to General Walker, Feb. 3, 1863, in Francis W. Pickens and Milledge L. Bonham Papers, Library of Congress.

158. For an overview of slave insurrections see Herbert Aptheker, *American Negro Slave Revolts*, 5th ed. (New York, 1983); Eugene D. Genovese, *From Rebellion to Revolution: Afro-American Slave Revolts in the Making of the Modern World* (Baton Rouge, 1979). In what has been called "one of the most remarkable feats of detective work achieved by a modern historian," Winthrop D. Jordan probes the 1861 Mississippi conspiracy in his *Tumult and Silence at Second Creek: An Inquiry into a Civil War Slave Conspiracy*, rev. ed. (Baton Rouge, 1995).

159. Henry Clay Bruce, *The New Man: Twenty-Nine Years a Slave, Twenty-Nine Years a Free Man, Recollections of H. C. Bruce* (York, Pa., 1895), 25–26.

160. Perdue, Barden, and Phillips, *Weevils in the Wheat*, 75–76.

161. Ibid., 35.

162. Jacobs, *Incidents in the Life of a Slave Girl*, 63.

163. Ibid., 64.

164. Perdue, Barden, and Phillips, *Weevils in the Wheat*, 75–76.

165. Henry Box Brown, *Narrative of the Life of Henry Box Brown, Written by Himself* (Boston, 1852) 19; Jacobs, *Incidents in the Life of a Slave Girl*, 66.

166. Perdue, Barden, and Phillips, *Weevils in the Wheat*, 76.

167. Rawick, Hillegas, and Lawrence, *American Slave, Supplement, Series 1*, vol. 7, pt. 2, 507.

168. Rawick, *American Slave*, vol. 7, 271 (Robinson); vol. 7, 103 (McAllum).

169. Ibid., vol. 6, 82.

170. Ibid., vol. 15, pt. 2, 346.

171. Ibid., vol. 11, pt. 7, 174.

172. Ibid., vol. 14, pt. 1, 157.

173. Yetman, *Life under the Peculiar Institution*, 149.

174. Rawick, Hillegas, and Lawrence, *American Slave Supplement, Series 1*, vol. 9, pt. 4, 1556.

175. Rawick, *American Slave*, vol. 6, 82.

176. Rawick, Hillegas, and Lawrence, *American Slave Supplement, Series 1*, vol. 8, pt. 3, 1254.

177. Ibid., vol. 6, pt. 1, 250–51.

178. Ibid., vol. 7, pt. 2, 604.

179. Rawick, *American Slave*, vol. 7, 231.

180. Rawick, Hillegas, and Lawrence, *American Slave, Supplement, Series 1*, vol. 8, pt. 3, 902.

181. Ibid., vol. 6, pt. 1, 324.

182. Rawick, *American Slave*, vol. 4, pt. 1, 280. For a variant transcription, see Yetman, *Life under the Peculiar Institution*, 70.

183. Ibid., vol. 6, 159.

Chapter 4: History as Ritual

1. Orlando Patterson, *Slavery and Social Death: A Comparative Study* (Cambridge, Mass., 1982), 37.

2. On the relationship between symbolic behavior and authority, see Raymond Firth, *Symbols: Public and Private* (Ithaca, 1973), 368–87; and Meyer Fortes, "Ritual and Office in Tribal Society," in *Essays on the Ritual of Social Relations*, ed. Max Gluckman (Manchester, 1962), 86.

3. Jack Goody, "Religion and Ritual: The Definitional Problem," *British Journal of Sociology* 12 (1961): 159.

4. Edmund Leach, *Rethinking Anthropology*, London School of Economics Monographs on Social Anthropology, no. 22 (London, 1961), 6.

5. Victor Turner, *The Ritual Process: Structure and Anti-Structure* (Ithaca, 1977), 66; idem, *The Forest of Symbols: Aspects of Ndembu Ritual* (Ithaca, 1967), 30–32.

6. For a historical ethnography of slavery in All Saints Parish, see Charles Joyner, *Down by the Riverside: A South Carolina Slave Community* (Urbana, 1984).

7. Plowden C. J. Weston, "Rules and Management for the Plantation, 1859," printed in Elizabeth Collins, *Memories of the Southern States* (Taunton, Eng., 1865), 105–7; Elizabeth Allston Pringle, *Chronicles of Chicora Wood* (New York, 1922), 152–54; *Rice Planter and Sportsman: The Recollections of J. Motte Alston*, ed. Arney R. Childs (Columbia, S.C., 1953), 10, 14; James R. Sparkman to Benjamin Allston, Mar. 10, 1858, in Robert F. W. Allston Papers, South Carolina Historical Society, Charleston; Adele Petigru Allston memorandum, Nov. 15, 1951, ibid.; Ben Horry, in Slave Narratives: A Folk History of Slavery from Interviews with Former Slaves (hereafter Slave Narratives), typewritten records prepared by the Federal Writers' Project, 1936–1938, Work Projects Administration, 14, part 2, 309–10; microfilm of original in Library of Congress.

8. Benjamin Allston to Robert F. W. Allston, Mar. 24, 1861, in Robert F. W. Allston Papers, South Carolina Historical Society; Fortes, "Ritual and Office in Tribal Society," 86.

9. For descriptions of slave weddings in All Saints Parish, see Louisa Brown, in Slave Narratives, 14, part 1, 115; William Wyndham Malet, *An Errand to the South in the Summer of 1862* (London, 1863), 68; Julia Peterkin, *Roll, Jordan, Roll* (New York, 1933), 10.

10. Hagar Brown, in Slave Narratives, 14, part 1, 113–14; Emily Weston Diary, Jan. 22, 1859, in private possession; personal interview with John Beese (son of an All Saints Parish slave), Pawleys Island, S.C., Jan. 22, 1972; personal interview with Mary Small (daughter of an All Saints Parish slave), Free Woods, S.C., Aug. 2, 1975.

11. John Hunter to Benjamin Allston, Mar. 6, 1858, in Benjamin Allston Papers, Duke University Library; James R. Sparkman to Benjamin Allston, Mar. 10, 1858, in Robert F. W. Allston Papers, South Carolina Historical Society; James R. Sparkman, "The Negro," in Sparkman Family Papers, Southern Historical Collection, University of North Carolina; Mariah Heywood, Slave Narratives, 14, part 2, 284.

12. Hagar Brown, in WPA Mss., South Caroliniana Library, University of South Carolina; Louisa Brown, in Slave Narratives, 14, part 1, 115; Ben Horry, in Slave Narratives, 14, part 2, 309–11; Adele Petigru Allston to Benjamin Allston, Jan. 1, 18, 1857, in Robert F. W. Allston Papers, South Carolina Historical Society; Andrew Hasell to Daniel W. Jordan, July 16, 1860, and Jordan's reply, July 19, 1860, Daniel W. Jordan Papers, Duke University Library. For more on slave uses of alcoholic beverages in All Saints Parish, see Weston, "Rules and Management for the Plantation," 144. For analyses of positive and negative functions of alcohol in social interaction, see Louis J. Chiaramonte, "Mumming in 'Deep Harbour': Aspects of Social Organization in Mumming and Drinking," esp. 84–88, and John F. Szwed, "The Mask of Friendship: Mumming as a Ritual of Social Relations," esp. 109–16, both in *Christmas Mumming in Newfoundland: Essays In Anthropology, Folklore and History*, ed. Herbert Halpert and G. M. Story (Toronto, 1969).

13. Margaret Bryant, in Slave Narratives, 14, part 1, 147; Albert Carolina, in Slave Narratives, 14, part 1, 113; Gabe Lance, in Slave Narratives, 14, part 3, 92; Ben Horry, in Slave Narratives, 14, part 2, 303, 305, 311; Hagar Brown, WPA Mss., South Caroliniana Library; Mariah Heywood, in Slave Narratives, 14, part 2, 286–97; Malet, *Errand to the South*, 68–69.

14. W. L. Westermann, "Slave Maintenance and Slave Revolts," *Classical Philology* 40 (1945): 8; Mary Douglas, *Purity and Danger: An Analysis of Concepts of Pollution* (London, 1966), 62–63. On "off time" in All Saints Parish, see Albert Carolina, in Slave Narratives, 14, part 1, 198; Mariah Heywood, in Slave Narratives, 14, part 2, 284; Ben Horry, in Slave Narratives, 14, part 2, 304, 309.

15. W. E. B. Du Bois, *The Souls of Black Folk* (Chicago, 1903), 378. On the symbolic dimension, see Kenneth Burke, *Language as Symbolic Action: Essays in Life,*

Literature, and Method (Berkeley, 1971), 391; Peter Berger and Thomas Luckmann, *The Social Construction of Reality: A Treatise in the Sociology of Knowledge* (New York, 1966), 47–49, 104; Joseph Church, *Language and the Discovery of Reality* (New York, 1961), 95. This interpretation is based upon the analysis of twenty-two animal trickster tales collected in All Saints Parish by Genevieve Willcox Chandler and published as part of *South Carolina Folk Tales*, compiled by Workers of the Writers Program of the Work Projects Administration in the State of South Carolina (Columbia, S.C., 1941); on Chandler's extensive collection of trickster tales in WPA Mss. in the South Caroliniana Library; and on my own field recordings of human trickster tales from children and grandchildren of slaves in All Saints Parish. Tale types in the All Saints repertory include 2, 15, 72, 175, 1074, 1525, and 1612. Motifs include A2325.1, A2232.4.1, A2494.4.4, H1376.5, J2413.42, K11.1, K72, K401.1, K471, K585, K607.3.2, K611, K1021, K1055, K1840, K1860, K1951, K1956, and K1961.

16. Erving Goffman, "The Neglected Situation," *American Anthropologist* 66 (1964): 133–36; Douglas, *Purity and Danger*, 62–63: Sabe Rutledge, in WPA Mss., South Caroliniana Library.

17. Turner, *Forest of Symbols*, 30; Roger D. Abrahams, "Trickster, the Outrageous Hero," in *Our Living Traditions*, ed. Tristram P. Coffin (New York, 1968), 170.

18. For a discussion of "symboling," see Leslie White, *The Science of Culture* (New York, 1949), 22–39. On trickster tales in Africa and America, see Ruth Finnegan, *Oral Literature in Africa* (Oxford, 1970), 341–51; Lawrence W. Levine, *Black Culture and Black Consciousness: Afro-American Folk Thought from Slavery to Freedom* (New York, 1977), 102–21; Janheinz Jahn, *Muntu: An Outline of the New African Culture* (New York, 1961), 221; E. E. Evans-Pritchard, *The Zande Trickster* (Oxford, 1967), 28–30; Mary Douglas, *Natural Symbols: Explorations in Cosmology* (New York, 1973).

19. WPA Mss., South Caroliniana Library.

20. *South Carolina Folk Tales*, 29–31, Tale Type 175, Motif K471. Alan Dundes makes a persuasive case for an African source for African-American versions of this tale in his "African and Afro-American Tales," in *African Folklore in the New World*, ed. Daniel J. Crowley (Austin, 1977), 43.

21. John tales from All Saints Parish are found in the WPA Mss., South Caroliniana Library. For an analysis of perspective by incongruity, see Kenneth Burke, *Permanence and Change* (Indianapolis, 1965), 69–70.

22. Hagar Brown, in Slave Narratives, 14, part 1, 110; Zackie Knox, in WPA Mss., South Caroliniana Library.

23. Eric Hobsbawm, *Primitive Rebels: Studies in Archaic Forms of Social Movement in the Nineteenth and Twentieth Centuries* (Manchester, 1959), 24–25.

24. The masters' stereotype of the slaves held that they were "docile, gentle under good treatment, capable of strong but superficial affection, incapable of deep thought, improvident and hating labor; vain, frivolous, apish and imitative;

slow to learn where thought is necessary; bestial in their desires; but cheerful and happy with light work and sufficient food to meet their slightest wants" (*Charleston Daily Courier*, June 27, 1855). Edward Thomas Heriot, who planted Mt. Arena Plantation on Sandy Island, epitomized the stereotype in a letter to his Scottish cousin: "I manage them as my children" (Heriot to Anna Bruce Cunningham, Apr. 20, 1853, in Edward Thomas Heriot Papers, Duke University Library). The stereotype was shared by such northern travelers in All Saints Parish as James Roberts Gilmore, who considered the blacks' reputed inferiority to be a *result* of slavery: "Slavery cramps the intellect and dwarfs the nature of a man, and where the dwarfing process has gone on, in father and son, for two centuries, it must surely be the case that the later generations are below the first." See his *Among the Pines*, 27. That the slaves did not accept the masters' stereotype is evident in the rapidity with which they attacked the most visible symbols of the slave regime after emancipation. See, for example, Elizabeth Weston to Adele Petigru Allston, May 17, 1865, in Robert F. W. Allston Papers, South Carolina Historical Society; Jane Pringle to Adele Petigru Allston, Apr. 1, 1865, in Robert F. W. Allston Papers, South Carolina Historical Society; and "Copy of Interview with Captain Stillwagen of U.S.S. Pawnee, Georgetown, S.C., Mar. 10, 1865, about lawlessness about the rice plantations," in the Sparkman Family Papers, Southern Historical Collection, University of North Carolina. A slave told Gilmore that "de black lub freedom as much as de white. . . . De blacks hab strong hands, and when de day come you'll see dey hab heads, too!" (*Among the Pines*, 20). On total institutions, see Erving Goffman, *Asylums: Essays on the Social Situation of Mental Patients and Other Inmates* (Chicago, 1962), xiii. On folklore as cultural action, see Roger D. Abrahams, "The Negro Stereotype: Negro Folklore and the Riots," *Journal of American Folklore* 83 (1970): 231; Clifford Geertz, *The Interpretation of Cultures* (New York, 1973), 449–53; Paul Ricoeur, "The Model of the Text: Meaningful Action Considered as Text," *Social Research* 38 (1971): 529–62.

Chapter 5: "Guilty of Holiest Crime"

1. *Baltimore American*, reprinted in the *Richmond Enquirer*, Dec. 6, 1859; affidavit of John Avis, Apr. 25, 1882, quoted in Oswald Garrison Villard, *John Brown, 1800–1859: A Biography Fifty Years After* (1885; rpt. New York, 1910), 670–71; Mary Ann Jackson, *Life and Letters of General Thomas J. Jackson* (New York, 1892), 130; Porte Crayon [David Hunter Strother], quoted in Boyd P. Studer, "An Eyewitness Describes the Hanging of John Brown," *American Heritage* 6 (Feb. 1955): 7–8. Journalist Strother's account was turned down by *Harper's Weekly*. A Virginia unionist and a relative of Brown's prosecutor, Strother became a brevet brigadier general in the Union Army and saw action in some thirty battles.

2. *Baltimore American*, reprinted in the *Richmond Enquirer*, Dec. 6, 1859; affidavit of John Avis, Apr. 25, 1882, quoted in Villard, *Biography*, 670–71.

3. *Baltimore American*, reprinted in the *Richmond Enquirer*, Dec. 6, 1859; Porte Crayon [David Hunter Strother], *Harper's Weekly*, Nov. 12, 1859; Jackson, *Life and Letters*, 390–91; Annie Brown Adams, quoted in Villard, *Biography*, 419; Israel Green, "The Capture of John Brown," *North American Review* 141 (Dec. 1885): 564–69; "Memoirs of Richard J. Hinton," in Richard Realf, *Poems of Richard Realf* (New York, 1898), xlii.

4. *Baltimore American*, reprinted in the *Richmond Enquirer*, Dec. 6, 1859.

5. Ibid.; affidavit of John Avis, Apr. 25, 1882, quoted in Villard, *Biography*, 671; Crayon [Strother], quoted in Studer, "An Eyewitness Describes the Hanging of John Brown," 8–9; Jackson, *Life and Letters*, 131–32; John Brown's last note, Dec. 2, 1859, quoted in Franklin B. Sanborn, *Memoirs of John Brown* (Concord, Mass., 1878), 94. The original is owned by the Chicago Historical Society.

6. *Baltimore American*, reprinted in the *Richmond Enquirer*, Dec. 6, 1859; Crayon [Strother], quoted in Studer, "An Eyewitness Describes the Hanging of John Brown," 8–9; Jackson, *Life and Letters*, 131–32.

7. Wendell Phillips, *Speeches and Lectures* (Boston, 1863), 289–93; see also Thomas Drew, *The John Brown Invasion* (Boston, 1860), 73–79.

8. Thomas Wentworth Higginson, one of Brown's close supporters, contends that Brown had "studied military strategy" for the express purpose of organizing a slave insurrection, "even making designs (which I have seen) for a new style of forest fortification, simple and ingenious, to be used by parties of fugitive slaves when brought to bay"; see Higginson, *Contemporaries* (Boston, 1899), 219–43.

9. Henry Ward Beecher, address, Brooklyn, New York, Oct. 30, 1859, quoted in James Redpath, *Echoes of Harper's Ferry* (Boston, 1860), 257–79.

10. See Victor Turner, *Dramas, Fields, and Metaphors: Symbolic Action in Hurnall Society* (Ithaca, 1974), 43, 61–71.

11. Ibid., 14, 36–40, 78–79.

12. Ibid., 35–36, 66–67, 96, 55.

13. Ibid., 45–46, 60–61.

14. Ibid., 37, 63–68. Turner links the root paradigm with the concept of "communitas," which he describes as "an 'essential we' . . . which is at the same time a generic human bond underlying or transcending all particular cultural definitions and normative orderings of social ties" (68).

15. Turner's social drama approach grows out of his studies of social structure, the phenomenon of communitas, and the concept of liminality. In his usage, structure is what separates people and constrains their actions, whereas communitas (or antistructure) is what unites people above and beyond customary, formal social bonds. The bonds of communitas are antistructural, in that they are "undifferentiated, equalitarian, direct, nonrational (though not irrational), I-thou or Essential We relations, in Martin Buber's sense" (ibid., 47). "Liminality" is the state of being "betwixt and between" successive positions or clearly demarcated modes of participation in the social structure. The condition of being outside of

or on the periphery of everyday life is thus considered "liminal," and a liminal phase is an essential component of the ritual process. Entire societies can be in liminal transition between different social structures, as the United States was in December of 1859, and may thus be in a fundamentally sacred condition. See Victor Turner, *The Ritual Process: Structure and Anti-Structure* (Chicago, 1969).

16. See Turner, *Dramas, Fields, and Metaphors*, 37 and 79. On Brown's lack of contact with or support from African Americans, see Stephen B. Oates, *To Purge This Land with Blood: A Biography of John Brown* (New York, 1970), 247–48 and 282–83; David M. Potter, *The South and the Sectional Conflict* (Baton Rouge, 1968), 201–18; Benjamin Quarles, *Blacks on John Brown* (Urbana, 1972), 29–30; idem, *Allies for Freedom: Blacks and John Brown* (New York, 1974), 43–51; and Merton Dillon, *Slavery Attacked: Southern Slaves and Their Allies, 1619–1865* (Baton Rouge, 1990), 235.

17. *Charleston Daily Courier*, Oct. 20, 1859; *Edgefield* (S.C.) *Advertiser*, Oct. 26, 1859. The *Advertiser* proudly published its prophetic motto beneath the paper's masthead: "We will cling to the pillars of the temple of our liberties, and if it must fall we will perish amid the ruins."

18. *New York Daily Tribune*, Oct. 19–22, 26, 31, and Nov. 12, 1859; *The Liberator*, quoted in the *Boston Journal*, Oct. 29, 1859; *Topeka Tribune* and *Atchison City (Kans.) Freedom's Champion*, both quoted in Villard, *Biography*, 473.

19. *New York Herald*, Oct. 19, 1859; see also the *Washington Star*, Oct. 17, 18, 20, 1859.

20. Robert C. Albrecht, "Thoreau and His Audience: 'A Plea for Capt. John Brown,'" *American Literature* 32 (1961): 395–99; James Ford Rhodes, *History of the United States from the Compromise of 1850*, 7 vols. (New York, 1893–1906), vol. 3, 383–416; Avery Craven, *The Coming of the Civil War*, 2d ed., rev. (Chicago, 1957), 408.

21. Robert A. Rusk, *The Life of Ralph Waldo Emerson* (New York, 1949), 402.

22. John Brown to H. L. Vaill, Nov. 16, 1859, in *John Brown: The Making of a Revolutionary, in His Own Words and Those of His Contemporaries*, ed. Louis Ruchames (New York, 1969), 143; John Brown to Mary Ann Day Brown, Nov. 10, 1859, quoted in Villard, *Biography*, 540–41. See also Turner, *Dramas, Fields, and Metaphors*, 37–38.

23. *Boston Journal* (supplement), Oct. 29, 1859; *New York Daily Tribune*, Oct. 19 and 31, 1859.

24. *South Carolina House Journal*, 1859, 32; *South Carolina Senate Journal*, 1859, 5 and 75; *Charleston Mercury*, Oct. 19, 1859. See also Bertram Wyatt-Brown, "John Brown's Antinomian War," in his *Yankee Saints and Southern Sinners* (Baton Rouge, 1985), 97–127; Harold S. Schultz, *Nationalism and Sectionalism in Carolina, 1852–1860: A Study of the Movement for Southern Independence* (Durham, N.C., 1950), 183–89; Jack Kenny Williams, "The Southern Movement to Reopen the African Slave Trade, 1854–1860: A Factor in Secession," *Proceedings of the South Carolina Historical Association*, 1960, 23–31; Percy L. Rainwater, "Economic Benefits of Secession: Opinions in Mississippi in the 1830s," *Journal of Southern History* 6 (Nov. 1935): 459–74.

25. *Savannah Republican*, quoted in Villard, *Biography*, 500; *Mobile (Ala.) Daily Register*, Oct. 25, 1859; *Richmond Enquirer*, Oct. 25, 1859.

26. *Salisbury (N.C.) Carolina Watchman*, Oct. 26, 1859. Bruner opposed secession, but once North Carolina seceded he quickly and completely supported the new Confederacy.

27. William Henry Trescot to William Porcher Miles, Feb. 8, 1859, in William Porcher Miles Papers, Southern Historical Collection, University of North Carolina (hereafter Miles Papers, UNC); William Henry Trescot to James Henry Hammond, Oct. 25, 1859, James Henry Hammond Papers, Library of Congress (hereafter Hammond Papers). In the meantime Hammond was urging his friend William Gilmore Simms to avoid a current literary feud. Would not "Harpers Ferry, and all that suffice, but South Carolina must have her bowels rent by these [illegible] unaccustomed feuds?" Hammond thought Simms had "a disposition to disparage his literary rivals," a disposition he ascribed to "a defect of his early education." Although Hammond described the writer as a "particular friend," he privately considered Simms to be lacking in "the delicacy of a thorough bred man." See James Henry Hammond to William Gilmore Simms, Oct. 24, 1859, in Hammond Papers; Carol Bleser, ed., *Secret and Sacred: The Diaries of James Henry Hammond, a Southern Slaveholder* (New York, 1988), 49.

28. See Turner, *Dramas, Fields, and Metaphors*, 38–41. The dilemma is at least partly inherent in the long controversy over slavery itself. Are there some questions that simply cannot be handled by democratic processes? If not, why did the contending parties resort to arms by 1861? If so, what are the implications for democracy today and tomorrow? See Charles Joyner, "From Civil War to Civil Rights," *Australasian Journal of American Studies* 10 (1991): 26–39. All that can be said with certainty is that neither the trial and execution of John Brown, nor congressional action, nor the electoral process in 1860, nor a combination of these, was successful in bringing this particular social drama to a peaceful conclusion.

29. Lawson Botts, quoted in the *National Intelligencer*, Oct. 29, 1859; John Brown, quoted, ibid.; Henry A. Wise, speech in Richmond, Va., Oct. 21, 1859, printed in the *Richmond Enquirer*, Oct. 25, 1859. See also Turner, *Dramas, Fields, and Metaphors*, 88–89. For the best discussion of Brown's mental health, see Wyatt-Brown, "Antinomian," 97–127. See also Potter, *Sectional*, esp. 211–15; and C. Vann Woodward, "John Brown's Private War," in his *The Burden of Southern History* (Baton Rouge, 1960), 41–68.

30. See Turner, *Dramas, Fields, and Metaphors*, 13–15, 53, 87. On loss of honor and social death, see Bertram Wyatt-Brown, *Southern Honor: Ethics and Behavior in the Old South* (New York, 1982); and Orlando Patterson, *Slavery and Social Death: A Comparative Study* (Cambridge, Mass., 1982).

31. See, for example, the *New York Herald*, Nov. 6, 13, 27, 1859; and the *Pittsburgh Gazette*, Dec. 1, 1859; Theodore Parker to Francis Jackson, Nov. 24, 1859, in Francis Power Cobbe, ed., *Collected Works of Theodore Parker* (London, 1862), 164–77.

32. *Frankfort Yeoman*, n.d., quoted in Villard, *Biography*, 502.

33. *Columbus (Ga.) Daily Enquirer*, Oct. 21 and 25, and Nov. 2, 5, 11, 30, 1859; *Charleston Daily Courier*, Oct. 20, 1859; *Charleston Mercury*, Oct. 31, Nov. 1, 2, 5, 26, and Dec. 10, 1859.

34. *Charlotte North Carolina Whig*, Nov. 1 and 8, 1859; *Salisbury Carolina Watchman*, Nov. 13, 1859; *Lancaster (S.C.) Ledger*, Nov. 2, 1859.

35. *Little Rock Arkansas Gazette*, Nov. 12, 1859; *Charleston Mercury*, Nov. 14, 1859; *Richmond Enquirer*, Nov. 5, 1859; *Raleigh Standard*, Oct. 26, 1859, and Nov. 12, 1859.

36. Beaufort T. Watts to James Henry Hammond, [Nov.] 1857, in Beaufort T. Watts Papers, South Caroliniana Library, University of South Carolina; *Congressional Globe*, 35th Cong., 1st Sess., appendix, 69–71. See also Drew Gilpin Faust, *James Henry Hammond and the Old South: A Design for Mastery* (Baton Rouge, 1982), 350–55.

37. *Charleston Evening News*, July 29, 1858; James Henry Hammond, *Speech of James H. Hammond Delivered at Barnwell C[ourt] H[ouse], October 29th, 1858* (Charleston, 1858).

38. James Henry Hammond to Edmund Ruffin, Feb. 8, 1859, Edmund Ruffin Papers, Southern Historical Collection, University of North Carolina; James Henry Hammond to William Gilmore Simms, Jan. 1, 1859, Hammond Papers; Bleser, *Secret and Sacred*, 275.

39. Bleser, *Secret and Sacred*, 273–75; James Henry Hammond to William Gilmore Simms, July 30, 1859, Hammond Papers; George P. Elliott to James Henry Hammond, Nov. 5, 1859, ibid. For a sophisticated analysis of Hammond's mental and physical health, see Faust, *James Henry Hammond and the Old South*, 181–84, 375–78.

40. Francis W. Pickens to Milledge Luke Bonham, Apr. 14, 1860, Milledge Luke Bonham Papers, South Caroliniana Library, University of South Carolina; John B. Edmunds Jr., *Francis W. Pickens and the Politics of Destruction* (Chapel Hill, 1986), 143–49.

41. Beaufort T. Watts to James Henry Hammond, Nov. 24, 1859, Hammond Papers; *Charlotte North Carolina Whig*, Nov. 29, 1859; *Salisbury Carolina Watchman*, Nov. 29, 1859.

42. *Charlotte North Carolina Whig*, Nov. 15, 1859; *Lancaster Ledger*, Nov. 21, 1859. See also Turner, *Dramas, Fields, and Metaphors*, 41.

43. James Buchanan, quoted in Varina Howell Davis, *Jefferson Davis: A Memoir by His Wife* (New York, 1890), 646.

44. *Salisbury Carolina Watchman*, Nov. 22, 1859; *Salisbury Carolina Watchman*, Nov. 22, 1859, in which the *Selma (Ala.) Reporter and Democrat*, n.d., is reprinted.

45. *Charlotte North Carolina Whig*, Nov. 29, 1859; *Natchez Mississippi Free Trader*, Dec. 1, 1859; *Richmond Whig*, reprinted in *Charlotte North Carolina Whig*, Nov. 29, 1859.

46. *Pickens (S.C.) Keowee Courier*, Oct. 29, Nov. 5, and Dec. 10, 1859; *Spartanburg (S.C.) Carolina Spartan*, Nov. 24, 1859.

47. See Turner, *Dramas, Fields, and Metaphors*, 71.

48. Ibid., 41–46.

49. Henry A. Wise, speech in Richmond, Va., Oct. 21, 1859, printed in the *Richmond Enquirer*, Oct. 25, 1859; John Brown, quoted in the *National Intelligencer*, Oct. 29, 1859. See also Turner, *Dramas, Fields, and Metaphors*, 69 and 92.

50. Louisa May Alcott, quoted in Rusk, *Life of Ralph Waldo Emerson*, 402; A. Bronson Alcott, "Sonnet XXIV," addressed to John Brown, Harpers Ferry, in his *Sonnets and Canzonets* (Boston, 1882), 141. See also Emerson's speech on Brown delivered a month later in Salem, Massachusetts, Jan. 6, 1860, in Redpath, *Echoes*, 118–22.

51. William Lloyd Garrison, quoted in Villard, *Biography*, 560; *New York Daily Tribune* Dec. 3, 1859.

52. John Knox McLean Papers, South Caroliniana Library, University of South Carolina; Theodore Tilton, quoted in *A John Brown Reader*, ed. Louis Ruchames (London, 1959), 272–75.

53. Moncure Daniel Conway, quoted in Ruchames, *Reader*, 278–80.

54. Sarah Grimké, quoted in William Birney, *James G. Birney and His Times* (New York, 1890), 282–83. For a remarkable study of the Grimké sisters' abolitionist career, see Gerda Lerner, *The Grimké Sisters from South Carolina: Rebels against Slavery* (Boston, 1967).

55. William H. Herndon to Charles Sumner, Dec. 10, 1860, in Charles Sumner Papers, Harvard University.

56. Abraham Lincoln, speech in Troy, Kansas, Dec. 2, 1859, quoted in Villard, *Biography*, 564; *New York Weekly Day Book*, quoted in the *Salisbury Carolina Watchman*, Dec. 6, 1859. On racism among Northern workers, see Eric Foner, *Free Soil, Free Labor, Free Men: The Ideology of the Republican Party before the Civil War* (New York, 1970).

57. Claude M. Fuess, *Life of Caleb Cushing* (New York, 1923), 235–37.

58. Edward Everett, speech in Boston, Massachusetts, Dec. 8, 1859, printed in the *Richmond Enquirer*, Dec. 16, 1859. The quotations in the following paragraph are from the same source.

59. Caleb Cushing, speech in Boston, Massachusetts, Dec. 8, 1859, printed in the *National Intelligencer*, Dec. 17, 1859; Cushing to Chairman, Democratic Party of Massachusetts, quoted in Fuess, *Life of Caleb Cushing*, 241–42.

60. Caleb Cushing to Chairman, Democratic Party of Massachusetts, quoted in Fuess, *Life of Caleb Cushing*, 241–42.

61. Wise, quoted in the *Charlotte North Carolina Whig*, Dec. 13, 1859.

62. *Raleigh Standard*, quoted in the *Charlotte North Carolina Whig*, Jan. 23, 1860; *Petersburg (Va.) Express*, Dec. 17, 1859, quoted in the *Salisbury Carolina Watchman*, Jan. 3, 1860.

63. W. Duncan to James Henry Hammond, Dec. 2, 1859, Hammond Papers.

64. *New Orleans Daily Picayune*, Dec. 2, 1859; James McKaye, *Mastership and Its*

Fruits: The Emancipated Slave Face to Face with His Old Master (New York, 1864), quoted in Janet Duitsman Cornelius, *When I Can Read My Title Clear: Literacy, Slavery, and Religion in the Antebellum South* (Columbia, S.C., 1991), 3, 84.

65. *Richmond Enquirer*, Dec. 23, 1859; *Salisbury Carolina Watchman*, Dec. 20, 1859; *Mississippi Free Trader*, Dec. 24, 1859; *Salisbury Carolina Watchman*, Dec. 12, 1859.

66. Christopher G. Memminger to William Porcher Miles, Jan. 3, 1860, in Miles Papers, UNC; D. H. Hamilton to William Porcher Miles, Dec. 9, 1859, in William Porcher Miles Papers, South Caroliniana Library, University of South Carolina (hereafter Miles Papers, USC); *South Carolina House Journal*, 1859, 72–73; Christopher G. Memminger to William Porcher Miles, Dec. 27,1859, Miles Papers, USC.

67. *Charleston Mercury*, Dec. 5, 1859; *Edgefield Advertiser*, Dec. 14, 1859; message of Governor William Henry Gist of South Carolina to Legislature, Nov. 29, 1859.

68. *South Carolina House Journal*, 1859, 12–24; *South Carolina Senate Journal*, 1859, 11–23; William Henry Gist to William Porcher Miles, Dec. 20, 1859, Miles Papers, USC; *South Carolina House Journal*, 1859, 263; *South Carolina Senate Journal*, 1859, 135; *South Carolina House Journal*, 1859, 174–75, 176, 191.

69. *South Carolina House Journal*, 1859, 196–97, 199, 201, 202, 204, 263, 268, 274, 276; *Reports and Resolutions of the General Assembly of the State of South Carolina, Passed at the Annual Session of 1859* (Columbia, S.C., 1859), 579; W. W. Boyce to Christopher G. Memminger, Jan. 14, 1860, Christopher G. Memminger Papers, Southern Historical Collection, University of North Carolina; Christopher G. Memminger to William Porcher Miles, Dec. 27, 1859, Jan. 3, 16, 24, 30, and Feb. 4, 1860, Miles Papers, UNC. On the nullification controversy, see William W. Freehling, *Prelude to Civil War: The Nullification Controversy in South Carolina, 1816–1836* (New York, 1966). On the secession crisis of 1850, see John Barnwell, *Love of Order: South Carolina's First Secession Crisis* (Chapel Hill, 1982). On Memminger's mission to Virginia, see Steven Channing, *Crisis of Fear: Secession in South Carolina* (New York, 1974), 112–30; and Ollinger Crenshaw, "Christopher G. Memminger's Mission to Virginia," *JSH* 8 (Nov. 1942): 334–49.

70. William Henry Trescot to James Henry Hammond, Dec. 30, 1859; James Henry Hammond, draft of proposed Constitutional Amendment, marked CONFIDENTIAL, Dec. 1859; I[saac] W. Hayne to James Henry Hammond, Jan. 5, 1860; and James Henry Hammond to William Gilmore Simms, Dec. 19, 1859; all in Hammond Papers.

71. James McCarty to William Porcher Miles, Jan. 16, 1860, Miles Papers, USC; Robert Barnwell Rhett to William Porcher Miles, Jan. 29, 1860, Miles Papers, UNC.

72. Ralph Waldo Emerson, address in Salem, Mass., Jan. 6, 1860, in *Emerson's Complete Works*, ed. James Elliot Cabot, 12 vols. (Boston, 1883), vol. 11, 257–63.

73. Charles Sumner, speech before U.S. Senate, June 4, 1860, entitled "The Barbarism of Slavery," in *The Works of Charles Sumner*, 15 vols. (Boston, 1874–83), vol. 5, 17–26 (quote on 26). On Brooks's caning of Sumner, see David Herbert Donald, *Charles Sumner and the Coming of the Civil War* (New York, 1960).

74. Henry David Thoreau, address at North Elba, N.Y., July 4, 1860, in *The Writings of Henry David Thoreau*, ed. Bradford Torrey and Franklin B. Sanborn, 20 vols. (orig. publ. 1894–95 in 7 vols.; repr. Boston, 1906), vol. 10, 237–48.

75. *New Orleans Daily Crescent*, Jan. 21, 1860; *Salisbury Carolina Watchman*, Mar. 27, 1860.

76. Abraham Lincoln, speech at Cooper Union, New York City, Feb. 27, 1860, in Roy P. Basler, ed. *The Collected Works of Abraham Lincoln*, 9 vols. (New Brunswick, N.J., 1953–55), vol. 3, 522–50.

77. Papers of the South Carolina Democratic Party, 1860, South Caroliniana Library, University of South Carolina.

78. Charles W. Johnson, ed., *Proceedings of the First Three Republican Conventions* (Minneapolis, 1893), 131–33.

79. *Charleston Mercury*, May 23, 1860.

80. *Salisbury Carolina Watchman*, May 22, 1860; Sept. 11, 1860.

81. Ibid., Sept. 11 and 18, 1860, and Oct. 9, 1860.

82. *New Orleans Daily Crescent*, Nov. 13, 1860; Mary Boykin Chesnut, entry for Nov. 8, 1860, *A Diary from Dixie*, ed. Isabella D. Martin and Myrta Lockett Avary (New York, 1905), 1. Chesnut's comment does not, however, appear in either the Ben Ames Williams edition of *A Diary from Dixie* (Boston, 1949) or in C. Vann Woodward's *Mary Chesnut's Civil War* (New Haven, 1981). For more of Chesnut's comments on John Brown, see Woodward, *Mary Chesnut's Civil War*, 114, 148, 245, 269, 409, 413, 428, 440, 466.

83. *Richmond Enquirer*, Jan. 21, 1860; for Simms's remarks, see the *Charleston Mercury*, Jan. 17, 1861.

84. *Charleston Courier*, Dec. 3, 1860; *Charleston Mercury*, Dec. 4, 1860; South Carolina's "Declaration of the Causes of Secession," Dec. 20, 1860, in *The Rebellion Record*, ed. Frank Moore, 12 vols. (New York, 1861–68), vol. 1, 3–4.

85. See Turner, *Dramas, Fields, and Metaphors*, 56 and 72.

86. John Brown's speech to the Virginia Court, Nov. 2, 1859, in Franklin B. Sanborn, ed., *The Life and Letters of John Brown, Liberator of Kansas, and Martyr of Virginia* (1885; rpt. New York, 1969), 585; see also Turner, *Dramas, Fields, and Metaphors*, 85–89, and idem, *Schism and Continuity in an African Society* (Manchester, Eng., 1957), 94.

Chapter 6: The South as a Folk Culture

1. See David M. Potter, "The Enigma of the South," *Yale Review* 51 (1961): 151; idem, *Lincoln and His Party in the Secession Crisis* (New Haven, 1942); idem, *The South and the Sectional Conflict* (Baton Rouge, 1968); idem, *The South and the Concurrent Majority*, ed. Don E. Fehrenbacher and Carl N. Degler (Baton Rouge, 1972); and idem, *The Impending Crisis, 1848–1861* (New York, 1976). Potter was not, of course, *always* right. For example, he insisted in 1967 that the topic of slavery had "been

worked to a point where diminishing returns now seem about to set in." The next two decades would see an extraordinary explosion of studies that virtually rewrote the history of slavery. The quotes in the text and this note are from his "Depletion and Renewal in Southern History," in *Perspectives on the South: Agenda for Research*, ed. Edgar T. Thompson (Durham, N.C., 1967), 78, 84–85.

2. Drew Gilpin Faust, "The Peculiar South Revisited: White Society, Culture, and Politics in the Antebellum Period, 1800–1860," in *Interpreting Southern History: Historiographical Essays in Honor of Sanford W. Higginbotham*, ed. John B. Boles and Evelyn Thomas Nolen (Baton Rouge, 1987), 78–79.

3. C. Vann Woodward, *The Burden of Southern History* (Baton Rouge, 1960), ix–xi, 167–70.

4. Potter, "Enigma of the South," 142–46, 149–51.

5. Robert Redfield, "The Folk Society," *American Journal of Sociology* 52 (1947): 297–98. See also George M. Foster's critique, "What Is Folk Culture?" *American Anthropologist* 55 (1953): 159–73.

6. Howard W. Odum, *The Way of the South: Toward the Regional Balance of America* (New York: Macmillan, 1947), 64; idem, *Folk, Region, and Society: Selected Essays of Howard Odum*, ed. Katherine Jocher et al. (Chapel Hill, 1964), 219–38, 253–54. See also the essays on Odum in Morton Sosna, *In Search of the Silent South* (New York, 1977), 42–59; Michael O'Brien, *The Idea of the American South, 1920–1941* (Baltimore, 1979), 31–96; Richard H. King, *A Southern Renaissance: The Cultural Awakening of the American South, 1930–1955* (New York, 1980), 39–51; Daniel Joseph Singal, *The War Within: From Victorian to Modernist Thought in the South, 1919–1945* (Chapel Hill, 1982), 115–52; Fred Hobson, *Tell About the South: The Southern Rage to Explain* (Baton Rouge, 1983), 180–202; and John Shelton Reed, "Howard Odum and Regional Sociology," in his *Surveying the South: Studies in Regional Sociology* (Columbia, Mo., 1993), 1–12.

7. Richard M. Dorson, "Is There a Folk in the City?" in *The Urban Experience and Folk Tradition*, ed. Américo Paredes and Ellen J. Steckert (Austin, 1971), 185–228; James Borchert, *Alley Life in Washington: Family, Community, Religion and Folklife in the City, 1850–1970* (Urbana, 1980); Charles Joyner, "A Model for the Analysis of Folklore Performance in Historical Context," *Journal of American Folklore* 88 (1975): 254–65.

8. Clifford Geertz, *The Interpretation of Cultures* (New York, 1973), 14, 89. Sidney Mintz and Richard Price apply the distinction between culture and society to good effect in their study of Africans in the New World, *The Birth of African-American Culture: An Anthropological Perspective* (Boston, 1992).

9. "Between the simple backward look and the simple progressive thrust," Raymond Williams notes, "there is room for long argument but none for enlightenment. We must begin differently; not in the idealizations of one order or another, but in the history to which they are only partial and misleading responses." See his *The Country and the City* (New York, 1973), 37.

10. Eric J. Hobsbawm, "From Social History to the History of Society," in *Historical Studies Today*, ed. Felix Gilbert and Stephan R. Graubard (New York, 1972), 20; E. P. Thompson, "Time, Work-Discipline, and Industrial Capitalism," *Past and Present* 38 (1967): 80. Examples of both the richness and the limitations of the contextual school of folklore performance studies include Dan Ben-Amos, "Toward a Definition of Folklore in Context," *Journal of American Folklore* 84 (1971): 3–15; Roger D. Abrahams, "Introductory Remarks to a Rhetorical Theory of Folklore," *Journal of American Folklore* 81 (1968): 144–34; Alan Dundes, "Texture, Text, and Context," *Southern Folklore Quarterly* 28 (1964): 251–65; and Dell Hymes, *Foundations in Sociolinguistics: An Ethnographic Approach* (Philadelphia, 1974), 3–66.

11. See Geertz, *Interpretation of Cultures;* his *Local Knowledge: Further Essays in Interpretive Anthropology* (New York, 1983); and his *Works and Lives: The Anthropologist as Author* (Stanford, 1988); Mary Douglas, *Purity and Danger: An Analysis of Concepts of Pollution* (London, 1966); and her *Natural Symbols: Explorations in Cosmology* (New York, 1973); Victor W. Turner, *The Forest of Symbols: Aspects of Ndembu Ritual* (Ithaca, 1967); his *The Drums of Affliction* (Oxford, 1968); his *The Ritual Process: Structure and Anti-Structure* (Ithaca, 1969); and his *Dramas, Fields, and Metaphors: Symbolic Action in Human Society* (Ithaca, 1974).

12. Among the most important works of *les annalistes* in English are Marc Bloch, *Land and Work in Medieval Europe*, trans. J. E. Anderson (New York, 1969); idem, *French Rural History: An Essay on Its Basic Characteristics*, trans. Janet Sondheimer (Berkeley, 1970); Peter Burke, ed., *A New Kind of History: From the Writings of Lucien Febvre*, trans. K. Folka (New York, 1973) 27–43; Fernand Braudel, *The Mediterranean and the Mediterranean World in the Age of Philip II*, 2 vols., trans. Sian Reynolds (New York, 1972–75); idem, *Civilization and Capitalism, Fifteenth to Eighteenth Century*, 3 vols., trans. Sian Reynolds (New York, 1982–85); Jacques Le Goff, *Time, Work, and Culture in the Middle Ages*, trans. Arthur Goldhammer (Chicago, 1980); Emmanuel Le Roy Ladurie, *The Peasants of Languedoc*, trans. John Day (Urbana, 1974).

13. W. J. Cash, *The Mind of the South* (1941; rpt., New York, 1991), xlviii, 29–58. See also Michael O'Brien, *Rethinking the South: Essays in Intellectual History* (Baltimore, 1988), 180–83.

14. Bertram Wyatt-Brown, "The Ideal Typology and Ante-bellum Southern History: A Testing of a New Approach," *Societas* 5 (1975): 1–21. The quotation is on page 14.

15. Bertram Wyatt-Brown, *Southern Honor: Ethics and Behavior in the Old South* (New York, 1982), 60, 45, 35, 53; and his *Yankee Saints and Southern Sinners* (Baton Rouge, 1985), 185.

16. Wyatt-Brown, *Southern Honor*, 71–72.

17. Kenneth S. Greenberg, *Masters and Statesmen: The Political Culture of American Slavery* (Baltimore, 1985); Geertz, *Interpretation of Cultures*, 216.

18. Edward L. Ayers, *Vengeance and Justice: Crime and Punishment in the Nineteenth-Century American South* (New York, 1984), 26, 19, 14, 13.

19. Clifford Geertz's famous description of culture as a "model for" and a "model of" human behavior is in his *Agricultural Involution: The Process of Ecological Change in Indonesia* (Berkeley, 1963), 11. Faust's comment on Geertz appears in her *Southern Stories: Slaveholders in Peace and War* (Columbia, Mo., 1992), 4–5. See also the following works by Faust: *A Sacred Circle: The Dilemma of the Intellectual in the Old South, 1840–1860* (Baltimore, 1977); *James Henry Hammond and the Old South: A Design for Mastery* (Baton Rouge, 1982); *The Creation of Confederate Nationalism: Ideology and Identity in the Civil War South* (Baton Rouge, 1988); *Mothers of Invention: Women of the Slaveholding South in the American Civil War* (Chapel Hill, 1996); and "The Rhetoric and Ritual of Agriculture in Antebellum South Carolina," *Journal of Southern History* 45 (1979): 63–79.

20. Rhys Isaac, *The Transformation of Virginia, 1740–1790* (Chapel Hill, 1982). See also three other works by Isaac: "On Explanation, Text, and Terrifying Power in Ethnographic History," *Yale Journal of Criticism* 6 (1993): 217–36; "Power and Meaning: Event and Text: History and Anthropology," in *Dangerous Liaisons: Essays in Honor of Greg Dening*, ed. Donna Merwick (Melbourne, Aus., 1994), 297–315; and "Stories of Enslavement: A Person-Centered Ethnography from an Eighteenth-Century Virginia Plantation," in *Varieties of Southern History: New Essays on a Region and Its People*, ed. Bruce Clayton and John Salmond (Westport, Conn., 1996), 3–20. Greg Dening's perceptive and thought-provoking books include *Islands and Beaches: Discourse on a Silent Land, Marquesas 1774–1880* (Honolulu, 1980); *History's Anthropology: The Death of William Gooch*, Association for Social Anthropology in Oceania Special Publications, no. 2 (Lanham, Md., 1988); *The Bounty: An Ethnographic History* (Melbourne, Aus., 1988); *Mr. Bligh's Bad Language: Passion, Power and Theatre on the Bounty* (Cambridge, 1992); and *Performances* (Chicago, 1996). Isaac also acknowledges the influence of such "historifying anthropologists" as Geertz, Marshal Sahlins, Richard Price, Maurice Bloch, Sherry Ortner, David Lan, and Valerio Valeri.

21. Dening, *The Bounty*, 111; idem, *History's Anthropology*, 1, 9, 15, 36, 99.

22. Dening, *History's Anthropology*, 99; idem, *Islands and Beaches*. See also Merwick, *Dangerous Liaisons*.

23. Charles Joyner, "Texts, Texture, and Context: Toward an Ethnographic History of Slave Resistance," in Clayton and Salmond, *Varieties of Southern History;* Stuart A. Marks, *Southern Hunting in Black and White: Nature, History, and Ritual in a Carolina Community* (Princeton, 1991), 8. See also J. David Sapir and J. Christopher Crocker, eds., *The Social Use of Metaphor: Essays on the Anthropology of Rhetoric* (Philadelphia, 1977), and James W. Fernandez, *Persuasions and Performances: The Play of Tropes in Culture* (Bloomington, Ind., 1986).

24. Anthony F. C. Wallace, "Culture and Cognition," *Science* 135 (1962): 351; Alfred Kroeber and Clyde Kluckhohn, *Culture: A Critical Review of Concepts and Definitions* (Cambridge, Mass.: Harvard University Press, 1952), 182; Ward H. Goodenough, *Description and Comparison in Cultural Anthropology* (Chicago, 1970),

110; Stephen Tyler, *Cognitive Anthropology* (New York, 1969), 6; William P. Mc-Ewen, *The Problem of Social Scientific Knowledge* (Totowa, N.J., 1963), 34–35; Benjamin N. Colby, "Ethnographic Semantics: A Preliminary Survey," *Current Anthropologist* 7 (1966): 3–32; Herbert Halpert, "American Regional Folklore," in "Folklore Research in North America," *Journal of American Folklore* 60 (1974): 355–56; idem, "The Functional Approach," in "Conference on the Character and State of Studies in Folklore," *Journal of American Folklore* 54 (1946): 510–12; Richard M. Dorson, "Standards of Collecting and Publishing American Folktales," in "The Folktale: A Symposium," *Journal of American Folklore* 80 (1957): 54; Kenneth S. Goldstein, *A Guide for Fieldworkers in Folklore* (Hatboro, Pa., 1964), 7.

25. Robert Redfield, *Peasant Society and Culture* (Chicago, 1956), 5; Foster, "What Is Folk Culture?" 164; Immanuel Wallerstein, "What Can One Mean by Southern Culture?" in *The Evolution of Southern Culture*, ed. Numan V. Bartley (Athens, Ga., 1988), 10. Here Wallerstein is only slightly softer in his natural and economic determinism in the formation of folklore than Leon Trotsky:

> The similarity of conditions in the development of the herding and agricultural and primarily peasant peoples, and the similarity in the character of their mutual influence upon one another, cannot but lead to the creation of a similar folklore. And from the point of view of the question that interests us here, it makes absolutely no difference whether these homogeneous themes arose independently upon different peoples [polygenesis], as the reflection of a life-experience which was homogeneous in its fundamental traits and which was reflected through the homogeneous prism of a peasant imagination, or whether the seeds of these fairy tales were carried by a favorable wind from place to place, striking root wherever the ground turned out to be favorable [monogenesis and diffusion]. It is very likely that in reality, these methods were combined.

See Leon Trotsky, "The Formalist School," *Literature and Revolution* [1924], trans. Rose Strunsky (New York, 1925), 174.

26. Charles Joyner, "African and European Roots of Southern Culture: The 'Central Theme' Revisited," in *Dixie Debates*, ed. Helen Taylor and Richard King (London, 1995); idem, "Southern Folklore as a Key to Southern Identity," *Southern Humanities Review* 1 (1967): 211–22; idem, *Folk Song in South Carolina* (Columbia, S.C., 1971); Winthrop D. Jordan, *White Over Black: American Attitudes Toward the Negro, 1550–1812* (Chapel Hill, 1958), 605.

27. John Shelton Reed, *The Enduring South: Subcultural Persistence in Mass Society*, rev. ed. (Chapel Hill, 1986).

Chapter 7: The Bold Fischer Man

1. David Hackett Fischer, *Albion's Seed: Four British Folkways in America* (New York, 1989), vii.

2. David Hackett Fischer, *Historians' Fallacies: Toward a Logic of Historical Thought* (New York, 1970). He discusses the "fallacy of elitism" on pages 230–32.

3. Fischer, *Albion's Seed*, 872.

4. Ibid., 256–65, 652–55, 470–75, 57–62.

5. Ibid., 264–74, 655–62, 475–81, 62–68.

6. Ibid., 274–80, 662–68, 481–85, 68–75.

7. Ibid., 669–75, 281–86, 75–82, 485–90.

8. Ibid., 286–97, 675–80, 490–98, 83–87.

9. Ibid., 298–306, 680–83, 498–502, 87–93.

10. Ibid., 97–102, 311–20, 507–13, 687–90.

11. Ibid., 306–10, 683–86, 93–97, 502–507.

12. Ibid., 321–26, 691–96, 103–11, 513–17.

13. Ibid., 111–17, 326–32, 517–22, 697–702.

14. Ibid., 332–40, 703–708, 117–25, 522–26.

15. Ibid., 125–30, 340–44, 526–30, 708–15.

16. Ibid., 715–27, 344–49, 130–34, 530–38.

17. Ibid., 349–54, 134–39, 538–44, 727–31.

18. Ibid., 732–35, 354–60, 544–52, 139–46.

19. Ibid., 735–40, 360–64, 146–51, 552–55.

20. Ibid., 740–43, 151–58, 365–68, 555–60.

21. Ibid., 158–66, 560–66, 368–73, 743–47.

22. Ibid., 759–65, 181–88, 389–97, 577–84.

23. Ibid., 382–89, 174–80, 573–77, 754–58.

24. Ibid., 166–74, 374–82, 566–73, 747–53.

25. Ibid., 772–76, 405–10, 196–99, 590–95.

26. Ibid., 189–96, 398–405, 584–89, 765–71.

27. Ibid., 777–82, 410–18, 205, 595–603.

28. Ibid., 3–4, 897–89.

29. Ibid., 810–12, 816–19.

30. Ibid., 811–12.

31. The quoted historian is Fischer. See his *Historians' Fallacies*, 226. He describes the practice of exaggerating the role of one's own group in interaction with other groups as constituting the "fallacy of ethnomorphism." In *Historians' Fallacies* he considers elevating Anglo-American culture to normative status to be "the most powerful form of ethnomorphism" (226–28).

32. In his *Historians' Fallacies*, Fischer denotes the "confusion of social and cultural groups of many kinds with geographical groups" to be the "fallacy of false culture" (239). "Reasoning improperly from a property of a member of a group to a property of the group itself" he calls the "fallacy of composition" (219). And "reasoning from a partial resemblance between two entities to an entire and exact correspondence" he terms "the fallacy of the perfect analogy" (247). Fischer's wise comment on culture is on page 237.

33. Fischer, *Albion's Seed*, 3.

34. Fischer discusses question-begging on pages 49–51 of *Historians' Fallacies*.

35. Fischer, *Albion's Seed*, 4–11.

36. Henry Glassie, *Folk Housing in Middle Virginia: A Structural Analysis of Historic Artifacts* (Knoxville, 1975); idem, *Passing the Time in Ballymenone* (Philadelphia, 1982); David J. Hufford, *The Terror That Comes in the Night: An Experience-Centered Study of Supernatural Assault Traditions* (Philadelphia, 1982); idem, "A New Approach to the 'Old Hag': The Nightmare Tradition Reexamined," in *American Folk Medicine: A Symposium*, ed. Wayland Hand (Berkeley, 1976), 73–85.

37. See the following by Michael Montgomery: "The Roots of Appalachian English," in *Methods in Dialectology*, ed. Alan R. Thomas (New York, 1988), 480–91; "Exploring the Roots of Appalachian English," *English World-Wide* 10 (1988): 227–78; "The Linguistic Value of Ulster Emigrant Letters," *Ulster Folklife* 41 (1995): 1–16; "How Scotch-Irish Is Your English?" *Journal of East Tennessee History* 67 (1995): 1–33.

38. Fischer discusses the "fallacy of circular proof" on pages 49–51 of *Historians' Fallacies*.

39. Fischer, *Albion's Seed*, 7–8.

40. Fernand Braudel, *The Mediterranean and the Mediterranean World in the Age of Philip II*, trans. Sian Reynolds (New York, 1972–75), 20.

41. Fischer, *Albion's Seed*, 819–20; Charles Joyner, *Down by the Riverside: A South Carolina Slave Community* (Urbana, 1984); Jack P. Greene, *Pursuits of Happiness: The Social Development of Early British Colonies and the Formation of American Culture* (Chapel Hill, 1988). Greene stresses the interplay of "inheritance" and "experience" through a three-stage sequence marked first by "social simplification," then by "social elaboration," and finally by "social replication." See also Fischer's brief discussion of a four-stage sequence in *Albion's Seed* (819–20): 1) the transit of culture from Britain to America; 2) a cultural crisis of great intensity; 3) a period of cultural consolidation; and finally, 4) a period of cultural devolution.

42. Fischer, *Historian's Fallacies*, 5.

Chapter 8: The Narrowing Gyre

1. Henry Glassie, *Passing the Time in Ballymenone: Culture and History of an Ulster Community* (Philadelphia, 1982; Bloomington, Ind., 1995).

2. Eric J. Hobsbawm, "From Social History to the History of Society," in *Historical Studies Today*, ed. Felix Gilbert and Stephen R. Graubard (New York, 1972), p. 19.

3. See Lindsay Anderson, *About John Ford* (London, 1981); John Baxter, *The Cinema of John Ford* (New York, 1971); Peter Bogdanovich, *John Ford* (Berkeley, 1978); Ronald R. Davis, *John Ford: Hollywood's Old Master* (Norman, Okla., 1995); Dan

Ford, *Pappy: The Life of John Ford* (Englewood Cliffs, N.J., 1979); Tag Gallagher, *John Ford: The Man and His Films* (Berkeley, 1986); Lee Lourdeaux, *Italian and Irish Film-makers in America: Ford, Capra, Coppola, and Scorsese* (Philadelphia, 1990); Charles J. Marland, *American Vision: The Films of Chaplin, Ford, Capra, and Welles* (New York, 1977); Janey Ann Place, *The Non-Western Films of John Ford* (Secaucus, N.J., 1979); Joseph L. Reed, *Three American Originals: John Ford, William Faulkner, and Charles Ives* (Middletown, Conn., 1984); Andrew Sinclair, *John Ford: A Biography* (New York, 1979); Peter Stowell, *John Ford* (Boston, 1986).

4. Henry Glassie, *Pattern in the Material Folk Culture of the Eastern United States* (Philadelphia, 1968); idem, *Folk Housing in Middle Virginia: A Structural Analysis of Historic Artifacts* (Knoxville, 1975); idem, *All Silver and No Brass: An Irish Christmas Mumming* (Bloomington, Ind., 1975).

5. Henry Glassie, "Take That Night Train to Selma," in *Folksongs and Their Makers*, ed. Henry Glassie, John F. Szwed, and Edward D. Ives (Bowling Green, Ohio, 1970).

6. Glassie, *All Silver and No Brass*, 148–49.

7. See Dan Ben-Amos, *Folklore Genres* (Austin, Tex., 1976); idem, *Folklore in Context: Essays* (New Delhi, 1982); idem, "Toward a Definition of Folklore in Context," *Journal of American Folklore* 84 (1971); idem, "Folklore in African Society," in *The Forms of Folklore in Africa: Narrative, Poetic, Gnomic, Dramatic*, ed. Bernth Lindfors (Austin, Tex., 1977), 22–29; idem, "The Elusive Audience of Benin Storytellers," *Journal of the Folklore Institute* 9 (1972): 39–43; Robert Plant Armstrong, *The Affecting Presence: An Essay in Humanistic Anthropology* (Urbana, 1971); Linda Degh, *Folktales and Society: Storytelling in a Hungarian Peasant Community*, trans. Emily M. Schossberger (Bloomington, Ind., 1969); Richard M. Dorson, *American Folklore* (Chicago, 1964); idem, *The British Folklorists: A History* (Chicago, 1968); idem, *American Folklore and the Historians* (Chicago, 1971); idem, *Folklore: Selected Essays* (Bloomington, Ind., 1972); idem, *American Negro Folk Tales* (New York, 1967); "A Theory for American Folklore," *Journal of American Folklore* 72 (1979); Dell Hymes, *Foundations in Sociolinguistics: An Ethnographic Approach* (Philadelphia, 1974); idem, "Breakthrough into Performance," in *Folklore Performance and Communication*, ed. Dan Ben-Amos and Kenneth S. Goldstein (The Hague, 1975), 11–74; Dennis Tedlock, *Finding the Center: Narrative Poetry of the Zuni Indians from Performances in the Zuni by Andrew Peynetsa and Walter Sanchez* (New York, 1972); James Deetz, *In Small Things Forgotten: The Archaeology of Early American Life* (New York, 1977); Estyn Evans, *The Personality of Ireland: Habitat, Heritage, and History* (Cambridge, 1973); idem, *Irish Heritage: The Landscape, the People, and Their Work* (Dundalk, 1963); Fred Kniffen, "American Cultural Geography and Folklife," in *American Folklife*, ed. Don Yoder (Austin, Tex., 1976), 51–70; and his "Louisiana House Types," *Annals of the Association of American Geographers* 26 (1936): 179–93.

8. Henry Glassie, *Irish Folk History: Texts from the North* (Philadelphia, 1982).

Chapter 9: A Community of Memory

1. "The conflict is deep in me," writes Eli Evans, "the Jew's involvement in history and his deep roots in the drama of man's struggle to understand deity and creation. But I respond to the Southerner's commitment to place, his loyalty to the land, to his own tortured history, to the strange bond beyond color that southern blacks and whites discover when they come to know one another." See his *The Provincials: A Personal History of Jews in the South* (New York, 1976), iv. See also Leonard Dinnerstein and Mary Dale Palsson, eds., *Jews in the South* (Baton Rouge, 1973); Melvin I. Urofsky and Nathan M. Kaganoff, eds., *"Turn to the South": Essays on Southern Jewry* (Charlottesville, 1978); and Myron Berman, *Richmond's Jewry, 1769–1976* (Charlottesville, 1978). Since publication of Irving Howe's monumental *World of Our Fathers*, the immigrant Jewish milieu of New York City during the late nineteenth and early twentieth centuries seemed to have become virtually synonymous, in some minds, with the American Jewish experience. Indeed, *How We Lived*, a massive collection of documents chronicling Jewish life in American during the same period, gives but two chapters to Jews outside of New York. See Irving Howe, *World of Our Fathers* (New York, 1976); and Irving Howe and Kenneth Libo, *How We Lived: A Documentary History of Immigrant Jews in America, 1880–1930* (New York, 1979). See also Allon Schoener, *Portal to America: The Lower East Side, 1870–1925* (New York, 1969); Moses Rischin, *The Promised City: New York's Jews, 1870–1914* (New York, 1970); Ronald Sanders, *The Downtown Jews* (New York, 1970); Richard L. Ehrlich, ed., *Immigrants in Industrial America, 1860–1920* (Charlottesville, 1977); Gary Goodman, *Choosing Sides* (New York, 1979); and Jeffrey S. Gurock, *When Harlem Was Jewish, 1870–1930* (New York, 1979). No depiction of American Jewish history can be complete without an understanding of the Jewish experience in the South.

2. America's 1790 census—its first—showed that the largest Jewish population in the country resided in South Carolina. The same was revealed by the 1800 census. See Ira Rosenswaike, "An Estimate and Analysis of the Jewish Population of the United States in 1790," *Publications of the American Jewish Historical Society* 30 (1960), reprinted in Abraham J. Karp, ed., *The Jewish Experience in America: Selected Studies from the Publications of the American Jewish Historical Society* (Waltham, Mass., 1969), vol. 1, 391–43; Ira Rosenswaike, "The Jewish Population of the United States as Estimated from the Census of 1820," in Karp, *Jewish Experience in America*, vol. 2, 9; Abram Vossen Goodman, "South Carolina from Shaftesbury to Salvador," in Dinnerstein and Palsson, *Jews in the South*, 29–46. The quote is on page 32. See also Dinnerstein and Palsson, *Jews in the South*, 26; Charles Reznikoff and Uriah Z. Engelman, *The Jews of Charleston* (Philadelphia, 1950); Jacob Rader Marcus, *Early American Jewry: The Jews of Pennsylvania and the South* (Philadelphia, 1953), 522–25; and James William Hagy, *"This Happy Land": The Jews of Colonial and Antebellum Charleston* (Tuscaloosa, 1993).

3. *South Carolina Gazette*, May 20, 1761; Barnet A. Elzas, *The Jews of South Carolina from the Earliest Times to the Present Day* (Philadelphia, 1905), 38–41, 241; Malcolm H. Stern, *First American Jewish Families: Six Hundred Genealogies, 1654–1877* (Waltham, Mass., 1979), 35, 205, 216; George C. Rogers Jr., *The History of Georgetown County, South Carolina* (Columbia, S.C., 1970), 167; Marcus, *Early American Jewry*, 266; Rosenswaike, "Estimate and Analysis," 400; idem, "Jewish Population of the United States," 10.

4. Marcus, *Early American Jewry*, 266, 421–22; Allan Tarshish, "The Economic Life of the American Jew in the Middle Nineteenth Century," in *Essays in American Jewish History* (Cincinnati, 1958), 278–83.

5. *Georgetown Gazette*, May 15, 1798–Dec. 28, 1800. See also Rosenswaike, "Jewish Population of the United States," 10; Stern, *First American Jewish Families*, 98, 139, 212, 216, 262, 276, 305; Elzas, *Jews of South Carolina*, 241–42; Rogers, *History of Georgetown County*, 221. In addition to the Abraham and Solomon Cohen families, the Jewish community in Georgetown included Mordecai Myers's sons Levi, Moses, Jacob, and Abraham, and their families, as well as the families of Nathan Hart, Levy Solomon, Isaac Moses, Jacob Woolf, Woolf Aronson, and Abraham Sasportas. Lizar Joseph, born in Mannheim, Germany, in 1762, was a partner with Levi Solomon in the auction and commission business as the new century dawned. A member of the Winyah Indigo Society, Joseph served as coroner of Georgetown in 1821 and was elected warden (councilman) in 1826. Lizar Joseph died in 1827 at the age of sixty-five. *Georgetown Gazette*, Apr. 10, 1799, and Apr. 9, 1800; Papers of the Winyah Indigo Society, Georgetown County Library. Lizar Joseph's birthplace and death date are recorded on his tombstone in the Hebrew Cemetery in Georgetown. See also Stern, *First American Jewish Families*, 139; Elzas, *Jews of South Carolina*, 142, 205, 242–43. The Hebrew community was enriched during the first quarter of the new century by the arrival in Georgetown of Aaron Lopez, Lewin Cohen, August Emsden, Maurice L. Henry, Solomon Myers, Henry and Joseph Joseph, and Israel, Sampson, Abraham, and Joseph Solomon, who became merchants, bankers, and active citizens of Georgetown. Aaron Lopez was elected a warden of Georgetown for three terms beginning in 1828 and served as intendant in 1836. Elzas (*Jews of South Carolina*, 132–40) compiled a directory of the Jews of South Carolina from 1800 to 1824, from the records of Beth Elohim in Charleston. According to Elzas the synagogue's records do not carefully distinguish among the names Solomon, Solomons, and Salomon. I have consistently written the name here as Solomon, following the current practice of that family in Georgetown. See Stern, *First American Jewish Families*, 84, 138–39, 176, 216, 259, 277. Lopez is indicated as intendant of Georgetown in 1836 by both Elzas (*Jews of South Carolina*, 194) and *For Love of a Rebel*, a publication of the Arthur Manigault Chapter, United Daughters of the Confederacy, in Georgetown (Charleston, 1964), 169. George Rogers, a careful professional historian, lists John Harrelson as intendant in 1836 (*History of Georgetown County*, 528).

6. *Georgetown Gazette*, June 5, 1798, Nov. 7, 1798, Feb. 20, 1799, Apr. 9, 1800, Dec. 13, 1800; *Statutes at Large of South Carolina*, vol. 8, 203; "Memorial of Sundry Inhabitants of Georgetown to the President of the Senate" (1785), South Caroliniana Library, University of South Carolina (hereafter SCL); Papers of the Winyah Indigo Society, Georgetown County Library; Stern, *First American Jewish Families*, 216; Elzas, *Jews of South Carolina*, 34, 106, 127–28, 242–43; Rogers, *History of Georgetown County*, 204.

7. *Georgetown Gazette*, May 15 and 22, 1798, Nov. 13, 1799, Dec. 28, 1800, May 2, 1801; *South Carolina and Georgia Almanac, 1794;* Papers of the Winyah Indigo Society; Elzas, *Jews of South Carolina*, 127, 143, 241–43; Rogers, *History of Georgetown County*, 528.

8. Archibald Henderson, *Washington's Southern Tour* (Boston, 1923), 125; Albert G. Mackey, *The History of Freemasonry in South Carolina* (Columbia, S.C., 1861), 226–27, 554; Elzas, *Jews of South Carolina*, 241; Rogers, *History of Georgetown County*, 218.

9. The Winyah Indigo Society, one of the oldest societies in South Carolina, included in its membership such prominent Georgetown Jews as Nathan Hart, Wolf Arsonson, Aaron Lopez, Solomon Joseph, Israel and Sampson Solomon, and Joseph and Samuel Sampson. Papers of the Winyah Indigo Society.

10. *Georgetown Gazette*, May 15, 1798, July 24, 1796, Feb. 20, 1799, Dec. 24, 1800; Papers of the Winyah Indigo Society; John Bolton O'Neill, *Biographical Sketches of the Bench and Bar of South Carolina*, 2 vols. (Charleston, 1859), vol. 2, 602. According to tombstone inscriptions in the Hebrew Cemetery in Georgetown, Jacob Myers married Miriam Etting of Lancaster, Pennsylvania, who died in 1808 at the age of twenty-one. See also Stern, *First American Jewish Families*, 216; Elzas, *Jews of South Carolina*, 128, 141, 242–43; Rogers, *History of Georgetown County*, 528.

11. Records of the Planters Club on Pee Dee, vol. 1, in James R. Sparkman Papers, SCL; Stern, *First American Jewish Families*, 35, 209; Elzas, *Jews of South Carolina*, 189; Rogers, *History of Georgetown County*, 195, 528. On the Gratz family, see Marcus, *Early American Jewry*, 422–23, and Stern, *First American Jewish Families*, 209. Miriam Gratz Moses, born in 1808, was the daughter of Solomon Moses and Rachel Gratz Moses. After Rachel's death in 1823, Miriam was reared by her aunt, Rebecca Gratz. Rebecca always regretted that her niece and her husband had been "confined to so small a community as Georgetown" and was certain that following their move to Savannah "he will feel as if his spirit was free to take a wider range among its peers and try its strength among more equal competiters [*sic*]." Joseph L. Blau and Salo W. Baron, eds., *The Jews of the United States, 1790–1840: A Documentary History* (New York, 1963), vol. 1, 227, 301. See also Saul Rubin, *Third to None: The Saga of Savannah Jewry* (Savannah, Ga., 1983).

12. John Ashe Alston to Richard Rush, Feb. 28, 1828, Records of the War Department, Record Group 94, National Archives; Stern, *First American Jewish Families*, 216; Elzas, *Jews of South Carolina*, 221; Blau and Baron, *The Jews of the United States*, vol. 1, 67, 301.

13. Bertram Wallace Korn, *American Jewry and the Civil War* (Philadelphia, 1951), chap. 2; *Winyah Intelligencer*, Feb. 8, Aug. 18, 1932; Election Returns, Georgetown District, legislative system, 1830–59, South Carolina Department of Archives and History; William W. Freehling, *Prelude to Civil War: The Nullification Controversy in South Carolina, 1816–1836* (New York, 1966); Chauncey S. Boucher, *The Nullification Controversy in South Carolina* (Chicago, 1916), 67, 78–79, 202–206; John Paul Ochenkowski, "The Origins of Nullification in South Carolina," *South Carolina Historical Magazine* 83 (1982): 138–39; *Proceedings of the States Rights and Free Trade Convention . . .* (Charleston, 1832), 3–4, 11; Morris Urman Schappes, ed., *A Documentary History of the Jews of the United States, 1654–1875*, rev. ed. (New York, 1952), 613.

14. Nathan Emanuel, for instance, owned four slaves in 1850—a single slave family. Benjamin Solomon, a sixty-year-old surveyor, owned only one slave, an eighteen-year-old mulatto female. But as the years passed there was a growing tendency toward slaveholding among Georgetown Jewry. For example, the families of Joseph and Samuel Sampson owned no slaves in 1850. By 1860, however, they had acquired them. U.S. Census, Slave Population Schedules, 1850 and 1860, National Archives; R. G. Dun Papers, Harvard Business School, 9b:110D; Rosenswaike, "Jewish Population of the United States," 18–19; Elzas, *Jews of South Carolina*, 241–43.

15. *Official Records of the War of the Rebellion*, Army, Series 1, vol. 14, 512–13; *For Love of a Rebel*, 23, 30–31, 33, 44, 169; Rod Gragg, "The Forgotten Front: A Military History of Georgetown County in the Civil War, 1861–1865," unpublished mss. in my possession, 10–26.

16. Sol Emanuel to Esther Alexander, in Sol Emanuel Scrapbook, presented to Miss Esther Alexander in 1868, SCL.

17. R. G. Dun Papers, 9b:128, 110R; Elzas, *Jews of South Carolina*, 205, 241–44; Rogers, *History of Georgetown County*, 221, 471–73; Thomas D. Clark, "The Post-Civil War Economy in the South," *American Jewish Historical Quarterly* 55 (1966): 427–29. The Sampsons were related to the Baruchs of Camden, S.C. See Bernard M. Baruch, *My Own Story* (New York, 1957).

18. Marcus Moses was described by the credit reporter for the R. G. Dun Company on the eve of the Civil War as a "Dutch Jew" who would "pay his debts promptly." The reporter cautioned that in his opinion, Moses—while "an active little fellow"—would "as soon think of investing money in the wildest speculation on foot as selling goods on time." R. G. Dun Papers, 9b:129, 10H.

19. In 1855 their firm, E. and H. Baum, was reported to have "no standing as business men in this community." R. G. Dun Papers, 9b:122, 123, 131, 110M. Baum's purchase of Willbrook is recorded in Deed Book E, Georgetown County Courthouse, 732–33. See also *Georgetown Times*, Aug. 19, 1965; Rogers, *History of Georgetown County*, 456–66.

20. R. G. Dun Papers, 9b:110N. Heiman Kaminski's holdings included the

Kaminski Hardware Company, the Taylor-Dickson Medical Dispensary, the Willow Bank Boat and Oar Company, and the Pee Dee Steamship Company. His partners in the *Linah C. Kaminski* were William L. Buck of Horry County and Capt. Stephen E. Woodbury. See *Georgetown Rice Milling Company, Georgetown, S.C.* (Charleston, 1880); J. C. Hemphill, *Men of Mark in South Carolina* (Washington, 1908), vol. 1, 202–3; *For Love of a Rebel*, 33; *Georgetown Times*, Aug. 19, 1965; Rogers, *History of Georgetown County*, 405, 465, 472.

21. Hemphill, *Men of Mark in South Carolina*, 1:202–3; David Duncan Wallace, *History of South Carolina* (New York, 1934), 4: 640; Rogers, *History of Georgetown County*, 472; U.S. Census, Mss. Population Schedules, 1850, 1860, 1870, 1880.

22. Minute Book, Georgetown Rifle Guards, SCL; Sol Emanuel, *An Historical Sketch of the Georgetown Rifle Guards . . .* ([Georgetown], 1909).

23. R. G. Dun Papers, 9b:128, 110R; Rogers, *History of Georgetown County*, 472, 529.

24. The 1866 indenture of Joseph and Samuel Sampson is detailed in Deed Book A, Georgetown County Courthouse, 54–87. The anonymous reporter for the R. G. Dun Company had already reported the weakness of the company prior to its bankruptcy. See R. G. Dun Papers, 9b:110F, 110U. But Sampson, described as a "man of good character & habits," was able to borrow enough money to establish a "small but safe business." A credit reporter for the R. G. Dun Company thought "he can pay a small amount promptly." By 1880 Sampson was sufficiently reestablished to become the Singer sewing machine agent in Georgetown.

25. The description of Ehrich is found in *Georgetown, South Carolina, As It Was, As It Is, As It Will Be* (Charleston, 1888). See also *Georgetown Rice Milling Company; Acts of the Legislature Relating to the Port and Harbor of Georgetown and Rules and Regulations Governing the Pilots of Said Port, 1886* (Charleston, 1887); and *Charter and Constitution of the Georgetown Building and Loan Association, Organized July 28, 1886* (Charleston, 1886). Bernard M. Baruch describes his cousin Joseph Sampson as a riverboat pilot in his *My Own Story*.

26. Alberta Morel Lachicotte, *Georgetown Rice Plantations* (Columbia, S.C., 1955), 9, 13–16; (Charleston) *News and Courier*, May 17, 1930.

27. A similar emphasis is challenged by Leonard Dinnerstein in a review of Myron Berman, *Richmond's Jewry, 1769–1976*, in *Journal of Southern History* 46 (1980): 461. Dinnerstein complains that the author "not only balances or goes over quickly any controversial or unpleasant experiences, but by doing so in effect distorts the Jewish past."

28. "Some Anti-Semitic Incidents in South Carolina," *Jewish Forum* 30 (1946): 19–20, 43–44, 66, 88, 104. For a comparative perspective, see Michael R. Marrus, *The Politics of Assimilation: A Study of the French Jewish Community at the Time of the Dreyfus Affair* (New York, 1971).

29. Charles P. Allston to Robert Lowndes, Jan. 8, 1894, Allston Family Papers, SCL.

30. R. G. Dun Papers, 9b:1oh.

31. Dinnerstein and Palsson, *Jews in the South*, 7, 21; Bertram Wallace Korn, "American Judaeophobia: Confederate Version," in Dinnerstein and Palsson, *Jews in the South*, 153–69; Leonard Dinnerstein, ed., *Anti-Semitism in the United States* (New York, 1971); Morton Borden, *Jews, Turks, and Infidels* (Chapel Hill, 1984), 36–50; and Howard N. Rabinowitz, "Nativism, Bigotry, and Anti-Semitism in the South," *American Jewish History* 77 (1988): 1–15. On the Leo Frank case, see Leonard Dinnerstein, *The Leo Frank Case* (New York, 1968); Louis Schmier, "'No Jew Can Murder': Memories of Tom Watson and the Lichtenstein Murder Case of 1901," *Georgia Historical Quarterly* 70 (1986): 433–55.

32. Rogers, *History of Georgetown County*, 472.

33. Harry Golden, "Jew and Gentile in the New South: Segregation at Sundown," *Commentary* 20 (1955): 403–4. See also his *Forgotten Pioneer* (Cleveland, 1963), 66–67; and his *A Little Girl Is Dead* (Cleveland, 1965), 226. See also Stephen J. Whitfield's wise and witty "Jews and Other Southerners: Counterpoint and Paradox," in Urofsky and Kaganoff, *"Turn to the South,"* 82–87.

34. See the insightful essay by Alfred Hero, "Southern Jews," in Dinnerstein and Pallson, *Jews in the South*, 217–50.

35. Evans, *Provincials*, 41–43. See also Seymour Martin Lipset and Earl Raab, *Jews and the New American Scene* (Cambridge, Mass., 1995); Dan V. Segre, *A Crisis of Identity: Israel and Zionism* (New York, 1980); Lionel Blue, *To Heaven with Scribes and Pharisees: The Jewish Path to God* (New York, 1967).

36. Charles E. Rosenberg, "History and Experience," introduction to *The Family in History*, ed. Charles E. Rosenberg·(Philadelphia, 1975), 1–11; Evans, *Provincials*, iv.

37. Interview with Judge Phil Ringel, Jacksonville, Fla., Nov. 22, 1980. See also Wyndham W. Malet, *An Errand to the South in the Summer of 1862* (London, 1863), 109–10; *For Love of a Rebel*, 168–69; *Georgetown Times*, Feb. 9, 1956; Thomas J. Tobias, "Joseph Tobias of Charles Town: 'Linguister,'" in Karp, *Jewish Experience in America*, vol. 1, 118; Rufus Learsi, *The Jews of America: A History* (Cleveland, 1954), 33; Evans, *Provincials*, 92. The absence of Jewish butchers in the manuscript federal census might seem to indicate nonobservance. The term *merchant*, however, likely subsumes a number of occupations, including butcher.

38. Ringel interview. See also Ruth Gruber Friedman, *The Passover Seder: Afikomen in Exile* (Philadelphia, 1980); J. B. Segal, *The Hebrew Passover from the Earliest Times to A.D. 70* (New York, 1963).

39. Ringel interview.

40. Ibid. See also Abram Vossen Goodman, *American Overture: Jewish Rights in Colonial Times* (Philadelphia, 1974), 176–92; Tobias, "Joseph Tobias of Charles Town," 114–19; Allan Tarshish, "The Charleston Organ Case," in Karp, *Jewish Experience in America*, vol. 2, 285–300.

41. Rischin, *The Promised City*, 95; Ehrlich, *Immigrants in Industrial America*, ix–

x; Gurock, *When Harlem Was Jewish;* Charles S. Liebman, "The Religion of American Jews," in *The Jew in American Society,* ed. Marshall Sklare (New York, 1974), 230; Thomas Kessner, *The Golden Door: Italian and Jewish Immigrant Mobility in New York City, 1880–1915* (New York, 1977). See also Barbara Kirshenblatt-Gimblett, "Traditional Storytelling in the Toronto Jewish Community: A Study in Performance and Creativity in an Immigrant Culture" (Ph.D. diss., Indiana University, 1972), 114–39.

42. Ringel interview.

43. Quoted in Yehuda Bauer, *The Holocaust in Historical Perspective* (Seattle, 1978), 44–45. The parable is associated with the Ba'al Shem Tov, the legendary founder of Hasidism. See Dan Ben-Amos and Jerome R. Mintz, trans. and eds., *In Praise of the Ba'al Shem Tov: The Earliest Collection of Legends about the Founder of Hasidism* (Bloomington, Ind., 1970), xv–xxx. See also Kirshenblatt-Gimblett, "Traditional Storytelling," 194–323.

Chapter 10: The Sounds of Southern Culture

1. Ulrich B. Phillips, "The Central Theme of Southern History," *American Historical Review* 34 (Oct. 1928): 30–43, reprinted in his *The Course of the South to Secession,* ed. E. Merton Coulter (New York, 1989), quote on page 152; George B. Tindall, "The Benighted South: Origins of a Modern Image," *Virginia Quarterly Review* 40 (Spring 1964): 281–94; Louis D. Rubin and James J. Kilpatrick, eds., *The Lasting South* (Chicago, 1957); David Smiley, "Quest for the Central Theme of Southern History," *South Atlantic Quarterly* 71 (Summer 1972): 307–25; C. Vann Woodward, *The Burden of Southern History* (Baton Rouge, 1960); Dan T. Carter, "From the Old South to the New: Another Look at the Theme of Change and Continuity," in *From the Old South to the New: Essays on the Transitional South,* ed. Walter J. Fraser Jr. and Winfred B. Moore Jr. (Westport, Conn., 1981), 34.

2. David M. Potter, "Enigma of the South," *Yale Review* 51 (1961): 142–51.

3. Mahalia Jackson (with Evan McLeod Wylie), *Movin' on Up* (New York, 1966), 32–33; Jules Victor Schwerin, *Got to Tell It: Mahalia Jackson, Queen of Gospel* (New York, 1992); Charles Joyner, *Folk Song in South Carolina* (Columbia, S.C., 1971), 62–94; idem, "A Single Southern Culture: Cultural Interaction in the Old South," in *Black and White: Cultural Interaction in the Antebellum South,* ed. Ted Ownby (Jackson, Miss., 1993), 3–22; See also Beverly Bush Patterson, *The Sound of the Dove: Singing in Appalachian Primitive Baptist Churches* (Urbana, 1995); *They All Sang Hallelujah: Plain-Folk Camp Meeting Religion, 1800–1845* (Knoxville, 1974); Buell E. Cobb Jr., *The Sacred Harp and Its Music* (Athens, Ga., 1978); Irving L. Sablosky, *American Music* (Chicago, 1969), 12–13, 36–45; H. Wiley Hitchcock, *Music in the United States: A Historical Introduction,* 2d ed. (Englewood Cliffs, N.J.), 7, 96–106; Gilbert Chase, *America's Music from the Pilgrims to the Present,* 2d ed., rev. (New York, 1966), 40, 41–52, 183–258; Bill C. Malone, *Country Music U.S.A.* 2d ed., rev. (Austin, 1985), 10–

14, 22. Malone details the influence of gospel music in such country singers as Kitty Wells and Wilma Lee Cooper (219), Red Foley (206), Jimmie Davis (224), the Statler Brothers (384–85), Hank Williams (239–41), and Elvis Presley (349). Examples could be picked virtually at random.

4. Roebuck Staples, quoted in Robert Palmer, *Deep Blues* (New York, 1981), 44; Booker T. Johnson ("Bukka") White, quoted in David Evans, *Big Road Blues: Tradition and Creativity in the Folk Blues* (Berkeley, 1982), 43; James Weldon Johnson mss., Beineke Library, Yale University. See also Dorothy Scarborough, "The 'Blues' as Folksongs," *Publications of the Texas Folklore Society* 2 (1917): 52–66; Guy B. Johnson, "Double Meaning in the Popular Negro Blues," *Journal of Abnormal and Social Psychology* 22 (1927): 12–20; Howard Odum, *Rainbow Round My Shoulder* (Indianapolis, 1938); W. C. Handy, *Father of the Blues: An Autobiography*, ed. Arna Bontemps (New York, 1942), 6; Samuel Charters, *The Country Blues* (New York, 1959); Charles Joyner, "Drink Small's Blues," *Egghead* 1 (1961): 4–5, 19; Paul Oliver, *Blues Fell This Morning: The Meaning of the Blues* (New York, 1961); Paul Oliver, *Conversation with the Blues* (London, 1965), 27, 45; Samuel Charters, *The Bluesmen: The Story and the Music of the Men Who Made the Blues* (New York, 1967), 52, 100–113; Paul Oliver, *The Story of the Blues* (Philadelphia, 1969); John Fahey, *Charley Patton* (London, 1970), 18; Paul Oliver, *Savannah Syncopators* (New York, 1970); Bruce Bastin, *Cryin' for the Carolines* (London, 1971); David Evans, *Tommy Johnson* (London, 1971); Jeff Todd Titon, *Early Downhome Blues: A Musical and Cultural Analysis* (Urbana, 1975; 2d ed., Chapel Hill, 1994); Lawrence W. Levine, *Black Culture and Black Consciousness: Afro-American Folk Thought from Slavery to Freedom* (New York, 1977), 217–38; William R. Ferris, *Blues from the Delta* (Garden City, N.Y., 1979); Cecilia Conway, *African Banjo Echoes in Appalachia: A Study of Folk Traditions* (Knoxville, 1995); Robert Palmer, *Deep Blues* (New York, 1981); Evans, *Big Road Blues*; Thomas G. Burton, *Tom Ashley, Sam McGee, Bukka White, Tennessee Traditional Singers* (Knoxville, 1981); Stephen Calt, *King of the Delta Blues: The Life and Music of Charley Patton* (Newton, N.J., 1988); Bruce Bastin, *Red River Blues: The Blues Tradition in the Southeast* (Urbana, 1986); James C. Cobb, *The Most Southern Place on Earth: The Mississippi Delta and the Roots of Regional Identity* (New York, 1992), 280–81; and Alan Lomax, *The Land Where the Blues Began* (New York, 1993). See also the following Library of Congress recordings: Benjamin A. Botkin, ed., *Negro Work Songs and Calls*, AAFS L8; Alan Lomax, ed., *Afro-American Spirituals, Work Songs, and Ballads*, AAFS L3; Marshall Stearns, ed., *Negro Blues and Hollers*, AAFS L59; Alan Lomax, ed., *Afro-American Blues and Game Songs*, AAFS L4.

5. Richard Wright, foreword to Paul Oliver, *Blues Fell This Morning* (Cambridge, 1990), xiii; Robert Johnson, "Hellhound on My Trail," in Charters, *Bluesmen*, 91; Alberta Hunter (b. 1897), quoted in Nat Shapiro and Nat Hentoff, *Hear Me Talkin' to Ya: The Story of Jazz as Told by the Men Who Made It* (New York, 1955), 246–471; Danny Barker (b. 1909), ibid., 243. Dizzy Gillespie made a similar point about jazz, insisting that "there is a parallel with jazz and religion." He is quoted in Neil Le-

onard, *Jazz: Myth and Religion* (New York, 1987), 41–42. On the "sorrow songs" see W. E. B. Du Bois, *The Souls of Black Folk* (Chicago, 1903), 252–56. See also James H. Cone, *The Spirituals and the Blues: An Interpretation* (New York, 1972), 112; Evans, *Big Road Blues*, 40; Pete Welding, "The Rise of Folk-Blues," *Down Beat*, Sept. 14, 1961, 14–17. Blues lyrics often focus on such knotty theological problems as the relationship between the sacred and the profane, good and evil, human beings and the spirit world, all within an essentially animistic cosmology (an expression of the blues' continuing connection to the earliest African-American creole culture and its religious expression—a fusion of African animism and Protestant Christianity). See Jon Michael Spencer, *Blues and Evil* (Knoxville, 1993).

6. Ralph Ellison, *Shadow and Act* (New York, 1964), 78–79; Bertha "Chippie" Hill (1905–50), "Two Nineteen Train" (1926), quoted in Levine, *Black Culture and Black Consciousness*, 230; W. C. Handy, "The Heart of the Blues," *Etude Music Magazine*, Mar. 1940, 152. On rebellion in the blues, see esp. William Barlow, *"Looking Up at Down": The Emergence of Blues Culture* (Philadelphia, 1989), 325–29. See also W. C. Handy, *Father of the Blues* (New York, 1970); Cobb, *Most Southern Place on Earth*, 1992), 276–305; Bill C. Malone, *Southern Music American Music* (Lexington, Ken., 1979), 41–51; Houston A. Baker, *Blues Ideology and Afro-American Literature: A Vernacular Theory* (Chicago, 1984); and Henry Louis Gates Jr., *The Signifying Monkey: A Vernacular Theory of African-American Literature* (New York, 1988).

7. Angela Davis, *Blues Legacies and Black Feminism: Gertrude "Ma" Rainey, Bessie Smith, and Billie Holiday* (New York, 1998); Alberta Hunter, in Shapiro and Hentoff, *Hear Me Talkin' to Ya*, 247; Buster Bailey, ibid., 244; Zutty Singleton, ibid., 244. On the musical form of the blues, see Evans, *Big Road Blues*; and Titon, *Early Downhome Blues*. On the literary qualities of the blues, see Oliver, *Blues Fell This Morning*; Baker, *Blues Ideology*; and Gates, *Signifying Monkey*. See also Derrick Stewart-Baxter, *Ma Rainey and the Classic Blues Singers* (New York, 1970); Sandra Lieb, *Mother of the Blues: A Study of Ma Rainey* (Amherst, 1981); Frank C. Taylor, *Alberta Hunter: A Study in Blues* (New York, 1987); Elaine Feldstein, *Bessie Smith* (London, 1985); Chris Albertson, *Bessie* (New York, 1972); Carmen Moore, *Angel Child: The Story of Bessie Smith* (New York, 1969); Paul Oliver, *Bessie Smith* (London, 1959); Derrick Stewart-Baxter, *Ma Rainey and the Classic Blues Singers* (New York, 1970); Daphne Harrison, *Black Pearls: Blues Queens of the 1920s* (New Brunswick, N.J., 1988); Linda Dahl, *Stormy Weather: The Music and Lives of a Century of Jazzwomen* (New York, 1984); Perry Bradford, *Born with the Blues* (Westport, Conn., 1973).

8. Rupert Hughes, "A Eulogy of Rag-Time," *Musical Record* (Boston) 447 (Apr. 1, 1899): 157–59; Rudi Blesh and Harriet Janis, *They All Played Ragtime*, 4th ed. (New York, 1971); William J. Schaefer and Johannes Riedel, *The Art of Ragtime* (Baton Rouge, 1973), 5; Susan Curtis, *Dancing to a Black Man's Tune: A Life of Scott Joplin* (Columbia, Mo., 1994); Edward A. Berlin, *Ragtime: A Musical and Cultural History* (Berkeley, 1980); idem, *King of Ragtime: Scott Joplin and His Era* (New York, 1977); Reid Badger, *A Life in Ragtime: A Biography of James Reese Europe* (New York, 1985);

On African-American piano music before ragtime, see Geneva H. Southall, *Blind Tom: The Post–Civil War Enslavement of a Black Musical Genius* (Minneapolis, 1979).

9. Henry A. Kmen, *Music in New Orleans: The Formative Years, 1791–1841* (Baton Rouge, 1977); Samuel Charters, *New Orleans, 1855–1963* (New York, 1964); Gunther Schuller, *Early Jazz: Its Roots and Musical Development* (New York, 1968); Edmund Souchon, *New Orleans Jazz: A Family Album* (Baton Rouge, 1967); Jack V. Buerkle and Danny Barker, *Bourbon Street Black: The New Orleans Black Jazzmen* (New York, 1973); Tom Bethell, *George Lewis: A Jazzman from New Orleans* (Berkeley, 1977).

10. Samuel Charters, *The Legacy of the Blues: Lives of Twelve Great Bluesmen* (New York, 1977), 85; Le Roi Jones [Imamu Amiri Baraka], *Blues People* (New York, 1963), 78–79; Barlow, *"Looking Up at Down,"* 26–32; Oliver, *Blues Fell This Morning;* and Charters, *New Orleans, 1855–1963.*

11. Louis Armstrong, in Shapiro and Hentoff, *Hear Me Talkin' to Ya,* 14; Barney Bigard and Barry Martyn, *With Louis and the Duke: The Autobiography of a Jazz Clarinetist* (New York, 1986), 7; George Lewis, interviewed by Richard B. Allen, New Orleans, Nov. 14, 1958, reel 4, Hogan Jazz Archive, Tulane University; Papa Jack Laine, interviewed by Richard B. Allen, New Orleans, Mar 26, 1957, reel 2, Apr. 25, 1964, reel 2, Hogan Jazz Archive, Tulane University; D. James LaRocca Collection, file 2, Hogan Jazz Archive, Tulane University. See also Bethell, *George Lewis: A Jazzman from New Orleans;* Ann Fairborn, *Call Him George* (New York, 1969); William J. Schafer, *Brass Bands and New Orleans Jazz* (Baton Rouge, 1977); Henry A. Kmen, "The Music of New Orleans," in *The Past as Prelude: New Orleans, 1718–1968,* ed. Hodding Carter Jr. (New Orleans, 1968), 231; Kmen, *Music in New Orleans,* 202–5.

12. William Geary "Bunk" Johnson to Frederic Ramsey Jr., quoted in Gilbert Chase, *America's Music from the Pilgrims to the Present,* 2d. ed., rev. (New York, 1966), 468; Louis Armstrong, quoted in Hugues Panassie, *The Real Jazz,* rev. and enlarged ed. (London, 1967), 77; Danny Barker, in Shapiro and Hentoff, *Hear Me Talkin' to Ya,* 38; Donald M. Marquis, *In Search of Buddy Bolden: First Man of Jazz* (Baton Rouge, 1978).

13. Thomas "Mutt" Carey, in Shapiro and Hentoff, *Hear Me Talkin' to Ya,* 45; Ferdinand Joseph ("Jelly Roll" Morton) La Menthe, in Alan Lomax, *Mister Jelly Roll,* 2d ed. (Berkeley, 1973), 125–26, 154; John Alexander ("Johnny") St. Cyr, quoted in Lomax, *Mister Jelly Roll,* 154n; Dan Morgenstern, "The Trumpet in Jazz," *Metronome,* Oct. 1961, 21; Chase, *America's Music,* 468.

14. Louis Armstrong, "Scanning the History of Jazz," *Jazz Review* 3 (July 1960): 7–8; Edmund Souchon II, "King Oliver: A Very Personal Memoir," *Jazz Review* 3 (May 1960): 8; idem, *New Orleans Jazz: A Family Album* (Baton Rouge, 1967); Hugues Panassie, "Louis Armstrong: His Records, His Influence," *Metronome,* Oct. 1961, 8; Lomax, *Mister Jelly Roll,* 154; Morgenstern, "Trumpet in Jazz," 21; Martin Williams, *Jazz Masters of New Orleans* (New York, 1967); Marshall W. Stearns, *The Story of Jazz* (New York, 1956), 160.

15. Louis Armstrong, in Shapiro and Hentoff, *Hear Me Talkin' to Ya*, 43; Armstrong, "Scanning the History of Jazz," 8. Beginning with its red-light origins, the jazz record producer Orrin Keepnews points out, jazz has "always had to struggle under the weight of a social stigma" often associated with what he denotes as "drunkenness, bawdiness, and other forms of immorality." See Keepnews, *The View from Within: Jazz Writings, 1948–1987* (New York, 1987), 36. But as Martin Williams notes, "anyone who thinks that jazz was born in a whore-house ought to be made aware of just whom he is insulting: the uptown Negro community, the downtown colored Creole community, and a segment of the white community in New Orleans." See his *Jazz in Its Time* (New York, 1989), 27.

16. George Vitelle (Papa Jack) Laine, interviewed by Richard B. Allen, New Orleans, Apr. 24, 1964, reel 1, Jan. 25, 1959, reel 2, Hogan Jazz Archive, Tulane University; Jelly Roll Morton, in Lomax, *Mister Jelly Roll*, 103. See also Arnold Loyacano, in Shapiro and Hentoff, *Hear Me Talkin' to Ya*, 58; Harry O. Brunn, *The Story of the Original Dixieland Jazz Band* (Baton Rouge, 1960).

17. Richard B. Allen, interview with Steve Brown, Apr. 22, 1958, reel 4, Hogan Jazz Archive, Tulane University; Stearns, *Story of Jazz*, 117; Leonard Feather, *The Book of Jazz* (New York, 1957), 155. A younger generation of New Orleans white musicians, such as George Girard, Pete Fountain, and the brothers Frank and Fred Assunto, frequented a place named Manny's Tavern in order to sit in with such black musicians as George Lewis. George Lewis, interviewed by Richard B. Allen, New Orleans, Jan. 25, 1960, reel 4, Hogan Jazz Archives, Tulane University.

18. Joseph L. Morrison, *Josephus Daniels: The Small-d Democrat* (Chapel Hill, 1966), 94–95; Lomax, *Mister Jelly Roll*, 179; Stearns, *Story of Jazz*, 112–13, 117; St. Clair Drake and Horace R. Cayton, *Black Metropolis: A Study of Negro Life in a Northern City* (Chicago, 1945, 1993); Allan H. Spear, *Black Chicago: The Masking of a Negro Ghetto, 1890–1920* (Chicago, 1967), 228.

19. Preston Jackson, in Shapiro and Hentoff, *Hear Me Talkin' to Ya*, 42; Brunn, *Story of the Original Dixieland Jazz Band; Schafer, *Brass Bands and New Orleans Jazz;* Jones, *Blues People*, 13, 100, 148–49. See also Andre Hodier, *Jazz: Its Evolution and Essence*, trans. David Noakes (New York, 1956), 22–23; Feather, *Book of Jazz*, 155; Stearns, *Story of Jazz*, 112–13. Although some white trumpeters, such as Bix Beiderbecke, learned to play jazz from the recordings of LaRocca and the ODJB without ever having heard black musicians, they were nevertheless indebted to such African-American musicians as King Oliver who had influenced LaRocca. "Though the legitimacy of its deviation can in no way be questioned," Amiri Baraka insists, "the fact that it is a deviation must be acknowledged." Perhaps *derivation* might have been a better word choice. Otherwise, it is unclear what Baraka could mean by "the legitimacy of its deviation." Nevertheless, his main point is sound: however legitimate its expression by white musicians may or may not be in any given case, jazz itself owes a profound debt to African-American music and to African-American culture. The fact that the debt was acknowledged by

serious white musicians (including LaRocca before the bitterness of age and neglect beset him) helped to elevate the recognition of African-American culture and society to a higher plane than it had ever previously known. See Jones, *Blues People*, 151.

20. Paul Mares, in Shapiro and Hentoff, *Hear Me Talkin' to Ya*, 123–24; Steve Brown interview.

21. Eric Hobsbawm (writing under the pen name Francis Newton), *The Jazz Scene* (Harmondsworth, Eng., 1961), 41.

22. Louis Armstrong, in Shapiro and Hentoff, *Hear Me Talkin' to Ya*, 103; Armstrong, "Scanning the History of Jazz," 8; Kid Ory, in Shapiro and Hentoff, *Hear Me Talkin' to Ya*, 48; Lomax, *Mister Jelly Roll*, 181; Larry Gushee, review of *Louis Armstrong 1923: With King Oliver's Creole Jazz Band* (Riverside RLP 12–122), *The Jazz Review* 1 (Sept. 1958): 36–37. See also Louis Goffin, *Horn of Plenty: The Story of Louis Armstrong*, trans. James F. Bezou (Westport, Conn., 1978); Hugues Panassie, *Louis Armstrong* (New York, 1979); Laurence Bergreen, *Louis Armstrong: An Extravagant Life* (New York, 1997); Louis Armstrong, *Swing That Music* (London, 1936); Bigard and Martyn, *With Louis and the Duke;* Morgenstern, "Trumpet in Jazz," 21.

23. Hoagy Carmichael, *The Stardust Road* (New York, 1946), 53; Eddie Condon, *We Called It Music* (New York, 1947), 107. Lawrence W. Levine uses the conversion experience metaphor in "Jazz and American Culture," in his *The Unpredictable Past: Explorations in American Cultural History* (New York, 1993), 181. See also Burton W. Paretti, *The Creation of Jazz: Music, Race, and Culture in Urban America* (Urbana, 1992), 53; Jones, *Blues People*, 147.

24. Steve Brown interview; George Lewis, interviewed by Richard B. Allen, New Orleans, Jan. 25, 1960, reel 4, Hogan Jazz Archive, Tulane University.

25. Houston A. Baker Jr., *Modernism and the Harlem Renaissance* (Chicago, 1987); Paul F. Berliner, *Thinking in Jazz: The Infinite Art of Improvisation* (Chicago, 1994); Jones, *Blues People*, 155.

26. Frank Buchmann-Moller, *You Just Fight for Your Life: The Story of Lester Young* (New York, 1990); Luc Delannoy, *Pres: The Story of Lester Young* (Fayetteville, Ark., 1993); Lewis Porter, ed., *A Lester Young Reader* (Washington, D.C., 1991); Charles Edward Smith, "Jack Teagarden," in Robert Gottlieb, ed., *Reading Jazz: A Gathering of Autobiography, Reportage, and Criticism from 1919 to Now* (New York, 1996), 361–76; Martin Williams, "Thoughts on Jazz Trombone," *Down Beat*, Jan. 18, 1962, 26; Gunther Schuller, *The Swing Era: The Development of Jazz, 1930–1945* (New York, 1989), 561–62; Lee Konitz, in Shapiro and Hentoff, *Hear Me Talkin' to Ya*, 310–11; Raymond Horricks, *Dizzy Gillespie and the Bebop Revolution* (New York, 1984). See also Jones, *Blues People*, 158–60, 183, 193; Ross Russell, "The Parent Style and Lester Young," in *The Art of Jazz: Essays on the Nature and Development of Jazz*, ed. Martin Williams (New York, 1960), 210; Raymond Horricks, *Count Basie and His Orchestra, Its Music and Its Musicians* (New York, 1957); Stanley Dance, *The World of Count Basie* (New York, 1980).

27. Leslie Gourse, *Straight, No Chaser: The Life and Genius of Thelonious Monk* (New York, 1997), 1–3, 19–31; Scott DeVeaux, *The Birth of Bebop: A Social and Musical History* (Berkeley, 1997), 199–201, 219–27, 437; Whitney Balliett, *Barney, Bradley, and Max: Sixteen Portraits in Jazz* (New York, 1989), 183–85; Nat Hentoff, *The Jazz Life* (New York, 1961), 195; William W. Savage Jr., *Singing Cowboys and All That Jazz: A Short History of Popular Music in Oklahoma* (Norman, 1983), 48–52; Dizzy Gillespie, *To Be or Not to Bop* (Garden City, N.J., 1979); Charles Joyner, conversations with Dizzy Gillespie, July 17, 1960, Baltimore, Md., Apr. 3, 1968, Laurinburg, N.C., Feb. 10, 1987, Oxford, Miss.

28. Milt Hinton, quoted in Shapiro and Hentoff, *Hear Me Talkin' to Ya*, 343, 337; Dizzy Gillespie, foreword to Feather, *Book of Jazz*, 6; Dizzy Gillespie, in Shapiro and Hentoff, *Hear Me Talkin' to Ya*, 337; DeVeaux, *Birth of Bebop*, 167–88, 225–27; Horricks, *Dizzy Gillespie;* Joachime Berendt, *O Jazz: do rag ao rock* (Sao Paulo, 1987), 84.

29. Thelonious Monk to Mary Lou Williams, quoted in Shapiro and Hentoff, *Hear Me Talkin' to Ya*, 341; Dizzy Gillespie, quoted in Stearns, *Story of Jazz*, 157; Dizzy Gillespie, quoted in Shapiro and Hentoff, *Hear Me Talkin' to Ya*, 337; Kenny Clarke, quoted, ibid., 337–38; Dave Tough, quoted in Stearns, *Story of Jazz*, 159; Joyner, Gillespie interviews, July 17, 1960, Feb. 10, 1987; Gourse, *Straight, No Chaser*, 19–31; Martin Williams, "Thelonious Monk: Arrival without Departure," *Saturday Review*, Apr. 13, 1963, 32–33; Horricks, *Dizzy Gillespie*, 18, 25–27; Jones, *Black Music*, 22–23.

30. Dizzy Gillespie, quoted in W. Royal Stokes, *The Jazz Scene: An Informal History from New Orleans to 1990* (New York, 1991), 64; Hodier, *Jazz*, 103; Jones, *Black Music*, 199; Williams "Thelonious Monk," 32; Horricks, *Dizzy Gillespie*, 21.

31. Bill C. Malone, *Singing Cowboys and Musical Mountaineers: Southern Culture and the Roots of Country Music* (Athens, Ga., 1994), esp. 69–74; Nat Hentoff, *Listen to the Stories* (New York, 1995); Cecilia Tichi, *High Lonesome: The American Culture of Country Music* (Chapel Hill, 1994); Melton A. McLaurin and Richard A. Peterson, eds. *You Wrote My Life: Lyrical Themes in Country Music*, Cultural Perspectives on the American South, vol. 6 (Philadelphia, 1992). The Faulkner quote is from his Nobel Prize acceptance speech, published in his *Essays, Speeches, and Public Letters*, ed. James B. Meriwether (New York, 1966), 119–21.

32. Malone, *Country Music U.S.A.*, 77–91; Tony Russell, *Blacks, Whites, and Blues* (New York, 1970), 59–69; Richard A. Peterson and Russell Davis, "The Fertile Crescent of Country Music," *Journal of Country Music* 6, no. 1 (Spring 1975): 19–25.

33. Nolan Porterfield, *Jimmie Rodgers: The Life and Times of America's Blue Yodeler* (Urbana, 1979); Mike Paris, *Jimmie the Kid: The Life of Jimmie Rodgers* (New York, 1977); Joyner, "Single Southern Culture," 4–5. See also D. K. Wilgus, "An Introduction to the Study of Hillbilly Music," *Journal of American Folklore* 78 (1965): 195–203; L. Mayne Smith, "An Introduction to Bluegrass," *Journal of American Folklore*

78 (1965): 246–56; Archie Green, "Hillbilly Music: Source and Symbol," *Journal of American Folklore* 78 (1965): 204–18; Ed Kahn, "Hillbilly Music: Source and Resource," *Journal of American Folklore* 78 (1965): 257–66; John Cohen, "The Folk Music Interchange: Negro and White," *Sing Out!* 14 (Jan. 1965): 42–49. Some have contended that the yodel in country music represents a borrowing from black singers. There is some musical evidence in support of the contention. Certainly sudden leaps into falsetto are characteristic of African-American musical style, especially in the field hollers. But comparison of the actual performance of country yodelers with such African-American changes of register suggests otherwise.

34. Charles K. Wolfe, "Ralph Peer at Work: The Victor 1927 Bristol Sessions," *Old Time Music* 5 (Summer 1972): 10–15; Ralph Peer, "Discovery of the First Hillbilly Great," *Billboard* 65 (May 16, 1953): 20; Ivan M. Tribe, *The Stonemans: An Appalachian Family and the Music That Shaped Their Lives* (Urbana, 1993), 57–62.

35. Savage, *Singing Cowboys and All That Jazz*, 13–15; William Ivey, "The Legacy of Bob Wills," liner notes to *The Bob Wills Anthology*, Historic Country Music Reissues, Columbia LP PG32416 (1973); Charles R. Townsend, *San Antonio Rose: The Life and Music of Bob Wills* (Urbana, 1976); idem, *From Folk to Popular Song to Folklore: The Story of Bob Wills' "San Antonio Rose"* (Dallas, 1985); idem, "Bob Wills, Fiddler," *Devil's Box* 16, no. 2 (1982): 16–22; Ruth Sheldon Knowles, *Bob Wills: Hubbin' It* (Nashville, 1995), originally published as *Hubbin' It: The Life of Bob Wills* (Kingsport, Tenn., 1938). See also Gary Ginell, with Roy Lee Brown, *Milton Brown and the Founding of Western Swing* (Urbana, 1994).

36. Monroe is quoted in Russell, *Blacks, Whites, and Blues*, 100; Charles Joyner, conversation with Mother Maybelle Carter, Concord, N.C., Aug. 1964; Malone, *Country Music U.S.A.*, 324, 67, 104, 105, 240; Russell, *Blacks, Whites, and Blues*, 41; Ed Kahn, "The Carter Family: A Reflection of Changes in Society" (Ph.D. diss., University of California, Los Angeles, 1970); June Carter, "I Remember the Carter Family," *Sing Out!* 17, no. 3 (June–July 1967): 6–11; Archie Green, "The Carter Family's 'Coal Miner's Blues,'" *Southern Folklore Quarterly* 25, no. 4 (Dec. 1961): 226–37; Neil V. Rosenberg, *Bluegrass: A History* (Urbana, 1985); Charles K. Wolfe and Neil V. Rosenberg, *Bluegrass 1950–1958: Bill Monroe* (Vollersode, Germ., 1989); Roger M. Williams, *Sing a Sad Song: The Life of Hank Williams* (Urbana, 1981), 28–29. See also John Wright, *Traveling the High Way Home: Ralph Stanley and the World of Traditional Bluegrass Music* (Urbana, 1995); Joyner, *Folk Song in South Carolina*, 97; and Norm and Anne Cohen, "The Legendary Jimmie Tarlton," *Sing Out!* 16, no. 4 (Sept. 1966): 16–19.

37. Porterfield, *Jimmie Rodgers*, 160, 409; Malone, *Country Music U.S.A.*, 77–91, 108; Russell, *Blacks, Whites, and Blues*, 59–69, 81–85; David Evans, "Black Musicians Remember Jimmie Rodgers," *Old Time Music* 7 (1972–73): 12–14; Jason Berry, "The Sunshine Man: A Tale of Stardom, Political Heat, and Legendary Music," *Reckon* 1, no. 3 (Fall 1995): 48–57.

38. Malone, *Country Music U.S.A.*, 246–47.

39. Peter Guralnik, *Last Train to Memphis: The Rise of Elvis Presley* (Boston, 1994), 289; Joe Esposito and Elena Oumano, *Good Rockin' Tonight* (New York, 1994); Greil Marcus, *Mystery Train: Images of America in Rock'n'Roll*, rev. ed. (New York, 1982); Dave Marsh, *Elvis* (New York, 1982); Jac Tharpe, ed., *Elvis: Images and Fancies* (Jackson, 1979); Colin Escott and Martin Hawkins, *Catalyst: The Sun Records Story* (New York, 1975); Craig Morrison, *Go Cat Go! Rockabilly Music and Its Makers* (Urbana, 1996); Johnny Cash, *Cash: The Autobiography* (San Francisco, 1997); Alan Clayson, *Only the Lonely: Roy Orbison's Life and Legacy* (New York, 1989); Ellis Amburn, *Dark Star: The Story of Roy Orbison* (New York, 1990); Malone, *Country Music U.S.A.*, 247–48; Joyner, "Single Southern Culture," 5.

40. Malone, *Country Music U.S.A.*, 313–14; David C. Morton with Charles K. Wolfe, *DeFord Bailey: A Black Star in Early Country Music* (Knoxville, 1992); Frye Gaillard, "An Opry Star Shines On," *Country Music*, Mar. 1979, 38; idem, "Sour Notes at the Grand Ole Opry," *Southern Voices*, May–June 1974 (no pagination); Charles Joyner, conversation with DeFord Bailey, Apr. 1966, Nashville, Tenn.; "DeFord Bailey Comes Home to the Opry," *Nashville Tennessean*, Dec. 16, 1974. See also Charlie Burton, "Charley Pride," *Rolling Stone* 83 (Mar. 1971): 102–5, 60, 66.

41. E. P. Thompson, "Time, Work-Discipline, and Industrial Capitalism," *Past and Present* 38 (1967): 80.

Chapter 11: Sweet Music

Part of the data for this essay is drawn from fieldwork in western North Carolina and eastern Tennessee, 1964–66, 1972–74.

1. Charles Joyner, "Dulcimer," *Encyclopedia of Southern Culture*, ed. Charles Reagan Wilson and William R. Ferris (Chapel Hill, 1989), 1055.

2. See Ronald Eller, *Miners, Millhands and Mountaineers: Industrialization of the Appalachian South, 1880–1930* (Knoxville, 1982).

3. On the 1960s folk revival see Neil V. Rosenberg, ed., *Transforming Tradition: Folk Music Revivals Examined* (Urbana, 1993); Jean Ritchie's *Singing Family of the Cumberlands* (New York, 1955) is a "folk-autobiography" by the educated "least-un" of a Kentucky mountain family. On Frank Proffitt see Frank M. Warner, *Folk Songs and Ballads of the Eastern Seaboard: From a Collector's Notebook* (Macon, Ga., 1963); Charles Joyner, "The Craftsmanship of Frank Proffitt: Tradition and the Individual Talent in Folklore," *Tennessee Folklore Society Bulletin* 32 (1966): 1–5; and Anne Warner, *Traditional American Folk Songs from the Anne and Frank Warner Collection* (Syracuse, 1984), 251–61.

4. The number of dulcimer instruction books is staggering. The following are but a few: A. W. Jeffreys, *Tuning and Playing the Appalachian Dulcimer* (Staunton, Va., 1964); Len and Sue MacEachron, *Playing the Dulcimer by Ear and Other Easy Ways* (Minneapolis, 1970); Lynn McSpadden, *Four and Twenty Songs for the Moun-*

tain Dulcimer (Mountain View, Ark., 1970); Odell Scott, "The Appalachian Dulcimer," *Festival of American Folklife 1968*, program booklet (Washington, 1968); John Pearse, *The Dulcimer Book* (London, 1970) and *Teach Yourself the Appalachian Dulcimer* (London, 1968); John F. Putnam, *The Plucked Dulcimer of the Southern Mountains* (Berea, Ky., 1961); Jean Ritchie, *The Dulcimer Book* (New York, 1963); Martha Schecter, *Dulcimer Tuning* (Cambridge, Mass., 1970); Ralph Lee Smith, "Some Pointers for Beginning Dulcimer Players," *Sing Out!* 20 (Nov.–Dec. 1970): 6–9; Margaret Witners, *How to Play the Dulcimer* (Boston, 1963); Lorraine Lee, *The Magic Dulcimer* (Brighton, Mass.), 1983.

5. Robert Redfield, *Peasant Society and Culture* (Chicago, 1956), 60–66; Roger D. Abrahams and George Foss, *Anglo-American Folksong Style* (Englewood Cliffs, N.J., 1968), 10–11, 15. See also George C. Foster, "What Is Folk Culture?" *American Anthropologist* 55 (1953): 159–73; Sidney W. Mintz, "The Folk-Urban Continuum and the Rural Proletarian Community," *American Journal of Sociology* 59 (1953–54): 136–43; and Henry H. Glassie, "Folk Art," in *Folklore and Folklife: An Introduction,* ed. Richard M. Dorson (Chicago, 1972), 259–60, 272.

6. I am indebted to Dell Hymes's teaching for this approach, derived from sociolinguistics. See especially his *Foundations in Sociolinguistics: An Ethnographic Approach* (Philadelphia, 1974), 3–66.

7. R. Gerald Alvey, *Dulcimer Maker: The Craft of Homer Ledford* (Lexington, Ky., 1984), 134.

8. Ibid., 9–13, 123–24.

9. Ibid., 10–12, 31, 123.

10. Ibid., 10–13.

11. Ibid., 13–16, 30–31.

12. Ibid., 12, 16–19.

13. Ibid., 21.

14. Ibid., 21–23, 36–38.

15. Ibid., 38–48.

16. Ibid., 34–35, 44.

17. Ibid., 42, 46, 50, 113.

18. The German folklorist Hermann Bausinger notes that the infusion of technology "creates not only a new world of objects, but also new social and spiritual realities," accompanied by "transformations which are different for each individual cultural good." See his *Folk Culture in a World of Technology*, trans. Elke Dettmer (Bloomington, Ind., 1990), 32, 47.

19. Unless otherwise attributed, all quotations from Stanley Hicks, Edd Presnell, Jim Sams, and B. F. Robison come from interviews I conducted in the early 1970s.

20. Although he could neither read nor write, Roby Hicks not only made dulcimers, banjos, and fiddles, but also barrels, wagon wheels, churns, tables and chairs, and kitchen utensils. He even made his own tools. Anne Warner described

one of Roby Hicks's fiddles: "The bottom and sides were one piece of wood, hollowed like a dug-out canoe, with the top nailed on. It is beautiful craftsmanship, and it plays with a tone rather like a hoarse viola." See her *Traditional American Folk Songs*, 105. See also Robert Isbell, *The Last Chivaree: The Hicks Family of Beech Mountain* (Chapel Hill, 1996), 1–26; and John Evans, note booklet for the LP recording *Stanley Hicks/Live* (Dallas, Tex., 1983). The album was issued on the Moonshine label.

21. The Brown-Hudson Folklore Award citation to Edd Presnell is published in *North Carolina Folklore Journal* 23 (1975): 21–22. The award is named for two distinguished North Carolina folksong collectors, Frank C. Brown of Duke and Arthur Palmer Hudson of the University of North Carolina at Chapel Hill.

22. Stanley Hicks and Edd Presnell essentially may have received patterns from the same source. Edd Presnell's father-in-law was Benjamin Hicks, whose brother Roby was Stanley's father. Nathan Hicks, Benjamin's son, was the father-in-law of Frank Proffitt. See Warner, *Traditional American Folk Songs*, 205, 9.

23. Note Walter Benjamin's observation that "the uniqueness of a work of art is inseparable from its being imbedded in the fabric of tradition," in his *Illuminations*, trans. Harry Zohn (New York, 1968), 223.

24. For varying opinions on the origins of the plucked dulcimer see Charles Seeger, "The Appalachian Dulcimer," *Journal of American Folklore* 71 (1938): 40–51; Charles Faulkner Bryan, "America's Folk Instrument: The Appalachian Dulcimer," *Tennessee Folklore Society Bulletin* 18 (1952): 1–5; idem, "Appalachian Mountain Dulcimer Enigma," *Tennessee Folklore Society Bulletin* 10 (1954): 86–90; Vernon H. Taylor, "From Fancy to Fact in Dulcimer Discoveries," *Tennessee Folklore Society Bulletin* 23 (1957): 86–90; Ritchie, *The Dulcimer Book;* Donald H. Winkleman, "The Gentle Side of Folk Music," *Christian Science Monitor*, Sept. 26, 1966; Roger Welsch, "American Antique Stringed Instruments, Part II," *Spinning Wheel* (Jan.–Feb. 1967): 12–13, 45. European antecedents of the dulcimer are treated in Henry C. Mercer, "Zithers of the Pennsylvania Germans," *A Collection of the Papers Read Before the Bucks County Historical Society* 5 (1926): 482–97.

25. L. Allen Smith, *A Catalogue of Pre-Revival Appalachian Dulcimers*, foreword by Jean Ritchie (Columbia, Mo., 1983), xiii, 10.

26. Ibid., 46–47, 64.

27. Jean Ritchie, foreword, ibid., ix–x; Cecil Sharp, *English Folksongs from the Southern Appalachians* (London, 1932).

28. Smith, *Catalogue*, 9; A. L. Lloyd, *Folk Song in England* (New York, 1967), 393–96. Smith also makes what he considers "some reasonable inferences" (p. 5) as to how the dulcimer evolved. One such inference is that the Appalachian dulcimer evolved from the type B (half bout) zither to the type D (single bout) dulcimer. This would seem something less than a "reasonable inference" given the rarity of type B zithers. And Smith's assumption that the process of evolution may have

been from straight-sided zithers A21 or A25 to dulcimer D39 (with double bouts) would seem dubious indeed given that he never even saw D39.

29. Jean Ritchie notes in her foreword that "what Allen Smith has done, simply, is to have taken many little pools of knowledge from around the country and assembled them into one concise and easily available source." Smith, *Catalogue*, xi.

30. For the Scots and Scotch-Irish in the South, see Ian C. C. Graham, *Colonists from Scotland: Emigration to North America, 1707–1783* (Ithaca, 1956); Duane Meyer, *The Highland Scots of North Carolina, 1732–1776* (Chapel Hill, 1961); James G. Leyburn, *The Scotch-Irish: A Social History* (Chapel Hill, 1962).

31. Michael Owen Jones, *Craftsmen of the Cumberlands: Tradition and Creativity* (Lexington, Ky., 1989). While continuing to focus on chairmaking, this exploration of creativity in context marks an extensive rethinking of Jones's earlier *The Hand Made Object and Its Maker* (Berkeley, 1975).

32. Erik H. Erikson, *Childhood and Society*, 2d ed. (New York, 1963), 285. Erikson labels these potentialities "polarities." Similarly, the theologian Reinhold Niebuhr describes the persistent interplay of innocence and guilt in American history; the sociologist David Riesman, the complex interaction of individualism and conformity; and the historian Carl Becker, the contradictory tugs of freedom and responsibility. See Niebuhr's *The Irony of American History* (New York, 1952); Riesman's *The Lonely Crowd* (New Haven, 1950); and Becker's *Freedom and Responsibility in the American Way of Life* (New York, 1945). The historian C. Vann Woodward, in *American Counterpoint* (Boston, 1971), applies the polarities approach to North-South relations in the United States, while his friend David M. Potter contrasts abundance and poverty in his *People of Plenty* (Chicago, 1954). And the historian Michael Kammen takes the concept of polarities itself as his subject for a study of colonial and Revolutionary American in *People of Paradox* (New York, 1972). The political scientist Stanley Hoffman finds these polarities so pervasive "that the nation's values (and leaders) point simultaneously in opposite directions." See his *"Gulliver's Troubles" Or the Setting of American Foreign Policy* (New York, 1968), 187–88.

33. Edmund R. Leach, *The Artist in Tribal Society* (London, 1957), 122; H. G. Barnett, *Innovation: The Basis of Cultural Change* (New York, 1953), 208–12, 233. For studies of creativity in southern folk arts see Roger D. Abrahams, "Afterword," in *A Singer and Her Songs: Almeda Riddle's Book of Ballads*, ed. Roger D. Abrahams (Baton Rouge, 1970), 147–60; John A. Burrison, *Brothers in Clay: The Story of Georgia Folk Pottery* (Athens, Ga., 1983); John A. Burrison, ed., *Creativity in Southern Folklore*, special issue of *Studies in the Literary Imagination* 3 (Apr. 1970); Allen H. Eaton, *Handicrafts of the Southern Highlands* (New York, 1973 [1937]); William R. Ferris, ed., *Afro-American Art and Crafts* (Boston, 1983); Catherine Wilson Horne, ed., *Crossroads of Clay: The Southern Alkaline-Glazed Stoneware Tradition* (Columbia,

S.C., 1990); Sally and Richard Price, *Afro-American Arts of the Suriname Rain Forest* (Berkeley, 1980); Nancy Sweezy, *Raised in Clay: The Southern Pottery Tradition* (Washington, D.C., 1984); John Michael Vlach, *Charleston Blacksmith: The Work of Philip Simmons* (Athens, Ga., 1981); idem, *The Afro-American Tradition in Decorative Arts* (Cleveland, 1978); idem, *By the Work of their Hands: Studies in Afro-American Folklife* (Charlottesville, 1991); and Charles G. Zug III, *Turners and Burners: The Folk Potters of North Carolina* (Chapel Hill, 1986).

34. Roger D. Abrahams, "Creativity, Individuality, and the Traditional Singer," *Studies in the Literary Imagination* 3 (1970): 122. See also Henry Glassie, "Take That Night Train to Selma," in *Folksongs and Their Makers*, ed. Henry Glassie, Edward D. Ives, and John F. Szwed (Bowling Green, Ohio, 1970), 60; Barnett, *Innovation*, 386–89. See also Abraham's collaboration with the Ozark ballad singer Almeda Riddle, *A Singer and Her Songs: Almeda Riddle's Book of Ballads* (Baton Rouge, 1970). Other important folk autobiographies are Robin Morton and John McGuire, *Come Day, Go Day, God Send Sunday* (London, 1973); Bessie Jones and Bess Lomax Hawes, *Step It Down* (New York, 1972); and Bob Copper, *A Song for Every Season: A Hundred Years of a Sussex Farming Family* (London, 1971).

35. Barnett, *Innovation*, 318–21.

36. Kay L. Cothran, "Participation in Tradition," *Keystone Folklore Quarterly* 18 (1973): 7–13; idem, "Such Stuff as Dreams: A Folkloristic Sociology of Fantasy in the Okefenokee Rim, Georgia" (Ph.D. diss., University of Pennsylvania, 1972); William Faulkner, *Requiem for a Nun*, Signet ed. (New York, 1951), 229; T. S. Eliot, "Tradition and the Individual Talent," in his *The Sacred Wood* (London, 1934), 48–49.

Chapter 12: Sea Island Legacy

1. I attended Sunday morning worship at Wesley United Methodist Church on Johns Island, May 15, 1988.

2. Quoted in Guy and Candie Carawan, *Ain't You Got a Right to the Tree of Life?* Brown Thrasher Edition (Athens, Ga., 1989), xv.

3. Abraham Jenkins, ibid., 183; Alice Wine, ibid., 207.

4. Septima Clark, *Ready from Within: Septima Clark and the Civil Rights Movement*, ed. with an introduction by Cynthia Stokes Brown (Navarro, Cal., 1986), 36–41.

5. Ibid., 42.

6. Carawan and Carawan, *Ain't You Got a Right*, xii–xiii.

7. Clark, *Ready from Within*, 45–46; Bernice Robinson, in Carawan and Carawan, *Ain't You Got A Right*, 203.

8. Myles Horton, in Carawan and Carawan, *Ain't You Got a Right*, 198; Clark, *Ready from Within*, 44–45.

9. Horton, in Carawan and Carawan, *Ain't You Got a Right*, 198; Robinson, ibid., 202–3.

10. Horton, ibid., 198; Robinson, ibid., 203; Guy Carawan, "Spiritual Singing in the South Carolina Sea Islands," *Caravan* no. 20 (Mar. 1960): 20.

11. Carawan, "Spiritual Singing in the South Carolina Sea Islands," 20–25.

12. Ibid.; Horton, in Carawan and Carawan, *Ain't You Got a Right*, 198.

13. Guy and Candie Carawan, *We Shall Overcome: Songs of the Southern Freedom Movement* (New York, 1963), 111; idem, "'Keep Your Eyes on the Prize': Cultural Work in the Sea Islands," *Sing Out!* 31, no. 4 (1985): 32–35.

14. Carawan, "Spiritual Singing in the South Carolina Sea Islands," 20–25.

15. Robinson, in Carawan and Carawan, *Ain't You Got a Right*, 203, 205; Clark, *Ready from Within*, 70.

16. Guy Carawan to Pete Seeger, quoted in Seeger, "Johnny Appleseed, Jr.," *Sing Out!* 15, no. 5 (1965): 95; *Been in the Storm So Long: Spirituals and Shouts and Children's Games*, Folkways LP 3942; Guy Carawan, "The Living Folk Heritage of the Sea Islands," *Sing Out!* 14, no. 2 (1964): 29–32; Guy and Candie Carawan, "John's Island," *Sing Out!* 16, no. 1 (1966): 25–30; idem, "'Keep Your Eyes on the Prize,'" 32–37.

17. Carawan and Carawan, *We Shall Overcome*, 111; idem, "'Keep Your Eyes on the Prize,'" 32–35.

18. William Saunders, in Carawan and Carawan, *Ain't You Got a Right*, 229; *Moving Star Hall Singers and Alan Lomax: Sea Island Folk Festival*, Folkways LP 3841; Guy Carawan, *Sea Island Folk Festival*, booklet included with Folkways LP 3841. I was present at the second of the Sea Island Folk Festivals.

19. Saunders, in Carawan and Carawan, *Ain't You Got a Right*, 184.

20. Ibid.

21. Abraham Jenkins, in Carawan and Carawan, *Ain't You Got a Right*, 180.

22. Ibid., 175.

23. Saunders, in Carawan and Carawan, *Ain't You Got a Right*, 179–80.

24. Carawan and Carawan, *Ain't You Got a Right*, xvi.

25. Esau Jenkins, ibid., xvi; Janie Hunter, ibid., 215.

26. Hunter, ibid., 230; Benjamin Bligen, ibid., 219; Elaine Jenkins, ibid., 214.

27. Saunders, ibid., 227.

28. Robinson, ibid., 189.

Chapter 13: "Alice of the Hermitage"

1. For a study of the rice plantations of All Saints Parish, see Charles Joyner, *Down by the Riverside: A South Carolina Slave Community* (Urbana, 1984).

2. The parenthetical numbers denoting motifs are likely to be incomprehensible to the nonspecialist in comparative folk narrative analysis. The development of the "Finnish Method" of such analysis depended upon creating standard reference works of tale types and motifs. One of the leading disciples of the Finnish pioneers Kaarle Krohn and Antti Aarne was Stith Thompson, an American. De-

spite limitations inherent in the method itself, Thompson's *Motif-Index of Folk Literature* (Bloomington, Ind., 1955–58) is a monumental reference tool that has made the comparative study of folk narratives possible. Its numbering system time and again has proven itself a reliable and useful place to start. I have applied Thompson's motif numbers to the Alice legend.

3. Max Luthi, "Aspects of the Märchen and the Legend," *Genre* 2 (1969): 162–78; Linda Degh, "The 'Belief Legend' in Modern Society: Form, Function, and Relationship to Other Genres," in *American Folk Legend: A Symposium*, ed. Wayland D. Hand (Berkeley, 1971); Lauri Honko, "Genre Analysis in Folkloristics and Comparative Religion," *Tenemos* 3 (1968): 48–66.

4. Degh, "The 'Belief Legend' in Modern Society," 55.

5. Linda Degh and Andrew Vazsonyi, "The Dialectics of the Legend," Folklore Preprint Series, vol. 1, no. 6 (Bloomington, Ind., 1971), and their "Legend and Belief," *Genre* 4 (1971): 281–304; Robert A. Georges, "The General Concept of Legend: Some Assumptions to be Reexamined and Reassessed," in Hand, *American Folk Legend*, 16–18.

6. Lauri Honko, "Memorates and the Study of Folk Beliefs," *Journal of the Folklore Institute* 1 (1964): 5–19.

7. Herbert Halpert, "Definition and Variation in Folk Legend," in Hand, *American Folk Legend*, 48–49.

8. For an elaboration of this position, see Charles Joyner, "A Model for the Analysis of Folklore Performance in Historical Context," *Journal of American Folklore* 88 (1975): 254–65.

9. Mircea Eliade, *The Myth of the Eternal Return* (New York, 1954), 141–59; Richard M. Dorson, "How Shall We Rewrite Charles M. Skinner Today?" in Hand, *American Folk Legend*, 70–72; Linda Degh, "Folk Narrative," in *Folklore and Folklife*, ed. Richard M. Dorson (Chicago, 1972), 76–77; Jan Harold Brunvand, *The Study of American Folklore*, 2d ed. (New York, 1978), 116–19.

10. Carl W. von Sydow, *Selected Papers in Folklore* (Copenhagen, 1948), 73–74, 87.

11. Ibid., 106–26.

12. The increasing importance of mixed forms is emphasized by Linda Degh in her "The 'Belief Legend' in Modern Society," 62, and by Kurt Ranke in his "Kategorienprobleme der Volksprosa," *Fabula* 9 (1967): 4–12.

13. Linda Degh emphasizes the necessity of "piecing together" a legend in her "The 'Belief Legend' in Modern Society," 62.

14. Luthi, "Aspects of the Märchen and the Legend," 162–78 See also Honko, "Genre Analysis in Folkloristics and Comparative Religion," 48–66. See also Jacob Grimm's metaphoric comparison of legend and *Märchen:* "The fairy tale flies, the legend knocks at your door; the one can draw freely out of the fullness of poetry, the other has almost the authority of history." *Deutsche Mythologie* (1844), quoted by Degh in "Folk Narrative," 72.

15. See J. R. Rayfield, "What Is a Story?" *American Anthropologist* 74 (1972): 1085–1106.

16. Robert A. Georges, "Toward an Understanding of Storytelling Events," *Journal of American Folklore* 82 (1969): 313–28. See also Erving Goffman, "The Neglected Situation," *American Anthropologist* 66 (1964): 133–36.

17. George C. Rogers Jr., *History of Georgetown County, South Carolina* (Columbia, S.C., 1970), 256; Alberta Morel Lachicotte, *Georgetown Rice Plantations* (Columbia, S.C., 1955), 64–68; Henry A. M. Smith, "Hobcaw Barony," *South Carolina Historical and Genealogical Magazine* 10 (1909): 79; Mabel L. Webber, "Moore of St. Thomas Parish," *South Carolina Historical and Genealogical Magazine* 27 (1926): 157–69.

18. Washington Allston was born at Brookgreen Plantation in All Saints Parish but lived much of his adult life in London and in Cambridge, Massachusetts, where he married into the Dana family and was an intimate of Coleridge and Washington Irving. See William H. Gerdts and Theodore E. Stebbins Jr., *"A Man of Genius": The Art of Washington Allston (1779–1843)* (Boston, 1979); E. P. Richardson, *Washington Allston: A Study of the Romantic Artist in America* (Chicago, 1948); Jared B. Flagg, *The Life and Letters of Washington Allston* (New York, 1892); and Rogers, *History of Georgetown County*, 521.

19. See especially Laurence Oliphant, *Patriots and Filibusters, or Incidents of Political and Exploratory Travel* (Edinburgh, 1860), 132–46; Anon., "Recollections of a Visit to the Waccamaw," *Living Age*, Aug. 1, 1857, 292–93; Elizabeth Collins, *Memories of the Southern States* (Taunton, Eng., 1865); William Wyndham Malet, *An Errand to the South in the Summer of 1862* (London, 1863); Edmund Kirke [James Roberts Gilmore], *Among the Pines: South in Secession-Time* (New York, 1862); Almira Coffin to Mrs. J. G. Osgood, May 10, 1851, in "South Carolina through New England Eyes," ed. J. Harold Easterby, *South Carolina Historical and Genealogical Magazine* 45 (1944): 127–36; An Anonymous Englishman, "Rambles at Random through the Southern States," *Blackwood's Magazine*, Jan. 1860.

20. Elizabeth W. Allston Pringle, *Chronicles of Chicora Wood* (New York, 1922), 67. Peter H. Wood indicates that the sickle-cell trait gave blacks a limited immunity to malaria. See his *Black Majority: Negroes in Colonial South Carolina from 1670 through the Stono Rebellion* (New York, 1975), 63–91.

21. Lawrence Fay Brewster, *Summer Migrations and Resorts of South Carolina Planters* (Durham, N.C., 1947), 3–6; J. H. Easterby, ed., *The South Carolina Rice Plantation as Revealed in the Papers of Robert F. W. Allston* (Chicago, 1945), 9; Rogers, *History of Georgetown County*, 312–23; Ben Horry, in "Slave Narratives: A Folk History of Slavery in the United States from interviews with Former Slaves," typewritten records prepared by the Federal Writers Project, 1936–38, Work Projects Administration, 14, part 2, 306, 317, 323, microfilm of original in Library of Congress.

22. See J. Fred Rippy, *Joel R. Poinsett: Versatile American* (Durham, 1935); Anthony Devereux, *The Life and Times of Robert F. W. Allston* (Charleston, 1976); Easterby, *South Carolina Rice Plantation*, 15, 155; Paul Straiti, "Samuel F. B. Morse in Charleston, 1818–1821," *South Carolina Historical Magazine* 79 (1978): 95–97. John Ashe Alston was Morse's most lavish patron. See also Pringle, *Chronicles of Chicora Wood*, 20–23, and *Catalogue of the Carolina Art Association* (1858).

23. Chalmers G. Davidson, *The Last Foray: The South Carolina Planters of 1860: A Sociological Study* (Columbia, S.C., 1971), 5.

24. *Charleston Yearbook*, 1894, 243–73.

25. Rogers, *History of Georgetown County*, 251.

26. All Saints Waccamaw Vestry Records, South Carolina Historical Society, Charleston, S.C.; Dr. E. B. Flagg Medical Day Book, no. 7, South Carolina Historical Society.

27. All Saints Waccamaw Vestry Records.

28. Julian Stevenson Bolick, *Waccamaw Plantations* (Clinton, S.C., 1946), 116; idem, *The Return of the Gray Man* (Clinton, S.C., 1956), 144; Nancy and Bruce Roberts, *Ghosts of the Carolinas* (Charlotte, N.C., 1971), 53–54; Clarke A. Willcox, *Musings of a Hermit*, 4th ed. (Charleston, S.C., 1973), 71. A report by the Waccamaw Regional Planning and Development Council, "Environmental, Historical, and Recreational Atlas of the Waccamaw Region" (Georgetown, 1973), gives the date as 1848. Attempts to determine the date of origin through a search of postwar transactions involving the Hermitage have been fruitless. See Deed Book P, 678, Deed Book G, 111, Deed Book X, 113, Deed Book C-1, 319, Georgetown County Court House.

29. Alice's brother Allard married Penelope Bentley Ward at All Saints a year later, on January 16, 1850. Their first child, a daughter born October 21, 1850, was named Alice. All Saints Waccamaw Vestry Records.

30. South Carolina Writers Project, *South Carolina: The WPA Guide to the Palmetto State*, with a new introduction by Walter B. Edgar (Columbia, S.C., 1988 [1941]); WPA mss., South Caroliniana Library, University of South Carolina, Columbia; South Carolina Writers Project, *South Carolina Folk Tales* (Columbia, S.C., 1941).

31. Degh, "The 'Belief Legend' in Modern Society," 55.

32. Personal interview, Genevieve Willcox Chandler and Genevieve Chandler Peterkin, Murrells Inlet, S.C., June 1978. Mrs. Chandler had never before revealed the origin of the legend publicly. Personal interview, H. Trez Willcox, Myrtle Beach, S.C., Sept. 1980.

33. Halpert, "Definition and Variation in Folk Legend," 48–49.

34. Bolick, *Waccamaw Plantations*, 116–17, and his *Return of the Gray Man*, 1–10, 141–50.

35. Roberts and Roberts, *Ghosts of the Carolinas*, 53–54.

36. [Robbie L. Alford], *GhostsGhostsGhostsGhosts*, Historic Georgetown County Leaflet no. 7 (Georgetown, 1975).

37. *Atlanta Journal*, Oct. 29, 1961; Frances Moore, "Belle Alice: Just an Apparition?" *Charlotte Observer*, Jan. 22, 1965, 10c; *Sandlapper* (Columbia, S.C.), 4 (Feb. 1971); *Sunday Sunrise* (Myrtle Beach, S.C.), Dec. 18, 1977, 2, 5; *Wild Flower* (Marion, S.C.), n.d., 1–2.

38. Degh, "The 'Belief Legend' in Modern Society," 62.

39. Clarke A. Willcox, *Musings of a Hermit* (Charleston, 1966; 4th ed., Charleston, 1973). Perhaps understandably, Clarke Willcox contended that the legend was already traditional when the Willcox family moved into the Hermitage.

40. Degh, "The 'Belief Legend' in Modern Society," 55.

41. Degh and Vazsonyi, "The Dialectics of the Legend."

42. Idem, "Legend and Belief," 281–304. See also Georges, "The General Concept of Legend," 16–18.

43. Degh, "The 'Belief Legend' in Modern Society," 62.

44. Bronislaw Malinowski anticipated this kind of definition by rhetorical characteristics when he defined legend as a narrative with a historical or pseudo-narrative basis, *told as supposedly true events* (my emphasis). See Bronislaw Malinowski, *"Magic, Science, and Religion" and Other Essays* (Garden City, N.Y., 1954).

45. Honko, "Memorates and the Study of Folk Beliefs," 5–19. See also Patrick B. Mullen, "The Relationship of Legend and Folk Belief," *Journal of American Folklore* 84 (1971): 406–13.

46. See also Bronislaw Malinowski's indication that the Trobriand Islanders used their legends of Tudava as evidence for belief, in *The Argonauts of the Pacific* (London, 1932), 302.

47. Degh, "The 'Belief Legend' in Modern Society," 63–64.

Chapter 14: The Analysis of Folklore Performance

1. Richard M. Dorson, "A Theory for American Folklore," *Journal of American Folklore* 62 (1959): 203.

2. Among Dorson's most significant writings for historical context are *African Folklore* (Bloomington, Ind., 1972); *America Begins: Early American Writings* (New York, 1950); *America in Legend: Folklore from the Colonial Period to the Present* (New York, 1972); *American Folklore* (Chicago, 1959); *American Folklore and the Historian* (Chicago, 1971).

3. Paredes's comment may be found in his foreword to "Toward New Perspectives in Folklore," a special issue of the *Journal of American Folklore* 84 (1971): iii, published separately as *Toward New Perspectives in Folklore* (Austin, 1971). A good summary of the historical-geographical approach may be found in Jouko Hautala, *Finnish Folklore Research, 1828–1918* (Helsinki, 1968), 63–272.

4. Dorson briefly summarizes the historical-reconstructional approach in his *Folklore and Folklife* (Chicago, 1972), 12–15. An outstanding work combining folklore and oral history is Jan Vansina, *Oral History: A Study in Historical Methodology*

(London, 1965). Lynwood Montell's preface to *The Saga of Coe Ridge: A Study in Oral History* (Knoxville, 1970), vii–xxi, is an excellent introduction to the problems of what he calls "oral folk history"; but see also Dorson, *African Folklore*, 44–58, for an important distinction between folklore and oral history. Daniel J. Crowley discussed his return to Grant's Town in "Bahamian Narrative after Twenty Years," a paper presented at the 1972 annual meeting of the American Folklore Society.

5. Dan Ben-Amos, "Toward a Definition of Folklore in Context," *Journal of American Folklore* 84 (1971): 9. D. K. Wilgus made a vigorous defense of the "things" of folklore in his 1972 presidential address to the American Folklore Society. See "The Text Is the Thing," *Journal of American Folklore* 86 (1973): 241–52.

6. Richard Bauman, "Introduction," *Journal of American Folklore* 84 (1971): v.

7. Robert Jerome Smith, review of *25 estudios de folklore: Homenage a Vicente T. Mendoza y Virginia Rodriguez Rivera*, *Journal of American Folklore* 85 (1972): 387.

8. Ben-Amos, "Toward a Definition of Folklore in Context," 7–8, 13. For an extended development of this approach, see his "Folklore in African Society," in *The Forms of Folklore in Africa: Narrative, Poetic, Gnomic, Dramatic*, ed. Bernth Lindfors (Austin, Tex., 1977), 22–29.

9. See Dell Hymes, "The Contribution of Folklore to Sociolinguistic Research," *Journal of American Folklore* 84 (1971): 42–50, and his *Foundations in Sociolinguistics: An Ethnographic Approach* (Philadelphia, 1974), esp. 1–66.

10. Roger D. Abrahams, "Personal Power and Social Restraint in the Definition of Folklore," *Journal of American Folklore* 84 (1971): 29; see also his "Introductory Remarks to a Rhetorical Theory of Folklore," *Journal of American Folklore* 81 (1968): 157.

11. Stephan Thernstrom, *Poverty and Progress: Social Mobility in a Nineteenth Century City* (New York, 1973), 225–26.

12. The quote is from E. R. Leach, *Political Systems of Highland Burma: A Study of Kachin Social Structure* (Cambridge, Mass., 1954), 282. For a critique of this school see E. E. Evans-Pritchard, "Social Anthropology: Past and Present," *Man* 198 (1950), 118–24.

13. M. G. Smith, "History and Social Anthropology," *Journal of the Royal Anthropological Institute* 9 (1962): 77.

14. The problem of cultural change is brilliantly addressed in Michael Kammen, *People of Paradox: An Inquiry Concerning the Origins of American Civilization* (New York, 1973). Several studies of cultural change by anthropologists are useful in various ways to folklorists: Melville J. Herskovits, *Acculturation: The Study of Culture Contact* (New York, 1938); Sol Tax, ed., *Acculturation in the Americas* (Chicago, 1952); Felix M. Keesing, *Culture Change* (Stanford, 1953); Manning Nash, *Machine Age Maya: The Industrialization of a Guatemalan Community* (Washington, 1958); Clifford Geertz, *Peddlers and Princes: Social Development and Economic Change in Two Indonesian Towns* (Chicago, 1963); Clifford Geertz, ed., *Old Societies, New States: The Quest for Modernity in Asia and Africa* (New York, 1963); Ward H. Good-

enough, *Cooperation in Change: An Anthropological Approach to Community Development* (New York, 1963); George M. Foster, *Traditional Cultures and the Impact of Technological Change* (New York, 1962).

15. Leslie L. Roos Jr., "The Focus of Comparative Inquiry," *Social Forces* 52 (1974): 559; I. M. Lewis, *History and Social Anthropology* (London, 1970), xvii.

16. Edwin C. Rozwenc, *The Making of American Society* (Boston, 1972), vol. 1, xiii–xiv.

17. Pier Paolo Giglioli, *Language and Social Context* (Harmondsworth, Eng., 1972), 13.

18. Rozwenc, *Making of American Society*, xiv.

19. Abrahams, "Introductory Remarks to a Rhetorical Theory of Folklore," 157; Clyde Klukhohn, "Parts and Wholes in Cultural Analysis," in *Parts and Wholes*, ed. Daniel Lerner (New York, 1963), 121; John J. Gumperz, "Introduction," in *Directions in Sociolinguistics: The Ethnography of Communication*, ed. John J. Gumperz and Dell Hymes (New York, 1972), 26.

20. Robert Redfield, *Peasant Society and Culture: An Anthropological Approach to Civilization* (Chicago, 1956), 5. See also Klukhohn, "Parts and Wholes in Cultural Analysis," esp. 115–21.

21. Robert F. Berkhofer Jr., *A Behavioral Approach to Historical Analysis* (New York, 1969), 169–210.

22. The psychiatrist Erik Erikson considers the life-cycle to be among the "indispensable co-ordinates of identity." See his *Identity: Youth and Crisis* (New York, 1968), 91, and his *Childhood and Society* (New York, 1963), 247–74.

23. Kenneth S. Goldstein, *A Guide for Field Workers in Folklore* (Hatboro, Pa., 1964), 106, 121–22, 126. The notion of "folkloric competence" is derived from Gumperz's theory of a speaker's "linguistic competence," or mastery of a set of abstract rules that allow the speaker to communicate. See his description in Gumperz and Hymes, *Directions in Sociolinguistics*, 9.

24. Talcott Parsons, *Structure and Process in Modern Societies* (Glencoe, Ill., 1960), 172.

25. I am using "folkloric repertory" in a sense parallel to Gumperz's concept of "linguistic repertory" as "the totality of linguistic forms regularly employed in the course of socially significant interaction." See his "Linguistic and Social Interaction in Two Communities," *American Anthropologist* 66 (1964): 137–38.

26. Karl Deutsch, *Nationalism and Social Communication* (New York, 1953), 151.

27. Harry Stack Sullivan, "A Theory of Interpersonal Relations: The Illusion of Personal Individuality," in *Varieties of Personality Theories*, ed. Hendrick M. Ruitenbeek (New York, 1964), 139–48. See also Sullivan's *Conceptions of Modern Psychiatry* (Washington, 1945).

28. For an important step in this direction see Ben-Amos, "Folklore in African Society." An extraordinary auto-ethnography from which such an aesthetic may be derived is *A Singer and Her Songs: Almeda Riddle's Book of Ballads*, ed. Roger D.

Abrahams (Baton Rouge, 1970). Other valuable auto-ethnographies are Bessie Jones and Bess Lomax Hawes, *Step It Down: Games, Plays, Songs and Stories from the Afro-American Heritage* (New York, 1972); Robin Morton, ed., *Come Day, Go Day, God Send Sunday: The Songs and Life Story of John McGuire, Traditional Singer and Farmer from County Fermanagh* (London, 1973); and Bob Copper, *A Song for Every Season: A Hundred Years of a Sussex Farming Family* (London, 1971).

29. See Anthony F. C. Wallace, "Culture and Cognition," *Science* 135 (1962): 351–57; James P. Spradley and David W. McCurdy, *The Cultural Experience: Ethnography in a Complex Society* (Chicago, 1972), 1–84; Ward H. Goodenough, *Description and Comparison in Cultural Anthropology* (Chicago, 1970); Stephen Tyler, *Cognitive Anthropology* (New York, 1969); William P. McEwen, *The Problem of Social Scientific Knowledge* (Totowa, N.J., 1963); B[enjamin] N. Colby, "Ethnographic Semantics: A Preliminary Survey," *Current Anthropologist* 7 (1966): 3–32.

30. See John L. Fischer, "Syntax and Social Structure: Truk and Ponape," in *Sociolinguistics*, ed. William Bright (The Hague, 1966), 182. See also "Creativity in Southern Folklore," ed. John A. Burrison, special issue of *Studies in the Literary Imagination* 3 (1970), esp. Roger D. Abrahams, "Creativity, Individuality, and the Traditional Singer," 5–34.

31. Erikson, *Identity*, 93.

32. George Herbert Mead, *Mind, Self, and Society: From the Standpoint of a Social Behaviorist* (Chicago, 1934).

33. See Dell Hymes, "Models of the Interaction of Language and Social Life," in Gumperz and Hymes, *Directions in Sociolinguistics*, 38–41; and Susan Ervin-Tripp, "On Sociolinguistic Rules: Alternation and Co-occurrence," ibid., 240–41.

34. Theodore M. Newcomb, *Social Psychology* (New York, 1950), 475.

35. Ben-Amos, "Toward a Definition of Folklore in Context," 7ff.

36. Kay L. Cothran calls it "the context of context." See her "Participation in Tradition," *Keystone Folklore* 18 (1973): 7. See also Michael Moerman, "Accomplishing Ethnicity," in *Ethnomethodology*, ed. Roy Turner (Harmondsworth, Eng., 1974), 54–68; and D. Lawrence Wieder, "Telling the Code," ibid., 144–72.

37. Cothran, "Participation in Tradition," 7–8.

38. Ibid., 7–13. See also Gumperz and Hymes, *Directions in Sociolinguistics*, 26; Gumperz, "Linguistic and Social Interaction in Two Communities," 137–54; Ervin-Tripp, "On Sociolinguistic Rules," 213–50.

39. Goldstein, *Guide for Fieldworkers in Folklore*, 32.

40. Vansina, *Oral History*, 170–71.

41. "We cannot define the organism operationally," Gardner Murphy notes, "except in reference to the situation." See his *Personality: A Behavioral Approach to Origins and Structure* (New York, 1947), 891.

42. Robert Jerome Smith, "The Structure of Esthetic Response," *Journal of American Folklore* 84 (1971): 68–79.

43. Kenneth S. Goldstein, "Bowdlerization and Expurgation: Academic and

Folk," *Journal of American Folklore* 80 (1967): 375–86, and his "On the Application of the Concepts of Active and Inactive Traditions to the Study of Repertory," *Journal of American Folklore* 84 (1971): 62–97.

44. J. Milton Yinger, *Toward a Field Theory of Behavior: Personality and Social Structure* (New York, 1965); Talcott Parsons, *The Structure of Social Action*, 2d ed. (New York, 1948); Arnold Rose, ed., *Human Behavior and Social Processes: An Interactionist Approach* (Boston, 1962), 3–19; Paul Meadows, "The Dialectic of the Situation: Some Notes on Situational Psychology," *Philosophy and Phenomenological Research* 5 (1944): 354–64.

45. Talcott Parsons and Edward Stills, *Toward a General Theory of Action* (Cambridge, Mass., 1957), 279.

46. See Uriel Weinreich, William Labov, and Marvin Herzog, "Empirical Foundations for a Theory of Language Change," in *Proceedings of the Texas Conference on Historical Linguistics*, ed. W. Lehman (Austin, 1968), 97–195.

Chapter 15: Folklore and Social Transformation

1. Charles Joyner, *Down by the Riverside: A South Carolina Slave Community* (Urbana, 1984), 128 (quote), 172–95.

2. Elisabeth Muhlenfeld, *Mary Boykin Chesnut: A Biography* (Baton Rouge, 1981), 15; Charles Joyner, *Folk Song in South Carolina* (Columbia, S.C., 1971), 8–24, 41–42.

3. See C. Vann Woodward, ed., *Mary Chesnut's Civil War* (New Haven, 1981).

4. See Reinhard Rurup, *The Bourgeois Revolution in Germany*, trans. Ruth Hein (Cambridge, Mass., 1988); David Hershberg, ed., *Literature and the Historical Process* (Lexington, Ky., 1988); Kevin Sharp and Steven N. Zwicker, eds., *Politics of Discourse: The Literature and History of Seventeenth-Century England* (Berkeley, 1988); Barton Friedman, *Fabricating History: English Writers on the French Revolution* (Cleveland, 1988); Lynn Hunt, *Politics, Culture, and Class in the French Revolution* (Berkeley, 1984); Lloyd S. Kramer, *Threshold of a New World: Intellectuals and the Exile Experience in Paris, 1830–1848* (Ithaca, 1988); J. Gerald Kennedy and Daniel Mark Fogel, *American Letters and the Historical Consciousness: Essays in Honor of Lewis P. Simpson* (Baton Rouge, 1988).

5. G. Lawrence Gomme, *Folklore as an Historical Science* (London, 1908), 1–22; Hector and Nora Chadwick, *The Heroic Age* (Cambridge, 1912); Lord Raglan, *The Hero: A Study in Tradition, Myth, and Drama* (New York, 1936); idem, "Folk Traditions as Historical Fact," *Journal of American Folklore* 73 (1960): 58–59; Charles Joyner, "Folklore and History: The Tangled Relationship," *The Newberry Papers in Family and Community History* (Chicago, 1978), 1–2.

6. Thomas D. Clark, *The Rampaging Frontier* (Indianapolis, 1939), xii; Theodore R. Blegen, *Grass Roots History* (Minneapolis, 1947); Américo Paredes, *"With His Pistol in His Hand": A Border Ballad and Its Hero* (Austin, 1958); idem, "History and Folklore," in *Singers and Storytellers*, ed. Mody C. Boatwright (Dallas, 1961), 58–61.

7. Richard M. Dorson, "A Theory for American Folklore," *Journal of American Folklore* 75 (1959): 203. History and folklore were considered by Gladys-Marie Fry and W. Lynwood Montell, two of Dorson's Ph.D. students. See Fry, *Night Riders in Black Folk History* (Knoxville, 1975); Montell, *The Saga of Coe Ridge: A Study in Oral History* (Knoxville, 1970); idem, *Don't Go Up Kettle Creek: Verbal Legacy from the Upper Cumberland* (Knoxville, 1983); and W. Lynwood Montell and Barbara Allen, *From Memory to History: Using Oral Sources in Local Historical Research* (Nashville, 1981).

8. See the various essays in George C. Iggers, *New Directions in European Historiography* (Middletown, Conn., 1975); Charles F. Delzell, ed., *The Future as History* (Nashville, 1977); Michael Kammen, ed., *The Past Before Us: Contemporary Historical Writing in the United States* (Ithaca, 1980); and Stanley I. Kutler and Stanley N. Katz, eds., *The Promise of American History: Progress and Prospects* (Baltimore, 1982).

9. Among the most important works of *les annalistes* in English are Marc Bloch, *Land and Work in Medieval Europe*, trans. J. E. Anderson (New York, 1969); idem, *French Rural History: An Essay on Its Basic Characteristics*, trans. Janet Sondheimer (Berkeley, 1970); Peter Burke, ed., *A New Kind of History: From the Writings of Lucien Febvre*, trans. K. Folka (New York, 1973), xii, 27–43; Fernand Braudel, *The Mediterranean and the Mediterranean World in the Age of Philip II*, 2 vols., trans. Sian Reynolds (New York, 1972–75); idem, *Civilization and Capitalism, Fifteenth to Eighteenth Century*, 3 vols., trans. Sian Reynolds (New York, 1982–85); Jacques LeGoff, *Time, Work, and Culture in the Middle Ages*, trans. Arthur Goldhammer (Chicago, 1980); Emmanuel LeRoy Ladurie, *The Peasants of Languedoc*, trans. John Day (Urbana, 1974); his *Montaillou: The Promised Land of Error*, trans. Barbara Bray (New York, 1978); idem, *Carnival in Romans*, trans. Mary Feeney (New York, 1979); idem, *Love, Death, and Money in the Pays d'Oc*, trans. Alan Sheridan (New York, 1982); Jean-Claude Schmitt, *The Holy Greyhound: Guinefort, Healer of Children since the Thirteenth Century*, trans. Martin Thom, Cambridge Studies in Oral Literature and Culture, no. 6 (Cambridge, 1983). See also Traian Stoianovich, *French Historical Method: The Annales Paradigm* (Ithaca, 1977); Daniel Chirot, "The Social and Historical Landscape of March Bloch," in *Vision and Method in Historical Sociology*, ed. Theda Skocpol (Cambridge, 1984), 22–46; Lynn Hunt, "Introduction: History, Culture, and Text," in her *The New Cultural History* (Berkeley, 1989), 1–8; Peter Burke, *The French Historical Revolution: The Annales School, 1929–89* (Stanford, 1990); and Françoise Dosse, *New History in France: The Triumph of the* Annales, trans. Peter V. Conroy Jr. (Urbana, 1994).

10. The best introduction to the folklife studies movement in America is Don Yoder, ed., *American Folklife* (Austin, 1976). See also his "The Folklife Studies Movement," *Pennsylvania Folklife* 13 (1963): 43–56; and his "Folklife," in *Our Living Traditions*, ed. Tristram P. Coffin (New York, 1968), 47–57. The classic work of folklife scholarship is Richard Weiss, *Volkskunde der Schweiz: Grundriss* (Erlenbach-Zurich, 1946). A monumental folklife study by an American scholar is Henry

Glassie, *Passing the Time in Balleymenone: Culture and History in an Ulster Community* (Philadelphia, 1982).

11. Lauri Honko, "Genre Theory Revisited," address given at World Congress of Folklorists, Helsinki, June 16–21, 1974, published in *NIF Newsletter* 2 (1974): 8. See also Alan Dundes, "Texture, Text, and Context," *Southern Folklore Quarterly* 28 (1964): 251–65; Roger D. Abrahams, "Introductory Remarks to a Rhetorical Theory of Folklore," *Journal of American Folklore* 81 (1968): 143–58; Dan Ben-Amos, "Toward a Definition of Folklore in Context," *Journal of American Folklore* 84 (1971); Dell Hymes, *Foundations in Sociolinguistics: An Ethnographic Approach* (Philadelphia, 1974), esp. 3–66; and Richard Bauman, *Verbal Art as Performance* (Rowley, Mass., 1978).

12. C. Vann Woodward, *Thinking Back: The Perils of Writing History* (Baton Rouge, 1986), 3; Thomas Bender, "Making History Whole Again," *New York Times Book Review*, Oct. 6, 1985, 1, 42; Karen J. Winkler, "'Disillusioned' with Numbers and Counting, Historians Are Telling Stories Again," *Chronicle of Higher Education*, June 13, 1984, 506; idem, "'Intellectual Splintering' Has Made Discipline of History Too Parochial, AHA President Says," *Chronicle of Higher Education*, Jan. 4, 1984, 7.

13. The indictment against the new social history was most forcefully and intemperately argued by Gertrude Himmelfarb in her *The New Social History and the Old* (Cambridge, Mass., 1987).

14. Braudel, *Mediterranean World*, 20, 1244. See also Fernand Braudel, *Afterthoughts on Material Civilization and Capitalism*, trans. Patricia Ranum (Baltimore, 1977).

15. See, for example, Bengt Holbek, "The Many Abodes of Fata Morgana, or the Quest for Meaning in Fairy Tales," in *Papers I: The Eighth Congress for the International Society for Folk Narrative Research*, ed. Reimund Kvideland and Torunn Selberg (Bergen, 1984), 5–27; and the following essays in *Papers II: The Eighth Congress for the International Society for Folk Narrative Research*, ed. Kvideland and Selberg (Bergen, 1984): Annikki Kaivola-Bregenhoi, "Personal Narrative: Drawing the Line between Idiosyncrasy and Tradition," 1–10; Consuelo Ruiz-Montero, "The Morphology of the 'Library' of Appolodorus," 163–70; Christiane Seydou, "La fille recluse: Etude comparative de cinq contes peuls," 181–202; Nai-tung Ting, "Singleness of Effect, Spontaneity, and Immediacy in the folktale," 239–48.

16. Salman Rushdie, *Shame* (London, 1984), 124; Michel Foucault, *The Archaeology of Knowledge and the Discourse on Language* (London, 1972), and his *Power/Knowledge: Selected Interviews and Other Writings, 1972–1977* (New York, 1979); Jacques Derrida, *The Post Card: From Socrates to Freud and Beyond* (Chicago, 1987), and his *The Truth in Painting*, trans. Geoffrey Bennington and Ian McLeod (Chicago, 1987); and James Clifford, *The Predicament of Culture: Twentieth-Century Ethnography, Literature, and Art* (Cambridge, Mass., 1988). See also Christopher Norris, *Derrida* (Cambridge, Mass., 1988); Mark C. Taylor, ed., *Deconstruction in*

Context: Literature and Philosophy (Chicago, 1986); Susan Noakes, *Timely Reading: Between Exegesis and Interpretation* (Ithaca, 1988); Stephen Cohen, *The Language of Power, the Power of Language: The Effects of Ambiguity on Sociopolitical Structures in Shakespeare's Plays* (Cambridge, Mass., 1988); Rebecca W. Bushnell, *Prophesying Tragedy: Sign and Voice in Sophocles' Theban Plays* (Ithaca, 1988); and William R. Paulson, *The Noise of Culture: Literary Texts in a World of Information* (Ithaca, 1988).

17. Interview by the author with Mary Burroughs, Bucksport, S.C., Nov. 28, 1987, recorded by Wesley Joyner.

Chapter 16: Endangered Traditions

1. I was present at an exchange between Charles E. Fraser and Emory Campbell (quoted later in this chapter) in Charleston on December 3, 1982. The occasion was a conference entitled "Coastal Development: Past, Present, and Future," organized by the Coastal Heritage Program of the South Carolina Sea Grant Consortium with support from the South Carolina Committee for the Humanities. Their remarks are printed in the proceedings of the conference, pages 55–56, 63. Additional comments by Campbell are taken from Vernie Singleton, "We Are an Endangered Species: An Interview with Emory Campbell," *Southern Exposure* 10 (May–June 1982): 37–39.

Index

Charles Joyner is Burroughs Distinguished Professor of Southern History and Culture at Coastal Carolina University. He is perhaps best known for his book *Down by the Riverside: A South Carolina Slave Community* (University of Illinois Press, 1984), which won the National University Press Book Award, presented by the Eugene M. Kayden Foundation. He earned a Ph.D. degree in history from the University of South Carolina and a Ph.D. in folklore and folklife from the University of Pennsylvania. He has lectured throughout the world about the American South and has published widely about that topic.

Typeset in Cycles 10.5/13, designed by Sumner Stone
Book design by Dennis Roberts
Composed at the University of Illinois Press
Manufactured by Cushing-Malloy, Inc.

University of Illinois Press
1325 South Oak Street
Champaign, IL 61820-6903
www.press.uillinois.edu